A Photographic Atlas
for the
Microbiology
LABORATORY

4th EDITION

Michael J. Leboffe
San Diego City College

Burton E. Pierce

MORTON
PUBLISHING

925 W. Kenyon Ave., Unit 12
Englewood, Colorado 80110
www.morton-pub.com

Book Team

Publisher:	Douglas N. Morton
Biology Editor:	David Ferguson
Production Manager:	Joanne Saliger
Production Assistant:	Desiree Coscia
Typography:	Ash Street Typecrafters, Inc.
Cover Design:	Bob Schram, Bookends, Inc.

This book is dedicated to
Michele Elaine Pierce (1950–2010)
Loving wife, mother, and grandmother,
former student,
and skilled and caring Nurse Practitioner

Preface

As my fingers hit the keys of my laptop, I realize that I am, after a long, seemingly endless process, within days of completing the fourth edition of *A Photographic Atlas for the Microbiology Laboratory*. At this stage of a book's life, a new edition ought to be just a matter of touching up the previous edition. Or so I thought. But, *PAML 4e* has presented its share of challenges.

First, and foremost, is the fact that this is the first project (out of three previous *Atlas* editions, three editions of *Microbiology Laboratory Theory and Application*, one edition of *Microbiology Laboratory Theory and Application—Brief Edition*, and three editions of *Exercises for the Laboratory Manual*) I have worked on without my longtime friend and colleague, **Burt Pierce**. Burt made the courageous and healthy decision to retire and move to Portland, OR, to enjoy life with his wife, three dogs, and two cats (notice the absence of any microbes in the family). Yet, while he was not an active participant, his influence remains in this edition. A majority of his written and photographic contributions are still here, and I have tried to live up to his eye for detail, his demand for excellence, and his dedication to knowing our readership. His philosophy was that even though we were writing for undergraduate students and not professionals, there was no excuse for "dumbing down the material"; he had a steadfast faith in the intelligence of our readers. Long ago, I was impressed by a speech made by a former San Diego City College president, in which she appealed for teamwork between faculty, staff and administration with the phrase, "None of us is as good as all of us." She was right about the college, and it has been equally applicable to the books Burt and I have co-authored. Our skills complemented one another and the books were clearly better because of it. But beyond the production of books, and the associated blood, sweat, and tears, what mattered most was the friendship and satisfaction of a collective "job well done." As the old beer commercial said, "(Burt), I love ya, man!"

A second challenge was that the *Atlas* has slowly accumulated much more text in support of the photos. When we did the first edition, the *Atlas* broke the mold at Morton Publishing by including much more explanatory text for the photos beyond captions. (In fact, the captions were criticized for not being very informative!) Burt and I maintained that microbiology, by nature, is very different from other disciplines and required background material; a photo album wouldn't suffice. While we have continued to add photos and expand coverage in each edition, the increase in text has considerably outpaced the photos. (For those of you who have been with us through all four editions, compare photograph sizes in the first edition to this one!) Writing is not easy for me. But, I've finished reading the proofs and somehow it got written. Chalk up another challenge being met.

In many ways, this edition is like a first edition. Coverage has expanded from being primarily a book with a medical microbiology emphasis to one with a more balanced emphasis of microbiology in general. Following is a summary of the major changes in this edition.

- The original artwork has been replaced with professional renderings. Many of the older photos have been replaced with newer ones, and many new photos have been added. Between the artwork and photos, over 200 new figures (representing approximately 25% of the total) can be found.

- Four new chapters have been added. Chapter 1 provides an introduction to microbiology and presents a perspective on the places *Bacteria* and *Archaea* occupy in the biological world. It also expands the justification for the book's reorganization (see the following paragraph). Chapter 11 covers some of the most important groups within the Domain *Bacteria*. Chapters 13 and 14 do the same for the Domains *Archaea* and *Eukarya*, respectively.

- Chapters have been resequenced to better reflect the process followed by a working microbiologist, so isolation techniques and selective media have been moved up to Chapter 2. The chapters that follow continue the process: growth patterns (Chapter 3), microscopy and staining (Chapters 4, 5, and 6), biochemical testing (Chapter 7), serological testing (Chapter 8), and molecular techniques (Chapter 9). The next chapters cover the microbes themselves, beginning with viruses (Chapter 10), and followed by chapters on Domain *Bacteria* (Chapters 11 and 12), Domain *Archaea* (Chapter 13), and Domain *Eukarya* (Chapters 14 through 17). The book finishes with chapters on quantitative techniques (Chapter 18), medical, environmental, and food microbiology (Chapter 19), and host defenses (Chapter 20). An appendix illustrating major metabolic pathways combined with tables to show reactants and products of each completes this edition.

● In addition to the brand new chapters, artwork, and photos, some new topics have been added to established chapters. Other topics have been expanded. Chapter 2 now includes *Bacteroides* Bile Esculin Agar, BIGGY Agar, Columbia CNA Agar, and *Pseudomonas* Isolation Agar. Cooked Meat Broth was added to Chapter 3 and the

anaerobic jar has been updated. Chapter 4 has expanded coverage of electron microscopy. Parasporal crystal stain and cell wall stain have been added to Chapter 6. DNase Test Agar has been expanded in Chapter 7. The Winogradsky column and sulfur cycle have been added to Chapter 19, and the nitrogen cycle has been expanded.

Speaking for both Burt and me, *we* hope you find this edition of the *Photographic Atlas for the Microbiology Laboratory* more useful than ever.

Mike
La Mesa, CA
December 2010

Acknowledgments

Each edition builds upon previous editions and the list of people to whom we are indebted for their generous help and support continues to get longer and longer. These gracious people have been acknowledged in previous editions and, sadly, due to space limitations, must be thanked collectively here. Please realize this doesn't mean we have forgotten you! That being said, following are the people who have contributed to this edition.

As always, thanks to the Morton Publishing team for their continued support and friendship. Specifically, thanks to Doug Morton, President, and Chrissy DeMier, Business Manager, for their outstanding business model; to David Ferguson, Biology Editor, for his advice, patience, and gentle nudging (keep the elbows and stick down, though); Carter Fenton, Sales and Marketing Manager for executing the business model; Desireé Coscia, Project Manager for her assistance and attention to details; and all of Morton Publishing Company employees for their hard work and good nature. Thanks also goes to the extended Morton Publishing book team: Joanne Saliger and Patricia Billiot of Ash Street Typecrafters, Inc. for their characteristically high quality production and proofreading talents; Bob Schram of Bookends, Inc. for the cover design; and Marina Siuchong of Imagineering Art for the new artwork.

Reviewers of the 3rd edition were Susan Koval (University of Western Ontario), Kathleen Richardson (Portland Community College), and Marva Volk (Tulsa Community College). Thanks to all of you for your thoughtful and useful comments for improving the *Atlas*.

Thanks to our colleagues in the Biology Department at San Diego City College for their understanding, support, and in some cases, participation. In alphabetical order: Donna DiPaolo, Anita Hettena, Tom Kaido, Sabine Kurz-Camacho, Roya Lahijani, Martha Myers, Debra Reed, Erin Rempala, David Singer, Minou Spradley (Acting Dean, but still one of us), Laura Steininger, Eri Suzuki, Carla Sweet, Hector Valtierra, Muu Vu, and Gary Wisehart.

Thanks to Patricia McVay, Lab Director, AnnaLiza Manlutack, and Let Negado of the San Diego Public Health Laboratory for supplying slide preparations.

The following people contributed materials, time, cultures, photographs, and/or expertise to this project: Esther Angert (Cornell University Department of Microbiology), Steve Barlow (San Diego State University Electron Microscope Facility), Steven Byers, John Crawley (Focus Design), Marlene DeMers (San Diego State University Microbiology Department), Tom Gibson (San Diego State University Microbiology Department), Christie Hendrix (National Park Service), Hisahi ITO (Mitsubishi Gas Chemical Company, Inc., Oxygen Absorbers Division), Ian and Todd Malloy (Crikey Adventure Tours), Chris Nutting (Ward's Natural Science), Robert van Ommering (van Ommering Dairy) Tammy Wert (National Park Service), and Karsten Zengler (University of California San Diego, Department of Bioengineering). Individuals whose public domain photos we used are acknowledged in the photo's caption.

We also appreciate the contributions made by General Microbiology classes at San Diego City College over the years. You have shown us firsthand how to improve our books.

I owe a lot to friends, many of whom have been mentioned previously, who have made valiant efforts to keep me grounded and maintain a healthy perspective on Life (which is still a work in progress). Thanks in particular to Kristine Rickards and Alexandria Murallo.

And finally, thanks to the ever-growing gang of Leboffes: wife Karen, children Nathan, Alicia, Eric, and by marriage, Jenny, and grandchildren Selah and Josiah. Special thanks go to Alicia for reading the manuscript with a fresh, well-educated eye. It really drove home the point that my babies have grown up when one is correcting my grammar!

Alas, even with all this help, I have come to grips with the realization that nothing is perfect, and that I am ultimately responsible for errors, omissions, and poor judgment in the final product. Comments for improvement are welcome. I can be reached through the publisher.

Contents

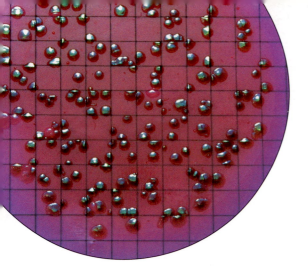

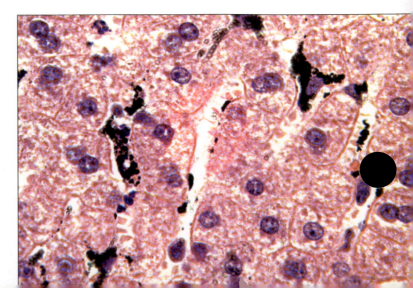

Introduction

A Tribute to the Past, a Moment in the Present, and an Openness to the Future

The authors are of the generation where biologists placed all organisms into two kingdoms: the Animal Kingdom and the Plant Kingdom. It was easy—anything that wasn't an animal was a plant, and so we had such diverse organisms as bacteria, yeast, and mushrooms placed in the same kingdom as roses and pine trees. Oh, and of course the simple nucleated cells (such as *Euglena* and *Amoeba*) were categorized based on their degree of resemblance to plants or animals.

Then came a big revolution based on information revealed by the electron microscope. It was found that some cells (subsequently called **prokaryotes**) do not have their genetic material encased inside a membranous nucleus. In fact, those that do (subsequently called **eukaryotes**) not only enclose their nucleus in membrane, but also have all kinds of membranous compartments within their cytoplasm. Endoplasmic reticulum, Golgi bodies, mitochondria, and many other structures were seen or clearly seen for the first time. Prokaryotes had none of these structures; their interior is very simple by comparison. (Figure 1-1 illustrates the obvious difference between prokaryotic and eukaryotic cells visible with the light microscope: size.) This led to a restructuring of biology at the kingdom level based on presence or absence of a nucleus, mode of nutrition (photosynthetic or not), and degree of complexity. All prokaryotes (bacteria) were placed in the Kingdom Monera. The eukaryotes were divided into four kingdoms: Fungi, Metaphyta (for the plants), Metazoa (for the animals), and Protista (for all the simple eukaryotes that didn't "fit" in the other three kingdoms). This system served us well over the second half of the 20th Century.

New technology allowing us to compare organisms at the molecular level led to another big revolution—including the addition of a taxonomic category more inclusive than Kingdom: the **Domain**. Based on comparisons of ribosomal RNA (rRNA), DNA, and proteins, the biological world is now seen to be composed of three Domains: *Bacteria* (comprising all bacteria), *Archaea* (formerly the archaeobacteria), and *Eukarya* (comprising

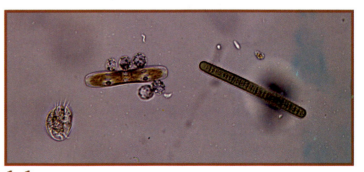

1-1 **COMPARISON OF PROKARYOTIC AND EUKARYOTIC CELL SIZES**
This micrograph is from a marine mud sample. Various cell types are bunched because the slide was drying out. The eukaryotic cells are the ciliate at the left, the golden brown diatom to its right, and the five, unidentified protists clinging to the diatom (gasping for oxygen it produces during photosynthesis!). Nuclei are not visible in these particular eukaryotes because the slide was unstained. The prokaryotes are the white specks (which are various bacteria) in the background and the greenish cyanobacterium at the right. The cyanobacterium looks to be the largest of the bunch, but it is a filament of cells stacked crosswise along the filament. Each cell is really small and lacks a nucleus.

TABLE 1-1 Comparison of the Three Domains

Characteristic (Present in at Least Some Species)	Bacteria	Archaea	Eukarya
Genetic			
Genome surrounded by nuclear membrane	No	No	Yes
Membrane-bound organelles	No	No	Yes
DNA molecule covalently bonded into circular form	Yes	Yes	No
Introns common	No	No	Yes
Operons present	Yes	Yes	No
Plasmids present	Yes	Yes	Rare
mRNA processing (poly-A tail and capping)	No	No	Yes
Metabolism			
Oxygenic photosynthesis	Yes	No	Yes
Anoxygenic photosynthesis	Yes	No	No
Methanogenesis	No	Yes	No
Nitrogen fixation	Yes	Yes	No
Chemolithotrophic metabolism	Yes	Yes	No
Cell Structure			
Cell wall of peptidoglycan	Most	Never	Never
Ester-linked, straight-chained fatty acids in membrane	Yes	No	Yes
Ether-linked, branched aliphatic chains in membrane	No	Yes	No
Ribosome type	70S	70S	80S

all eukaryotes.) A short list of defining characteristics for each domain is given in Table 1-1; Figure 1-2 illustrates their evolutionary history (**phylogeny**) as currently perceived by many biologists.[1] Examples are shown in Figures 1-3 through 1-6.

In the past editions we have ignored this new system, in large part because our emphasis had been on medical bacteriology. But now we have expanded coverage of the *Atlas* to include more aspects of general microbiology and this demands that we address the current taxonomy. Of course, we realize that even as this is being written, microbial taxonomy itself is being rewritten to be in line with new information gathered by working microbiologists. This is the way of Science.

A final note relates to the use of the term "prokaryote." There is a growing sentiment among microbiologists that "prokaryote" is not a valid designation because it includes representatives (*Bacteria* and *Archaea*) on different, ancient lineages. This is an argument to be settled by others more knowledgeable than we. So, until a decision is reached, we will continue to use "prokaryote" because it is such a convenient term!

The Working Microbiologist

Traditionally, the role of microbiologists has been to isolate a microbe from a mixed culture, grow the isolate in a pure culture, and then identify the isolate. A **culture** is composed of one or more kinds of organisms grown under artificial, but suitable conditions. If more than one species is present, it is said to be a **mixed culture**. If only one species is present, it is said to be a **pure culture**. Cultures may be grown in or on different kinds of **media**. A medium is the material that contains essential resources for growth (a carbon source, a nitrogen source, a sulfur source, and so on). Gases, such as oxygen, carbon dioxide, or diatomic nitrogen are generally not supplied by the medium, but must be made available in the culture container. A medium may be solid with nutrients

[1] Other interpretations for the relationships between the three domains have been made. No consensus has been reached on which, if any, is most correct.

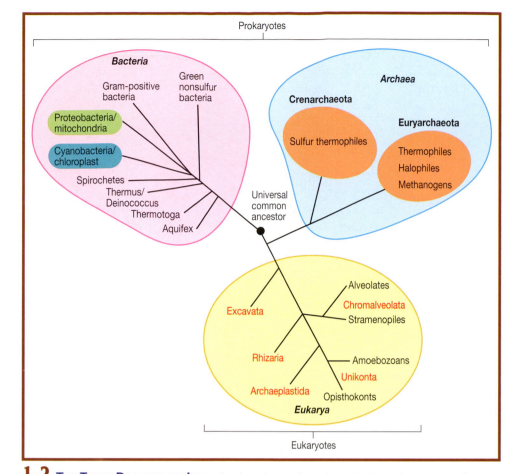

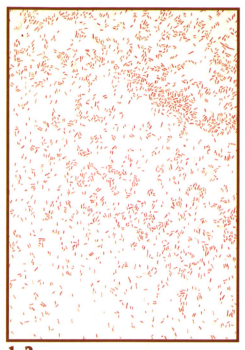

1-3 **ESCHERICHIA COLI—A BACTERIUM**
E. coli is the most studied and most well known of the *Bacteria*. It is a natural inhabitant of mammalian colons. Cells are about 1.0 µm wide by 2.0 to 4.0 µm long.

1-2 **THE THREE DOMAINS OF LIFE** The domains are based on 16S (in prokaryotes) and 18S (in eukaryotes) rRNA sequence comparisons. The *Archaea* and *Bacteria* are prokaryotic domains, each containing an as yet undetermined number of kingdoms. (*Bacteria* may comprise as many as 50 kingdoms, *Archaea* perhaps only 3.) Kingdom *Eukarya* includes all the eukaryotic organisms and is divided into the familiar Fungus, Plant, and Animal Kingdoms. The remaining eukaryotes ("Protists") will probably be broken up into 5 or more kingdoms as we learn more. Every kingdom has species that are "microbial" with the exception of the Plant and Animal Kingdoms.

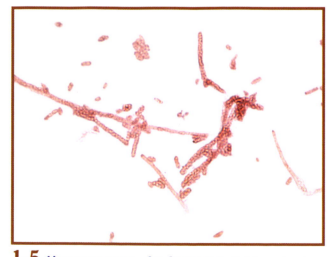

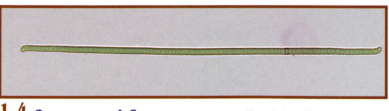

1-4 **OSCILLATORIA—A CYANOBACTERIUM** *Oscillatoria* is a filamentous cyanobacterium. That is, the organism is made of cells stacked together. This specimen is about 90 cells long, with individual cells about 7 µm wide. These *Bacteria* are capable of photosynthesis that produces oxygen, just like plants.

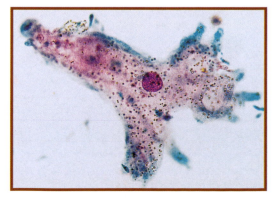

1-6 **AMOEBA—A EUKARYOTIC MICROBE**
Amoebas are characterized by the ability to stream their cytoplasm and produce **pseudopods** that allow them to move and engulf prey. Notice the nucleus within the cell.

1-5 **HALOBACTERIUM—AN ARCHAEAN** *Halobacterium* is an **extreme halophile**. That is, it grows in environments with salt concentrations approaching 25%. Gas vacuoles in the cells cause them to float to the surface.

suspended in the solidifying agent (usually **agar**) or it may be a liquid **broth**. Examples are shown in Figures 1-7 and 1-8.

Identification requires a pure culture because most microbes are not identified based on appearance or possession of unique physical structures (Figure 1-9). Rather, the identification (**diagnostic**) process usually involves running biochemical tests and recording the results. When enough relevant tests are run, the results are compared to a standard database of test results. The best fit leads to a provisional identification of the isolate. If the tests are run on a mixed culture, *the results will be a composite of both organisms' positive results and will most likely lead to misidentification!* The famous German physician and microbiologist Robert Koch said, "The pure culture is the foundation for all research on infectious disease." He was right.

All this background is a way of giving this edition of the *Atlas* some structure that wasn't present in previous editions. The earlier sections are devoted primarily to bacteriology and progress as a working microbiologist would as he/she tries to identify an isolate. Section 2 addresses methods by which bacteria can be isolated. Once isolation is achieved,

Section 3 provides information on how species can be differentiated based on macroscopic features. Sections 4, 5, and 6 carry this preliminary identification process on to include microscopic features. Section 7 presents differential physiological tests commonly used during the identification process. Section 8 does the same for diagnostic serological tests. This is followed by Molecular Techniques (Section 9), which includes an introduction to some techniques used in identification and a couple of others that are not. From here, we depart from the process of diagnostics to the subjects: the microbes themselves. Section 10 covers viruses, Sections 11 and 12 are devoted to *Bacteria*, and Section 13 addresses *Archaea*. Eukaryotic microbes, which are identified in large part by microscopic structural features, are covered in Sections 14 through 17. The *Atlas* concludes with three sections devoted to miscellaneous, albeit important, topics: Quantitative Techniques (Section 18), Medical, Environmental, and Food Microbiology, (Section 19), and Host Defenses (Section 20).

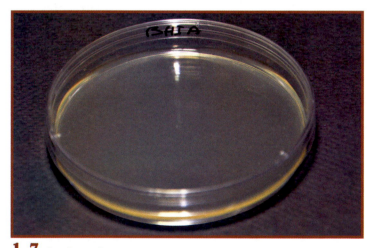

1-7 **AN AGAR PLATE** *BHIA stands for "Brain Heart Infusion Agar."* The 1.5–2% agar in the medium acts as a solidifying agent to suspend the nutrients—extracts of brain and heart tissues. Agar plates are usually used for isolating organisms from a mixed culture (Section 2).

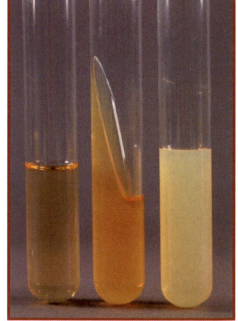

1-8 **TUBED MEDIA** From left to right: a broth, an agar slant, and an agar deep tube. The solid media are liquid when they are removed from the autoclave (where they get sterilized). Agar deeps are allowed to cool and solidify in an upright position, whereas agar slants are cooled and solidified on an angle. Broths are often used to produce fresh cultures, slants are used to maintain stock cultures, and agar deeps are used for many biochemical tests requiring low oxygen levels.

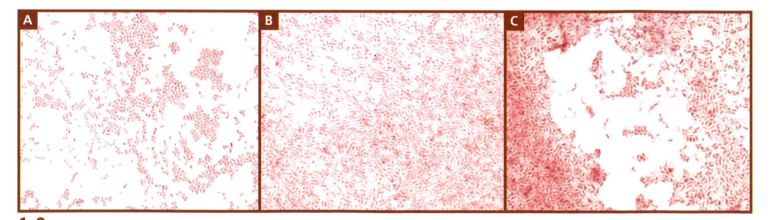

1-9 **IMAGINE TRYING TO IDENTIFY THESE THREE BACTERIAL GENERA USING ONLY THEIR MICROSCOPIC APPEARANCE!** **A** *Alcaligenes faecalis.* **B** *Citrobacter koseri.* **C** *Salmonella typhimurium.*

Isolation Techniques and Selective Media

Streak Plate Methods of Isolation

● Purpose

The identification process of an unknown microbe relies on obtaining a pure culture of that organism. The streak plate method produces individual colonies on an agar plate. A portion of an isolated colony then may be transferred to a sterile medium to start a pure culture.

● Principle

A microbial culture consisting of two or more species is said to be a **mixed culture**, whereas a **pure culture** contains only a single species. Obtaining isolation of individual species from a mixed sample is generally the first step in identifying an organism. A commonly used **isolation technique** is the **streak plate**.

In the streak plate method of isolation, a bacterial sample (always assumed to be a mixed culture) is streaked over the surface of a plated agar medium (Figure 2-1). During streaking, the cell density decreases, eventually leading to individual cells being deposited separately on the agar surface. Cells that have been sufficiently isolated will grow into **colonies** consisting only of the original cell type. Because some colonies form from individual cells and others from pairs, chains, or clusters of cells, the term **colony-forming unit (CFU)** is a more correct description of the colony origin.

A common streaking technique is the **quadrant method**, which uses the four-streak pattern shown in Figures 2-2 and 2-3. Streaking for isolation is frequently performed on **selective media**

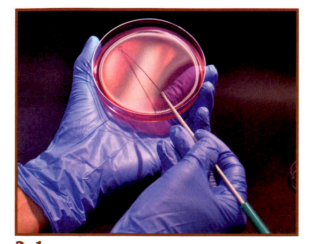

2-1 STREAKING A PLATE Hold the plate comfortably and streak with the edge of the loop. Be careful not to cut the agar.

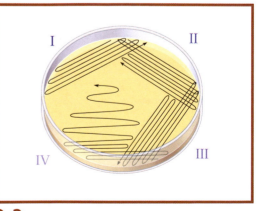

2-2 THE QUADRANT METHOD As shown, the quadrant method of streaking for isolation involves four individual streaks. The best results are obtained when the loop is flamed between streaks.

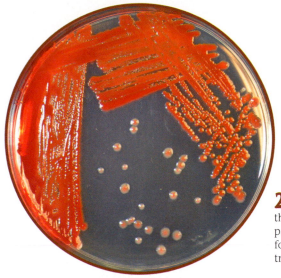

designed to encourage growth of certain types of organisms while inhibiting growth of others. The selective media considered in this section are used specifically to isolate pathogenic bacteria and yeast from human or environmental samples containing a mixture of organisms. Some selective media contain indicators that expose differences between organisms. Such media are considered to be selective and **differential**. See Tables 2-1, 2-2, and 2-3 for summaries of terms related to organisms and media, and roles of common ingredients found in selective media.

2-3 STREAK PLATE OF *SERRATIA MARCESCENS* Note the decreasing density of growth in the four streak patterns. On this plate, isolation is first obtained in the fourth streak. A portion of an individual colony may be transferred to a sterile medium to start a pure culture.

TABLE 2-1 Terms Related to Media

Term	Definition
Defined medium	A medium in which the chemical identity and exact amounts of all ingredients are known.
Undefined (complex) medium	A medium in which at least one ingredient is of unknown identity or amount.
Selective medium	A medium that contains an inhibitor to prevent or slow the growth of undesired organisms.
Differential medium	A medium that is formulated in such a way that differences in the biochemistry/physiology between organisms will be detected.

TABLE 2-2 Terms Related to Organisms

Term	Definition
Enteric	Refers to any gut bacterium, but usually to members of the *Enterobacteriaceae*, which are Gram-negative rods that ferment glucose and share other features in common.
Coliform	A member of the *Enterobacteriaceae* that produces acid (and gas) from lactose fermentation. (*Note:* this shared ability is useful for identification purposes, but is not of taxonomic significance.)
Noncoliform	A member of the *Enterobacteriaceae* that does not ferment lactose.

TABLE 2-3 Common Ingredients in Selective Media and Their Roles

Ingredient	Role
pH indicator	Plays a major role in making a medium differential; it detects acid or base production, depending on the medium.
Bile salts (oxgall)	Used to select against organisms incapable of surviving passage through the gut, especially Gram-positives.
Lactose	Used as the fermentable carbohydrate in media that differentiate between coliforms and noncoliforms.
Thiosulfate (in some form)	Used as an electron acceptor by organisms capable of reducing sulfur to H_2S.
Ferric ion	Used as an indicator of sulfur reduction by reacting with H_2S to form a black precipitate.

Bacteroides Bile Esculin (BBE) Agar

Purpose

Bacteroides fragilis is the most abundant bacterium found in the human colon, reaching densities of 10^{11} cells per gram of feces! It also is the most common anaerobic human pathogen. BBE Agar is a selective and differential medium used for the isolation and presumptive identification of *B. fragilis* and its close relatives (*B. fragilis* group).

Principle

Nutrition is supplied by a base medium of tryptic soy agar, which includes digests of casein (milk protein) and soybean meal. Other anaerobes in the sample are inhibited by oxgall (bile). Facultative anaerobes, also abundant in feces, compete with obligate anaerobes when grown anaerobically. These are inhibited by the antibiotic gentamicin. The medium also includes **esculin**, which *B. fragilis* is capable of hydrolyzing to produce **esculetin**. Esculetin in turn reacts with ferric ion in the medium to produce a brown coloration around *B. fragilis* growth (Figures 7-7 and 7-8). Presumptive identification of *B. fragilis* is based on its ability to grow on BBE and darken the medium (Figure 2-4).

2-4 *Bacteroides* **Bile Esculin Agar** This is a streak plate of a fecal specimen on BBE. The larger colonies within the darkened medium are presumptively identified as *B. fragilis* group. The smaller, lighter colonies not producing darkening of the medium are something other than *B. fragilis*.

Bismuth Sulfite Glucose Glycine Yeast (BiGGY) Agar

Purpose

BiGGY Agar is a selective and differential medium used to isolate species of the yeast *Candida*. Presumptive identification of *Candida spp.* is also possible because of the differential results. *Candida albicans* is a common inhabitant of the normal flora of the oral cavity, gastrointestinal tract, and vagina, but it is also an opportunistic pathogen, especially in immunocompromised individuals. For more information, please refer to page 183.

Principle

Carbon, nitrogen, and other nutrients are supplied by yeast extract and dextrose, whereas glycine stimulates growth. During autoclaving, sodium sulfite and bismuth ammonium citrate react to form bismuth sulfite, which is inhibitory to most bacteria, but not *Candida* species. *Candida* species reduce the bismuth sulfite (at slightly acidic or neutral pH) and produce a brown pigment within, and sometimes around, the colonies (Figure 2-5).

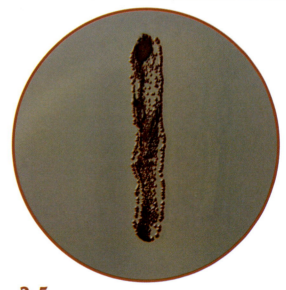

2-5 **BiGGY Agar** The ability to grow combined with the brown color (due to bismuth sulfite reduction) provides provisional identification of *Candida albicans*.

Chocolate II Agar

● Purpose

Chocolate II Agar is used for isolation and cultivation of *Neisseria* (Figures 2-6 and 2-7) and *Haemophilus* (Figure 2-8) species.

● Principle

Chocolate II Agar is made with a blend of casein, peptones, phosphate buffer, corn starch, and bovine hemoglobin. It also contains an enrichment supplement of amino and nucleic acids to encourage growth of *Neisseria* species and provide the **X** and **V blood factors** required by *Haemophilus* species (Figure 12-28).

　　This plated medium is typically streaked for isolation and incubated at 37°C in an aerobic environment enriched with carbon dioxide. Subcultures of colonies can then be grown on slanted media and used for diagnostic purposes.

2-6 *Neisseria gonorrhoeae* on Chocolate II Agar Compare colony size with Figure 2-7. *N. gonorrhoeae* colonies on Chocolate Agar are typically colorless.

2-7 *Neisseria meningitidis* on Chocolate II Agar Compare colony size with Figure 2-6. *N. meningitidis* colonies on Chocolate II Agar are typically large, blue-gray and mucoid.

2-8 *Haemophilus influenzae* on Chocolate II Agar Notice the large, smooth, mucoid colonies.

Columbia CNA With 5% Sheep Blood Agar

● Purpose

Columbia CNA with 5% Sheep Blood Agar is used to isolate and differentiate staphylococci, streptococci, and enterococci, primarily from clinical specimens.

● Principle

Columbia CNA with 5% Sheep Blood Agar is an undefined, differential, and selective medium that allows growth of Gram-positive organisms (especially staphylococci, streptococci, and enterococci) and stops or inhibits growth of most Gram-negative organisms (Figure 2-9). Casein, digest of animal tissue, beef extract, yeast extract, corn starch, and sheep blood provide a range of carbon and energy sources to support a wide variety of organisms. In addition, sheep blood supplies the X factor (heme) and yeast extract provides B-vitamins. The antibiotics colistin and nalidixic acid (CNA) act as selective agents against Gram-negative organisms by affecting membrane integrity and interfering with DNA replication, respectively. They are particularly effective against *Klebsiella*, *Proteus*, and *Pseudomonas* species. Further, sheep blood makes possible differentiation of Gram-positive organisms based on hemolytic reaction (Figures 7-10 to 7-12).

2-9 COLUMBIA CNA WITH 5% SHEEP BLOOD AGAR This plate was inoculated with four organisms—two Gram-positive cocci, and two Gram-negative rods. Only the Gram-positive organisms (left and top quadrants) grow well on the Columbia CNA agar. The two Gram-negatives either didn't grow (bottom) or grew poorly (right). Further, the top Gram-positive is β-hemolytic, whereas the one on the left is nonhemolytic.

Desoxycholate Agar

● Purpose

Desoxycholate (DOC) Agar is used for isolation and differentiation among the *Enterobacteriaceae*. It is also used to detect coliform bacteria in dairy products.

● Principle

Desoxycholate Agar is a selective and differential medium containing lactose, sodium desoxycholate, and neutral red dye. Lactose is a fermentable carbohydrate, desoxycholate is a Gram-positive inhibitor, and neutral red, which is colorless above pH 6.8 and red below, is added as a pH indicator.

Neutral red will reveal lactose fermentation (Figure 2-10) by turning the bacterial growth red where acid products have lowered the pH (Figures 2-11 and 2-12). Lactose nonfermenters will remain their natural color or the color of the medium. Thus, the characteristics to look for on DOC are the quality of growth and color production.

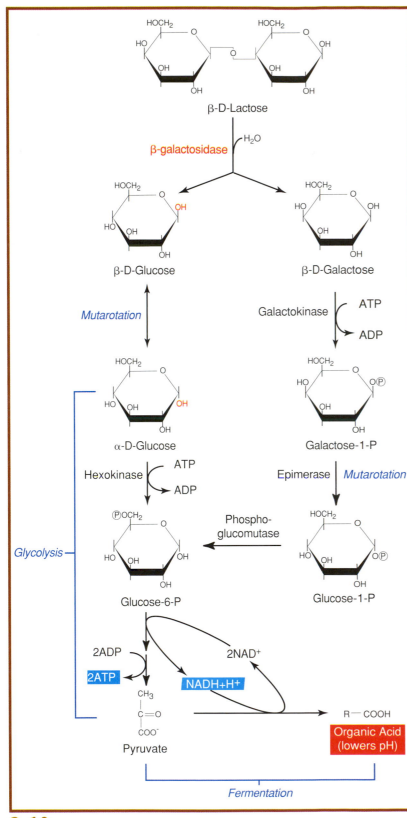

β-D-Lactose

β-galactosidase ⟶ H₂O

β-D-Glucose   β-D-Galactose

Mutarotation   Galactokinase ⟶ ATP ⟶ ADP

α-D-Glucose   Galactose-1-P

Hexokinase ⟶ ATP ⟶ ADP   Epimerase *Mutarotation*

Glycolysis   Phospho-glucomutase   Glucose-1-P

Glucose-6-P

2ADP   2NAD⁺

2ATP   NADH+H⁺

Pyruvate   R—COOH   Organic Acid (lowers pH)

Fermentation

2-10 LACTOSE FERMENTATION WITH ACID END PRODUCTS

2-11 DESOXYCHOLATE AGAR DOC medium inoculated with (clockwise from top): *Escherichia coli*, *Enterobacter aerogenes*, *Shigella flexneri*, and *Enterococcus faecalis*. Note the inhibition of the Gram-positive *E. faecalis*. Note also the red coloring of the lactose fermenting coliforms *E. coli* and *E. aerogenes*.

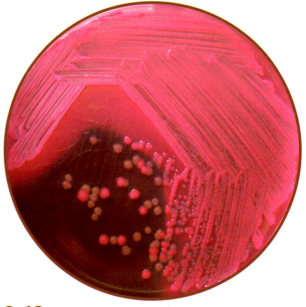

2-12 DESOXYCHOLATE AGAR STREAKED FOR ISOLATION DOC medium inoculated with the coliform *Escherichia coli* (pink) and *Shigella flexneri* (buff). The color difference is because *Shigella* is a noncoliform and doesn't ferment lactose.

Endo Agar

● Purpose

Endo agar is used to detect fecal contamination in water and dairy products. Whereas its current use is to isolate and identify the presence of enteric lactose fermenters (coliforms), its original use was to isolate and identify *Salmonella typhi*, a lactose nonfermenter (noncoliform).

● Principle

Endo Agar contains color indicators sodium sulfite and basic fuchsin (which also double as Gram-positive inhibitors). Lactose is included as a fermentable carbohydrate. Lactose fermenters (Figure 2-10) growing on the medium will appear red or pink and darken the medium slightly due to the reaction of sodium sulfite with the fermentation intermediate acetaldehyde. Refer to the Appendix for more details on fermentation. Lactose nonfermenters produce colorless to slightly pink growth (Figure 2-13). Some lactose fermenters, such as *Escherichia coli* and *Klebsiella pneumoniae* produce large amounts of acid, which gives the colonies a metallic sheen (Figure 2-14).

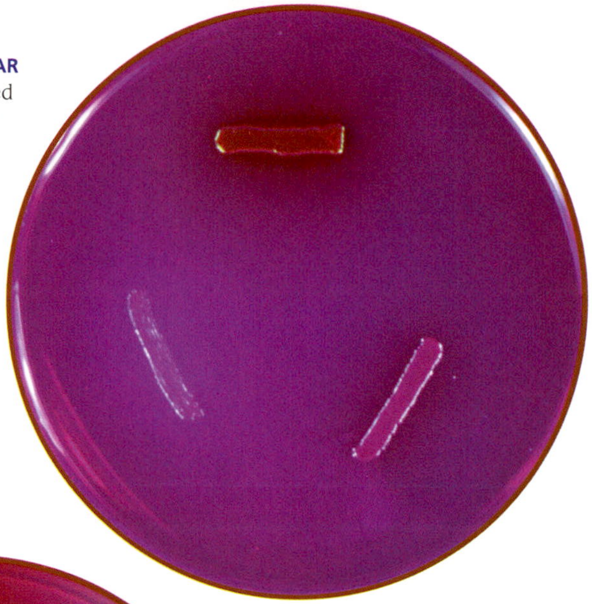

2-13 ENDO AGAR
Endo Agar inoculated with *Escherichia coli* (top), *Enterobacter aerogenes* (lower right) and *Shigella sonnei* (lower left). Notice the difference in the intensity of the pink between *E. aerogenes* (a coliform) and *S. sonnei* (a noncoliform).

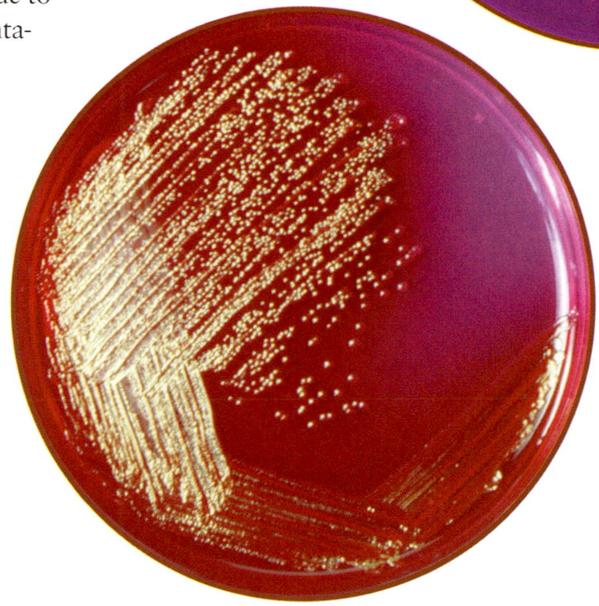

2-14 METALLIC SHEEN
Endo Agar streaked with *Escherichia coli* to illustrate the metallic sheen resulting from large amounts of acid produced during lactose fermentation.

Eosin Methylene Blue Agar

● Purpose

Eosin Methylene Blue (EMB) Agar is used for isolation of fecal coliforms. EMB Agar can be streaked for isolation or used in the Membrane Filter Technique as discussed on page 228.

● Principle

Eosin Methylene Blue agar contains peptone, lactose, sucrose, and the dyes eosin Y and methylene blue. The sugars provide fermentable substrates to encourage growth of fecal coliforms. The dyes inhibit growth of Gram-positive organisms and, under acidic conditions, also produce a dark purple complex usually accompanied by a green metallic sheen. This green metallic sheen serves as an indicator of the vigorous lactose and/or sucrose fermentation typical of fecal coliforms. Smaller amounts of acid production (typical of *Enterobacter aerogenes* and slow lactose fermenters) result in a pink coloration of the growth. Nonfermenters remain their normal color or take on the coloration of the medium (Figures 2-15 and 2-16).

2-15 **EOSIN METHYLENE BLUE AGAR** EMB agar inoculated with (clockwise from top) *Escherichia coli, Enterobacter aerogenes, Salmonella typhimurium,* and *Enterococcus faecalis*. Note the characteristic green metallic sheen of *E. coli* and the pink coloration with slight darkening of *E. aerogenes*. Both organisms are coliforms; the difference in color is due to the degree of acid production. Some *E. coli* strains appear black without the green sheen or produce colonies with dark centers. See Figure 2-16.

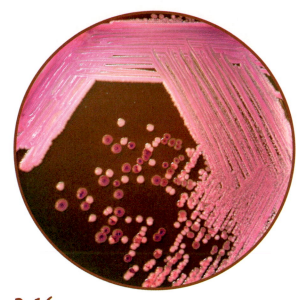

2-16 **EOSIN METHYLENE BLUE AGAR STREAKED FOR ISOLATION** EMB agar inoculated with *Escherichia coli* and *Salmonella typhimurium*. Note the dark centers in the *E. coli* colonies. *S. typhimurium* is a noncoliform and remains its natural color.

Hektoen Enteric Agar

● Purpose

Hektoen Enteric (HE) Agar is used to isolate and differentiate *Salmonella* and *Shigella* species from other Gram-negative enteric organisms.

● Principle

Hektoen Enteric Agar is an undefined medium designed to isolate *Salmonella* and *Shigella* species from other enterics based on the ability to ferment lactose, sucrose, or salicin, and to reduce sulfur to hydrogen sulfide gas (H_2S). In addition to the three sugars, sodium thiosulfate is included as a source of sulfur. Ferric ammonium citrate is added to react with H_2S and form a black precipitate. Bile salts are included to inhibit most Gram-positive cocci. Bromthymol blue and acid fuchsin dyes are added as color indicators.

Differentiation is possible as a result of the various colors produced in the colonies and in the agar. Enterics that produce acid from fermentation will produce yellow to salmon-pink colonies. Organisms like *Salmonella*, *Shigella*, and *Proteus* that do not ferment any of the sugars produce blue-green colonies. *Proteus* and *Salmonella* species that reduce sulfur to H_2S form colonies containing a black precipitate. Refer to Figures 2-17 and 2-18.

2-17 **HEKTOEN ENTERIC AGAR** HE Agar inoculated with (clockwise from top), *Escherichia coli*, *Proteus mirabilis*, *Shigella flexneri*, and *Enterococcus faecalis*. *E. coli* produces yellow color because acid is an end-product of its fermentation of lactose. *P. mirabilis* does not ferment lactose but does produce a black precipitate from the reaction between ferric ammonium citrate in the medium and H_2S from sulfur reduction. *Shigella* is also a lactose nonfermenter and is blue-green; it is not a sulfur reducer. *E. faecalis* is inhibited by the bile salts.

2-18 HEKTOEN ENTERIC AGAR STREAKED FOR ISOLATION HE agar streaked with *Salmonella typhimurium* and *Escherichia coli*. Note the black *Salmonella* colonies due to sulfur reduction and the yellow *E. coli* colonies due to lactose fermentation with acid end-products.

MacConkey Agar

● Purpose

MacConkey Agar is used to isolate and differentiate members of the *Enterobacteriaceae* based on the ability to ferment lactose. Variations on the standard medium include MacConkey Agar w/o CV (without crystal violet) to allow detection of Gram-positive cocci or MacConkey Agar CS to control swarming bacteria (such as *Proteus*) that interfere with other results.

● Principle

MacConkey Agar is a selective and differential medium containing lactose, bile salts, neutral red, and crystal violet. Bile salts and crystal violet inhibit growth of Gram-positive bacteria. Neutral red dye is a pH indicator that is colorless above a pH of 6.8 and red at a pH below 6.8. Acid accumulating from lactose fermentation turns the dye red. Lactose fermenters turn a shade of red on MacConkey agar whereas lactose nonfermenters remain their normal color or the color of the medium (Figures 2-19 and 2-20). Formulations without crystal violet allow growth of *Enterococcus* and some species of *Staphylococcus*, which ferment the lactose and appear pink on the medium.

2-19 MACCONKEY AGAR MacConkey Agar inoculated with (clockwise from top) *Escherichia coli, Enterobacter aerogenes, Shigella sonnei,* and *Proteus mirabilis. E. coli* and *E. aerogenes* produce pink color from acid-producing lactose fermentation. *S. sonnei* and *P. mirabilis,* both lactose nonfermenters, remain their normal color. Note the precipitated bile salts around the *E. coli,* also shown in Figure 2-20.

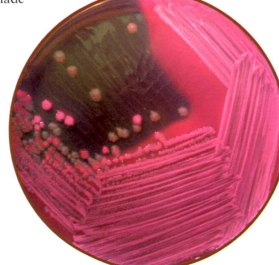

2-20 MACCONKEY AGAR STREAKED FOR ISOLATION MacConkey Agar inoculated with *Escherichia coli* and *Shigella flexneri.* Note the precipitated bile salts around the *E. coli* caused by acid from lactose fermentation.

Mannitol Salt Agar

● Purpose

Mannitol Salt Agar (MSA) is used for isolation and differentiation of pathogenic staphylococci, principally *Staphylococcus aureus*.

● Principle

Mannitol Salt Agar contains the carbohydrate mannitol, 7.5% sodium chloride (NaCl), and the pH indicator phenol red. Phenol red is yellow below pH 6.8, red at pH 7.4 to 8.4, and pink above 8.4. The sodium chloride makes this medium selective for staphylococci since most other bacteria cannot survive in this level of salinity. The pathogenic

species of *Staphylococcus* ferment mannitol (Figure 2-21) and produce acid, which turns the pH indicator yellow. Nonpathogenic staphylococcal species grow, but produce no color change. Refer to pages 71–73 and Figure A-5 in the Appendix for more information on fermentation.

The development of yellow halos around the bacterial growth is presumptive evidence that the organism is a pathogenic *Staphylococcus* (usually *S. aureus*). Good growth that produces no color change is presumptive evidence for nonpathogenic *Staphylococcus* (Figures 2-22 and 2-23). With few exceptions, organisms that grow poorly on the medium are not staphylococci.

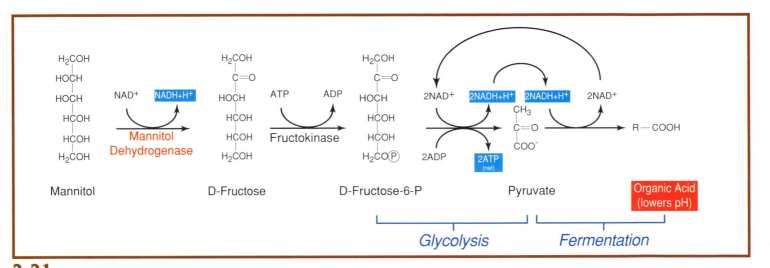

2-21 MANNITOL FERMENTATION WITH ACID END-PRODUCTS The organic acids produced lower the pH and turn the medium yellow.

2-22 MANNITOL SALT AGAR MSA inoculated with *Staphylococcus aureus* (top) and *S. epidermidis* (bottom). (*Note:* Some strains of *S. epidermidis* are inhibited by this medium). The yellow halo around *S. aureus* is due to mannitol fermentation with acid end products.

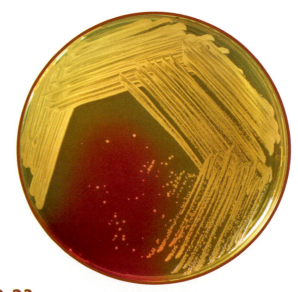

2-23 MANNITOL SALT AGAR STREAKED FOR ISOLATION MSA inoculated with *Staphylococcus aureus* and *Staphylococcus epidermidis*. The growth shown in this photo is typical of the two species on this medium; the colonies of *S. epidermidis* are small and red whereas those of *S. aureus* are slightly larger and yellow.

Phenylethyl Alcohol Agar

● Purpose

Phenylethyl (PEA) Alcohol Agar is used to isolate staphylococci and streptococci from specimens containing mixtures of bacterial flora. It is typically used for specimens thought to also contain *Escherichia coli*, or strains of *Proteus*. When prepared with 5% sheep blood, it is used for cultivation of Gram-positive anaerobes.

● Principle

PEA is an undefined, selective medium that allows growth of Gram-positive organisms and stops or inhibits growth of most Gram-negative organisms (Figure 2-24). The active ingredient, phenylethyl alcohol, functions by interfering with DNA synthesis in Gram-negative organisms.

2-24 **BRAIN HEART INFUSION AGAR *VS.* PHENYLETHYL ALCOHOL AGAR** **A** Growth on Brain Heart Infusion Agar. Clockwise from the top: *Staphylococcus aureus, Escherichia coli, Enterococcus faecium,* and *Klebsiella pneumoniae.* All show decent growth on BHIA. **B** The same organisms inoculated in the same positions of PEA. Notice that *S. aureus* and *E. faecium* grow well on both plates. *E. coli* and *K. pneumoniae* are inhibited by PEA, but *E. coli* is not completely stopped from growing.

Pseudomonas Isolation Agar

● Purpose

Pseudomonas Isolation Agar (PIA) is a selective and differential medium used to isolate nonfermenting Gram-negative bacteria in clinical samples, especially *Pseudomonas* species. It also allows differentiation of *P. aeruginosa*, a major cause of nosocomial infections (often from contamination of hospital equipment), from other pseudomonads based on its production of the pigment **pyocyanin**.

● Principle

The fatty acid synthesis inhibitor, Irgasan®[1] (also known as Triclosan), is inhibitory to many Gram-positive and Gram-negative species. *Pseudomonas* species are not affected by its activity (at its concentration in the medium) due to a membrane efflux pump. Carbon and nitrogen are provided by peptone and glycerol. Pyocyanin production is promoted by potassium sulfate, magnesium chloride, and glycerol.

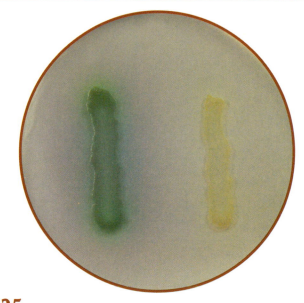

2-25 **PSEUDOMONAS ISOLATION AGAR** *Pseudomonas aeruginosa* is on the left; *P. fluorescens* is on the right. Notice the greenish color of *P. aeruginosa* due to the pigment pyocyanin.

---

[1] Irgasan is a registered trademark of Ciba-Geigy.

Salmonella–Shigella Agar

● Purpose

Salmonella-Shigella (SS) Agar is a selective medium originally used for the isolation of *Salmonella* and many *Shigella* species (*i.e.*, lactose non-fermenting enteric bacteria) from the lactose fermenting enterics (the coliforms). It is no longer recommended for isolation of *Shigella*, since Hektoen and XLD agars are more effective, but is still of use in isolating *Salmonella* species.

● Principle

Salmonella-Shigella Agar is an undefined, differential, and selective medium with bile salts and brilliant green dye acting as the selective agents against Gram-positives and many Gram-negatives. Lactose is included as a fermentable carbohydrate and sodium thiosulfate provides a source of reduceable sulfur. Neutral red is the pH indicator and ferric citrate reacts with H_2S to form a black precipitate, thus indicating sulfur reduction. Lactose fermenters will produce reddish colonies as neutral red changes from colorless to red in the low pH. *Salmonella* and *Shigella* species will be their natural color due to their inability to ferment lactose. *Salmonella* and *Proteus* species typically reduce sulfur, which is indicated by colonies with black centers. Refer to Figures 2-26 and 2-27.

2-26 *SALMONELLA-SHIGELLA AGAR* SS Agar inoculated with (clockwise from top) *Escherichia coli*, *Shigella flexneri*, *Salmonella typhimurium*, and *Enterococcus faecalis*. Note the pink color of *E. coli* due to acid production during lactose fermentation. Note also the black precipitate in the *Salmonella* growth due to the reaction of ferric citrate in the medium with H_2S produced from sulfur reduction. This phenomenon produces black colonies when the organism is streaked for isolation (Figure 2-27). Growth of *E. faecalis* is inhibited by bile salts and brilliant green dye.

2-27 *SALMONELLA-SHIGELLA AGAR* **STREAKED FOR ISOLATION** SS Agar inoculated with *Salmonella typhimurium* and *Shigella flexneri*. Note the colonies with black centers and clear edges characteristic of *Salmonella* on this medium.

Tellurite Glycine Agar

● Purpose

Tellurite Glycine Agar is an undefined, selective, and differential medium used for the isolation of coagulase-positive staphylococci from various sources. The most common and clinically important coagulase-positive staphylococcus is *Staphylococcus aureus*.

● Principle

Among the ingredients of Tellurite Glycine Agar are the carbohydrate mannitol, potassium tellurite, and lithium chloride. Organisms, such as the coagulase-positive *Staphylococcus aureus*, are able to ferment the mannitol and reduce the tellurite. When tellurite is reduced it produces a precipitate that turns the colonies black. Therefore, an organism that grows well on the medium and produces black colonies is likely *S. aureus* and is thus differentiated from coagulase-negative staphylococci and Gram-negative bacteria (Figure 2-28).

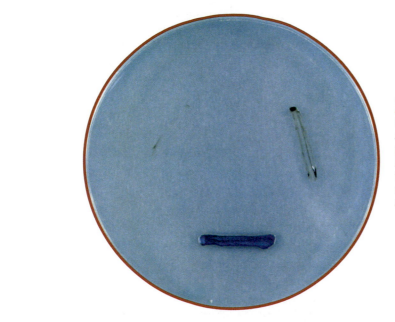

2-28 TELLURITE GLYCINE AGAR Clockwise from the top right: Gram-positive, coagulase-negative *Staphylococcus epidermidis,* Gram-positive, coagulase-positive *Staphylococcus aureus,* and Gram-negative *Escherichia coli,* grown on Tellurite Glycine Agar. Notice that *E. coli* is inhibited, and that the two staphylococci may be differentiated by their ability to reduce sulfur and turn the growth black.

TCBS Agar

● Purpose

Thiosulfate Citrate Bile Sucrose (TCBS) Agar is an undefined, selective, and differential medium used for the primary isolation of *Vibrio* species. Clinical and nonclinical specimens suspected of fecal contamination are streaked on TCBS in an effort to recover *Vibrio cholerae,* the most important pathogen of the genus.

● Principle

The medium's alkaline pH (8.6) promotes growth of *Vibrio spp.,* especially that of *V. cholerae.* Oxgall and sodium cholate are included to inhibit the growth of Gram-positive bacteria. Sucrose is the fermentable carbohydrate and sodium thiosulfate is included as an electron acceptor for sulfur reducers. Bromthymol blue is the pH indicator and ferric ammonium citrate is included to indicate sulfur reduction.

Sucrose fermenters producing acid end-products (such as *Vibrio cholerae*) form yellow colonies (Figure 2-29) while those of sucrose nonfermenters are blue. Some *Enterococci* ferment sucrose but are inhibited by the oxgall. These organisms, as shown in Figure 2-30, produce small yellow colonies. Species able to reduce thiosulfate to H_2S produce black colonies due to the reaction of H_2S with the ferric ion in the medium.

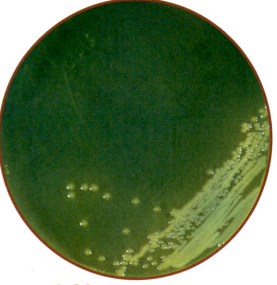

2-29 *VIBRIO CHOLERAE* STREAKED ON TCBS AGAR The large, yellow colonies are indicative of *Vibrio cholerae.*

2-30 *ENTEROCOCCUS FAECALIS* STREAKED ON TCBS AGAR This Gram-positive coccus may also be recovered from fecally contaminated samples; however, its yellow colonies are much smaller than those of *V. cholerae.* Compare the *E. faecalis* colonies with those in Figure 2-29.

Xylose Lysine Desoxycholate Agar

● Purpose

Xylose Lysine Desoxycholate (XLD) Agar is a selective and differential medium used to isolate and identify *Shigella* and *Providencia* from stool samples.

● Principle

XLD Agar is a selective and differential medium containing sodium desoxycholate, xylose, L-lysine, and ferric ammonium citrate. Desoxycholate is a Gram-positive inhibitor, xylose is a fermentable carbohydrate, L-lysine is an amino acid provided for decarboxylation (See Decarboxylation, page 67), and ferric ammonium citrate is an indicator to mark the presence of hydrogen sulfide gas (H_2S) from sulfur reduction. Phenol red, which is yellow when acidic and red or pink when alkaline, is added as a pH indicator.

Organisms that ferment xylose will acidify the medium and produce yellow colonies. Organisms able to remove the carboxyl group from (decarboxylate) L-lysine will release alkaline products and produce red colonies. Organisms able to reduce sulfur will produce a black precipitate in the growth due to the reaction of ferric ammonium citrate with H_2S.

Shigella and *Providencia*, which do not ferment xylose but decarboxylate lysine, appear red on the medium. *Salmonella* species, which ferment xylose but then decarboxylate the lysine also appear as red colonies but with black centers due to the reduction of sulfur to H_2S. Other enterics that would ordinarily revert to decarboxylation after exhausting the sugar and alkalinize the medium are prevented from doing so by the high sugar content and the short incubation time. These organisms appear yellow on the medium (Figure 2-31).

2-31 XYLOSE LYSINE DESOXYCHOLATE AGAR
XLD agar inoculated with (clockwise from top): *Proteus mirabilis* (positive for sulfur reduction), *Salmonella typhimurium* (atypically negative for sulfur reduction), and *Escherichia coli* (positive for lactose fermentation).

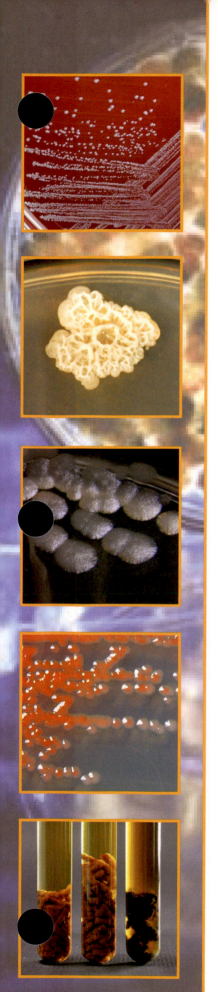

Bacterial Growth

3

Growth Patterns on Agar

● Purpose

Recognizing different bacterial growth morphologies on agar plates is a useful and often crucial step in the identification process. Agar slants are typically used for cultivation of pure cultures. Bacteria also frequently display distinct morphological color and texture on agar slants.

● Principle

When a single bacterial cell is deposited on a solid nutrient medium, it begins to divide. One cell makes two, two make four, four make eight . . . one million make two million, and so on. Eventually a **colony** appears where the original cell was deposited. Once the purity of a colony has been confirmed by an appropriate staining procedure (Sections 5 and 6), cells can then be transferred to a sterile medium to begin a **pure culture**.

Color, size, shape, and texture of microbial growth are determined by the genetic makeup of the organism. However, organismal genetic expression is also greatly influenced by environmental factors including nutrient availability, temperature, and incubation time. Colony characteristics may be viewed with the naked eye or with the assistance of a colony counter (Figure 3-1).

The basic categories of growth include colony shape, margin (edge), elevation, color, and texture (Figure 3-2). Colony shape may be described as **circular**, **irregular**, or **punctiform** (tiny). The margin may be **entire** (smooth, with no irregularities), **undulate** (wavy), **lobate** (lobed), **filamentous**, or **rhizoid** (branched like roots). Colony elevations include **flat**, **raised**, **convex**, **pulvinate** (very convex), and **umbonate** (raised in the center). Colony texture may be **moist**, **mucoid**, or **dry**. Pigment production is another useful characteristic and may be combined with optical properties such as **opaque**, **translucent**, **shiny**, or **dull**.

3-1 THE COLONY COUNTER Subtle differences in colony shape and size can best be viewed on the colony counter. The **transmitted light** and magnifying glass allow observation of greater detail, however, colony color is best determined with **reflected** light. The grid in the background is used as a counting aid. Each big square is a square centimeter.

19

Figures 3-3 through 3-31 show a variety of bacterial colony forms and characteristics. Where applicable, contrasting environmental factors are indicated. Figures 3-32 and 3-34 show growth characteristics on agar slants.

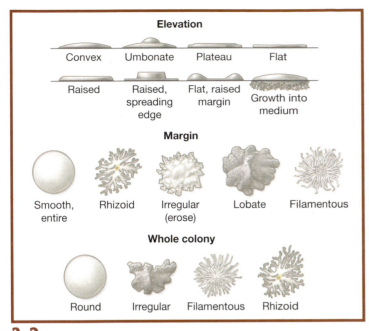

3-2 A SAMPLING OF BACTERIAL COLONY FEATURES These terms are used to describe colonial morphology. Descriptions also should include color, surface characteristics (dull or shiny), consistency (dry, butyrous-buttery, or moist) and optical properties (opaque or translucent).

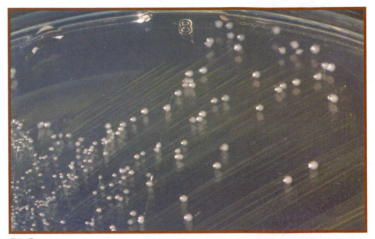

3-3 *ENTEROCOCCUS FAECIUM* GROWN ON NUTRIENT AGAR The colonies are white, circular, convex, smooth, and have an entire margin. *E. faecium* (formerly known as *Streptococcus faecium*) is found in human and animal feces.

3-4 *STAPHYLOCOCCUS EPIDERMIDIS* GROWN ON SHEEP BLOOD AGAR The colonies are white, raised, circular, and entire. *S. epidermidis* is an opportunistic pathogen.

3-5 *MICROCOCCUS LUTEUS* GROWN ON BRAIN HEART INFUSION AGAR These colonies are yellow, smooth, and convex with a regular margin. They range in size from 1 to 3 mm. *M. luteus* is common in soil, dust, and on human skin.

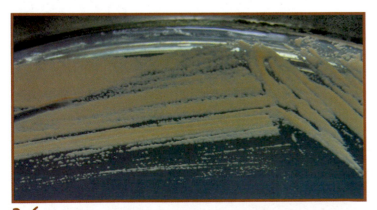

3-6 *KOCURIA ROSEA* GROWN ON BRAIN HEART INFUSION AGAR Pink, punctiform (these are less than 1 mm in diameter), smooth, regular colonies typify *K. rosea*, an inhabitant of water, dust, and salty foods.

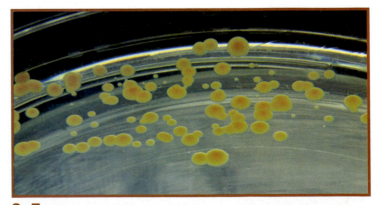

3-7 *SARCINA AURANTIACA* GROWN ON BRAIN HEART INFUSION AGAR *S. aurantiaca* produced yellow-orange, smooth, convex, regular colonies on BHIA. These are between 1 to 3 mm in diameter.

3-8 *RHODOCOCCUS RHODOCHROUS* **GROWN ON BRAIN HEART INFUSION AGAR** These colonies are reddish-pink, smooth, and convex with a regular margin. They are about 1 mm in diameter. *Rhodococcus* species are soil organisms.

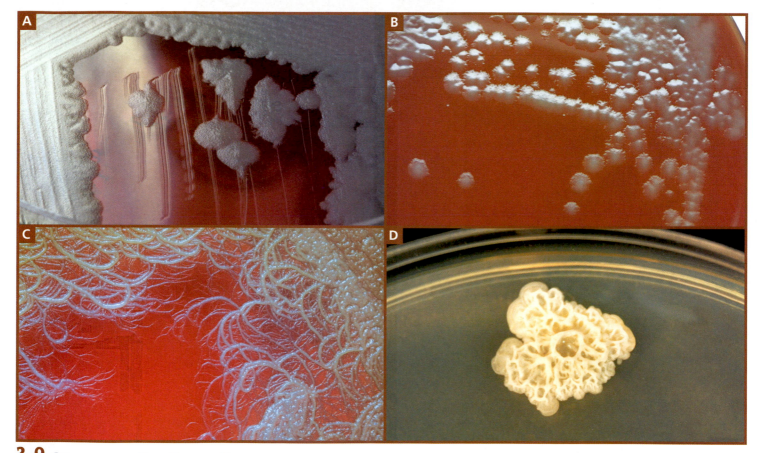

3-9 **COMPARISON OF FOUR** *BACILLUS* **SPECIES** **A** *B. cereus* grown on Blood Agar produces distinctively large (up to 7 mm), gray, granular, irregular colonies. They often produce a "mousy" smell. Also note the extensions of growth along the streak line. **B** *B. anthracis* colonies resemble *B. cereus*, but are usually smaller and adhere to the medium more tenaciously. **C** *B. mycoides* produces rapidly spreading, rhizoid colonies. **D** This unknown *Bacillus* isolated as a laboratory contaminant produced wrinkled, irregular colonies with an undulate (wavy) margin.

3-10 "MEDUSA HEAD" COLONIES OF *CLOSTRIDIUM SPOROGENES* ON BLOOD AGAR These irregularly circular colonies have a raised, yellow center and a flat, spreading edge of tangled filaments (reminiscent of the mythological creature Medusa, who had snakes for hair!). They vary in size from 2 to 6 mm.

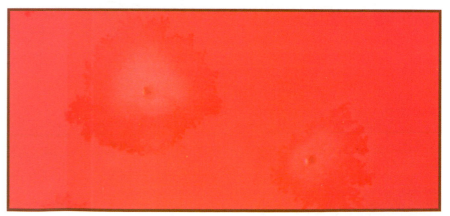

3-11 *PROVIDENCIA STUARTII* **GROWN ON NUTRIENT AGAR** The colonies are shiny, buff, and convex. *P. stuartii* is a frequent isolate in urine samples obtained from hospitalized and catheterized patients. *P. stuartii* is highly resistant to antibiotics.

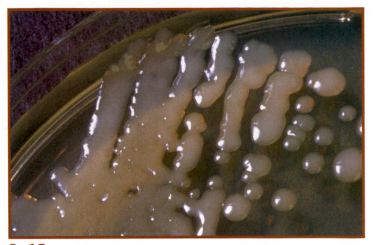

3-12 *KLEBSIELLA PNEUMONIAE* **GROWN ON NUTRIENT AGAR** The colonies are mucoid, raised, and shiny. While it is a normal inhabitant of the human intestinal tract, it is associated with community-acquired pneumonia and nososomial urinary tract infections.

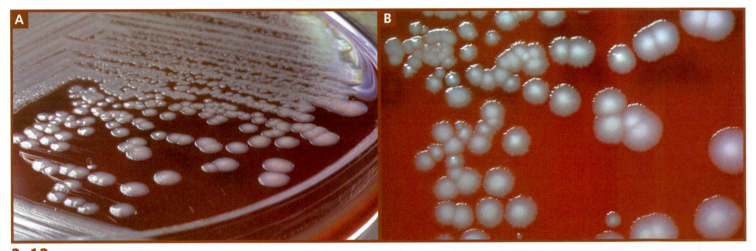

3-13 *ALCALIGENES FAECALIS* **COLONIES ON SHEEP BLOOD AGAR** The colonies of this opportunistic pathogen are umbonate with an opaque center and a spreading edge. **A** Side view. Note the raised center. **B** Close-up of the *A. faecalis* colonies showing spreading edge.

3-14 *CITROBACTER KOSERI* **GROWN ON SHEEP BLOOD AGAR** The colonies are round, smooth, and opaque with a regular margin. This species is also able to partially hemolyze red blood cells (α-hemolytic), as evidenced by the greening around each colony. They range in size from 1 to 2 mm.

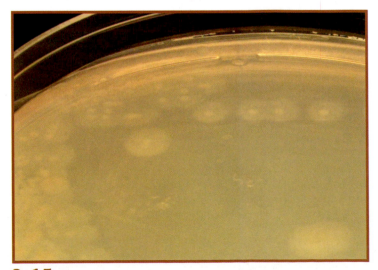

3-15 *ERWINIA AMYLOVORA* **GROWN ON BRAIN HEART INFUSION AGAR** These colonies are whitish, transluscent, spreading, and umbonate. *Erwinia* species are plant pathogens.

3-16 *RHIZOBIUM LEGUMINOSARUM* **GROWN ON BRAIN HEART INFUSION AGAR** The colonies are convex, circular, and filamentous. They are translucent at the edges and about 5 mm in diameter. *R. leguminosarum* is capable of producing root nodules (tumors) in many legumes and subsequently fixing atmospheric nitrogen.

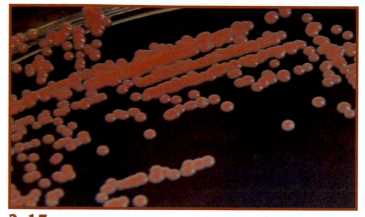

3-17 *DEINOCOCCUS RADIODURANS* **GROWN ON TRYTPICASE SOY AGAR** These small (between 1 and 2 mm in diameter), round, convex, and regular colonies took 36 hours to develop the orange color. This species is highly resistant to ionizing radiation.

3-18 *MYCOBACTERIUM SMEGMATIS* **GROWN ON SHEEP BLOOD AGAR** The colonies of this slow growing relative of *M. tuberculosis* are punctiform.

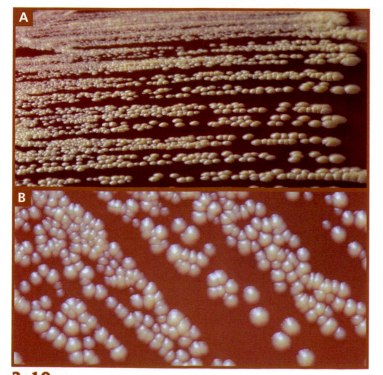

3-19 *CORYNEBACTERIUM XEROSIS* **GROWN ON SHEEP BLOOD AGAR** **A** As seen in this view from the side, the colonies are dull, buff, and convex. **B** Close-up of circular *C. xerosis* colonies. *C. xerosis* is rarely an opportunistic pathogen.

3-20 **UMBONATE COLONY OF AN ANAEROBIC LAB CONTAMINANT** The colony on the left is truly umbonate. The one on the right is getting there. Their diameters are about 3 mm.

3-21 *STREPTOMYCES GRISEUS* **GROWN ON BRAIN HEART INFUSION AGAR** These colonies are circular and ridged with a granular appearance. At a later stage of development, they produce yellow reproductive spores. Growth of streptomycetes is associated with an "earthy" smell. This one plate fragranced the entire incubator!

3-22 **SWARMING GROWTH PATTERN** Members of the genus *Proteus* will swarm at certain intervals and produce a pattern of concentric rings due to their motility. This is a photograph of *P. vulgaris* demonstrating swarming behavior on DNase agar.

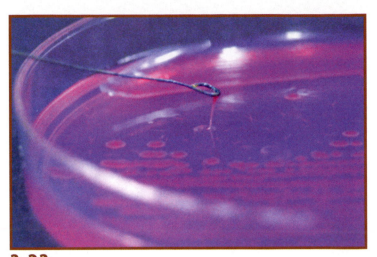

3-23 **MUCOID COLONIES** *Pseudomonas aeruginosa* grown on Endo agar demonstrates a mucoid texture. *P. aeruginosa* is found in soil and water, and can cause infections in burn patients.

3-24 **BUTYROUS COLONY OF AN UNKNOWN SOIL ISOLATE** This 12 mm colony was found on a Glycerol Yeast Extract plate inoculated with a diluted soil sample. It was almost liquid in composition, something that is indicated by its contact with the yellow colony to its right.

3-25 **CHROMOBACTERIUM VIOLACEUM GROWN ON SHEEP BLOOD AGAR** *C. violaceum* produces shiny, purple, convex colonies. It is found in soil and water, and rarely produces infections in humans.

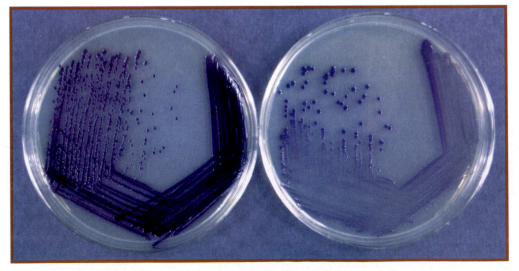

3-26 **INFLUENCE OF NUTRIENT AVAILABILITY ON PIGMENT PRODUCTION** Pigment production may be influenced by environmental factors such as nutrient availability. *Chromobacterium violaceum* produces a much more intense purple pigment when grown on Trypticase Soy Agar (left) than when grown on Nutrient Agar, a less nutritious medium (right).

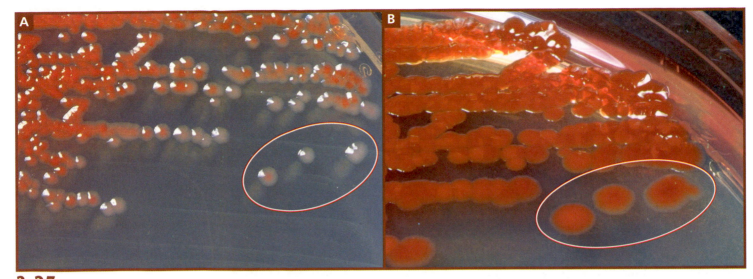

3-27 **INFLUENCE OF AGE ON PIGMENT PRODUCTION** **A** *Serratia marcescens* grown on Sheep Blood Agar after 24 hours. **B** The same plate of *S. marcescens* after 48 hours. Note in particular the change in the 3 colonies in the lower right (encircled).

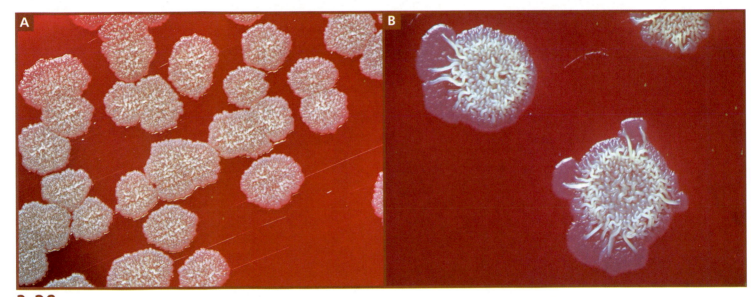

3-28 **EFFECT OF AGE ON COLONY MORPHOLOGY** **A** Close-up of *Bacillus subtilis* on Sheep Blood Agar after 24 hours of incubation. **B** Close-up of *B. subtilis* on Sheep Blood Agar after 48 hours. Note the wormlike appearance.

3-29 **DIFFUSIBLE PIGMENT OF *PSEUDOMONAS AERUGINOSA*** The blue-green pigment pyocyanin often makes *P. aeruginosa* easy to identify.

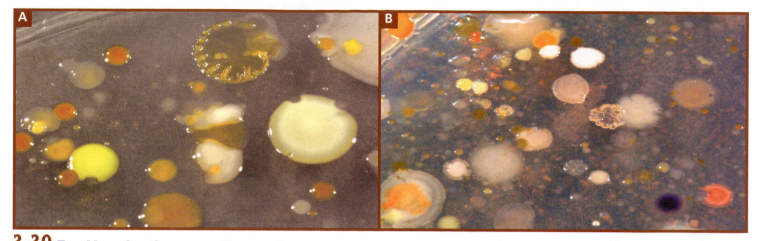

3-30 **TWO MIXED SOIL CULTURES ON NUTRIENT AGAR** These plates show the morphological diversity present in two soil samples.

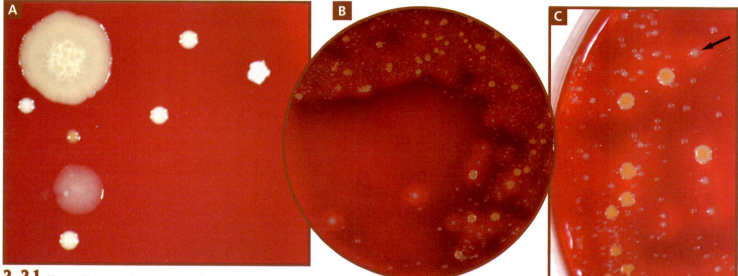

3-31 **THREE THROAT CULTURES ON SHEEP BLOOD AGAR**
A There are probably five different species on this plate. **B** Note the α-hemolysis (darkening of the agar; see page 61 for more information) shown by much of the growth. **C** This is a close-up of the same plate as in **B**. Note the weak β-hemolysis of the white colony in the upper right (**arrow**). White growth with β-hemolysis is characteristic of *Staphylococcus aureus*.

3-32 **PIGMENT PRODUCTION ON SLANTS** From left to right, *Staphylococcus epidermidis* (white), *Pseudomonas aeruginosa* (green), *Chromobacterium violaceum* (violet), *Serratia marcescens* (red/orange), *Kocuria rosea* (rose), and *Micrococcus luteus* (yellow).

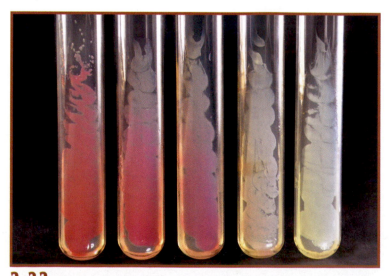

3-33 **INFLUENCE OF TEMPERATURE ON PIGMENT PRODUCTION** *Serratia marcescens* was grown for 48 hours on Trypticase Soy Agar slants at five different temperatures. From left to right: 25°C, 30°C, 33°C, 35°C, and 37°C. A difference of 2°C makes the difference between being pigmented or not!

3-34 GROWTH TEXTURE ON SLANTS From left to right, *Bacillus* spp. (flat, dry), *Alcaligenes faecalis* (spreading edge), *Mycobacterium phlei* (crusty/friable), *Lactobacillus plantarum* (transparent, barely visible).

Growth Patterns in Broth

● Purpose

Bacterial genera—and frequently different species within a genus—demonstrate characteristic growth patterns in broth that provide useful information when attempting to identify an organism.

● Principle

Microorganisms cultivated in broth display a variety of growth characteristics. Some organisms float on top of the medium and produce a type of surface membrane called a **pellicle**; others sink to the bottom as **sediment**. Some bacteria produce **uniform fine turbidity** while others appear to clump in what is called **flocculent** growth. Refer to Figures 3-35 and 3-36. Figure 3-37 shows an example of a pigmented species (*Rhodospirillum rubrum*) in broth.

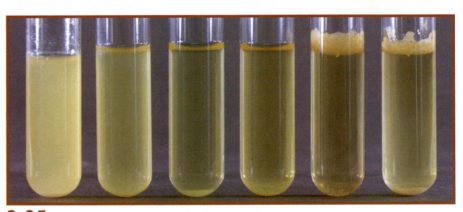

3-35 GROWTH PATTERNS IN BROTH From left to right in pairs (by type of organism): *Enterobacter aerogenes* and *Citrobacter diversus*—motile members of *Enterobacteriaceae* (uniform fine turbidity), *Enterococcus faecalis* and *Staphylococcus aureus*—nonmotile Gram-positive cocci (sediment), *Mycobacterium phlei* and *Mycobacterium smegmatis* (relatives of *Mycobacterium tuberculosis*)—nonmotile with a waxy cell wall (pellicle).

3-36 FLOCCULENCE IN BROTH
This is a *Streptococcus* species from a throat culture demonstrating flocculence in Todd-Hewitt Broth.

3-37 PIGMENT IN BROTH *Rhodospirillum rubrum* has a red color due to carotenoid pigments. It grows as a photoheterotroph in the presence of light and the absence of oxygen.

Aerotolerance

● Purpose

The two procedures discussed here—**agar deep stabs** and **agar shakes**—are good visual indicators of oxygen tolerance (aerotolerance) in microorganisms.

● Principle

Most microorganisms can survive within a range of environmental conditions, but not surprisingly, tend to produce growth with the greatest density in the areas where conditions are most favorable. One important resource influencing microbial growth is oxygen. Some organisms require oxygen for their metabolic needs. Some other organisms are not affected by it at all. Still other organisms cannot even survive in its presence. This ability or inability to live in the presence of oxygen is called **aerotolerance**.

Most growth media are sterilized in an autoclave during preparation. This process not only kills unwanted microbes, but also removes most of the free oxygen from the medium as well. After the medium is removed from the autoclave and allowed to cool, the oxygen begins to diffuse back in. In tubed media (both liquid and solid) this process creates a gradient of oxygen concentrations, ranging from **aerobic** at the top, nearest the source of oxygen, to **anaerobic** at the bottom. Because of microorganisms' natural tendency to proliferate where the oxygen concentration best suits their metabolic needs, differing degrees of population density will develop in the medium over time that can be used to visually examine their aerotolerance.

Obligate (strict) aerobes, organisms that require oxygen for respiration, grow at the top where oxygen is most plentiful. **Facultative anaerobes** grow in the presence or absence of oxygen. When oxygen is available, they respire aerobically. When oxygen is not available, they either respire anaerobically (reducing sulfur or nitrate instead of oxygen) or ferment an available substrate. Refer to the Appendix and Section 7 for more information on anaerobic respiration and fermentation. Where an oxygen gradient exists, facultative anaerobes grow throughout the medium but are more dense at the top. **Aerotolerant anaerobes** (or simply "aerotolerants"—not to be confused with "aerotolerance"), organisms that don't require oxygen and are not adversely affected by it, live uniformly throughout the medium. Aerotolerant anaerobes ferment even in the presence of free oxygen. **Microaerophiles**, as the name suggests, survive only in environments containing lower than atmospheric levels of oxygen. Some

microaerophiles called **capnophiles** can survive only if carbon dioxide levels are elevated. Microaerophiles will be seen somewhere near the middle or upper middle region of the medium. Finally, **obligate (strict) anaerobes** are organisms for which even small amounts of oxygen are lethal and, therefore, will be seen only in the lower regions of the medium, depending on how far into the medium the oxygen has diffused.

Agar deep stabs are prepared with Tryptic Soy Agar (TSA) enriched with yeast extract to promote growth of a broad range of organisms. Oxygen, which is removed from the medium during preparation and autoclaving, immediately begins to diffuse back in as the agar cools and solidifies. This process creates a gradient of oxygen concentrations in the medium, ranging from aerobic at the top to anaerobic at the bottom.

Agar deeps are stab-inoculated with an inoculating needle to introduce as little air as possible. The location of growth that develops indicates the organism's aerotolerance (Figure 3-38).

Agar shakes are also prepared with enriched TSA, but differ from agar deep stabs in that, after autoclaving, they are cooled to 45°C and placed in a warm water bath until time for inoculation. Agar shakes are inoculated in liquid form, mixed gently to distribute the bacteria evenly throughout the medium, and allowed to solidify. Like agar deep stabs, the location of growth that develops in agar shakes indicates the aerotolerance of the organism (Figure 3-39).

3-38 AGAR DEEP STAB TUBES From left to right: *Clostridium butyricum* (strict anaerobe), *Staphylococcus aureus* (facultative anaerobe), and *Pseudomonas aeruginosa* (strict aerobe).

3-39 AGAR SHAKE TUBES From left to right, *Clostridium butyricum* (strict anaerobe), *Escherichia coli* (facultative anaerobe), uninoculated control, and *Pseudomonas aeruginosa* (strict aerobe).

Cultivation of Anaerobes—Anaerobic Jar

● Purpose

Cultivation of obligate anaerobes and microaerophiles requires providing an environment in which oxygen is either absent or considerably reduced. Various methods have been devised to provide these environments, three of which are covered in the remainder of Section 3.

The anaerobic jar (Figure 3-40) is used to grow obligate anaerobes and microaerophiles. Because it is the atmosphere within the jar that is anaerobic, the jar can be incubated in a normal incubator alongside aerobically grown cultures.

● Principle

Inoculated plates or tubes are placed in the jar and the appropriate gas-generating sachet is activated. In the case of the Anaerogen™ Gas Generating System by Oxoid, simply opening the packet inside the jar and immediately clamping the lid on the jar is all that is necessary. Ascorbic acid in the packet reacts with free oxygen and in turn releases CO_2. Within 30 minutes, the atmosphere inside the jar is less than 1% O_2 and between 9 and 13% CO_2. A methylene blue (or some other) indicator strip is also placed inside the jar. It will turn blue if exposed to air, thus acting as a control to ensure anaerobic conditions have been produced. Figure 3-41 shows two plates inoculated with the same organisms, but one was incubated anaerobically while the other was incubated aerobically.

The Oxoid Campygen™ sachet works in a similar way, but produces 5% O_2, 10% CO_2, and 85% N_2. It is designed for growing microaerophiles, such as *Campylobacter jejuni*.

3-40 THE ANAEROBIC JAR Note the sachet and the white indicator strip inside the jar. The sachet has performed properly, reducing the oxygen level within the jar to less than 1%, as evidenced by the indicator strip. If the indicator were blue, it would mean free oxygen remained in the jar and the resulting growth would be in question relative to its ability to survive in anaerobic conditions.

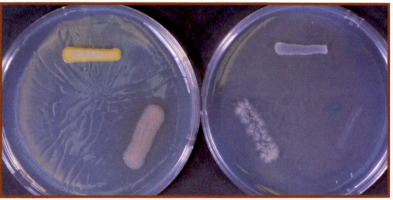

3-41 PLATES INCUBATED INSIDE AND OUTSIDE THE ANAEROBIC JAR Both Nutrient Agar plates were inoculated with *Staphylococcus aureus* (top), *Pseudomonas aeruginosa* (right), and *Clostridium sporogenes* (left). The plate on the left was incubated aerobically outside the jar; the plate on the right was incubated inside the anaerobic jar. Note the relative amounts of growth of the three organisms.

Cultivation of Anaerobes—Thioglycollate Broth

● Purpose

Fluid Thioglycollate Medium is a simple, inexpensive system for cultivating small numbers of anaerobic or microaerophilic bacteria. It is a liquid medium formulated to promote growth of a wide variety of fastidious anaerobic and microaerophilic microorganisms.

● Principle

Fluid Thioglycollate Medium is prepared as a basic medium or with a variety of supplements, depending on the specific needs of organisms being cultivated. As such, it is appropriate for a broad variety of aerobic and anaerobic, fastidious and nonfastidious organisms. It is particularly well adapted for cultivation of strict anaerobes and microaerophiles.

Key components of the medium are yeast extract, pancreatic digest of casein, dextrose, sodium thioglycollate, L-cystine, and resazurin. Yeast extract and pancreatic digest of casein provide nutrients; sodium thioglycollate and L-cystine reduce oxygen to water; and resazurin (pink when oxidized, colorless when reduced) acts as an indicator. A small amount of agar is included to slow oxygen diffusion.

3-42 **AEROBIC ZONE IN THIOGLYCOLLATE MEDIUM** Note the pink region in the top (oxidized) portion of the broth. The bottom (reduced) portion of the medium remains colorless.

Oxygen is removed from the medium during autoclaving but begins to diffuse back in as the tubes cool to room temperature. This produces a gradient of concentrations from fully aerobic at the top to anaerobic at the bottom. Thus, fresh media will appear clear to straw colored with a pink region at the top where the dye has become oxidized (Figure 3-42). Figure 3-43 demonstrates some basic bacterial growth patterns in the medium as influenced by the oxygen gradient.

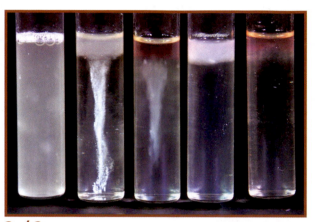

3-43 **GROWTH PATTERNS IN THIOGLYCOLLATE MEDIUM** Growth patterns of a variety of organisms are shown in these Fluid Thioglycollate Broths. Pictured from left to right are: aerotolerant anaerobe, facultative anaerobe, strict anaerobe, strict aerobe, and microaerophile. Compare these tubes with the uninoculated broth in Figure 3-42.

Cultivation of Anaerobes—Cooked Meat Broth

● Purpose

The purpose of Cooked Meat Broth is to grow anaerobes, especially pathogenic clostridia such as *Clostridium perfringens*, *C. tetani*, *C. botulinum*, and *C. difficile*. Certain clostridia are proteolytic, whereas others are saccharolytic.

Because it is the medium that becomes anaerobic, these tubes can be incubated in an aerobic incubator, thus eliminating the need for expensive equipment.

● Principle

Cooked Meat Broth (Figure 3-44) is a nutrient rich medium, with beef heart, peptone, and dextrose acting as carbon and nitrogen sources. The beef heart is in the form of meat particles, whereas the other ingredients are dissolved in the broth. Anaerobic conditions occur as a result of several factors. One, cardiac muscle contains glutathione, a tripeptide that can reduce free molecular oxygen in the medium. Two, the meat is cooked prior to use. This denatures proteins and exposes their sulfhydryl groups, which perform the same function—oxygen reduction. Lastly, the medium with caps loosened is either incubated in an anaerobic jar for 24 hours to remove O_2 or boiled to drive off the O_2. Caps are immediately tightened to prevent the reentry of O_2. Blackening and disintegration of the meat particles indicate proteolytic growth. Acid (not indicated directly) and gas production indicate saccharolytic growth.

3-44 **COOKED MEAT BROTH** The meat particles are visible in each broth. From left to right: *Clostridium butyricum*, uninoculated, *C. sporogenes*. Blackening of the meat particles by *C. sporogenes* is indicative of proteolytic activity. *C. butyricum* grew, but is not proteolytic.

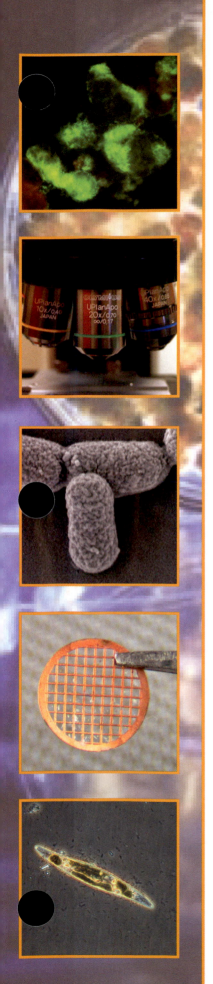

Microscopy

Types of Microscopy

The earliest microscopes used visible light to create images and were little more than magnifying glasses. Today, more sophisticated compound light microscopes (Figure 4-1) are routinely used in microbiology laboratories. The various types of light microscopy include bright-field, dark-field, fluorescence, and phase contrast microscopy (Figure 4-2). Although each method has specific applications and advantages, bright-field microscopy is most commonly used in introductory classes and clinical laboratories. Many research applications use electron microscopy because of its ability to produce higher quality images of greater magnification.

Light Microscopes

Bright-field microscopy produces an image made from light that is transmitted through a specimen (Figure 4-2A). The specimen restricts light transmission and appears "shadowy" against a bright background (where light enters the microscope unimpeded). Because most biological specimens are transparent, contrast between the specimen and the background can be improved with the application of stains to the specimen (see Sections 5 and 6). The price of improved contrast is that the staining process usually kills cells. This is especially true of bacterial staining protocols.

Image formation begins with light coming from an internal or an external light source (Figure 4-3). It passes through the **condenser** lens, which concentrates the light and makes illumination of the specimen more uniform. **Refraction** (bending) of light as it passes

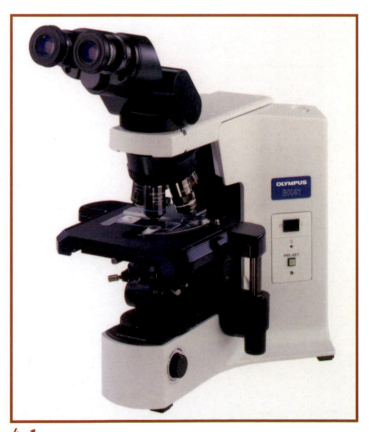

4-1 A BINOCULAR COMPOUND MICROSCOPE A quality microscope is an essential tool for microbiologists. Most are assembled with exchangeable component parts and can be customized to suit the particular needs of the user. Photograph courtesy of Olympus America Inc.

4-2 TYPES OF LIGHT MICROSCOPY A This is a bright-field micrograph of an entire diatom (called a "whole mount"). Because of its thickness, the entire organism will not be in focus at once. Continually adjusting the fine focus to clearly observe different levels of the organism will give a sense of its three-dimensional structure. The bright rods around the diatom are bacteria. **B** The same diatom viewed with dark-field microscopy. Notice that dark-field is especially good at providing contrast between the organism's edge and its interior and the background. Notice also that the bacteria are not visible, though this would not always be the case. **C** This phase contrast image of the same diatom shows different details of the interior than what is seen in the other two micrographs. Also, notice the bacteria are dark. **D** This is a fluorescence micrograph of *Mycobacterium kansasii*. The apple green is one of the characteristic colors of fluorescence microscopy.

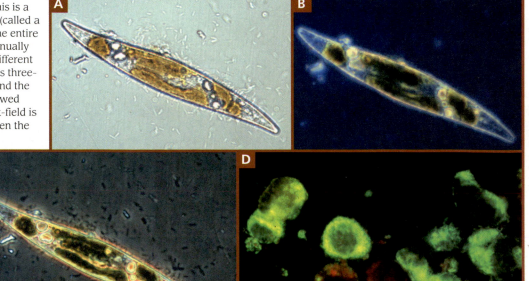

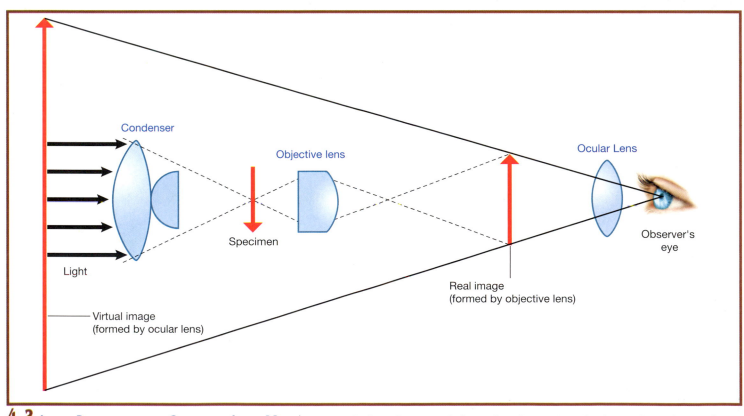

4-3 IMAGE PRODUCTION IN A COMPOUND LIGHT MICROSCOPE Light from the source is focused on the specimen by the condenser lens. It then enters the objective lens, where it is magnified to produce a real image. The real image is magnified again by the ocular lens to produce a virtual image that is seen by the eye.

(After Chan, et al., 1986)

through the **objective lens** from the specimen produces a magnified **real image.** This image is magnified again as it passes through the **ocular lens** to produce a **virtual image** that appears below or within the microscope. The amount of magnification produced by each lens is marked on the lens (Figure 4-4A and B). Total magnification of the specimen can be calculated by using the following formula:

Total Magnification = Magnification of the Objective Lens × Magnification of the Ocular Lens

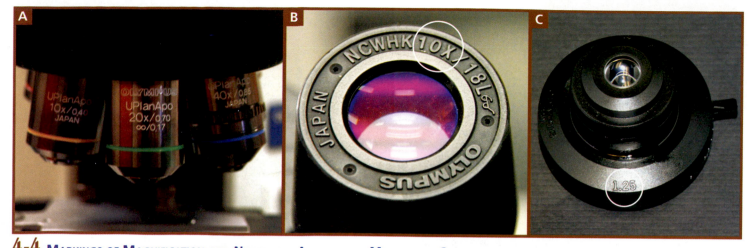

4-4 **MARKINGS OF MAGNIFICATION AND NUMERICAL APERTURE ON MICROSCOPE COMPONENTS** **A** Three plan apochromatic objective lenses on the nosepiece of a light microscope. *Plan* means the lens produces a flat field of view. *Apochromatic* lenses are made in such a way that chromatic aberration is reduced to a minimum. From left to right, the lenses magnify 10X, 20X, and 40X, and have numerical apertures of 0.40, 0.70, and 0.85. The 20X lens has other markings on it. The mechanical tube length is the distance from the nosepiece to the ocular and is usually between 160 to 210 mm. However, this 20X lens has been corrected so the light rays are made parallel, effectively creating an infinitely long mechanical tube length (∞). This allows insertion of accessories into the light path without decreasing image quality. The thickness of cover glass to be used is also given (0.17 ± 0.01 mm). **B** A 10X ocular lens. **C** A condenser (removed from the microscope) with a numerical aperture of 1.25. The lever at the right is used to open and close the iris diaphragm and adjust the amount of light entering the specimen.

The practical limit to magnification with a light microscope is around 1300X. Although higher magnifications are possible, image clarity is more difficult to maintain as the magnification increases. Clarity of an image is called **resolution** (Figure 4-5). The **limit of resolution** (or **resolving power**) is an actual measurement of how far apart two points must be in order for the microscope to view them as being separate. Notice that resolution improves as resolving power is made smaller.

The best limit of resolution achieved by a light microscope is about 0.2 μm. (That is, at its absolute best, a light microscope cannot distinguish between two points closer together than 0.2 μm.) For a specific microscope, the actual limit of resolution can be calculated with the following formula:[1]

$$D = \frac{\lambda}{NA_{Condenser} + NA_{Objective}}$$

where D is the minimum distance at which two points can be resolved, λ is the wavelength of light used, and $NA_{condenser}$ and $NA_{objective}$ are the numerical apertures of the condenser lens and objective lens, respectively. Because numerical aperture has no units, the units for D are the same as the units for wavelength, which typically are in nanometers (nm).

Numerical aperture is a measure of a lens's ability to "capture" light coming from the specimen and use it to make the image. As with magnification, it is marked on

4-5 **RESOLUTION AND LIMIT OF RESOLUTION** The headlights of most automobiles are around 1.5 m apart. As you look at the cars in the foreground of the photo, it is easy to see both headlights as separate objects. The automobiles in the distance appear smaller (but really aren't) as does the apparent distance between the headlights. When the apparent distance between automobile headlights reaches about 0.1 mm, they blur into one because that is the limit of resolution of the human eye.

the lens (Figures 4-4A and C). Using immersion oil between the specimen and the objective lens increases its numerical aperture and in turn, makes its limit of resolution smaller. (If necessary, oil may also be placed between the condenser lens and the slide.) The result is better resolution.

The light microscope may be modified to improve its ability to produce images with contrast without staining, which often distorts or kills the specimen. In **dark-field microscopy** (Figure 4-2B), a special condenser is used so only the light reflected off of the specimen enters the objective.

---

[1] Different equations have been developed to determine approximate limit of resolution, each made from different assumptions. The one used here assumes the $NA_{Objective} \geq NA_{Condenser}$.

The appearance is of a brightly lit specimen against a dark background, and often with better resolution than that of the bright field microscope.

Phase contrast microscopy (Figure 4-2C) uses special optical components to exploit subtle differences in the refractive indices of water and cytoplasmic components to produce contrast. Light waves that are in phase (that is, their peaks and valleys exactly coincide) reinforce one another and their total intensity (because of the summed amplitudes) increases. Light waves that are out of phase by exactly one-half wavelength cancel each other and result in no intensity—that is, darkness. Wavelengths that are out of phase by any amount will produce some degree of cancellation and result in brightness that is less than maximum but more than darkness. Thus, contrast is provided by differences in light intensity that result from differences in refractive indices in parts of the specimen that put light waves more or less out of phase. As a result, the specimen and its parts appear as various levels of darks and lights.

Fluorescence microscopy (Figure 4-2D) uses a fluorescent dye on the specimen that emits fluorescence when illuminated with ultraviolet radiation. In some cases, specimens possess naturally fluorescing chemicals and no dye is needed.

The Electron Microscope

The **electron microscope** uses an electron beam to create an image, with electromagnets acting as lenses. The limit of resolution is improved by a factor of 1000 (theoretically down to 0.1 nm, but more realistically down to 2 nm) over the light microscope.

The **transmission electron microscope (TEM)** (Figure 4-6) produces a two-dimensional image of an ultrathin section by capturing electrons that have passed through the specimen. The degree of interaction between the electrons and the heavy metal stain affects the kinetic energy of the electrons, which are collected by a fluorescent plate. The light of varying intensity emitted from the plate is directly proportional to the electron's kinetic energy and is used to produce the image. The TEM is useful for studying a cell's interior, its **ultrastructure**. A sample transmission electron micrograph is shown in Figure 4-7.

The previous paragraph gave a brief overview of how the TEM works. However, a key to successful transmission electron microscopy is excellent sample preparation. Following is an overview of sample preparation. The specimen is fixed by one of various methods (treatment with formaldehyde, glutaraldehyde, or osmium tetroxide) to prevent cell decomposition, stained with an electron dense material (lead, uranium, or osmium compounds), dehydrated, and embedded in a plastic block (Figure 4-8). It is then cut into thin slices using an ultramicrotome (Figure 4-9) armed with a glass or diamond blade. The slices are captured on a grid

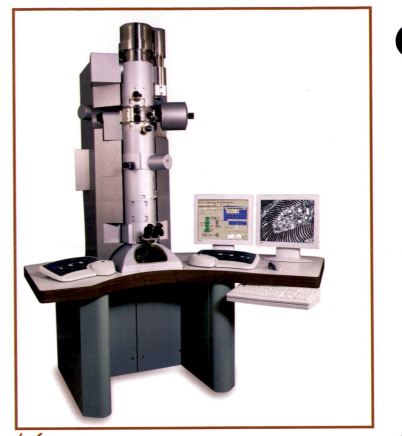

4-6 TRANSMISSION ELECTRON MICROSCOPE The transmission electron microscope produces an image using electrons that pass through the specimen. The image is then viewed on the monitor. This particular model magnifies from 8X up to 630,000X.

Photograph courtesy of Carl Zeiss NTS GmbH

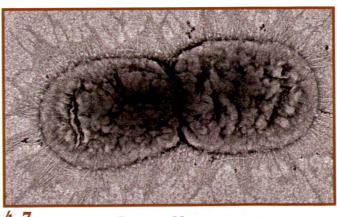

4-7 TRANSMISSION ELECTRON MICROGRAPH The TEM produces images of sectioned specimens. Since light is not used, the image is not in color. These cells were magnified 12,500X.

Photograph courtesy of Carl Zeiss NTS GmbH

(Figure 4-10), which is inserted into the TEM so it rests in the electron beam path. Figure 4-11 shows what the microscopist sees when working.

A **scanning electron microscope (SEM)** (Figure 4-12) is used to make a three-dimensional image of the specimen's surface. In this technique, a beam of electrons is passed over

4-8 **TEM Specimen Embedded in a Plastic Block** These plastic resin blocks contain specimens, the black spots within the blocks. On the right is a trimmed block that has had excess resin cut away to produce a minute piece of specimen that extends from the block. This is the portion of specimen to be sectioned (Figure 4-9).

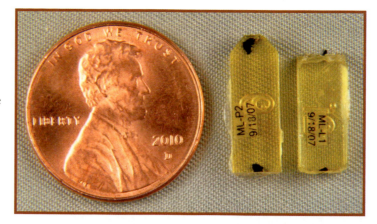

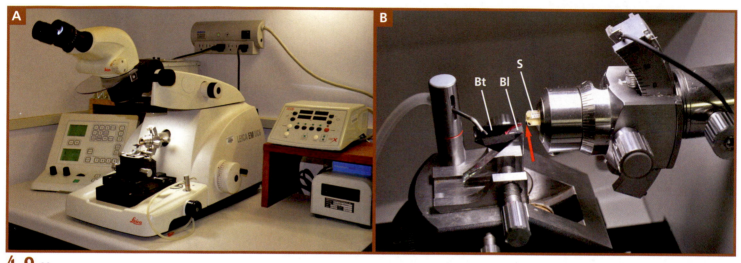

4-9 **Ultramicrotome** **A** This ultramicrotome is capable of producing specimen slices 100 nm in thickness (and less). The arm holding the specimen traces an elliptical path as it approaches and is withdrawn from the sample. In each cycle, it is advanced the distance equal to the desired section thickness, often 100 nm. **B** The specimen block (**S**), with the tiny, trimmed down specimen (**arrow**) facing the blade (**Bl**), is held in the ultramicrotome chuck. As the specimen moves forward and passes by the glass or diamond blade a thin slice is made, which is caught and floated on water in the boat (**Bt**) behind the blade. The specimen holder is withdrawn, returned to the starting position, and advanced by the desired thickness and another cut is made. The process is repeated to produce multiple sections of the same thickness.

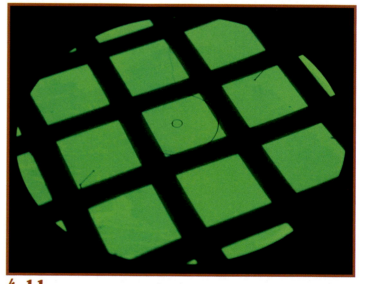

4-10 **The Grid and Grid Holder** The thin sections are picked up by a grid (shown), which acts as the equivalent of a glass slide in light microscopy. The shiny material between grid bars is a plastic film that fills in the openings and keeps specimens from dropping through. The grid is placed in a grid holder that is inserted into the TEM. The grid with its specimens is thus positioned in the electron beam path.

4-11 **The Viewing Screen** Electron beams do not produce an image visible to the human eye. In order for the image to be seen, the microscopist views the specimen on this screen coated with a phosphorescent material. The kinetic energy of the electrons hitting the screen is converted to light, which makes the specimen visible. The thick, dark lines are the grid bars at very low magnification. The image is also captured by a digital camera and viewed on a computer monitor.

the stained surface of the specimen. Some electrons are reflected (**backscatter electrons**), whereas other electrons (**secondary electrons**) are emitted from the metallic stain. These electrons are captured and used to produce the three-dimensional image. A sample scanning electron micrograph is shown in Figure 4-13.

As with the TEM, sample preparation involves fixation, dehydration, and staining (but not sectioning). Once the sample is fixed and dehydrated, it is mounted on a stub (Figure 4-14) and coated with the "stain" (usually gold) by a process known as "sputter coating." A simple explanation of this process is as follows. Argon gas is ionized in an electric field within an evacuated chamber. The positively charged argon ions bombard a gold foil, which releases gold atoms that are free to coat the sample. Figure 4-15 shows a sputter coater.

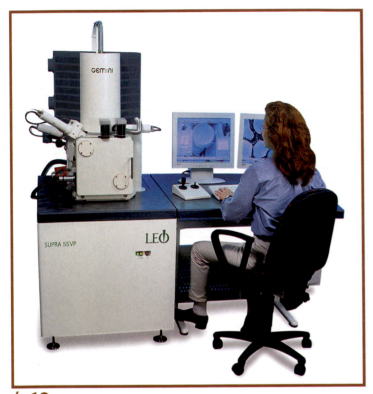

4-12 SCANNING ELECTRON MICROSCOPE This scanning electron microscope has the ability to magnify from 12X to 900,000X with a resolving power as low as 1.0 nm.

Photograph courtesy of Carl Zeiss NTS GmbH

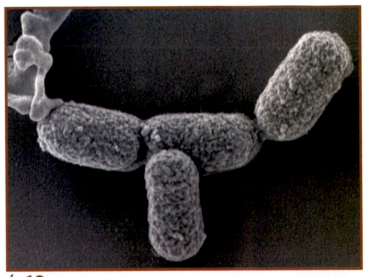

4-13 SCANNING ELECTRON MICROGRAPH Like the TEM, the image produced by the SEM has no color, but it is three-dimensional. This micrograph is of *E. coli*.   Photograph courtesy of Carl Zeiss NTS GmbH

4-14 SEM SPECIMEN MOUNTED ON A STUB This is a gold-coated pill bug resting on its back upon the platform of the stub. The larger cylinder is a holder for the stub.

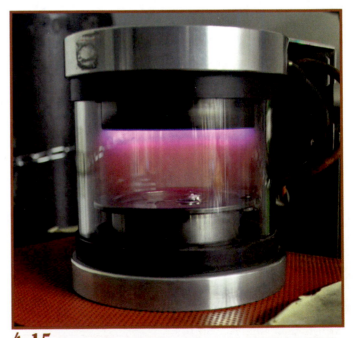

4-15 SPUTTER COATER Stubs with specimens are placed in the sputter coater chamber, which is then evacuated. Sputtering with gold occurs when ionized argon gas bombards a gold foil to release gold atoms. Two specimens are visible within; the purple is the argon gas.

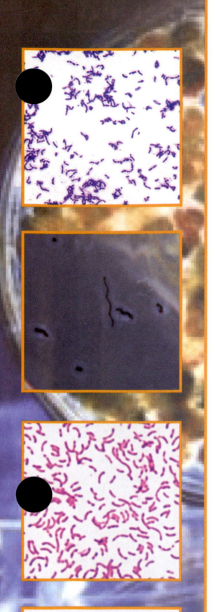

Bacterial Cellular Morphology and Simple Stains

Simple Stains

● Purpose

In Section 4 you were introduced to two of the three important features of a microscope and microscopy: magnification and resolution. A third feature is **contrast**. To be visible, the specimen must contrast with the background of the microscope field. Because cytoplasm is essentially transparent, viewing cells with the standard light microscope is difficult without stains to provide that contrast. Once stained, cell morphology, size, and arrangement then may be determined.

● Principle

Stains are solutions consisting of a solvent (usually water or ethanol) and a colored molecule (often a benzene derivative), the **chromogen**. The portion of the chromogen that gives it its color is the **chromophore**. A chromogen may have multiple chromophores, with each intensifying the color. The **auxochrome** is the charged portion of a chromogen and allows it to stain the cell through ionic or covalent bonds. **Basic stains**[1] (where the auxochrome becomes positively charged as a result of picking up a hydrogen ion or losing a hydroxide ion) are attracted to the negative charges on the surface of most bacterial cells. Thus, the cell becomes colored (Figure 5-1). Common basic stains include methylene blue, crystal violet, and safranin. Examples of basic stains may be seen in Figures 5-2 and 5-3, and in A Gallery of Bacterial Cell Diversity (pages 39–44).

---

[1] Notice that the term "basic" means "alkaline," not "elementary," although coincidentally basic stains can be used for simple staining procedures.

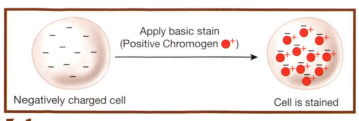

5-1 **CHEMISTRY OF BASIC STAINS** Basic stains have a positively charged chromogen (●+), which forms an ionic bond with the negatively charged bacterial cell, thus colorizing the cell.

5-2 **A SIMPLE STAIN USING SAFRANIN** Safranin is a basic stain. Notice that the stain is associated with the cells and not the background. The organism is *Klebsiella mobilis* (formerly *Enterobacter aerogenes*), grown in culture. Cell dimensions are 0.3–1.0 μm wide by 0.6–6.0 μm long.

Basic stains are applied to bacterial smears that have been **heat-fixed**. Heat-fixing kills most of the bacteria, makes them adhere to the slide, and coagulates cytoplasmic proteins to make them more visible. It also distorts the cells to some extent.

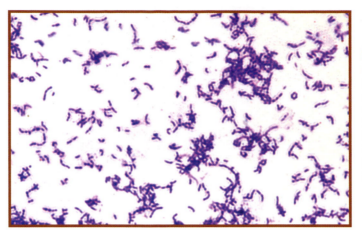

5-3 A SIMPLE STAIN USING CRYSTAL VIOLET This micrograph shows *Propionibacterium acnes* stained with the basic stain crystal violet. *P. acnes* is a commensal living on the skin of most humans. It has been associated with the skin condition acne. Cell dimensions are 0.5–0.8 μm wide by 1–5 μm long.

Negative Stain

● Purpose

The negative staining technique is used to determine morphology and cellular arrangement in bacteria that are too delicate to withstand heat-fixing. A primary example is the spirochete *Treponema*, which is distorted by the heat-fixing of other staining techniques. Also, where determining the accurate size is crucial, a negative stain can be used because it produces minimal cell shrinkage.

● Principle

The negative staining technique uses a dye solution in which the chromogen is acidic and carries a negative charge. (An acidic chromogen gives up a hydrogen ion, which leaves it with a negative charge.) The negative charge on the bacterial surface repels the negatively charged chromogen, so the cell remains unstained against a colored background (Figure 5-4). Examples of acidic staining solutions used in negative stains are Nigrosin and Congo red (Figures 5-5 and 5-6).

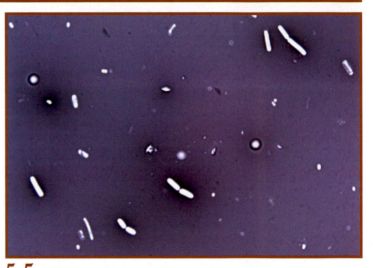

5-5 A NIGROSIN NEGATIVE STAIN Notice that the *Bacillus megaterium* cells are unstained against a dark background. Cell dimensions are 1.2–1.5 μm wide by 2.0–5.0 μm long. The small, irregularly-shaped white spots are bubbles or other artifacts.

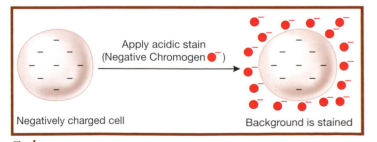

5-4 CHEMISTRY OF ACIDIC STAINS Acidic stains have a negatively charged chromogen (●-) that is repelled by negatively charged cells. Thus, the background is colored and the cell remains transparent.

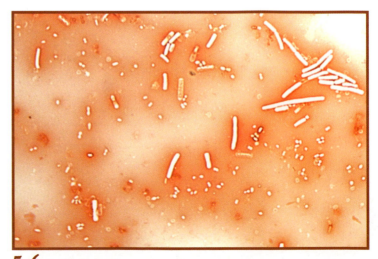

5-6 A NEGATIVE STAIN WITH CONGO RED Compare this negative stain of *Bacillus megaterium* to Figure 5-5. *B. megaterium* is a soil organism. Cell dimensions are 1.2–1.5 μm wide by 2.0–5.0 μm long.

A Gallery of Bacterial Cell Diversity

Bacterial cells are much smaller than eukaryotic cells (Figure 5-7) and come in a variety of **morphologies** (shapes) and **arrangements**. Determining cell morphology is an important first step in identifying a bacterial species. Cells may be spheres (**cocci**, singular **coccus**), rods (**bacilli**, singular **bacillus**), or spirals (**spirilla**, singular **spirillum**). Variations of these shapes include slightly curved rods (**vibrios**), short rods (**coccobacilli**), and flexible spirals (**spirochetes**). Examples

of cell shapes are shown in Figures 5-8 through 5-17. In Figure 5-17, *Corynebacterium xerosis* illustrates **pleomorphism**, where a variety of cell shapes—slender, ellipsoidal, or ovoid rods—may be seen in a given sample.

Cell arrangement, determined by the number of planes in which division occurs and whether the cells separate after division, is also useful in identifying bacteria. Spirilla rarely are seen as anything other than single cells, but cocci and bacilli do form multicellular associations. Because cocci exhibit the most variety in arrangements, they are used for illustration in Figure 5-18. If the two daughter cells remain attached after a coccus divides, a **diplococcus** is formed. The same process happens in bacilli that produce **diplobacilli**. If the cells continue to divide in the same plane and remain attached, they exhibit a **streptococcus** or **streptobacillus** arrangement.

If a second division occurs in a plane perpendicular to the first, a **tetrad** is formed from a diplococcus. A third division plane perpendicular to the other two produces a cube-shaped arrangement of eight cells called a **sarcina**. Tetrads and sarcinae are seen only in cocci. If the division planes of a coccus are irregular, a cluster of cells is produced to form a **staphylococcus**. Figures 5-19 through 5-26 illustrate common cell arrangements.

Some organisms produce more unique arrangements. **Snapping division** in corynebacteria produces either a **palisade** or **angular** arrangement of cells (Figures 5-27 and 5-28). Figure 5-29 illustrates a phenomenon characteristic of virulent strains of *Mycobacterium tuberculosis* in which they grow in parallel chains called **cords**.

Arrangement and morphology are often easier to see when the organisms are grown in a broth rather than on a

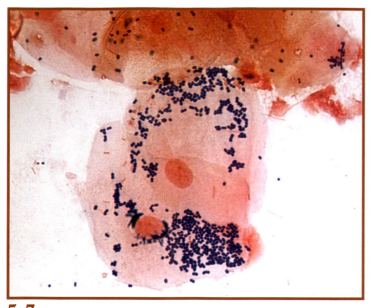

5-7 **PROKARYOTIC AND EUKARYOTIC CELLS (GRAM STAIN)** This is a direct smear specimen taken from around the base of the teeth below the gum line. The large, pink cells are human epithelial cells and are eukaryotic (notice the prominent nuclei). The small, purple cells are prokaryotic bacteria. Typically, prokaryotic cells range in size from 1–10 μm, whereas eukaryotic cells are in the 10–100 μm range.

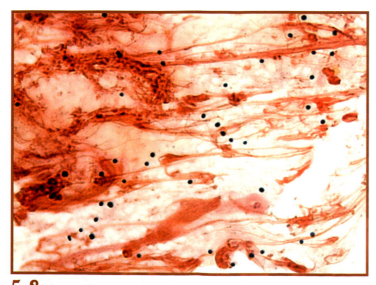

5-8 **SINGLE COCCI FROM A NASAL SWAB (GRAM STAIN)** This direct smear of a nasal swab illustrates unidentified cocci (dark circles) stained with crystal violet. The red background material is mostly mucus.

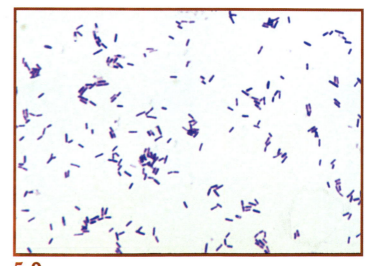

5-9 **A "TYPICAL" BACILLUS (CRYSTAL VIOLET STAIN)** Notice the variability in rod length (due to different ages of the cells) in this stain of the soil organism *Bacillus subtilis* grown in culture. Cell dimensions are 0.7 μm wide by 2.0–3.0 μm long.

solid medium (Figures 5-13 and 5-14), or are observed from a direct smear. If you have difficulty identifying cell morphology or arrangement, consider transferring the organism (isolate) to a broth culture and trying again.

One last bit of advice: don't expect Nature to perfectly conform to our categories of morphology and cell arrangement. These are convenient descriptive categories that will not easily be applied in all cases. When examining a slide, look for the most common morphology and most complex arrangement. Do not be afraid to report what you see. For instance, it's okay to say, "Cocci in singles, pairs, and chains."

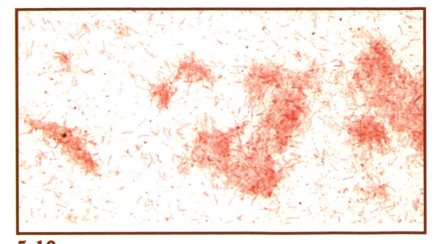

5-10 A Long, Thin *Bacillus* (Gram Stain) The cells of *Aeromonas sobria*, a freshwater organism, are considerably longer than wide. Notice that a cell can be a bacillus without being in the genus *Bacillus*. Cell dimensions are about 0.5 μm wide by 1–3.5 μm long. These cells were grown in culture.

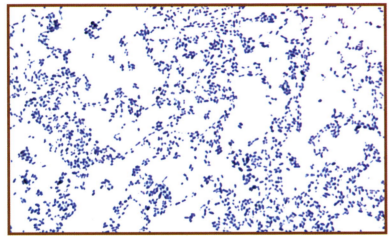

5-11 Ovoid Coccus (Gram Stain) *Lactococcus lactis* is an elongated coccus that a beginning microbiologist might confuse with a rod. Notice the slight elongation of the cells, and also that most cells are not more than twice as long as they are wide. *L. lactis* is found naturally in raw milk and milk products, but these cells were grown in culture. Cell dimensions are about 1 μm wide by 1–2 μm long.

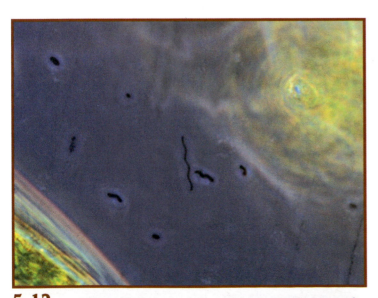

5-12 Two Different Spirilla (Phase Contrast Wet Mount) The two different spirilla are undoubtedly different species based on their different morphologies: one is long and slender with loose spirals, the other is shorter and fatter with tighter coils. Cell dimensions are less than 1 μm wide and up to 35 μm long.

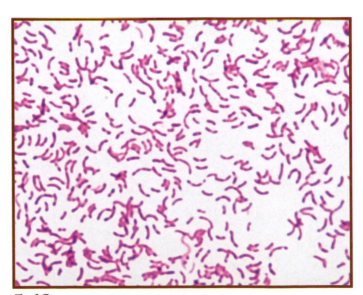

5-13 A Spirillum from a Solid Medium (Carbolfuchsin Stain) Sometimes the organism's source affects its morphology. Shown is *Rhodospirillum rubrum* grown on an agar slant and stained with carbolfuchsin. Notice that the cells are not spiral shaped and that most are curved rods. Compare their size and shape with Figure 5-14. Cell dimensions are about 1 μm wide by 10 μm long.

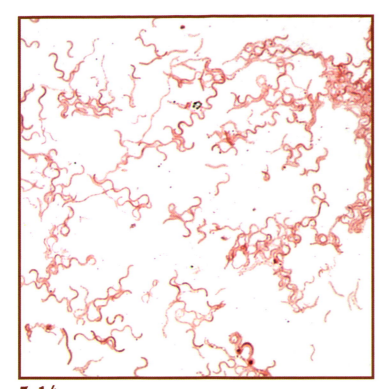

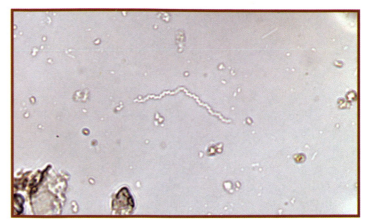

5-15 A **SPIROCHAETE** Spirochaetes are tightly coiled, flexible rods. This bright field micrograph shows a marine species of *Spirochaeta*. Notice the bend in the center of the cell. Cell dimensions of the genus are less than 1 µm wide by 5–500 µm long.

5-14 A **SPIRILLUM GROWN IN BROTH** Shown is *Rhodospirillum rubrum*, grown in broth and stained with safranin. Compare the size and shape of these cells with those shown in Figure 5-13.

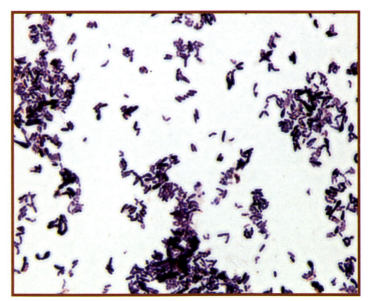

5-17 **BACTERIAL PLEOMORPHISM (GRAM STAIN)** Some organisms grow in a variety of shapes and are said to be **pleomorphic**. Notice the rods of *Corynebacterium xerosis* range from almost spherical to many times longer than wide. This organism is normally an inhabitant of skin and mucous membranes and may be an opportunistic pathogen in compromised patients.

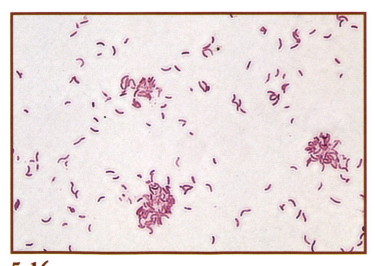

5-16 A **VIBRIO (GRAM STAIN)** *Vibrio cholerae* is the causative agent of cholera in humans. Careful examination of the smear will reveal most rods as curved. These cells are from culture and range in size from less than 1 µm wide by 1.5–2.5 µm long.

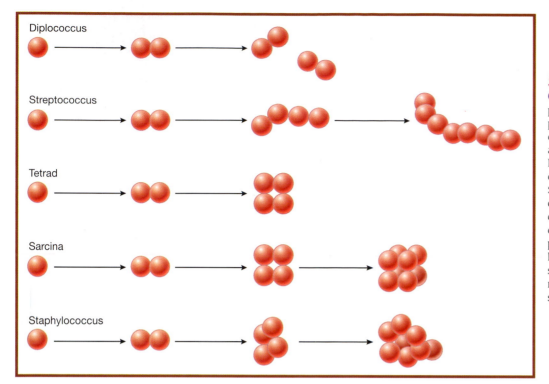

Diplococcus

Streptococcus

Tetrad

Sarcina

Staphylococcus

5-18 **DIVISION PATTERNS AMONG COCCI** Diplococci have a single division plane and the cells generally occur in pairs. Streptococci also have a single division plane, but the cells remain attached to form chains of variable length. If there are two perpendicular division planes, the cells form tetrads. Sarcinae have divided in three perpendicular planes to produce a regular cuboidal arrangement of cells. Staphylococci have divided in more than three planes to produce a characteristic grape-like cluster of cells. (*Note:* Rarely will a sample be composed of just one arrangement. Report what you see, and emphasize the most complex arrangement.)

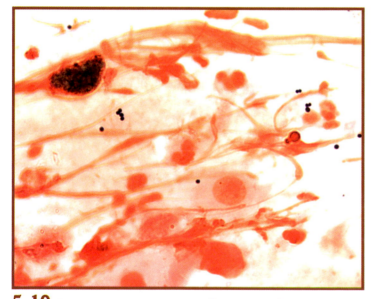

5-19 **DIPLOCOCCUS ARRANGEMENT (GRAM STAIN)** A few unidentified diplococci are visible in this nasal swab. Single cocci may be the same organism (and haven't divided yet) or something else. The red background material is host epithelial cells and mucus.

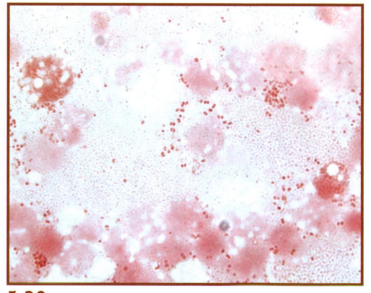

5-20 **ANOTHER DIPLOCOCCUS ARRANGEMENT (GRAM STAIN)** *Neisseria gonorrhoeae* is a diplococcus that causes gonorrhea in humans. Members of this genus produce diplococci with flattened adjacent sides. Each cell is less than 1 μm in diameter.

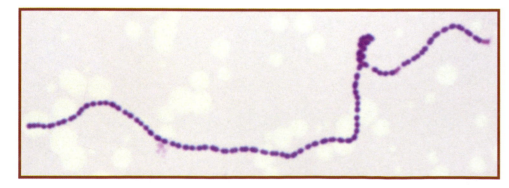

5-21 **STREPTOCOCCUS ARRANGEMENT (GRAM STAIN)** *Enterococcus faecium* is a streptococcus that inhabits the digestive tract of mammals. This specimen is from a broth culture (which enables the cells to form long chains) and was stained with crystal violet. Notice the slight elongation of these cells along the axis of the chain. Cells are up to 2 μm wide by 2.5 μm long.

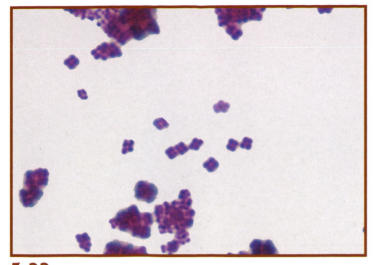

5-22 TETRAD ARRANGEMENT (GRAM STAIN) *Micrococcus roseus* grows in squared packets of cells evident even when they are bunched together. The normal habitat for *Micrococcus* species is the skin, but these were obtained from culture. Each cell is approximately 1μm in diameter.

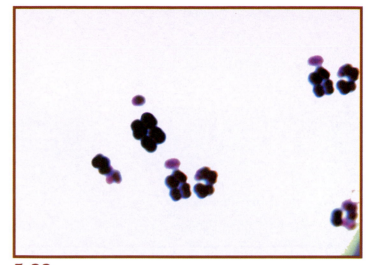

5-23 A SARCINA (CRYSTAL VIOLET STAIN) *Sarcina maxima* exhibits the sarcina organization. As usual, not all will exhibit the sarcina arrangement—a variety of arrangements leading up to the most complex arrangement are seen. Each cell is 2–3 μm in diameter.

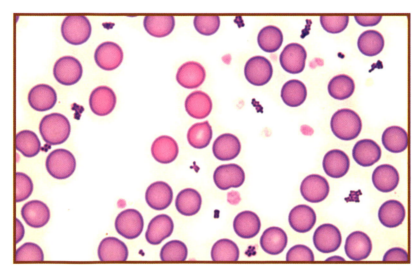

5-24 STAPHYLOCOCCUS ARRANGEMENT *Staphylococcus aureus* is shown in a blood smear. Note the staphylococci interspersed between the erythrocytes. *S. aureus* is a common opportunistic pathogen of humans. Cells are approximately 1μm in diameter.

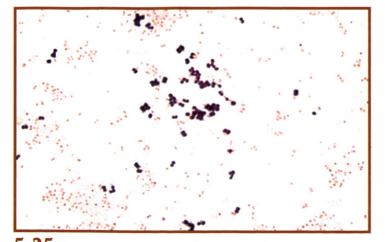

5-25 TWO EXAMPLES OF COCCI (GRAM STAIN) Compare *Moraxella catarrhalis* (pink stain) and *Micrococcus luteus* (purple), both grown in culture. *M. catarrhalis* is a diplococcus with flattened adjacent sides. It is an inhabitant of the human upper respiratory tract, especially the nasal cavity, and is rarely pathogenic. *M. luteus* is a larger coccus that grows in pairs and tetrads, and is found on the skin and other membranes.

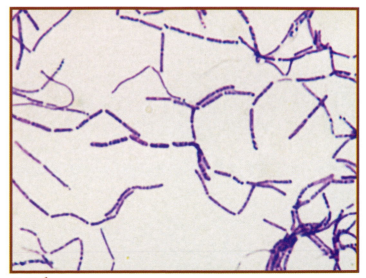

5-26 STREPTOBACILLUS ARRANGEMENT (CRYSTAL VIOLET STAIN) *Bacillus megaterium* is a streptobacillus. These cells were obtained from culture and are 1.2–1.5 μm wide by 2–5 μm long.

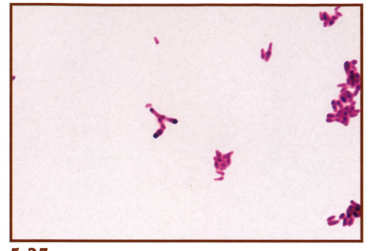

5-27 ANGULAR ARRANGEMENT OF *CORYNEBACTERIUM* (CARBOL-FUCHSIN STAIN) *Corynebacterium diphtheriae* exhibits an angular arrangement of cells produced by snapping division typical of the genus. Cell dimensions are 0.3–0.8 μm wide by 1.0–8.0 μm long. *C. diphtheriae* produces an exotoxin that causes the symptoms of diphtheria.

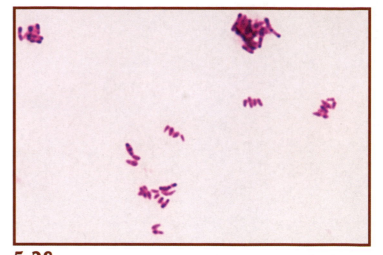

5-28 PALISADE ARRANGEMENT OF *CORYNEBACTERIUM* (CARBOL-FUCHSIN STAIN) In this micrograph, *Corynebacterium diphtheriae* illustrates its characteristic palisade arrangement of cells. Notice how the cells are stacked lengthwise and are not in an irregular arrangement, as in staphylococci.

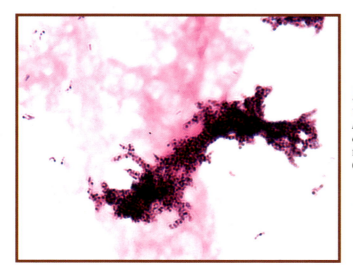

5-29 CORDING OF *MYCOBACTERIUM TUBERCULOSIS* (ACID-FAST STAIN) *M. tuberculosis* aggregates in characteristic cords due to the adhesion of the waxy, acid-fast cell walls of the organisms. Cells measure 0.2–0.6 μm wide by 1-10 μm long.

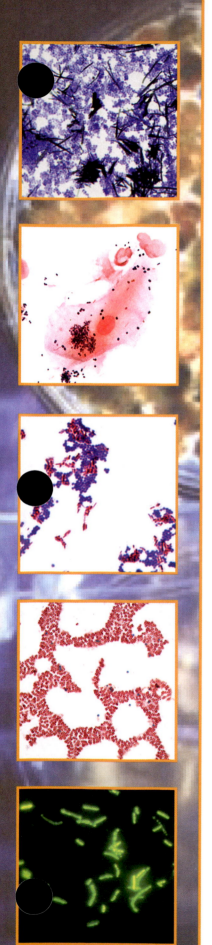

Bacterial Cell Structures and Differential Stains

Gram Stain

● Purpose

The Gram stain, used to distinguish between Gram-positive and Gram-negative cells, is the most important and widely used microbiological differential stain. In addition to Gram reaction, this stain also allows determination of cell morphology, size, and arrangement. It is typically the first differential test run on a specimen brought into the laboratory for identification. In some cases, a rapid, presumptive identification of the organism or elimination of a particular organism is possible.

● Principle

The Gram stain is a differential stain in which a **decolorization** step occurs between the application of two basic stains. The Gram stain has many variations, but they all work in basically the same way (Figure 6-1). The **primary stain** is crystal violet. Iodine is added as a **mordant** to enhance crystal violet staining by forming a **crystal violet–iodine complex**. Decolorization follows and is the most critical step in the procedure. Gram-negative cells are decolorized by the solution (of variable composition—generally alcohol or acetone) whereas Gram-positive cells are not. Gram-negative cells can thus be colorized by the **counterstain** safranin. Upon successful completion of a Gram stain, Gram-positive cells appear purple and Gram-negative cells appear reddish-pink (Figure 6-2).

Electron microscopy and other evidence indicate that the ability to resist decolorization or not is based on the different wall constructions of Gram-positive and Gram-negative cells. Gram-negative cell walls have a higher lipid content (because of the outer membrane) and a thinner peptidoglycan layer than Gram-positive cell walls (Figure 6-3). The alcohol/acetone in the decolorizer

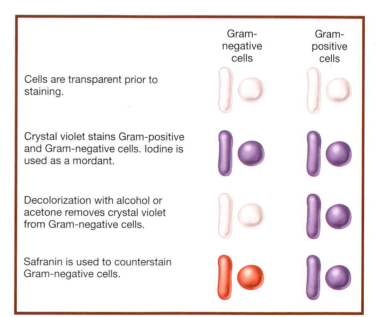

6-1 GRAM STAIN After application of the primary stain (crystal violet), decolorization, and counterstaining with safranin, Gram-positive cells stain violet and Gram-negative cells stain pink/red. Notice that crystal violet and safranin are both basic stains, and that it is the decolorization step that makes the Gram stain differential.

Within the figure:
- Gram-negative cells / Gram-positive cells
- Cells are transparent prior to staining.
- Crystal violet stains Gram-positive and Gram-negative cells. Iodine is used as a mordant.
- Decolorization with alcohol or acetone removes crystal violet from Gram-negative cells.
- Safranin is used to counterstain Gram-negative cells.

extracts the lipid, making the Gram-negative wall more porous and incapable of retaining the crystal violet–iodine complex, thereby decolorizing it. The thicker peptidoglycan and greater degree of cross-linking (because of teichoic acids)

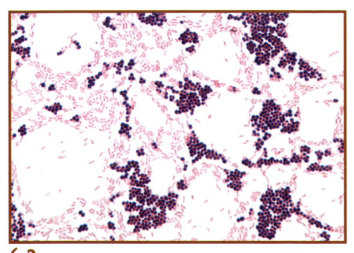

6-2 **GRAM STAIN OF *STAPHYLOCOCCUS EPIDERMIDIS* (+) AND *CITROBACTER DIVERSUS* (−)** *S. epidermidis* has a staphylococcal arrangement, whereas *C. diversus* is a bacillus of varying lengths.

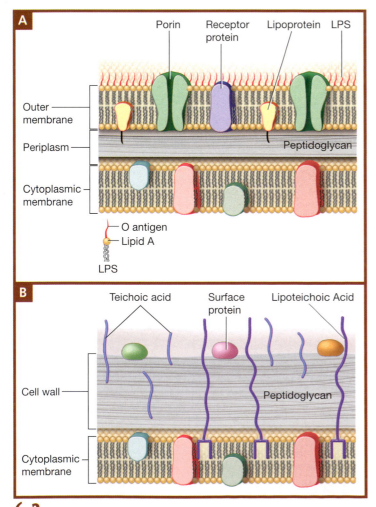

6-3 **BACTERIAL CELL WALLS** **A** The Gram-negative wall is composed of less peptidoglycan (as little as a single layer) and more lipid (due to the outer membrane) than the Gram-positive wall **B**.

trap the crystal violet–iodine complex more effectively, making the Gram-positive wall less susceptible to decolorization.

Although some organisms give Gram-variable results, most variable results are a consequence of poor technique. The decolorization step is the most crucial and most likely source of Gram stain inconsistency. It is possible to **over-decolorize** by leaving the alcohol on too long and get reddish Gram-*positive* cells. It also is possible to **under-decolorize** and produce purple Gram-*negative* cells. Neither of these situations changes the actual Gram reaction for the organism being stained. Rather, these are false results because of poor technique.

A second source of poor Gram stains is inconsistency in preparation of the emulsion. Remember, a good emulsion dries to a faint haze on the slide.

Until correct results are obtained consistently, it is recommended that control smears of Gram-positive and Gram-negative organisms be stained along with the organism in question (Figure 6-4). As an alternative control, a direct smear made from the gumline may be Gram-stained (Figure 6-5) with the expectation that both Gram-positive and

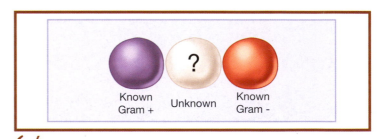

6-4 **POSITIVE CONTROLS TO CHECK YOUR TECHNIQUE** Staining known Gram-positive and Gram-negative organisms on either side of your unknown organism act as positive controls for your technique. Try to make the emulsions as close to one another as possible. Spreading them out across the slide makes it difficult to stain and decolorize them equally.

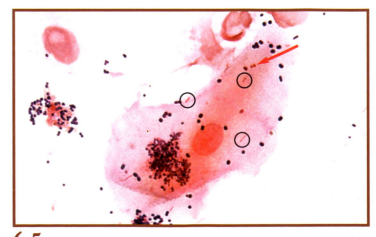

6-5 **DIRECT SMEAR POSITIVE CONTROL (GRAM STAIN)** A direct smear made from the gumline may also be used as a Gram stain control. Expect numerous Gram-positive bacteria (especially cocci) and some Gram-negative cells, including your own epithelial cells. In this slide, Gram-positive cocci predominate, but a few Gram-negative cells are visible, including Gram-negative rods (circled) and a Gram-negative diplococcus (**arrow**) on the surface of the epithelial cell.

Gram-negative organisms will be seen. Over-decolorized and under-decolorized gumline direct smears are shown for comparison (Figures 6-6 and 6-7). Positive controls also should be run when using new reagent batches.

Age of the culture also affects Gram stain consistency. Older Gram-positive cultures may lose their ability to resist decolorization and give an artifactual Gram-negative result. The genus *Bacillus* is notorious for this. *Staphylococcus* can also be a culprit. Cultures 24 hours old or less are best for this procedure.

Potassium hydroxide provides a nonstain test to confirm Gram reaction for particularly difficult species. Part of a colony is emulsified in a drop of KOH for one minute, then the loop is slowly withdrawn. Release of chromosomal material by Gram-negative cells makes the suspension viscous, stringy, and adhesive (Figure 6-8). Gram-positives are unchanged and the emulsion remains watery.

Interpretation of Gram stains can be complicated by nonbacterial elements. For instance, stain crystals from an old or improperly made stain solution can disrupt the field (Figure 6-9) or stain precipitate may be mistakenly identified as bacteria (Figure 6-10). In direct smears host cells or noncellular material may be seen (Figures 6-11 to 6-14).

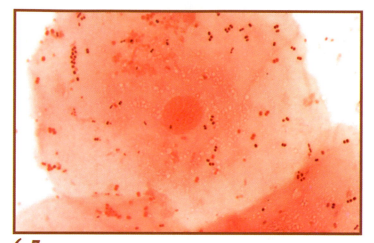

6-7 AN OVER-DECOLORIZED GRAM STAIN This also is a direct smear from the gum line. Notice the virtual absence of any purple cells, a certain indication of over-decoloration.

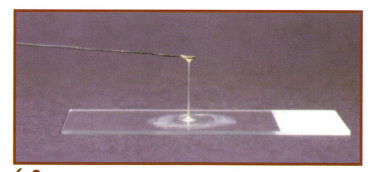

6-8 THE KOH TEST FOR GRAM REACTION This preparation of *Escherichia coli*, a Gram-negative organism, has been emulsified in KOH for one minute. The solution has become viscous and stringy due to the release of chromosomal material from the cells.

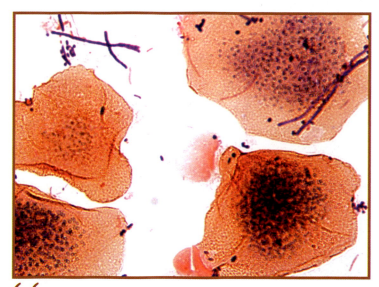

6-6 AN UNDER-DECOLORIZED GRAM STAIN This is a direct smear from the gum line. Notice the purple patches of stain on the epithelial cells. Also notice the variable quality of this stain—the epithelial cell to the left of center is stained better than the others.

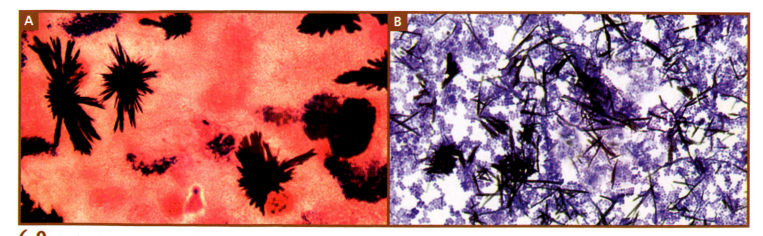

6-9 CRYSTAL VIOLET CRYSTALS (GRAM STAIN) If the staining solution is old or inadequately filtered, crystal violet crystals may appear. Although they are pleasing to the eye, they obstruct your view of the specimen. Crystals from two different Gram stains are shown here. **A** This specimen is of a gum line direct smear; **B** *Micrococcus roseus* grown in culture.

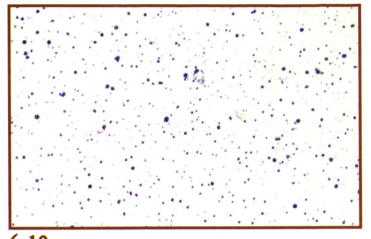

6-10 STAIN PRECIPITATE (GRAM STAIN) If the slide is not rinsed thoroughly or the stain is allowed to dry on the slide, spots of stain precipitate may form and may be confused with bacterial cells. Their variability in size is a clue that they are not bacteria.

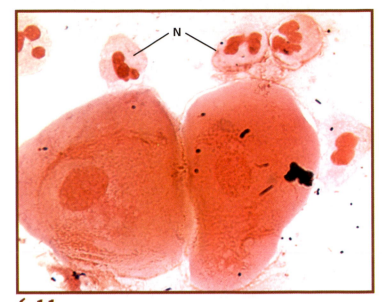

6-11 NEUTROPHILS IN DIRECT SMEARS (GRAM STAIN) This gum line smear illustrates neutrophils (**N**), cells typically found in inflamed tissue. Notice their size relative to the epithelial cells, their lobed nucleus, and Gram-negative staining reaction. In some preparations, they are very distorted and only the nuclei make them identifiable (Figure 6-14).

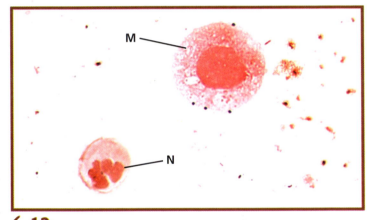

6-12 MACROPHAGE (GRAM STAIN) In some direct smears, macrophages (**M**) are visible. Compare the size of this macrophage to the single neutrophil (**N**) below it. Notice its spherical nucleus and vacuolated cytoplasm (containing bacteria in the process of digestion). Also notice the Gram-positive cocci on its surface, probably caught in the act of being engulfed.

6-13 RESPIRATORY EPITHELIAL CELLS (GRAM STAIN) Two distorted respiratory epithelial cells are seen in this direct smear of a nasal swab. Their columnar and irregular shape, nucleus, and cilia (what are left) provide clues to their identity.

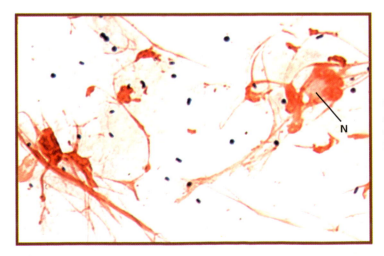

6-14 MUCUS (GRAM STAIN) Mucus strands dominate the field in this Gram-stained nasal swab. Gram-positive cocci and a deteriorating neutrophil (**N**) are also visible.

Acid-fast Stain

● Purpose

The acid-fast stain is a differential stain used to detect cells capable of retaining a primary stain when treated with an acid alcohol. It is an important differential stain used to identify bacteria in the genus *Mycobacterium,* some of which are pathogens (*e.g.,* *M. leprae* and *M. tuberculosis,* causative agents of leprosy and tuberculosis, respectively). Members of the actinomycete genus *Nocardia* (*N. brasiliensis* and *N. asteroides* are opportunistic pathogens) are partially acid-fast. Oocysts of coccidian parasites, such as *Crypto-sporidium* and *Isospora,* are also acid-fast. Because so few organisms are acid-fast, the acid-fast stain is run only when infection by an acid-fast organism is suspected.

Acid-fast stains are useful in identification of **acid-fast bacilli (AFB)** and rapid, preliminary diagnosis of tuberculosis (with greater than 90% predictive value from sputum samples). It also can be performed on patient samples to track the progress of antibiotic therapy and determine their degree of contagiousness. A prescribed number of microscopic fields is examined and the number of AFB is determined and reported using a standard scoring system (Table 6-1).

● Principle

The presence of mycolic acids in the cell walls of acid-fast organisms is the cytological basis for this differential stain. Mycolic acid is a waxy substance that gives acid-fast cells a higher affinity for the primary stain and resistance to decolorization by an acid alcohol solution. A variety of acid-fast staining procedures are employed, two of which are the Ziehl-Neelsen (ZN) method and the Kinyoun (K)

method. These differ primarily in that the ZN method uses heat as part of the staining process, whereas the K method is a "cold" stain. In both protocols, the bacterial smear may be prepared in a drop of serum to help the "slippery" acid-fast cells adhere to the slide. The two methods provide comparable results.

The waxy wall of acid-fast cells repels typical aqueous stains. (As a result, most acid-fast positive organisms are only weakly Gram-positive.) In the ZN method (Figure 6-15),

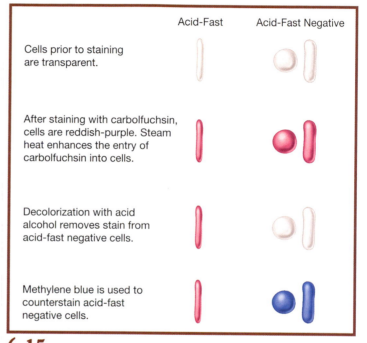

6-15 THE ZIEHL-NEELSEN ACID-FAST STAIN Acid-fast cells stain reddish-purple; nonacid-fast cells stain blue or the color of the counterstain if a different one is used.

TABLE 6-1 Acid-fast Smear Reporting Standards*

Number of AFB Seen Fuchsin Stain 1000X Magnification	Number of AFB Seen Fluorochrome Stain 450X Magnification	Number of AFB Seen Fluorochrome Stain 250X Magnification	Reported As
0 AFB per Field	0 AFB per Field	0 AFB per Field	No AFB Seen
1–2 AFB per 300 Fields	1–2 AFB per 70 Fields	1–2 AFB per 30 Fields	Doubtful; repeat with another specimen
1–9 AFB per 100 Fields	2–18 AFB per 50 Fields	1–9 AFB per 10 Fields	1+
1–9 AFB per 10 Fields	4–36 AFB per 10 Fields	1–9 AFB per Field	2+
1–9 per Field	4–36 AFB per Field	10–90 AFB per Field	3+
>9 per Field	>36 AFB per Field	> 90 AFB per Field	4+

*Modified from Kent, P.T. and G.P. Kubica. 1985. *Public Health Mycobacteriology: A Guide for the Level III Laboratory.* U.S. Department of Health and Human Services, Centers for Disease Control, Atlanta, GA.

the phenolic compound carbolfuchsin is used as the primary stain because it is lipid soluble and penetrates the waxy cell wall. Staining by carbolfuchsin is further enhanced by steam heating the preparation to melt the wax and allow the stain to move into the cell. Acid alcohol is used to decolorize nonacid-fast cells; acid-fast cells resist this decolorization. A counterstain, such as methylene blue, is then applied. Acid-fast cells are reddish-purple; nonacid-fast cells are blue (Figure 6-16).

The Kinyoun method (Figure 6-17) uses a slightly more lipid soluble and concentrated carbolfuchsin as the primary stain. These properties allow the stain to penetrate the acid-fast walls without the use of heat, but make this method

slightly less sensitive than the ZN method. Decolorization with acid alcohol is followed by a contrasting counterstain, such as brilliant green (Figure 6-18) or methylene blue.

Fluorescent dyes, such as auramine or rhodamine, are used in many clinical laboratories and are actually preferable to traditional carbolfuchsin stains for examination of direct smears because of their higher sensitivity. The **fluorochrome** combines specifically with mycolic acid. Acid alcohol is used for decolorization and potassium permanganate is the counterstain. When observed under the microscope with UV illumination, acid-fast cells are yellow against a dark background and nonacid-fast cells are not seen (Figure 6-19).

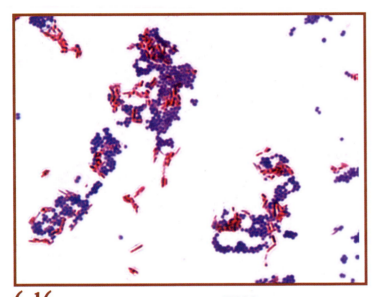

6-16 An Acid-fast Stain Using the ZN Method   Notice how most of the *Mycobacterium phlei* (AF+) cells are in clumps, an unusual state for most rods. They do this because their waxy cell walls make them sticky. A few individual cells are visible, however, and they clearly are rods. The *Staphylococcus epidermidis* cells (AF−) are also in clumps, but that is because they grow as grape-like clusters. Each cell's diameter is approximately 1 μm. Compare this micrograph with Figure 6-18.

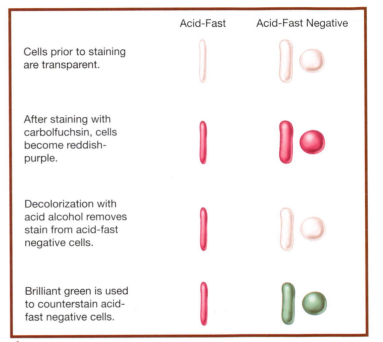

	Acid-Fast	Acid-Fast Negative
Cells prior to staining are transparent.		
After staining with carbolfuchsin, cells become reddish-purple.		
Decolorization with acid alcohol removes stain from acid-fast negative cells.		
Brilliant green is used to counterstain acid-fast negative cells.		

6-17 The Kinyoun Acid-fast Stain   Acid-fast cells stain reddish-purple; nonacid-fast cells stain green or the color of the counterstain if a different one is used.

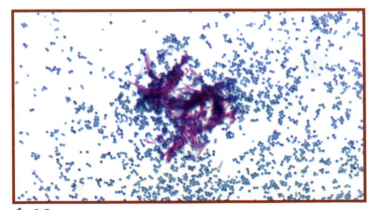

6-18 An Acid-fast Stain Using the Kinyoun Method   This is an acid-fast stain of *Mycobacterium smegmatis* (+) and *Staphylococcus epidermidis* (−) from cultures. Again, notice the clumping of the acid-fast organisms. It is not uncommon for brilliant green dye to stain more of a gray color, but it still contrasts with the carbolfuchsin of acid-fast positive cells. Compare this micrograph with Figure 6-16.

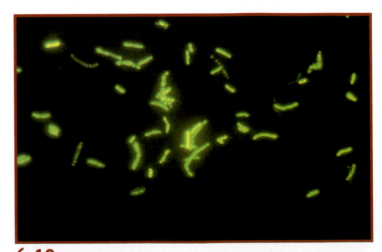

6-19 Fluorochrome Stain of *Mycobacterium kansasii* Using Auramine O Dye and Observed Under Ultraviolet Light   Notice the characteristic "beaded" appearance and nonuniform staining of these cells. *M. kansasii* causes chronic pulmonary disease.

Capsule Stain

● Purpose

The capsule stain is a differential stain used to detect cells capable of producing an extracellular capsule. Capsule production increases virulence in some microbes (such as the anthrax bacillus *Bacillus anthracis* and the pneumococcus *Streptococcus pneumoniae*) by making them less vulnerable to phagocytosis.

● Principle

Capsules are composed of mucoid polysaccharides or polypeptides that repel most stains. The capsule stain technique takes advantage of this phenomenon by staining *around* the cells. Typically, an acidic stain, such as Congo red or nigrosin that stains the background, and a basic stain that colorizes the cell proper, are used. The capsule remains unstained and appears as a white halo between the cells and the colored background (Figures 6-20 and 6-21).

This technique begins by spreading the cells in a film of an acidic stain and serum. The smear is allowed to air dry and is not heat-fixed. Heat-fixing causes shrinkage of the cells, leaving an artifactual white halo around them that might be interpreted as a capsule when counterstained. In place of heat-fixing, cells may be emulsified in a drop of serum to promote adherence to the glass slide.

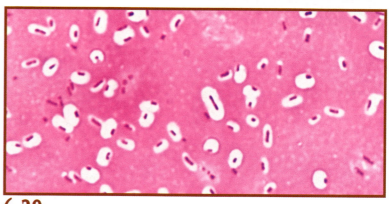

6-20 CAPSULE STAIN OF *KLEBSIELLA PNEUMONIAE* The acidic stain colorizes the background while the basic stain colorizes the cell, leaving the capsules as unstained, and white clearings around the cells. Notice the lack of uniform capsule size, and even the absence of a capsule in some cells. Compare this micrograph to Figure 6-21. The difference in cell size between the two photos is due to enlargement of the micrograph, not to the staining.

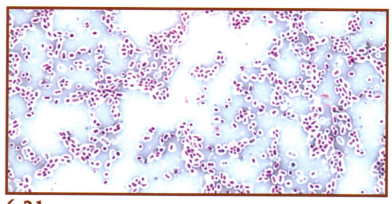

6-21 AN ALTERNATIVE CAPSULE STAIN OF *KLEBSIELLA PNEUMONIAE* In this capsule stain, Congo red is the acidic stain and Maneval's is the basic stain. After staining, the Congo red often looks bluish or gray. *K. pneumoniae* is an inhabitant of the intestinal tract of humans and is associated with urinary and respiratory tract infections, but this specimen was grown on an agar slant. The cells are approximately 1 μm wide by 2–4 μm long. Compare this micrograph to Figure 6-20.

Endospore Stain

● Purpose

The spore stain is a differential stain used to detect the presence and location of spores in bacterial cells. Only a few genera produce spores. Among them are the genera *Bacillus* and *Clostridium*. Most members of *Bacillus* are soil, freshwater, or marine **saprophytes**, but a few are pathogens, such as *B. anthracis*, the causative agent of anthrax. Most members of *Clostridium* are soil or aquatic saprophytes or inhabitants of human intestines, but four pathogens are fairly well known: *C. tetani, C. botulinum, C. perfringens,* and *C. difficile,* which produce tetanus, botulism, gas gangrene, and pseudomembranous colitis, respectively.

● Principle

An **endospore** is a dormant form of the bacterium that allows it to survive poor environmental conditions. Spores are resistant to heat and chemicals because of a tough outer covering made of the protein **keratin**. The keratin also resists staining, so extreme measures must be taken to stain the spore. In the Schaeffer-Fulton method (Figure 6-22), a primary stain of malachite green is forced into the spore by steaming the bacterial emulsion. Alternatively, malachite green can be left on the slide for 15 minutes or more to stain the spores. Malachite green is water-soluble and has a low affinity for cellular material, so **vegetative cells** and **spore**

	Spore producer	Spore nonproducer
Cells and spores prior to staining are transparent.		
After staining with malachite green, cells and spores are green. Heat is used to force the stain into spores, if present.		
Decolorization with water removes stain from cells, but not spores.		
Safranin is used to counterstain cells.		

6-22 THE SCHAEFFER-FULTON SPORE STAIN Upon completion, spores are green, and vegetative and spore mother cells are red.

mother cells can be decolorized with water and counterstained with safranin (Figures 6-23 and 6-24).

Spores may be located in the middle of the cell (**central**), at the end of the cell (**terminal**), or between the end and middle of the cell (**subterminal**). Spores also may be differentiated based on shape—either **spherical** or **elliptical (oval)**—and size relative to the cell (*i.e.*, whether they cause the cell to look swollen or not). These structural features are shown in Figures 6-25 through 6-27.

A special stain is not required to visualize endospores. Figure 6-28 is a phase contrast micrograph of estuarine mud

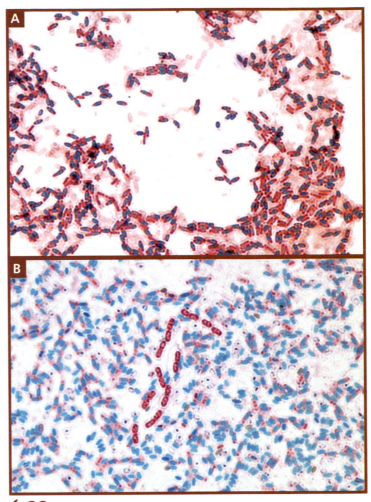

6-23 CULTURE AGE CAN AFFECT SPORULATION Bacteria capable of producing spores don't do so uniformly during their culture's growth. Sporulation is done in response to nutrient depletion, and so is characteristic of older cultures. These two *Bacillus* cultures illustrate different degrees of sporulation. **A** Most cells in this specimen contain spores; very few have been released. **B** This specimen consists mostly of released spores.

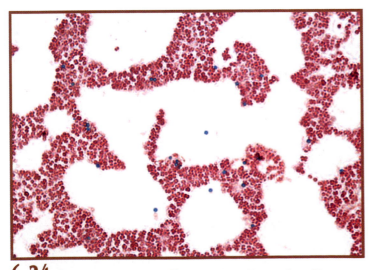

6-24 *SPOROSARCINA UREAE* SPORES *Clostridium* and *Bacillus* are the largest and most commonly encountered endospore forming genera, but there are at least a half-dozen others. *Sporosarcina* cells are spherical or slightly elongated and are approximately 2 μm in diameter.

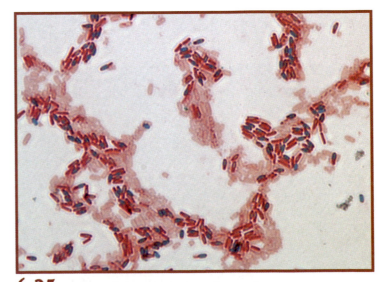

6-25 CENTRAL ELLIPTICAL ENDOSPORES Most of these *Bacillus megaterium* spores are centrally positioned, but all are elliptical. The spore does not distend the mother cell.

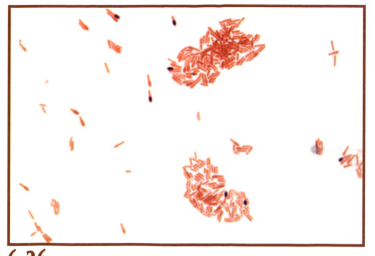

6-26 **SUBTERMINAL SPORES** This is a stained preparation of *Clostridium botulinum* using an alternative procedure. The black spores slightly distend the cell.

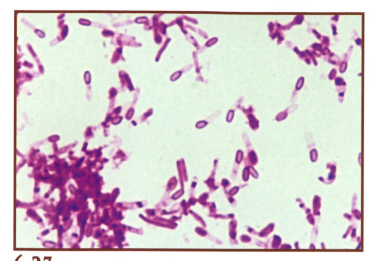

6-27 **ELLIPTICAL TERMINAL SPORES** *Clostridium tetani* stained by a different spore stain protocol using carbolfuchsin. Notice how the spores have caused the ends of the cells to swell.

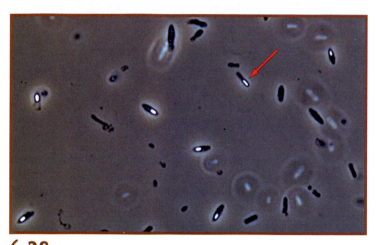

6-28 **SPORES AS SEEN WITH PHASE CONTRAST MICROSCOPY** The white, elliptical spores are easily seen in these unidentified, anaerobic rods found in an estuarine mud sample. Because they are anaerobic, it is likely they are one or more species of *Clostridium*. Note the difference in morphology between the cell marked with the **arrow** and the others.

in which several spore-forming bacteria are visible. Without staining, however, one must be careful not to confuse inclusions, such as sulfur (Figure 6-29A) or lipid (Figure 6-29B) granules, with true endospores. The spore stain will definitively identify true endospores. *Corynebacterium* species may also be a source of confusion, because they often have club-shaped swellings (Figure 6-30).

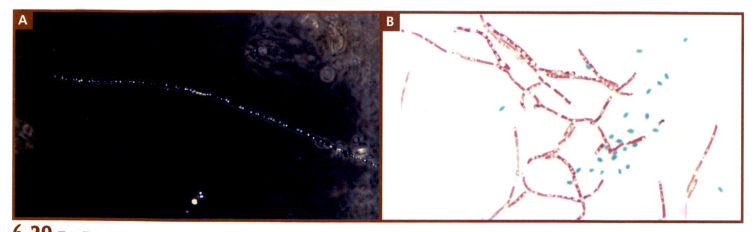

6-29 **THE ENDOSPORE STAIN ALLOWS DIFFERENTIATION BETWEEN TRUE ENDOSPORES AND CELLULAR INCLUSIONS** **A** The bright spots in this filamentous bacterium (possibly *Thiothrix*) are sulfur granules, but they might be confused with endospores in this phase contrast micrograph. Their irregular size and the presence of more than one per cell are clues that they are not endospores, but an endospore stain would remove any doubt. **B** This micrograph is an endospore stain of *Bacillus cereus* grown in culture. The spores are green, but notice all the unstained, white spots inside the cells! They are lipid granules. Now, imagine looking at this specimen using a simple stain or a Gram stain. Would you be able to identify the spores or would the lipid granules mislead you?

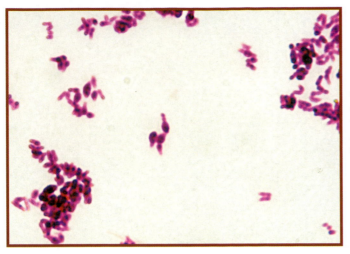

6-30 CORYNEBACTERIA HAVE TERMINAL, CLUB-SHAPED SWELLINGS In a simple stain, these might be misinterpreted as spores. This is a slide of *Corynebacterium diphtheriae* grown in culture.

Flagella Stain

● Purpose

The flagella stain allows direct observation of flagella. Presence and arrangement of flagella may be useful in identifying bacterial species.

● Principle

Although phase contrast microscopy permits visualization of bacterial flagella (Figure 6-31), they are too thin to be observed with the bright field microscope and ordinary stains. Various special flagella stains have been developed that use a **mordant** to assist in encrusting flagella with stain to a visible thickness. Most require experience and advanced techniques, and are typically not performed in beginning microbiology classes.

The number and arrangement of flagella may be observed with a flagella stain. A single flagellum is said to be **polar** and the cell has a **monotrichous** arrangement (Figure 6-32). Other arrangements (shown in Figures 6-33

through 6-35) include **amphitrichous**, with flagella at both ends of the cell; **lophotrichous**, with tufts of flagella at the end of the cell; and **peritrichous**, with flagella emerging from the entire cell surface.

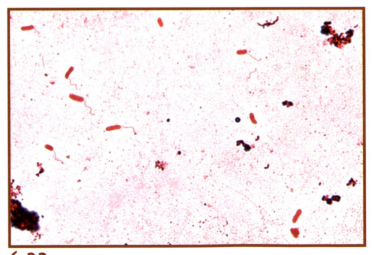

6-32 POLAR FLAGELLA *Pseudomonas aeruginosa* is often suggested as a positive control for flagella stains. Notice the single flagellum emerging from the ends of many (but not all) cells. This is due to the fragile nature of flagella, which can be broken from the cells during slide preparation.

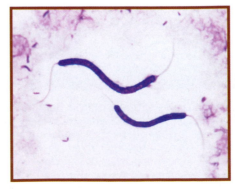

6-33 AMPHITRICHOUS FLAGELLA *Spirillum volutans* has a flagellum at both ends.

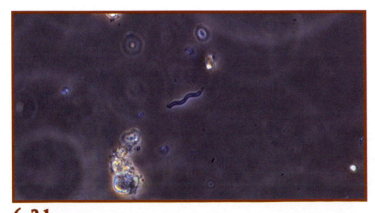

6-31 BACTERIAL FLAGELLA ARE THIN! The flagella of this aquatic spirillum are barely visible at each end of the cell in this phase contrast micrograph.

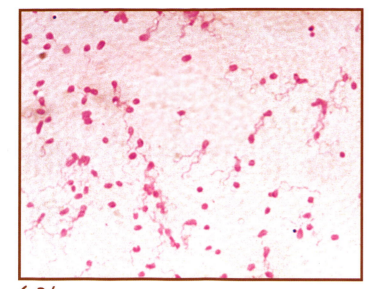

6-34 **LOPHOTRICHOUS FLAGELLA** Several flagella emerge from one end of this *Pseudomonas* species. Again, not all cells have flagella because they were too delicate to stay intact during the staining procedure.

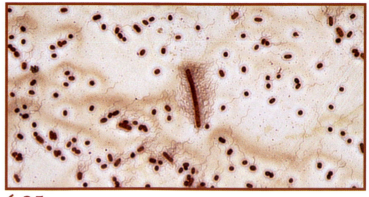

6-35 **PERITRICHOUS FLAGELLA OF *PROTEUS VULGARIS*** Notice the flagella emerging from the entire cell surface. *P. vulgaris* is capable of swarming motility (Figure 3-22), in which the cells spread across the agar surface at specific intervals, and then remain in place until the next swarm. The smaller cells are called "swimmers" and are the form seen when grown in a liquid medium. When transferred to a solid medium or under certain environmental conditions, swimmers differentiate into "swarmers." A swarmer is seen in the center of this micrograph. Swarmers are larger, contain multiple nucleoids (the site of DNA), and produce an extracellular slime or capsule that assists in swarming. After swarming, they break up into swimmer cells. Swarmers are the more virulent form.

Wet Mount and Hanging Drop Preparations

● Purpose

Most bacterial microscopic preparations result in death of the microorganisms due to heat-fixing and staining. Simple **wet mounts** and the **hanging drop technique** allow observation of living cells to determine motility. They also are used to see natural cell size, arrangement, and shape. All of these may be useful characteristics in the identification of a microbe.

● Principle

A wet mount preparation is made by placing the specimen in a drop of water on a microscope slide and covering it with a cover glass. Because no stain is used and most cells are transparent, viewing is best done with as little illumination as possible (Figure 6-36). Motility often can be observed at low or high dry magnification, but viewing must be done quickly due to drying of the preparation. As the water recedes, bacteria will appear to be herded across the field. This is not motility. You should look for independent darting motion of the cells.

A hanging drop preparation allows longer observation of the specimen since it doesn't dry out as quickly. A thin ring of petroleum jelly is applied around the well of a depression slide. A drop of water is then placed in the center of the cover glass and living microbes are transferred into it. The depression microscope slide is carefully placed over the cover glass in such a way that the drop is received into the depression and is undisturbed. The petroleum jelly causes the cover glass to stick to the slide.

The preparation may then be picked up, inverted so the cover glass is on top, and placed under the microscope for examination. As with the wet mount, viewing is best done with as little illumination as possible. The petroleum jelly forms an air-tight seal that slows drying of the drop, allowing a long period for observation of cell size, shape, binary fission, and motility.

If these techniques are done to determine motility, the observer must be careful to distinguish between true motility and **Brownian motion** created by collisions with water molecules. In the latter, cells will appear to vibrate in place. With true motility, cells will exhibit independent movement over greater distances.

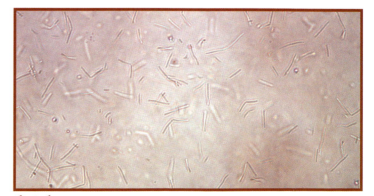

6-36 **THE WET MOUNT** Shown is an unstained wet mount preparation of *Aeromonas sobria*, a motile Gram-negative rod. Because of the thickness of the water in the wet mount, cells show up in many different focal planes and are mostly out of focus. To get the best possible image, adjust the condenser height and reduce the light intensity with the iris diaphragm.

Miscellaneous Structures

Bacterial cellular structure is simple compared to eukaryotic cells. However, differentiation of cytoplasmic components is possible to a certain degree. Figures 6-37 through 6-42 illustrate some of these structures.

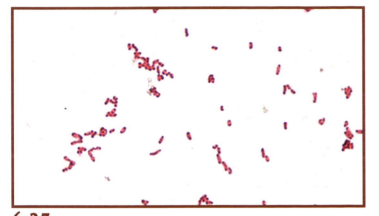

6-37 BIPOLAR STAINING (GRAM STAIN) Some cells in the *Enterobacteriaceae* (Gram-negative rods often found in the large intestine) exhibit bipolar staining, in which the ends stain more darkly than the center. These cells are said to be "vacuolated," but they do not have true, membrane-bound vacuoles.

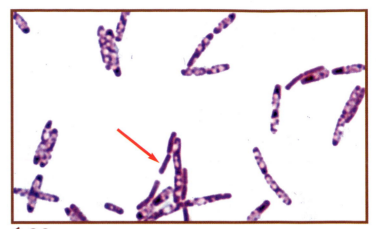

6-38 VACUOLATED CYTOPLASM (GRAM STAIN) *Bacillus* cells may stain uniformly (**arrow**) or they may have a foamy, vacuolated appearance (most cells in the field). The larger white regions within the cell are probably developing endospores. This is *Bacillus cereus* grown in culture.

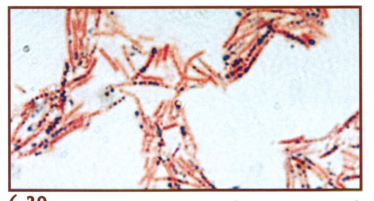

6-39 ORGANIC CYTOPLASMIC GRANULES (SUDAN BLACK B STAIN) Dark staining poly-β-hydroxybutyrate (PHB) granules serve as a carbon and energy reserve. This specimen is *Bacillus cereus;* other organisms store carbon in the form of starch or glycogen.

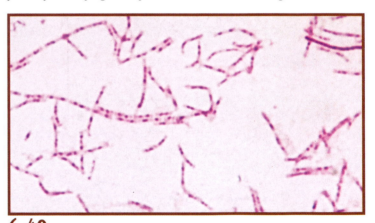

6-40 THE NUCLEOPLASM *Bacillus cereus* stained to show the nucleoplasm. Remember that what appears to be a nucleus is not. There is no membrane separating the nucleoid from the cytoplasm.

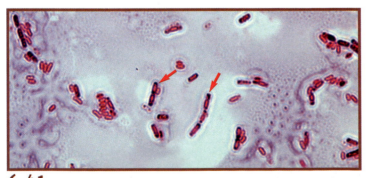

6-41 PARASPORAL CRYSTALS *Bacillus thuringiensis* produces proteinaceous bodies near its spores called parasporal crystals (the dark objects indicated by **arrows**). These crystals kill the larvae of various insect groups (especially Lepidopterans). After ingestion of the crystal, it is activated in the larval gut by a protease enzyme. The result is cytolysis of larval cells and, presumably, a ready nutrient source for the endospore when it germinates. These crystals have been commercially marketed as Bt toxin.

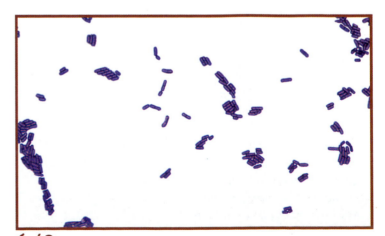

6-42 CELL WALL STAIN This is a micrograph of *Bacillus coagulans* showing its cell walls. Notice the wall separating cells that form a chain. This indicates that they are in the process of dividing or have recently completed a division.

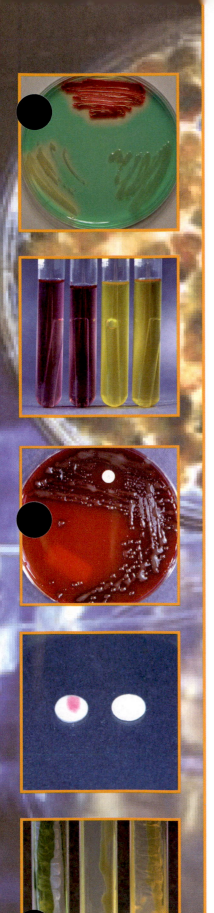

Differential Media

API 20 E Identification System for *Enterobacteriaceae* and Other Gram-negative Rods

● Purpose

The API 20 E multitest system (available from bioMérieux, Inc.) is used clinically for the rapid identification of *Enterobacteriaceae* (more than 5,500 strains) and other Gram-negative rods (more than 2,300 strains).

● Principle

The API 20 E system is a plastic strip of 20 microtubes and cupules, partially filled with different dehydrated substrates. Bacterial suspension is added to the microtubes, rehydrating the media and inoculating them at the same time. As with the other biochemical tests in this section, color changes take place in the tubes either during incubation or after addition of reagents. These color changes reveal the presence or absence of chemical action and, thus, a positive or negative result (Figure 7-1).

After incubation, spontaneous reactions—those that do not require addition of reagents—are evaluated first. Then tests that require addition of reagents are performed and evaluated. Finally, the results are entered on the Result Sheet (Figure 7-2). An oxidase test is performed separately and constitutes the 21st test.

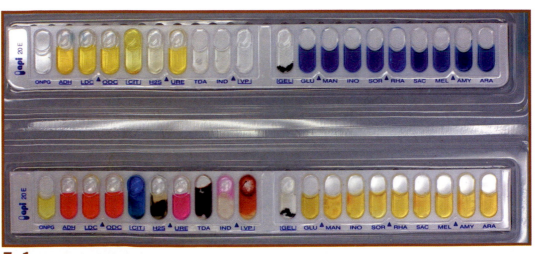

7-1 API 20 E TEST STRIPS The top strip is uninoculated. The bottom strip (with the exception of GEL) is positive for all results.

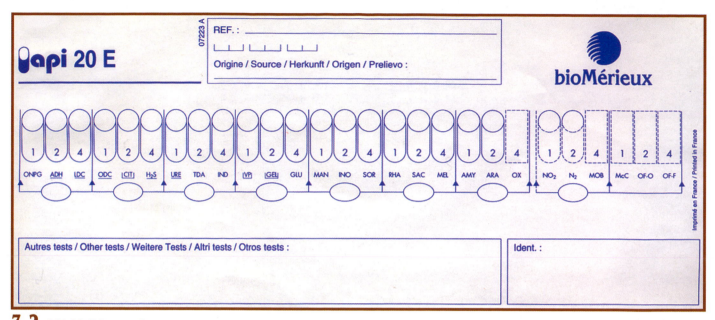

7-2 API 20 E RESULT SHEET The API 20 E Result Sheet divides the tests into groups of three, assigning each member of a group a numerical value of 1, 2, or 4. The values for positive results in each group are added together to produce a single-digit number. This number, when combined with the numbers from other groups, produces a seven-digit code that then is interpreted using the Analytical Profile Index supplied by the company (visit http://www.BioMérieux-USA.com).

As shown in Figure 7-2, the Result Sheet divides the tests into groups of three, with the members of a group having numerical values of 1, 2, or 4, respectively. These numbers are assigned for positive (+) results only. Negative (−) results are not counted. The values for positive results in each group are added together to produce a number from 0 to 7, which is entered in the oval below the three tests. The totals from each group are combined sequentially to produce a seven-digit code, which can then be interpreted on the Analytical Profile Index[*].

_____
* The index is now available by subscription only through Bio-Mérieux-USA.com.

In rare instances, information from the 21 tests (and the 7-digit code) is not discriminatory enough to identify an organism. When this occurs, the organism is grown and examined on MacConkey Agar and supplemental tests are performed for nitrate reduction, oxidation/reduction of glucose, and motility. The results are entered separately in the supplemental spaces on the Result Sheet and used for final identification.

Bacitracin Susceptibility Test

● Purpose

The Bacitracin Susceptibility Test is used to differentiate and presumptively identify β-hemolytic group A streptococci (*Streptococcus pyogenes*-susceptible) from other β-hemolytic streptococci (resistant). It also differentiates the genus *Staphylococcus* (resistant) from the susceptible *Micrococcus* and *Stomatococcus*.

● Principle

Antibiotics, as discussed in Section 19, are antimicrobial substances produced by microorganisms. Bacitracin, produced by *Bacillus licheniformis*, is a powerful peptide antibiotic that inhibits bacterial cell wall synthesis (Figure 7-3).

Thus, it is effective only on bacteria that have cell walls and are in the process of growing.

The Bacitracin Test is a simple test performed by placing a bacitracin-impregnated disk on an agar plate inoculated to produce a bacterial lawn. The bacitracin diffuses into

$$CH_3\text{-}C(CH_3)\text{=}CH\text{-}CH_2\text{-}[CH_2\text{-}C(CH_3)\text{=}CH\text{-}CH_2]_9\text{-}CH_2\text{-}C(CH_3)\text{=}CH\text{-}CH_2\text{-}O\text{-}P(\text{=}O)(O^-)O^-$$

7-3 UNDECAPRENYL PHOSPHATE Undecaprenyl phosphate is involved in transport of peptidoglycan subunits across the cell membrane during cell wall synthesis. Bacitracin interferes with its release from the peptidoglycan subunit. It is a C_{55} molecule derived from eleven isoprene subunits plus a phosphate.

the agar and, where its concentration is sufficient, inhibits growth of susceptible bacteria. Inhibition of bacterial growth will appear as a clearing on the agar plate. Any zone of clearing 10 mm in diameter or greater around the disk is interpreted as bacitracin susceptibility (Figure 7-4). For more information on antimicrobial susceptibility, refer to the Antimicrobial Susceptibility Test, page 223.

7-4 BACITRACIN SUSCEPTIBILITY ON A SHEEP BLOOD AGAR PLATE *Staphylococcus aureus* (Resistant, R) is above and *Micrococcus luteus* (Susceptible, S) is below.

β-Lactamase Test

 ### Purpose

The β-Lactamase Test is used to quickly identify if patient isolates are resistant to penicillins and cephalosporins. It is especially useful in identifying resistant strains of *Neisseria gonorrhoeae*, *Staphylococcus spp.*, and members of genus *Enterococcus*.

Principle

Penicillins and cephalosporins—called β-**lactam antibiotics** because of the β-lactam ring in their chemical structure—kill bacteria by interfering with cell wall synthesis. The bacterial enzyme **transpeptidase** catalyzes cross-linking between peptidoglycan subunits thus adding rigidity to the cell wall. By competing for sites on transpeptidase, β-lactam antibiotics prevent essential cross-linking of the peptidoglycan. Many bacteria have developed resistance to these antibiotics by producing enzymes called β-**lactamases**. β-lactamases hydrolyze the β-lactam ring, thus destroying the structure of the antibiotic. Partial chemical structures of β-lactam antibiotics are shown in Figure 7-5.

The β-Lactamase Test is one of many tests used to identify β-lactamase production by measuring resistance to β-lactam antibiotics. In this test, a paper disk containing nitrocefin is smeared with the test organism. Nitrocefin is a cephalosporin, susceptible to most β-lactamases, that turns pink when it is hydrolyzed. Therefore, if the test organism produces β-lactamase, it will hydrolyze the nitrocefin and produce a pink spot on the disk (Figure 7-6).

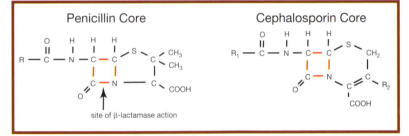

7-5 β-LACTAM ANTIBIOTIC STRUCTURE Although penicillins and cephalosporins have unique structures, their bactericidal effects are similar in that they both contain a β-lactam ring and interfere with peptidoglycan cross-linking. The **arrow** indicates the site of β-lactamase activity.

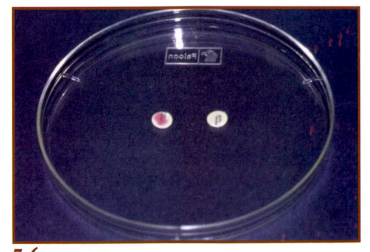

7-6 CEFINASE® DISKS A β-lactam resistant strain is on the left and a susceptible strain is on the right.
(Disks available from Becton-Dickinson Microbiology Systems, Sparks, MD)

Bile Esculin Test

● Purpose

The Bile Esculin Test is most commonly used for presumptive identification of enterococci and members of the *Streptococcus bovis* group, all of which are positive.

● Principle

Bile Esculin Agar is an undefined, selective, and differential medium containing beef extract, digest of gelatin, esculin, oxgall (bile), and ferric citrate. Esculin, extracted from the bark of the Horse Chestnut tree, is a glycoside composed of glucose and esculetin. Beef extract and gelatin provide nutrients and energy; bile is the selective agent added to separate the *Streptococcus bovis* group and enterococci from other streptococci (see Table 2-3, page 6). Ferric citrate is added as a source of oxidized iron to indicate a positive test.

Many bacteria can hydrolyze esculin under acidic conditions (Figure 7-7), and many bacteria, especially Gram-negative enterics, demonstrate tolerance to bile. However, among the streptococci, typically only enterococci and members of the *Streptococcus bovis* group (*S. equinus*, *S. gallolyticus*, *S. infantarius*, and *S. alactolyticus*) tolerate bile and hydrolyze esculin.

In this test, when esculin molecules are split, esculetin reacts with the Fe^{3+} from the ferric citrate and forms a dark brown precipitate (Figure 7-8). This precipitate darkens the medium surrounding the growth. An organism that darkens the medium even slightly is Bile Esculin-positive (Figure 7-9). An organism that does not darken the medium is negative.

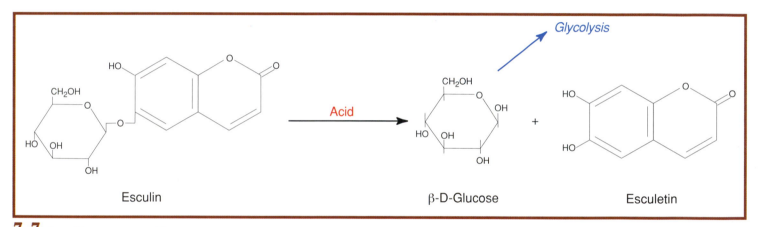

Esculin → (Acid) → β-D-Glucose + Esculetin → Glycolysis

7-7 **ACID HYDROLYSIS OF ESCULIN** Many organisms have the ability to produce esculetin. However, the group D streptococci and enterococci are unique in their ability to do this in the presence of bile salts.

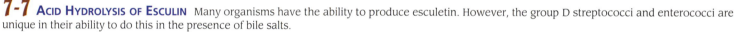

Esculetin + Fe^{3+} ⟶ **Dark Brown Color**

7-8 **BILE ESCULIN TEST INDICATOR REACTION** This test involves the reaction of esculetin, produced during the hydrolysis of esculin, with Fe^{3+}. The result is a dark brown to black color in the medium.

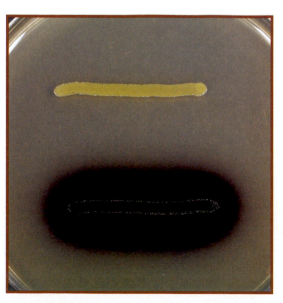

7-9 **BILE ESCULIN TEST RESULTS** This plate was inoculated with *Staphylococcus aureus* (top) and *Enterococcus faecium* (bottom). The darkening of the medium around *E. faecium* indicates a positive result.

Blood Agar

● Purpose

Blood agar is used for isolation and cultivation of many types of fastidious bacteria. It is also used to differentiate bacteria based on their hemolytic characteristics, especially within the genera *Streptococcus*, *Enterococcus*, and *Aerococcus*.

● Principle

Several species of Gram-positive cocci produce exotoxins called **hemolysins,** which are able to destroy red blood cells (RBCs) and hemoglobin. Blood Agar, sometimes called Sheep Blood Agar because it includes 5% sheep blood in a Tryptic Soy Agar base, allows differentiation of bacteria based on their ability to hemolyze RBCs.

The three major types of hemolysis are β-hemolysis, α-hemolysis, and γ-hemolysis. β-hemolysis, the complete destruction of RBCs and hemoglobin, results in a clearing of the medium around the colonies (Figure 7-10). α-hemolysis is the partial destruction of RBCs and produces a greenish discoloration of the agar around the colonies (Figure 7-11). γ-hemolysis is actually nonhemolysis and appears as simple growth with no change to the medium (Figure 7-12).

Hemolysins produced by streptococci are called **streptolysins.** They come in two forms—type O and type S. **Streptolysin O** is oxygen-labile and expresses maximal activity under anaerobic conditions. **Streptolysin S** is oxygen-stable but expresses itself optimally under anaerobic conditions as well. The easiest method of providing an environment favorable for streptolysins on Blood Agar is what is called the **streak–stab technique.** In this procedure, the Blood Agar plate is streaked for isolation and then stabbed with a loop. The stabs encourage streptolysin activity because of the reduced oxygen concentration of the subsurface environment (Figure 7-13).

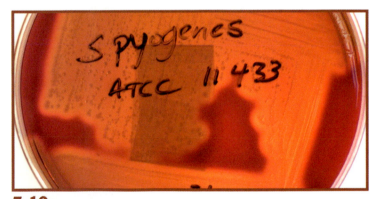

7-10 β-**HEMOLYSIS** *Streptococcus pyogenes* demonstrates β-hemolysis. The clearing around the growth is a result of complete lysis of red blood cells. This photograph was taken with transmitted light.

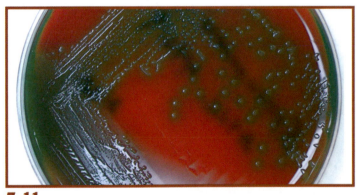

7-11 α-**HEMOLYSIS** This is a streak plate of *Streptococcus pneumoniae* demonstrating α-hemolysis. The greenish zone around the colonies results from incomplete lysis of red blood cells.

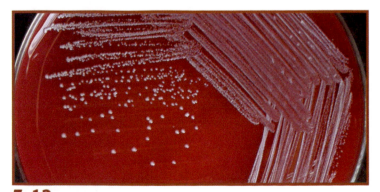

7-12 γ-**HEMOLYSIS** This streak plate of *Staphylococcus epidermidis* on a Sheep Blood Agar illustrates no hemolysis.

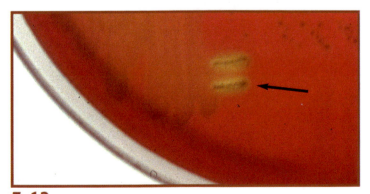

7-13 **AEROBIC** *VS.* **ANAEROBIC HEMOLYSIS** An unidentified throat culture isolate demonstrates α-hemolysis when growing on the surface, but β-hemolysis beneath the surface surrounding the stabs (**arrow**). This results from production of an oxygen-labile hemolysin.

CAMP Test

● Purpose

The CAMP test (an acronym of the developers of the test—Christie, Atkins, and Munch-Peterson) is used to differentiate Group B *Streptococcus agalactiae* (+) from other *Streptococcus* species (−).

● Principle

Group B *Streptococcus agalactiae* produces the CAMP factor—a hemolytic protein that acts synergistically with the β-hemolysin of *Staphylococcus aureus* subsp. *aureus*. When streaked perpendicularly to an *S. aureus* subsp. *aureus* streak on blood agar (Figure 7-14), an arrowhead-shaped zone of hemolysis forms and is a positive result (Figure 7-15).

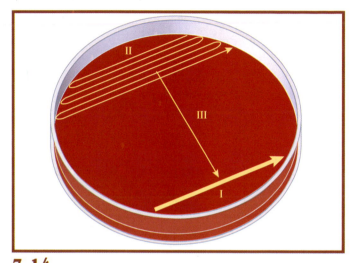

7-14 CAMP Test Inoculation Two inoculations are made. First *Staphylococcus aureus* subsp. *aureus* is streaked along one edge of a fresh Blood Agar plate (I). Then the isolate (when testing an unknown organism) is inoculated densely in the other half of the plate opposite *S. aureus* (II). Finally, a single streak is made from inside Streak II toward, but not touching, *S. aureus* (III).

7-15 Positive CAMP Test Results Note the arrowhead zone of clearing in the region where the CAMP factor of *Streptococcus agalactiae* acts synergistically with the β-hemolysin of *Staphylococcus aureus* subsp. *aureus*.

Casein Hydrolysis Test

● Purpose

The Casein Hydrolysis Test is used to identify bacteria capable of hydrolyzing casein with the enzyme **casease**.

● Principle

Many bacteria require proteins as a source of amino acids and other components for synthetic processes. Some bacteria have the ability to produce and secrete enzymes (exoenzymes) into the environment that catalyze the hydrolysis (break-down) of large proteins to smaller peptides or individual amino acids, thus enabling their uptake across the membrane.

Casease is an enzyme some bacteria produce to hydrolyze the milk protein **casein** (Figure 7-16), the molecule that gives milk its white color. When broken down into smaller fragments, the ordinarily white casein loses its opacity and becomes clear.

The presence of casease can be detected easily with the test medium Milk Agar (Figure 7-17). Milk Agar is an undefined medium containing pancreatic digest of casein, yeast extract, dextrose, and powdered milk. When plated Milk Agar is inoculated with a casease-positive organism, secreted casease will diffuse into the medium around the colonies and create a zone of clearing where the casein has been hydrolyzed. Casease-negative organisms do not secrete casease and, thus, do not produce clear zones around the growth.

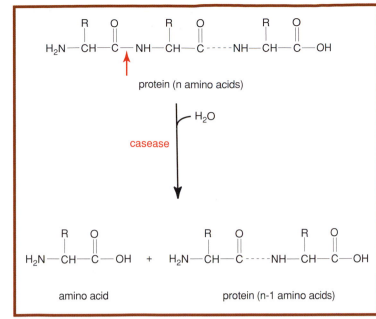

7-16 CASEIN HYDROLYSIS Hydrolysis of any protein occurs by breaking peptide bonds (**red arrow**) between adjacent amino acids to produce short peptides or individual amino acids.

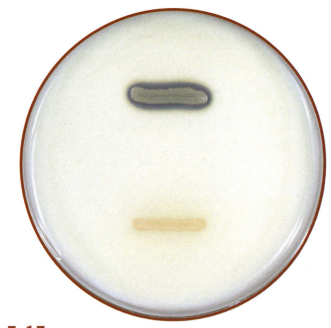

7-17 CASEIN HYDROLYSIS TEST RESULTS This Milk Agar plate was inoculated with *Bacillus megaterium* (casease-positive) above and *Micrococcus roseus* (casease-negative) below.

Catalase Test

● Purpose

The Catalase Test is used to identify organisms that produce the enzyme **catalase**. It is most commonly used to differentiate members of the catalase-positive *Micrococcaceae* from the catalase-negative *Streptococcaceae*. Variations on this test may also be used in identification of *Mycobacterium* species.

● Principle

The electron transport chains of aerobic and facultatively anaerobic bacteria are composed of molecules capable of accepting and donating electrons as conditions dictate. As such, these molecules alternate between the oxidized and reduced form, passing electrons down the chain to the final electron acceptor (FEA). Energy lost by electrons in this sequential transfer is used to perform oxidative phosphorylation (*i.e.*, produce ATP from ADP).

One carrier molecule in the ETC called **flavoprotein** can bypass the next carrier in the chain and transfer electrons directly to oxygen (Figure 7-18). This alternate pathway produces two very potent cellular toxins—hydrogen peroxide (H_2O_2) and superoxide radical (O_2^-).

Aerobic and facultatively anaerobic bacteria produce enzymes capable of detoxifying these compounds. **Superoxide dismutase** catalyzes conversion of superoxide radicals (the more lethal of the two compounds) to hydrogen peroxide (Figure 7-18). Catalase converts hydrogen peroxide into water and gaseous oxygen (Figure 7-19).

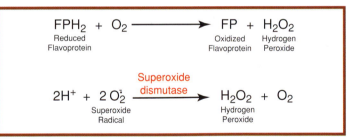

$$FPH_2 + O_2 \longrightarrow FP + H_2O_2$$

Reduced Flavoprotein → Oxidized Flavoprotein, Hydrogen Peroxide

$$2H^+ + 2O_2^- \xrightarrow{\text{Superoxide dismutase}} H_2O_2 + O_2$$

Superoxide Radical → Hydrogen Peroxide

7-18 MICROBIAL PRODUCTION OF H_2O_2 Hydrogen peroxide may be formed through the transfer of electrons from reduced flavoprotein to oxygen or from the action of superoxide dismutase.

$$2H_2O_2 \xrightarrow{\text{Catalase}} 2H_2O + O_{2\,(g)}$$

Hydrogen Peroxide

7-19 CATALASE MEDIATED CONVERSION OF H_2O_2 Catalase is an enzyme of aerobes, microaerophiles, and facultative anaerobes that converts hydrogen peroxide to water and oxygen gas.

Bacteria that produce catalase can be detected easily using typical store-grade hydrogen peroxide. When hydrogen peroxide is added to a catalase-positive culture, oxygen gas bubbles form immediately (Figures 7-20 and 7-21). If no bubbles appear, the organism is catalase-negative. This test can be performed on a microscope slide or by adding hydrogen peroxide directly to the bacterial growth.

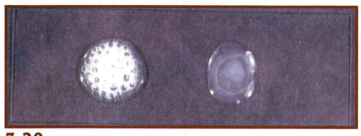

7-20 **CATALASE SLIDE TEST** Shown is the catalase slide test in which visible bubble production indicates a positive result. *Staphylococcus aureus* (+) is on the left, *Enterococcus faecium* (−) is on the right. It is a good idea to cover the slide with a Petri dish lid immediately after addition of peroxide to contain aerosols produced in positive reactions.

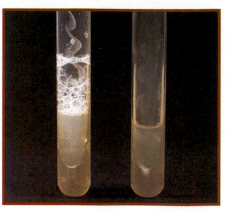

7-21 **CATALASE TUBE TEST** The catalase test may also be performed on an agar slant. *Staphylococcus aureus* (+) is on the left, *Enterococcus faecium* (−) is on the right.

Citrate Utilization Test

● Purpose

The Citrate Utilization Test is used to determine the ability of an organism to use citrate as its sole source of carbon. Citrate utilization is one part of a test series referred to as the IMViC (*Indole, Methyl Red, Voges-Proskauer and Citrate tests*) that distinguishes between members of the family *Enterobacteriaceae* and differentiates them from other Gram-negative rods.

● Principle

In many bacteria, citrate (citric acid) is produced as acetyl coenzyme A (from the oxidation of pyruvate or the β-oxidation of fatty acids) reacts with oxaloacetate at the entry to the Krebs cycle. Citrate is then converted through a complex series of reactions back to oxaloacetate, which begins the cycle anew. Refer to the Appendix (Figures A-1 and A-4) and Figure 7-51 for more information on the Krebs cycle and fatty acid metabolism.

In a medium containing citrate as the only available carbon source, bacteria that possess **citrate-permease** can transport the molecules into the cell and enzymatically convert it to pyruvate. Pyruvate can then be converted to a variety of products, depending on the pH of the environment (Figure 7-22).

Simmons Citrate Agar is a defined medium that contains sodium citrate as the sole carbon source and ammonium phosphate as the sole nitrogen source. Bromthymol blue dye, which is green at pH 6.9 and blue at pH 7.6, is added as an indicator. Bacteria that survive in the medium and utilize the citrate also convert the ammonium phosphate to ammonia (NH_3) and ammonium hydroxide (NH_4OH), both of which tend to alkalinize the agar. As the pH goes up, the medium changes from green to blue (Figure 7-23). Thus, conversion of the medium to blue is a positive citrate test result.

Occasionally a citrate-positive organism will grow on a Simmons Citrate slant without producing a change in color.

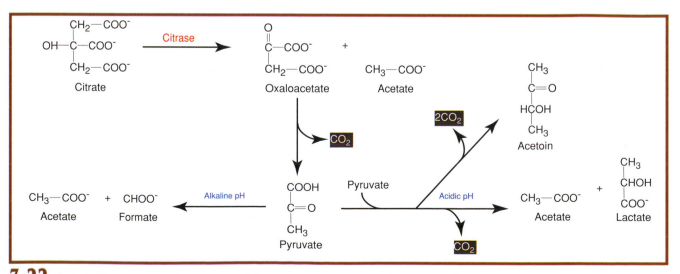

7-22 **CITRATE CHEMISTRY** In the presence of citrate-permease enzyme, citrate enters the cell and is converted to pyruvate. The pyruvate is then converted to a variety of products depending on the pH of the environment.

In most cases, this is because of incomplete incubation. In the absence of color change, growth on the slant indicates that citrate is being utilized and is evidence of a positive reaction. To avoid confusion between actual growth and heavy inoculum, which may appear as growth, citrate slants typically are inoculated lightly with an inoculating needle rather than a loop.

7-23 CITRATE TEST RESULTS Simmons citrate agar inoculated *Citrobacter diversus* (+) on the left, *Bacillus cereus* (−) in the center, and an uninoculated control on the right.

Coagulase Tests

● Purpose

The Coagulase Test is typically used to differentiate *Staphylococcus aureus* from other Gram-positive cocci.

● Principle

Staphylococcus aureus is an opportunistic pathogen that can be highly resistant to both the normal immune response and antimicrobial agents. Its resistance is due, in part, to the production of a **coagulase** enzyme. Coagulase works in conjunction with normal plasma components to form protective fibrin barriers around individual bacterial cells or groups of cells, shielding them from phagocytosis and other types of attack.

Coagulase enzymes occur in two forms—**bound coagulase** and **free coagulase**. Bound coagulase, also called **clumping factor**, is attached to the bacterial cell wall and reacts directly with fibrinogen in plasma. The fibrinogen then precipitates causing the cells to clump together in a visible mass. Free coagulase is an extracellular enzyme (released from the cell) that reacts with a plasma component called **coagulase-reacting factor** (CRF). The resulting reaction is similar to the conversion of prothrombin and fibrinogen in the normal clotting mechanism.

Two forms of the Coagulase Test have been devised to detect the enzymes: the Tube Test and the Slide Test. The Tube Test detects the presence of either bound or free coagulase, while the Slide Test detects only bound coagulase. Both tests utilize rabbit plasma treated with anticoagulant to interrupt normal clotting mechanisms.

The Tube Test is performed by adding the test organism to rabbit plasma in a test tube. Coagulation of the plasma (including any thickening or formation of fibrin threads) within 24 hours indicates a positive reaction (Figure 7-24). The plasma is typically examined for clotting (without shaking) after about 4 hours because it is possible for coagulation to take place early and revert to liquid within 24 hours.

In the slide test, bacteria are transferred to a slide containing a small amount of plasma. Agglutination of the cells on the slide within one to two minutes indicates the presence of bound coagulase (Figure 7-25). Equivocal or negative Slide Test results are typically confirmed using the Tube Test.

7-24 COAGULASE TUBE TEST Coagulase-negative *Staphylococcus epidermidis* below and the more pathogenic coagulase-positive *S. aureus* above. Coagulase increases bacterial resistance to phagocytosis and antibodies by surrounding infecting organisms with a clot.

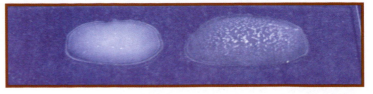

7-25 COAGULASE SLIDE TEST Emulsions of *Staphylococcus epidermidis* (−) on the left and *S. aureus* (+) on the right were prepared in sterile saline. Agglutination of the coagulase plasma is indicative of a positive result for bound coagulase.

BBL CRYSTAL™ Identification System—Enteric/Nonfermenter (E/NF)

● Purpose

The BBL CRYSTAL™ E/NF (Becton Dickinson Microbiology Systems) is a multitest system used to identify aerobic Gram-negative rods of the family *Enterobacteriaceae*, as well as other Gram-negative bacilli recovered from human samples. Identification is based on the results of 30 biochemical tests.

● Principle

The BBL CRYSTAL™ E/NF (Figure 7-26) test system panel consists of a base with 30 wells and a lid with 30 plastic tabs, each with a dehydrated substrate on its tip and which fits into a different well when the lid is in place. The organism to be identified is first suspended in an inoculum fluid, then dispensed into the 30 wells of the base. Placement of the lid onto the base immerses the plastic tabs in inoculum and reconstitutes the dehydrated substrates. Separate oxidase and indole tests must also be run.

After 18 to 20 hours incubation, the panel may be read using a light box and comparing the results to a standard color reaction chart. As can be seen in Figure 7-26, there are three rows of ten tests each (A through J). Numerical values of 4, 2, or 1 are assigned to any positive results for any test in the top, middle, or bottom rows, respectively, on the score sheet (Figure 7-27). By adding the values in the ten columns, a 10-digit BBL CRYSTAL™

profile number is obtained. The profile number is then matched to a computer data base of approximately 100 taxa for identification.

7-27 THE BBL CRYSTAL™ E/NF SCORE SHEET Positive test results are assigned a value of 4, 2, or 1, depending on its row. Columns are added and a ten digit number is made from the sums. This number is then matched to a database containing approximately 100 taxa for identification. The ten-digit number (5664677157) on this score sheet identifies the organism as *Enterobacter cloacae*.

7-26 THE BBL CRYSTAL™ E/NF The top row tests for carbohydrate utilization with acid end products. Positive tests are indicated by a gold or yellow color and are given a value of 4. The carbohydrates are: ARA= Arabinose, MNS=Mannose, SUC=Sucrose, MEL=Melibiose, RHA=Rhamnose, SOR=Sorbitol, MNT=Mannitol, ADO=Adonitol, GAL=Galactose, and INO= Inositol. The second row consists of tests that detect the ability to hydrolyze the various substrates with the production of a yellow compound (either *p*-nitrophenol or *p*-nitroaniline). Each positive is assigned a value of 2. The substrates are: PHO=*p*-nitrophenyl phosphate, BGL=*p*-nitrophenyl α-β-glucoside, NPG=*p*-nitrophenyl β-galactoside, PRO=Proline nitroanilide, BPH=*p*-nitrophenyl bis-phosphate, BXY=*p*-nitrophenyl xyloside, AAR=*p*-nitrophenyl α-arabinoside, PHC=*p*-nitrophenyl phosphorylcholine, GLR=*p*-nitrophenyl β-glucuronide, and NAG=*p*-nitrophenyl-N-acetyl glucosamide. The third row consists of various biochemical tests with each positive result being given a value of 1. The tests are as follows with the positive result in parentheses: GGL=γ-L-glutamyl *p*-nitroanilide hydrolysis (yellow), ESC=Esculin hydrolysis (black), PHE-Phenylalanine deamination (brown), URE=Urea hydrolysis (blue), GLY=Glycine degradation (blue), CIT=Citrate utilization (blue), MLO=Malonate utilization (blue), TTC=Tetrazolium reduction (red), ARG=Arginine catabolism (purple), and LYS=Lysine catabolism (purple).

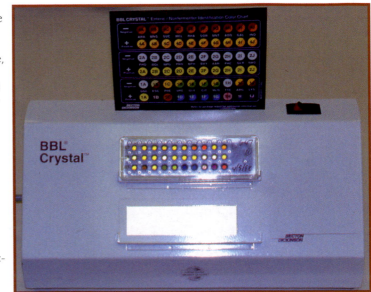

Decarboxylation Test

● Purpose

Decarboxylase media can include any one of several amino acids and each detects the presence of a different **decarboxylase** enzyme. Typically, these media are used to differentiate organisms in the family *Enterobacteriaceae* and to distinguish them from other Gram-negative rods.

● Principle

Møller's Decarboxylase Base Medium contains peptone, glucose, the pH indicator bromcresol purple, and the **coenzyme** pyridoxal phosphate. Bromcresol purple is purple at pH 6.8 and above, and yellow below pH 5.2. Base medium can be used with one of a number of specific amino acid substrates, depending on the decarboxylase to be identified.

After inoculation, an overlay of mineral oil is used to seal the medium from external oxygen and promote fermentation. Glucose fermentation (all *Enterobacteriaceae* ferment glucose) in the anaerobic medium initially turns it yellow due to the accumulation of acid end products. The low pH and presence of the specific amino acid induces **decarboxylase-positive** organisms to produce the enzyme. (That is, the specific decarboxylase gene is "switched on.")

Decarboxylation of the amino acid results in accumulation of alkaline end products that turn the medium purple (refer to Figures 7-28 through 7-31). If the organism is a glucose fermenter but does not produce the appropriate decarboxylase, the medium will turn yellow and remain so. If the organism does

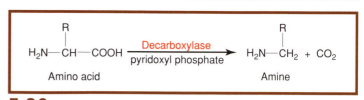

7-28 AMINO ACID DECARBOXYLATION Removal of an amino acid's carboxyl group results in the formation of an amine and carbon dioxide.

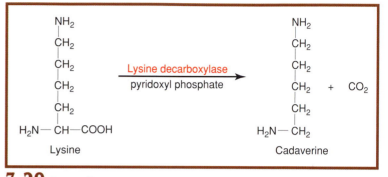

7-29 LYSINE DECARBOXYLATION Decarboxylation of the amino acid lysine produces cadaverine and CO_2.

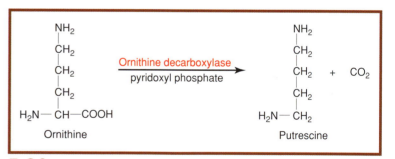

7-30 ORNITHINE DECARBOXYLATION Decarboxylation of the amino acid ornithine produces putrescine and CO_2.

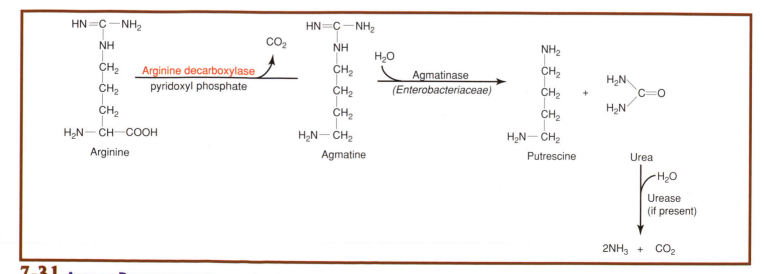

7-31 ARGININE DECARBOXYLATION Decarboxylation of the amino acid arginine produces the amine agmatine. Members of *Enterobacteriaceae* are capable of degrading agmatine into putrescine and urea. Those strains with urease can further break down the urea into ammonia and carbon dioxide. Thus, the end products of arginine catabolism are carbon dioxide, putrescine, and urea, or carbon dioxide, putrescine, and ammonia.

not ferment glucose the medium will exhibit no color change. Purple color is the only result that is considered positive; all others are negative (Figure 7-32).

7-32 **DECARBOXYLATION TEST RESULTS**
Lysine decarboxylase test results are shown here, but the colors are the same for all amino acids in Møller's medium. *Pseudomonas aeruginosa* (+) is on the left and *Proteus vulgaris* (−) is on the right. An uninoculated control is in the center.

DNase Test Agars

● Purpose

DNase Test Agar is used to distinguish *Serratia* species (+) from *Enterobacter* species, *Moraxella catarrhalis* (+) from *Neisseria* species, and *Staphylococcus aureus* (+) from other *Staphylococcus* species.

● Principle

An enzyme that catalyzes the hydrolysis of DNA into small fragments (oligonucleotides) or single nucleotides is called a **deoxyribonuclease** or **DNase** (Figure 7-33). DNase is an **exoenzyme**, that is, an enzyme that is secreted by a cell and

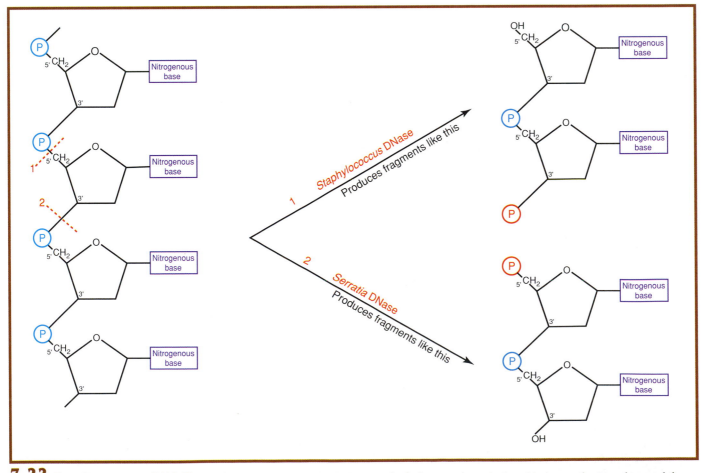

7-33 **TWO PATTERNS OF DNA HYDROLYSIS** DNase from *Staphylococcus* hydrolyzes DNA at the bond between the 5'-carbon and the phosphate (illustrated by line 1), thereby producing fragments with a free 3'-phosphate (shown in red on the upper fragment). Most fragments are one or two nucleotides long. A dinucleotide is shown here. *Serratia* DNase cleaves the bond between the phosphate and the 3'-carbon (illustrated by line 2) and produces fragments with free 5'-phosphates (shown in red on the lower fragment). Most fragments are two to four nucleotides in length. A dinucleotide is shown here.

acts on the substrate extracellularly. This extracellular diges-tion allows utilization of a macromolecule too large to be transported into the cell. Ability to produce this enzyme can be determined by culturing and observing a suspected organism on a DNase Test Agar plate. Three versions of the test are available.

One formulation for DNase Agar consists of peptides derived from soybean and casein that serve as carbon and nitrogen sources, sodium chloride for osmotic balance, and DNA as the substrate. After incubation, 1N HCl is added. Intact DNA will form a cloudy precipitate with the HCl, but not with nucleotides. Therefore, clearing around the growth is an indication of DNase activity (DNA hydrolysis) (Figure 7-34).

A modification of DNase test agar includes toluidine blue, which forms a blue complex with intact DNA, but appears pinkish when complexed with nucleotides. DNase activity is indicated by a pink coloration around the growth (Figure 7-35). While this medium has the advantage of not using 1N HCl reagent, toluidine blue may inhibit some Gram-positive cocci, so it is recommended for use with *Enterobacteriaceae*.

An alternate modification of DNase Test Agar contains methyl green dye. The dye forms a complex with poly-merized DNA that gives the agar a blue-green color at pH 7.5, but no complex is formed with nucleotides. Bacterial colonies that secrete DNase produce clearing around the growth of DNase positive organisms (Figure 7-36). The advantage to this medium is that adding 1N HCl is not necessary and it is appropriate for use with both Gram-positive cocci and *Enterobacteriaceae*.

7-34 DNASE AGAR Clockwise from the top: *Staphylo-coccus aureus* (+), *Staphylococcus epidermidis* (−), *Serratia marcescens* (+), and *Enterobacter aerogenes* (−).

7-35 DNASE AGAR WITH TOLUIDINE BLUE Clockwise from the top: *Serratia marcescens* (+), *Staphylococcus aureus* (+), and *Enterobacter aerogenes* (−). *S. aureus* strains often grow poorly on this medium. For this reason, DNase plus TB is recommended for use with *Enterobacteriaceae*.

7-36 DNASE AGAR WITH METHYL GREEN Clock-wise from the top: *Serratia marcescens* (+), *Enterobacter aerogenes* (−), and *Staphylococcus aureus* (+).

Enterotube® II

● Purpose

The Enterotube® II is a multiple test system used for rapid identification of bacteria from the family *Enterobacteriaceae*.

● Principle

The Enterotube® II is a multiple test system designed to identify enteric bacteria based on: glucose, adonitol, lactose, arabinose, sorbitol and dulcitol fermentation, lysine and ornithine decarboxylation, sulfur reduction, indole production, acetoin production from glucose fermentation, phenylalanine deamination, urea hydrolysis, and citrate utilization.

The Enterotube® II, as diagrammed in Figure 7-37, is a tube containing 12 individual chambers. Inside the tube, running lengthwise through its center, is a removable wire. After the end-caps are aseptically removed, one end of the wire is touched to an isolated colony on a streak plate and drawn back through the tube to inoculate the media in each chamber.

After 18 to 24 hours incubation, the results are interpreted, the indole test is performed, and the tube is scored on an Enterotube® II Results Sheet (Figure 7-38). As shown in the figure, the combination of positives entered on the score sheet results in a five-digit numeric code. This code is used for identification in the Enterotube® II Computer Coding and Identification System (CCIS).

The CCIS is a master list of all enterics and their assigned numeric codes. In most cases the five-digit number applies to a single organism, but when two or more species share the same code, a confirmatory VP test is performed to further differentiate the organisms. Figure 7-39 shows an Enterotube® II before and after inoculation.

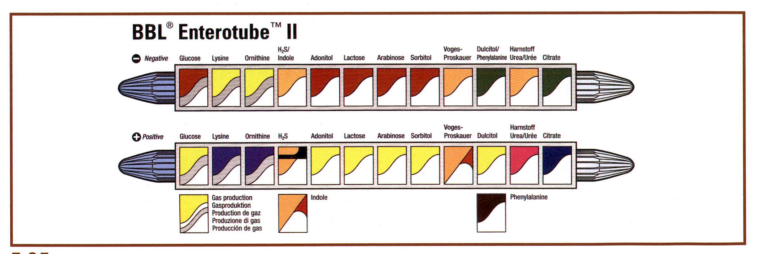

7-37 ENTEROTUBE® II TEST RESULT DIAGRAM

Illustration courtesy of Becton Dickinson and Company

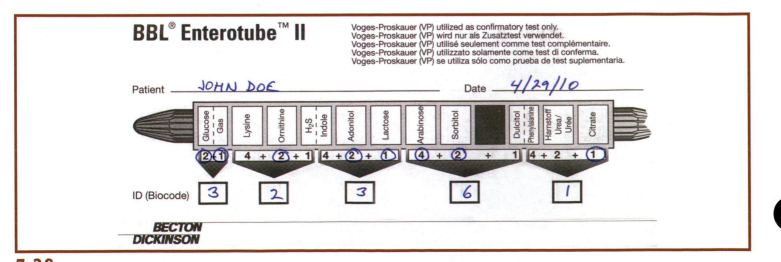

7-38 BBL ENTEROTUBE® II RESULT SHEET This is the result sheet for the tube in Figure 7-39B. The ID value obtained was 32361, which identifies the organism as *Enterobacter aerogenes*.

7-39 ENTEROTUBE® II TEST
RESULTS **A** Uninoculated tube.
B Tube inoculated with *Enterobacter
aerogenes* after 24 hours incubation.
This tube shows atypical negative
results for lysine decarboxylase; after
an additional 24 hours incubation, the
lysine medium turned purple (+).

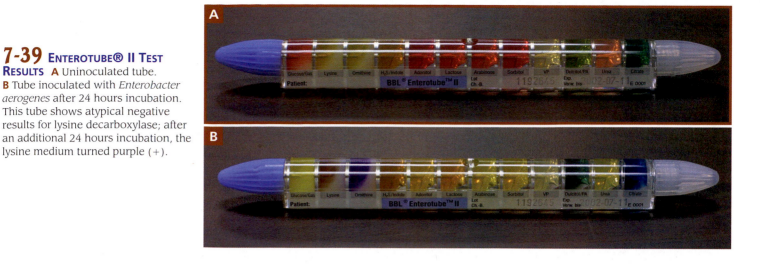

Fermentation Tests (Purple Broth and Phenol Red Broth)

● Purpose

Purple Broth and Phenol Red Broth Fermentation Tests are used to differentiate members of *Enterobacteriaceae* and to distinguish them from other Gram-negative rods.

● Principle

Carbohydrate fermentation is the metabolic process by which an organic molecule acts as an electron donor and one or more of its organic products act as the final electron acceptor. Fermentation of glucose begins with the production of pyruvate. Although some organisms use alternative pathways, most bacteria accomplish this by glycolysis (Appendix Figure A-1). The end products of pyruvate fermentation include a variety of acids, alcohols, and H_2 or CO_2 gases. The specific end products depend on the specific organism and the substrate fermented (Figure 7-40 and the Appendix Figure A-5).

The principle behind Purple Broth and Phenol Red Broth is the same. Each medium consists of a basal recipe to which a single fermentable carbohydrate is added. Both basal media include peptone and a pH indicator. Purple Broth includes bromcresol purple as the pH indicator, which is yellow below pH 6.8 and purple above; PR Broth includes phenol red, which is yellow below pH 6.8, pink above pH 7.4, and red in between. Any carbohydrate can be used, but glucose, lactose, and sucrose are common choices. Finally, an inverted Durham tube is placed in each tube as an indicator of gas production.

Acid production from fermentation of the carbohydrate lowers the pH below the neutral range of the indicator and turns the medium yellow (Figures 7-41 and 7-42). Deamination of the peptone amino acids produces ammonia (NH_3), which raises the pH and turns PR broth pink or, in the case of Purple Broth, produces no color change. Gas production is indicated by a bubble or pocket in the Durham tube where the broth has been displaced.

The ability of these media to detect acid production is largely dependent upon incubation time and the ability of the fermenter to produce an excess of acid relative to the ammonia produced from deamination. If the medium is examined at 18 hours after inoculation, a pink color (PR Broth) or purple color (Purple Broth) indicates that the organism has not fermented the substrate and has likely deaminated the peptone amino acids. Readings after 18–24 hours may be unreliable. If the tube indicates acid production, there is no problem. However, no color change or an indication of alkalinity may be due to a **reversion**. A reversion is what happens in the medium when an organism only performs deamination due to the consumption of carbohydrate. The subsequent pH shift from acid to alkaline may mask any evidence of fermentation because once the PR Broth turns pink or Purple Broth returns to purple, it is impossible to visually distinguish a reversion from the reaction of a true nonfermenter.

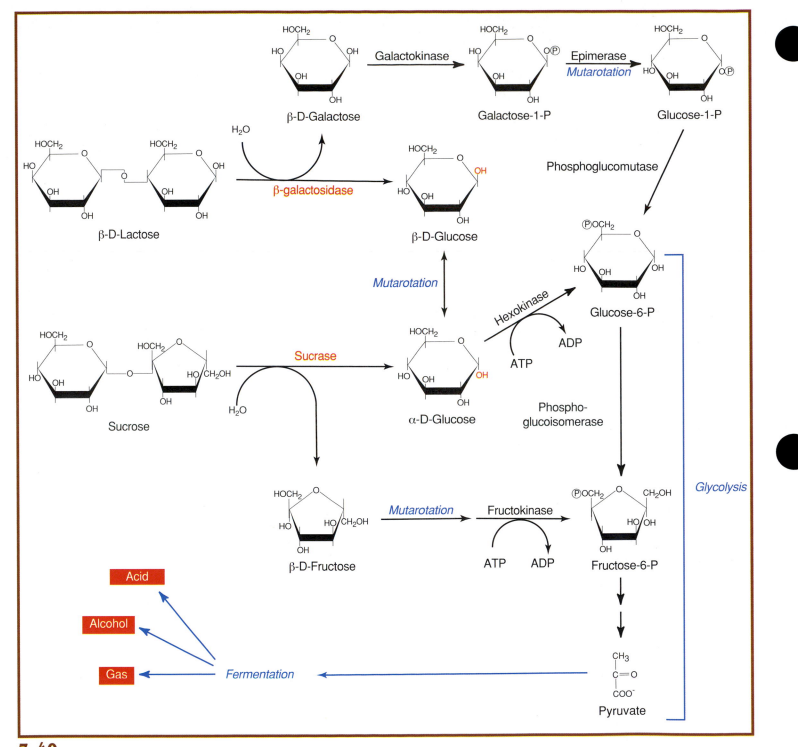

7-40 **FERMENTATION OF THE DISACCHARIDES LACTOSE AND SUCROSE** Sucrose and lactose fermentation do not follow unique pathways. Rather, fermentation of each sugar only requires one or two additional enzymes to convert them into monosaccharides capable of entering glycolysis.

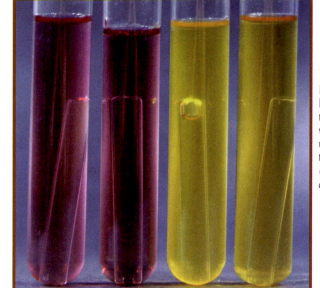

7-41 PURPLE LACTOSE BROTH RESULTS From left to right are *Proteus vulgaris* (–/–), an uninoculated control, *Escherichia coli* (A/G), and *Staphylococcus aureus* (A/–).

7-42 PR GLUCOSE BROTH RESULTS From left to right are *Escherichia coli* (A/G), *Staphylococcus aureus* (A/–), uninoculated control, *Micrococcus luteus* (–/–) and *Alcaligenes faecalis* (K).

Gelatin Hydrolysis Test

● Purpose

The Gelatin Hydrolysis Test is used to determine the ability of a microbe to produce **gelatinases**. *Staphylococcus aureus*, which is gelatinase-positive can be differentiated from *S. epidermidis* (gelatinase-negative). *Serratia* and *Proteus* species are positive members of *Enterobacteriaceae* while most others in the family are negative. *Bacillus anthracis*, *B. cereus*, and several other members of the genus are gelatinase-positive, as are *Clostridium tetani* and *C. perfringens*.

● Principle

Gelatin is a protein derived from collagen—a component of vertebrate connective tissue. Gelatinases comprise a family of extracellular enzymes produced and secreted by some microorganisms to hydrolyze gelatin. Subsequently, the cell can take up individual amino acids and use them for metabolic purposes. Bacterial hydrolysis of gelatin occurs in two sequential reactions, as shown in Figure 7-43.

The presence of gelatinases can be detected using Nutrient Gelatin, a simple test medium composed of gelatin, peptone, and beef extract. Nutrient Gelatin differs from most other solid media in that the solidifying agent (gelatin) is also the substrate for enzymatic activity. Consequently, when a tube of Nutrient Gelatin is stab-inoculated with a gelatinase-positive organism, secreted gelatinase (or gelatinases) will liquefy the medium. Gelatinase-negative organisms do not secrete the enzyme and do not liquefy the medium (Figure

7-44 and Figure 7-45). A 7-day incubation period is usually sufficient to see liquefaction of the medium. However, gelatinase activity is very slow in some organisms. All tubes still negative after 7 days should be incubated an additional 7 days.

A slight disadvantage of Nutrient Gelatin is that it melts at 28°C (82°F). Therefore, inoculated stabs are typically incubated at 25°C along with an uninoculated control to verify that any liquefaction is not temperature-related.

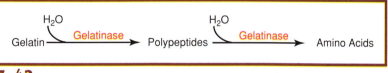
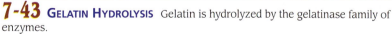

7-43 GELATIN HYDROLYSIS Gelatin is hydrolyzed by the gelatinase family of enzymes.

7-44 NUTRIENT GELATIN STABS *Aeromonas hydrophila* (+) above and *Micrococcus roseus* (–) below.

7-45 **CRATERIFORM LIQUEFACTION** This form of liquefaction may also be of diagnostic use because not all gelatinase-positive microbes liquefy the gelatin completely. Shown here is *Micrococcus luteus* liquefying the gelatin in the shape of a crater.

Indole Test (SIM Medium)

● Purpose

The Indole Test identifies bacteria capable of producing indole using the enzyme **tryptophanase**. The Indole Test is one component of the IMViC battery of tests (*Indole*, *Methyl Red*, *Voges-Proskauer*, and *Citrate*) used to differentiate the *Enterobacteriaceae*.

● Principle

The Indole Test, as it appears in this manual, is performed using SIM medium. SIM medium also tests for motility and sulfur reduction (SIM is an acronym for Sugar-Indole-Motility). It is a semi-solid medium that is formulated with casein and animal tissue as sources of amino acids, an iron-containing compound, and sulfur in the form of sodium thiosulfate.

Indole production in the medium is made possible by the presence of tryptophan (contained in casein and animal protein). Bacteria possessing the enzyme tryptophanase can hydrolyze tryptophan to pyruvate, ammonia (by deamination), and indole (Figure 7-46).

The hydrolysis of tryptophan in SIM medium can be detected by the addition of Kovacs' reagent after a period of incubation. Kovacs' reagent contains dimethylamino-benzaldehyde (DMABA) and HCl dissolved in amyl alcohol. When a few drops of Kovacs' reagent are added to the tube, it forms a liquid layer over the solid medium. DMABA then reacts with any indole present and produces a quinoidal compound that turns the reagent layer red (Figures 7-47 and 7-48). The formation of red color in the reagent layer indicates a positive reaction and the presence of tryptophanase. No red color is indole-negative.

An instantaneous indole test is available and done by placing bacterial growth on a paper slide impregnated with 5% DMABA (Figure 7-49). A positive result is formation of pink on the paper slide.

7-46 **TRYPTOPHAN CATABOLISM IN INDOLE-POSITIVE ORGANISMS** Tryptophanase hydrolyzes the amino acid tryptophan to indole, ammonia, and pyruvate. Subsequently, pyruvate can be used in the Krebs Cycle.

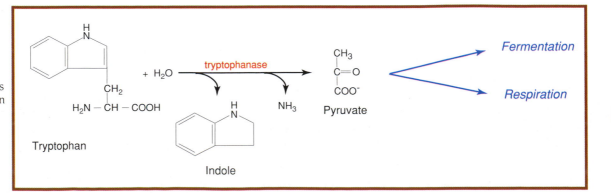

7-47 INDOLE REACTION WITH KOVACS' REAGENT

Kovacs' Reagent is added to the medium following incubation. If the organism is indole-positive, a red color is produced by this reaction.

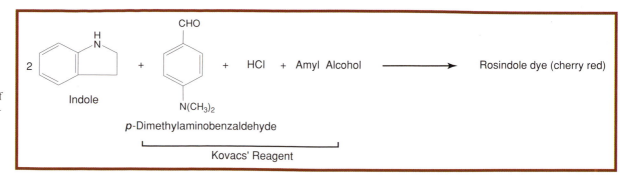

7-48 INDOLE TEST RESULTS

This is SIM medium inoculated with *Morganella morganii* (+) on the right and *Enterobacter aerogenes* (−) on the left.

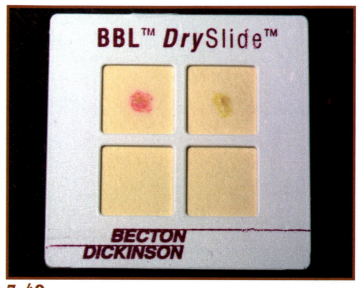

7-49 RAPID INDOLE TEST

BBL™ *Dry*Slide™ (Available from Becton-Dickinson, Sparks, MD.) This slide was inoculated with *Escherichia coli* (+) on the left and *Enterobacter aerogenes* (−) on the right.

Kligler's Iron Agar

● Purpose

Kligler's Iron Agar (KIA) is primarily used to differentiate members of *Enterobacteriaceae* and to distinguish them from other Gram-negative bacilli such as *Pseudomonas* or *Alcaligenes*.

● Principle

KIA is a rich medium designed to differentiate bacteria on the basis of glucose fermentation, lactose fermentation, and sulfur reduction. In addition to the two carbohydrates, it includes beef extract, yeast extract, and peptone as carbon and nitrogen sources, and sodium thiosulfate as an electron acceptor. Phenol red is the pH indicator and ferrous sulfate is the hydrogen sulfide indicator.

The medium is prepared as a shallow agar slant with a deep butt, thereby providing both aerobic and anaerobic growth environments. It is inoculated by a stab in the agar butt followed by a fishtail streak of the slant. The incubation period is 18 to 24 hours for carbohydrate fermentation and up to 48 hours for hydrogen sulfide reactions. Many reactions in various combinations are possible (Figure 7-50 and Table 7-1).

When KIA is inoculated with a glucose-only fermenter, acid products lower the pH and turn the entire medium yellow within a few hours. Because glucose is in short supply (0.1%), it will be exhausted within about 12 hours. As the glucose is used up, the organisms located in the aerobic region (slant) will begin to break down available amino acids, producing NH_3 and raising the pH. This process, which takes 18 to 24 hours to complete, is called a **reversion** and only occurs in the slant because of the anaerobic conditions in the butt. Thus, a KIA with a red slant and yellow butt after a 24-hour incubation period indicates that the organism ferments glucose but not lactose.

Organisms that are able to ferment glucose *and* lactose also turn the medium yellow throughout. However, because the lactose concentration is ten times higher than that of glucose, greater acid production results and both slant and butt will remain yellow after 24 hours. Therefore, a KIA with a yellow slant and butt at 24 hours indicates that the organism ferments glucose and lactose. Gas produced by carbohydrate fermentation will appear as fissures in the medium or will lift the agar off the bottom of the tube.

Hydrogen sulfide (H_2S) may be produced by the reduction of thiosulfate in the medium or by the breakdown of cysteine in the peptone (Figures 7-87 and 7-88). Ferrous sulfate in the medium reacts with the H_2S to form a black precipitate (Figure 7-89), usually seen in the butt. Acid conditions must exist for thiosulfate reduction; therefore, black precipitate in the medium is an indication of sulfur reduction *and* fermentation. If the black precipitate obscures the color of the butt, the color of the slant determines which carbohydrates have been fermented (*i.e.*, red slant = glucose fermentation, yellow slant = glucose and lactose fermentation).

An organism that does not ferment either carbohydrate but utilizes peptone and amino acids will alkalinize the medium and turn it red. If the organism can use the peptone aerobically and anaerobically, both the slant and butt will appear red. An obligate aerobe will turn only the slant red. Refer to Figure 7-50 for the various results.

Timing is critical in reading KIA results. An early reading could reveal yellow throughout the medium, leading one to conclude that the organism is a lactose fermenter when it simply may not yet have exhausted the glucose. A reading after the lactose has been depleted could reveal a yellow butt and red slant leading one to falsely conclude that the organism is a glucose-only fermenter. Tubes that have been interpreted for carbohydrate fermentation can be re-incubated for 24 hours before H_2S determination. Refer to Table 7-1 for information on the correct symbols and method of reporting the various reactions.

7-50 KIA RESULTS   From left to right: *Morganella morganii* (K/A, atypically not producing gas), *Pseudomonas aeruginosa* (K/NC), uninoculated control, *Proteus mirabilis* (K/A,H_2S), and *Escherichia coli* (A/A,G).

TABLE 7-1   **KIA Results and Interpretations**

TABLE OF RESULTS		
Result	**Interpretation**	**Symbol**
Yellow slant/yellow butt	Glucose and lactose fermentation with acid accumulation in slant and butt.	A/A
Red slant/yellow butt	Glucose fermentation with acid production. Proteins catabolized aerobically (in the slant) with alkaline products (reversion).	K/A
Red slant/red butt	No fermentation. Peptone catabolized aerobically and anaerobically with alkaline products. Not from *Enterobacteriaceae*.	K/K
Red slant/no change in butt	No fermentation. Peptone catabolized aerobically with alkaline products. Not from *Enterobacteriaceae*.	K/NC
No change in slant / no change in butt	Organism is growing slowly or not at all. Not from *Enterobacteriaceae*.	NC/NC
Black precipitate in the agar	Sulfur reduction. (An acid condition, from fermentation of glucose or lactose, exists in the butt even if the yellow color is obscured by the black precipitate.)	H_2S
Cracks in or lifting of agar	Gas production.	G

Lipase Test

Purpose

The Lipase Test is used to detect and enumerate lipolytic bacteria, especially in high-fat dairy products. A variety of other lipid substrates, including corn oil, olive oil, and soybean oil, are used to detect differential characteristics among members of *Enterobacteriaceae*, *Clostridium*, *Staphylococcus*, and *Neisseria*. Several fungal species also demonstrate lipolytic ability.

Principle

Lipid is the word generally used to describe all types of fats. The enzymes that hydrolyze fats are called **lipases**. Bacteria can be differentiated based on their ability to produce and secrete lipases. Although a variety of simple fats can be used for this determination, tributyrin oil is the most common constituent of lipase-testing media because it is the simplest triglyceride found in natural fats and oils.

Simple fats are known as **triglycerides**, or **triacylglycerols** (Figure 7-51). Triglycerides are composed of glycerol and three long-chain fatty acids. As is true of many biochemicals, tributyrin is too large to enter the cell, so some cells have the ability to secrete a lipase to break it down prior to cellular uptake. After lipolysis (hydrolysis), the glycerol can be converted to dihydroxyacetone phosphate, an intermediate of glycolysis (see Appendix Figure A-1). The fatty acids are catabolized by a process called β-oxidation. Two carbon fragments from the fatty acid are combined with Coenzyme A to produce Acetyl-CoA, which then may be used in the Krebs cycle to produce energy. Each Acetyl-CoA produced by this process also yields one NADH and one $FADH_2$ (important coenzymes in the electron transport chain). Glycerol and fatty acids may be used alternatively in anabolic pathways.

Tributyrin Agar is prepared as an emulsion that makes the agar appear opaque. When the plate is inoculated with a lipase-positive organism, clear zones will appear around the growth as evidence of lipolytic activity. If no clear zones appear, the organism is lipase-negative (Figure 7-52).

Spirit Blue Agar is prepared as an emulsion with tributyrin oil, but also contains spirit blue dye as a color

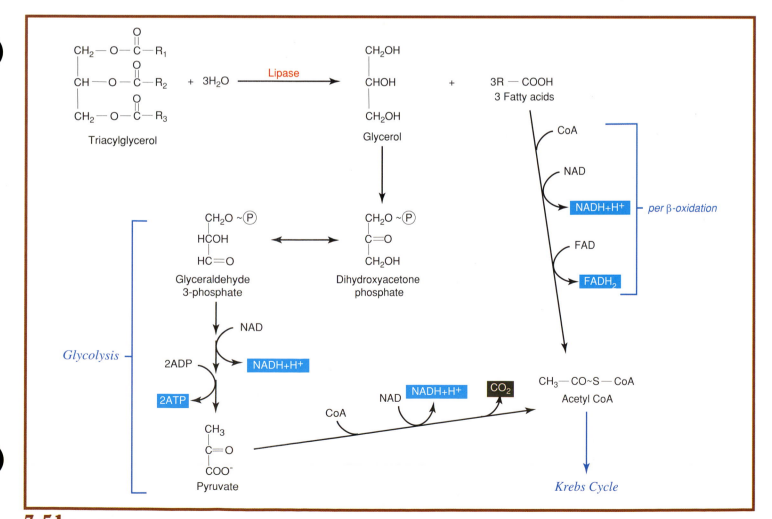

7-51 LIPID METABOLISM Triacylglycerols can be hydrolyzed by lipase into glycerol and three fatty acids. Glycerol can then be converted into dihydroxyacetone phosphate, an intermediate of glycolysis. The fatty acids can be broken down, two carbons at a time (by β-oxidation), to form Acetyl-CoA, a reactant of the Krebs Cycle.

indicator. The oil and dye form a complex that gives the medium an opaque light blue appearance. Lipase-positive bacteria growing on the medium hydrolyze the oil and

produce clear halos surrounding the growth. Lightening of the medium such as that produced around *P. mirabilis* is not a positive result (Figure 7-53).

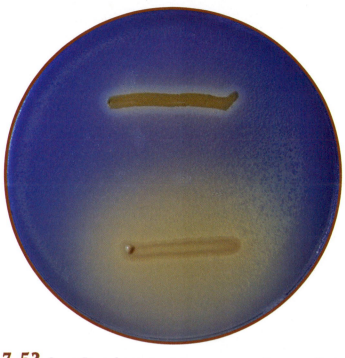

7-52 **TRIBUTYRIN AGAR** *Staphylococcus aureus* (lipase-positive) is above and *Proteus mirabilis* (lipase-negative) is below.

7-53 **SPIRIT BLUE AGAR** *Staphylococcus aureus* (lipase-positive) is above and *Proteus mirabilis* (lipase-negative) is below. Clearing, not lightening of the medium (as with *P. mirabilis*) is considered a positive result.

Litmus Milk Medium

● Purpose

Litmus Milk is used primarily to differentiate members within the genus *Clostridium*. It differentiates *Enterobacteriaceae* from other Gram-negative bacilli based on the ability of enterics to reduce litmus. Litmus Milk also is used to cultivate and maintain cultures of lactic acid bacteria.

● Principle

Litmus Milk is an undefined medium consisting of skim milk and the pH indicator azolitmin. Skim milk provides nutrients for growth, lactose for fermentation, and protein in the form of casein. Azolitmin (litmus) is pink at pH 4.5 and blue at pH 8.3. Between these extremes it is purple.

Four basic reactions occur in Litmus Milk: lactose fermentation, reduction of litmus, casein coagulation, and casein hydrolysis. In combination these reactions yield a variety of results, each of which can be used to differentiate bacteria. Several possible combinations are described in Table 7-2.

Lactose fermentation acidifies the medium and turns the litmus pink (Figure 7-54, second tube from the right).

This **acid reaction** typically begins with the splitting of the disaccharide into the monosaccharides glucose and galactose by the enzyme β-galactosidase (Figure 7-40). Accumulating acid may cause the casein to precipitate and form an **acid clot** (Figures 7-56 and 7-57). Acid clots solidify the medium and can appear pink or white with a pink band at the top (Figure 7-54, tube on far right) depending on the oxidation-reduction status of litmus. Reduced litmus is white; oxidized litmus is purple. Acid clots can be dissolved in alkaline conditions. Fissures or cracks in the clot are evidence of **gas** production (Figure 7-54, third tube from right). Heavy gas production that breaks up the clot is called **stormy fermentation.**

In addition to being a pH indicator, litmus is an E_h (oxidation-reduction) indicator. As mentioned above, reduced litmus is white. If litmus becomes reduced during lactose fermentation it will turn the medium white in the lower portion of the tube where the reduction rate is greatest.

Some bacteria produce proteolytic enzymes (caseases) such as rennin, pepsin, or chymotrypsin that coagulate casein and produce a **curd** (Figure 7-58). A curd differs from an acid clot in that it will not dissolve in alkaline conditions

TABLE 7-2 Litmus Milk Results and Interpretations*

TABLE OF RESULTS		
Result	**Interpretation**	**Symbol**
Pink color	Acid reaction	A
Pink and solid (white in the lower portion if the litmus is reduced); clot not movable	Acid clot	AC
Fissures in clot	Gas	G
Clot broken apart	Stormy fermentation	S
White color (lower portion of medium)	Reduction of litmus	R
Semisolid and not pink; clear to gray fluid at top	Curd	C
Clarification of medium; loss of "body"	Digestion of peptone; peptonization	P or D
Blue medium or blue band at top	Alkaline reaction	K
No change	None of the above reactions	NC

*These results may appear together in a variety of combinations.

and tends to retract from the sides of the tube revealing a straw-colored fluid called **whey**.

Certain caseases can digest both acid clots and curds. A **digestion** reaction leaves only a clear to brownish fluid behind (Figure 7-54, center tube). Bacteria that are able only to partially digest the casein typically produce ammonia (NH_3) which raises the pH of the medium and turns the litmus blue. Formation of a blue or purple ring at the top of the clear fluid or bluing of the entire medium indicates an **alkaline reaction** (Figure 7-54, tube at far left and third from left).

7-54 REACTIONS IN LITMUS MILK From left to right: *Alcaligenes faecalis* (K), uninoculated control, *Pseudomonas aeruginosa* (K), *Clostridium sporogenes* (D), *Clostridium acetobutylicum* (AGCR), *Escherichia coli* (A), and *Lactococcus lactis* (ACR). The clear fluid on the surface of the two *Clostridium* cultures is mineral oil used to make the medium anaerobic.

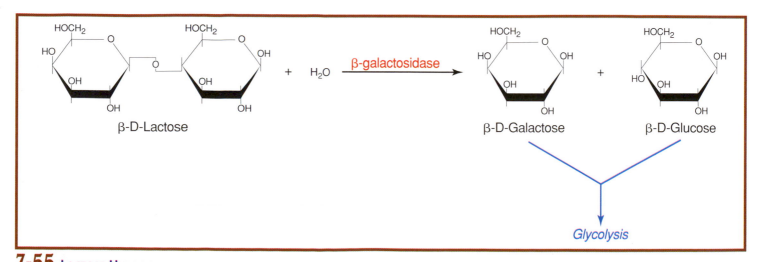

7-55 LACTOSE HYDROLYSIS Lactose hydrolysis requires the enzyme β-galactosidase and produces glucose and galactose—two fermentable sugars.

7-56 ACID CLOT FORMATION An acid clot is due to casease catalyzing the formation of caseinogen, an insoluble precipitate, under acidic conditions.

calcium caseinate →casease low pH→ caseinogen—an acid clot
(soluble salt of casein)   (insoluble precipitate)

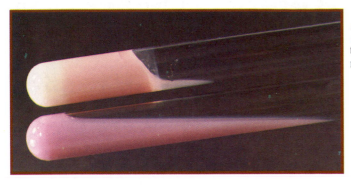

7-57 ACID CLOT An acid clot in the top tube, an uninoculated control below. Note the reduced litmus (white) at the bottom of the clot.

casein →rennin Ca⁺⁺→ paracasein—a soft curd
(soluble)   (insoluble precipitate)

7-58 CURD FORMATION Rennin converts casein to paracasein to form a soft curd.

Lysine Iron Agar

● Purpose

Lysine Iron Agar (LIA) is used to differentiate enterics based on their ability to decarboxylate or deaminate lysine and produce hydrogen sulfide (H_2S). LIA also is used in combination with Triple Sugar Iron Agar to identify members of *Salmonella* and *Shigella*.

● Principle

LIA is a combination medium that detects bacterial ability to decarboxylate or deaminate lysine and to reduce sulfur. It contains peptone and yeast extract to support growth, the amino acid lysine for deamination and decarboxylation reactions, and sodium thiosulfate—a source of reducible sulfur. A small amount of glucose (0.1%) is included as a fermentable carbohydrate. Ferric ammonium citrate is included as a sulfur reduction indicator and bromcresol purple is the pH indicator. Bromcresol purple is purple at pH 6.8 and yellow at or below pH 5.2.

LIA is prepared as a slant with a deep butt. This results in an aerobic zone in the slant and an anaerobic zone in the butt. After it is inoculated with two stabs of the butt and a fishtail streak of the slant, the tube is tightly capped and incubated for 18 to 24 hours.

If the medium has been inoculated with a lysine decarboxylase-positive organism, acid production from glucose fermentation will induce production of decarboxylase enzymes. The acidic pH will turn the medium yellow, but subsequent decarboxylation of the lysine will alkalinize the agar and return it to purple. Purple color throughout indicates lysine decarboxylation. Purple color in the slant with a yellow (acidic) butt indicates no lysine decarboxylation took place.

If the organism produces lysine deaminase, the resulting deamination reaction will produce compounds that react with the ferric ammonium citrate and produce a dark red color. Deamination reactions require the presence of oxygen. Therefore, any evidence of deamination will be seen only in the slant. A red slant with yellow (acidic) butt indicates lysine deamination.

Hydrogen sulfide (H_2S) is produced in LIA by the anaerobic reduction of thiosulfate. Ferric ions in the medium react with the H_2S to form a black precipitate in the butt (Figure 7-89). Refer to Figure 7-59 and Table 7-3 for the various reactions and symbols used to record them.

7-59 LIA RESULTS Lysine Iron Agar tubes illustrating typical results. From left to right: *Proteus mirabilis*, (R/A); *Citrobacter freundii*, (K/A, H_2S, [note the small amount of black precipitate near the middle and the gas production from glucose fermentation at the base]); uninoculated control; and *Salmonella typhimurium* (K/K [obscured by the black precipitate], H_2S).

TABLE 7-3 LIA Results and Interpretations

TABLE OF RESULTS		
Result	Interpretation	Symbol
Purple slant/purple butt	Lysine deaminase negative; Lysine decarboxylase positive	K/K
Purple slant/yellow butt	Lysine deaminase negative; Lysine decarboxylase negative; Glucose fermentation	K/A
Red slant/yellow butt	Lysine deaminase positive; Lysine decarboxylase negative; Glucose fermentation	R/A
Black precipitate	Sulfur reduction	H₂S

Malonate Test

● Purpose

The Malonate Test was originally designed to differentiate between *Escherichia*, which will not grow in the medium, and *Enterobacter*. Its use as a differential medium has now broadened to include other members of *Enterobacteriaceae*.

● Principle

One of the many enzymatic reactions of the Krebs cycle, as illustrated in the Appendix (Figure A-4), is the oxidation of succinate to fumarate. In the reaction, which requires the enzyme **succinate dehydrogenase**, the coenzyme FAD is reduced to FADH₂. Refer to the upper reaction in Figure 7-60.

Malonate (malonic acid), which can be added to growth media, is similar enough to succinate to replace it as the substrate in the reaction (Figure 7-60, lower reaction). This **competitive inhibition** of succinate dehydrogenase, in combination with the subsequent buildup of succinate in the cell, shuts down the Krebs cycle and will kill the organism unless it can ferment or utilize malonate as its sole remaining carbon source.

Malonate Broth is the medium used to make this determination. It contains a high concentration of sodium malonate, yeast extract, and a very small amount of glucose to promote growth of organisms that otherwise are slow to respond. Buffers are added to stabilize the medium at pH 6.7. Bromthymol blue dye, which is green in uninoculated media, is added to indicate any shift in pH. If an organism cannot utilize malonate but manages to ferment a small amount of glucose, it may turn the medium slightly yellow or produce no color change at all. These are negative results. If the organism utilizes malonate, it will alkalinize the medium and change the indicator from green to deep blue (Figure 7-61). Deep blue is positive.

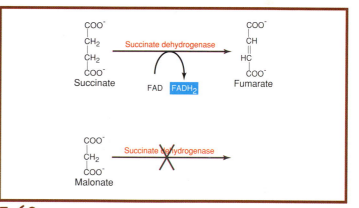

7-60 **COMPETITIVE INHIBITION OF SUCCINATE** The attachment of malonate to the enzyme succinate dehydrogenase prevents the attachment of succinate and thus, the conversion of succinate to fumarate.

7-61 **MALONATE TEST RESULTS** Malonate broth inoculated with *Enterobacter aerogenes* (+) on the left and *Escherichia coli* (−) in the center. An uninoculated control is on the right.

Methyl Red Test

● Purpose

The Methyl Red Test is a component of the IMViC battery of tests (*I*ndole, *M*ethyl Red, *V*oges-Proskauer, and *C*itrate) used to differentiate the *Enterobacteriaceae*. It identifies bacterial ability to produce stable acid end products by means of a **mixed-acid fermentation** of glucose.

● Principle

MR-VP Broth is a combination medium used for both Methyl Red (MR) and Voges-Proskauer (VP) tests. (Refer to page 98 for the VP test.) It is a simple solution containing only peptone, glucose, and a phosphate buffer. The peptone and glucose provide protein and a fermentable carbohydrate, respectively, and the potassium phosphate resists pH changes in the medium.

The MR test is designed to detect organisms capable of performing a **mixed acid fermentation**, which overcomes the phosphate buffer in the medium and lowers the pH (Figure 7-62). The acids produced by these organisms tend to be stable, whereas acids produced by other organisms tend to

be unstable and subsequently are converted to more neutral products.

Mixed acid fermentation is verified by the addition of methyl red indicator dye following incubation. Methyl red is red at pH 4.4 and yellow at pH 6.2. Between these two pH values, it is various shades of orange. Red color is the only true indication of a positive result. Orange is negative or inconclusive. Yellow is negative (Figure 7-63).

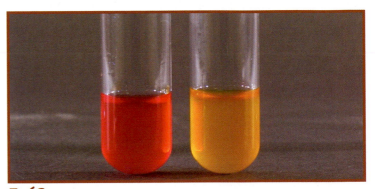

7-63 THE METHYL RED TEST *Escherichia coli* (MR-positive) on the left and *Enterobacter aerogenes* (MR-negative) on the right.

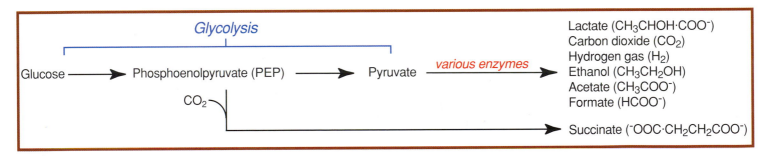

7-62 MIXED ACID FERMENTATION OF *E. COLI* *E. coli* is a representative Methyl Red-positive organism and is recommended as a positive control for the test. Its mixed acid fermentation produces the end products listed in order of abundance. Most of the formate is converted to H_2 and CO_2 gases. Note: The amount of succinate falls between acetate and formate, but is derived from PEP, not pyruvate. *Salmonella* and *Shigella* are also Methyl Red positive.

Motility Test

● Purpose

This test is used to detect bacterial motility. Motility is an important differential characteristic of *Enterobacteriaceae* and many other groups.

● Principle

Motility Test Agar is a semisolid medium designed to detect bacterial motility. Its agar concentration is reduced from the typical 1.5% to 0.4%—just enough to maintain its form while allowing movement of motile bacteria. It is inoculated

by stabbing with a straight transfer needle. Motility is detectable as diffuse growth radiating from the central stab line (Figure 7-64).

A tetrazolium salt (TTC) is sometimes added to the medium to make interpretation easier. TTC is used by the bacteria as an electron acceptor. In its oxidized form, TTC is colorless and soluble; when reduced it is red and insoluble (Figure 7-65). A positive result for motility is indicated when the red (reduced) TTC is seen radiating outward from the central stab. A negative result shows red only along the stab line (Figure 7-66).

7-64 MOTILITY TEST IN SIM MEDIUM WITHOUT TTC On the left is *Proteus vulgaris* (motile); *Shigella sonnei* (nonmotile) is on the right. Notice that motility of *P. vulgaris* is seen only as haziness in the medium. Tubes must be compared to uninoculated controls to discriminate between faint haziness and motility. Compare with Figure 7-66.

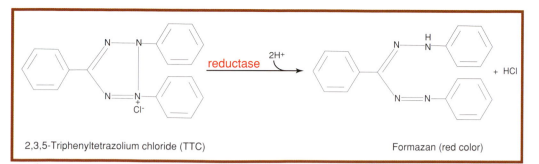

2,3,5-Triphenyltetrazolium chloride (TTC)   Formazan (red color)

7-65 REDUCTION OF TTC Reduction of 2,3,5-Triphenyltetrazolium chloride by metabolizing bacteria results in its conversion from colorless and soluble to the red and insoluble compound formazan. The location of the growing bacteria can be easily determined by the location of the formazan in the medium.

7-66 MOTILITY TEST RESULTS Motility Test Medium tubes containing TTC inoculated with *Enterobacter aerogenes* (+) on the left and *Micrococcus luteus* (−) on the right. Compare with Figure 7-64.

Nitrate Reduction Test

Purpose

Virtually all members of *Enterobacteriaceae* perform a one-step reduction of nitrate to nitrite. The Nitrate Test differentiates them from Gram-negative rods that either do not reduce nitrate or reduce it beyond nitrite to N_2 or other compounds.

Principle

Anaerobic respiration involves the reduction of (*i.e.*, transfer of electrons to) an inorganic molecule other than oxygen. Nitrate reduction is one such example. Many Gram-negative bacteria (including most *Enterobacteriaceae*) contain the enzyme **nitrate reductase** and perform a single-step reduction of nitrate to nitrite ($NO_3 \rightarrow NO_2$). Other bacteria, in a multi-step process known as **denitrification**, are capable of enzymatically converting nitrate to molecular nitrogen (N_2). Some products of nitrate reduction are shown in Figure 7-67.

Nitrate broth is an undefined medium of beef extract, peptone, and potassium nitrate (KNO_3). An inverted Durham tube is placed in each broth to trap a portion of any gas produced. In contrast to many differential media, no color indicators are included. The color reactions obtained in Nitrate Broth take place as a result of reactions between

7-67 POSSIBLE END PRODUCTS OF NITRATE REDUCTION Nitrate reduction is complex. Many different organisms under many different circumstances perform nitrate reduction with many different outcomes. Members of the *Enterobacteriaceae* simply reduce NO_3 to NO_2. Other bacteria, functionally known as "denitrifiers," reduce NO_3 all the way to N_2 via the intermediates shown, and are important ecologically in the nitrogen cycle. Both of these are anaerobic respiration pathways (also known as "nitrate respiration"). Other organisms are capable of assimilatory nitrate reduction, in which NO_3 is reduced to NH_4, which can be used in amino acid synthesis. The oxidation state of nitrogen in each compound is shown in parentheses.

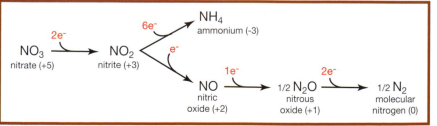

metabolic products and reagents added after incubation (Figure 7-68).

Before a broth can be tested for nitrate reductase activity (nitrate reduction to nitrite), it must be examined for evidence of denitrification. This is simply a visual inspection for the presence of gas in the Durham tube (Figure 7-69). If the Durham tube contains gas and the organism is known not to be a fermenter (as evidenced by a fermentation test), the test is complete. Denitrification has taken place. Gas produced in a nitrate reduction test by an organism capable of fermenting is not determinative because the source of the gas is unknown.

If there is no visual evidence of denitrification, **sulfanilic acid** and **α-naphthylamine** are added to the medium to test for nitrate reduction to nitrite. If present, nitrite will form

nitrous acid (HNO_2) in the aqueous medium. Nitrous acid reacts with the added reagents to produce a red, water-soluble compound (Figure 7-70). Therefore, red color formation after the addition of reagents indicates that the organism reduced nitrate to nitrite. If no color change takes place with the addition of reagents, the nitrate either *was not reduced* or *was reduced to one of the other nitrogenous compounds* shown in Figure 7-67. Because it is impossible to visually distinguish between these two occurrences, an additional test is necessary.

In this stage of the test, a small amount of powdered zinc is added to the broth to catalyze the (nonbiologic) reduction of any nitrate (which still may be present as KNO_3) to nitrite. If nitrate is present at the time zinc is added, it will be converted immediately to nitrite, and the

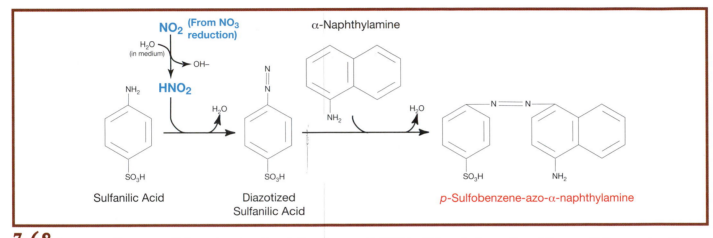

7-68 INDICATOR REACTION If nitrate is reduced to nitrite, nitrous acid (HNO_2) will form in the medium. Nitrous acid then reacts with sulfanilic acid to form diazotized sulfanilic acid, which reacts with the α-naphthylamine to form *p*-sulfobenzene-azo-α-naphthylamine, which is red. Thus, a red color indicates the presence of nitrite and is considered a positive result for nitrate reduction to nitrite.

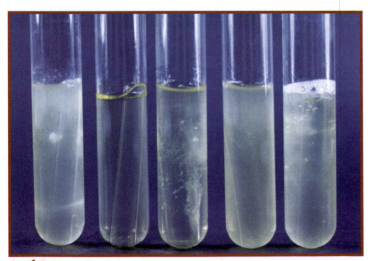

7-69 INCUBATED NITRATE BROTH BEFORE ADDITION OF REAGENTS These tubes have been incubated, but no reagents have been added. From left to right: *Enterobacter aerogenes*, an uninoculated control, *Enterococcus faecalis*, and two different strains of *Pseudomonas aeruginosa*. Note the gas produced by the *P. aeruginosa* strain on the far right indicating a positive result. (*P. aeruginosa* is a nonfermenter, therefore, the gas produced is an indication of denitrification.) The four tubes on the left must now receive reagents.

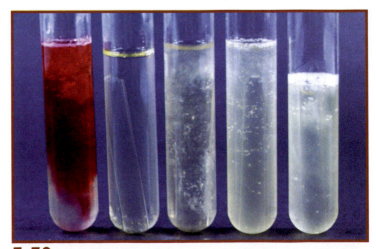

7-70 INCUBATED NITRATE BROTHS AFTER ADDITION OF REAGENTS These are the same tubes as in Figure 7-69 after the addition of sulfanilic acid and α-naphthalamine to the first four tubes. Red color is a positive result for reduction of nitrate to nitrite. From left to right: *E. aerogenes* is positive; the uninoculated control, *E. faecalis*, and *P. aeruginosa* are inconclusive at this point. No reagents were added to the *P. aeruginosa* tube on the far right because it was previously determined to be positive for denitrification (based on gas production). Zinc must now be added to the inconclusive tubes.

above-described reaction between nitrous acid and reagents will follow and turn the medium red. In this instance, the red color indicates that nitrate was *not* reduced by the organism (Figure 7-71). No color change after the addition of zinc indicates that the organism reduced the nitrate to NH_3, NO, N_2O, or some other nongaseous nitrogenous compound.

7-71 INCUBATED NITRATE BROTH AFTER ADDITION OF REAGENTS AND ZINC These are the same tubes as in Figure 7-70 after the addition of zinc to the middle three tubes. The control tubes and *E. faecalis* turned red. This is a negative result because it indicates that nitrate is still present in the tube. *P. aeruginosa* did not change color, which indicates that the nitrate was reduced by the organism beyond nitrite to some other nitrogenous compound. This is a positive result.

Novobiocin Susceptibility Test

● Purpose

The Novobiocin Test is used to differentiate coagulase-negative staphylococci. Most frequently it is used to presumptively identify the novobiocin-resistant *Staphylococcus saprophyticus*, a common urinary tract pathogen in young sexually active females.

● Principle

With the exception of *Staphylococcus saprophyticus*, most clinically important staphylococci are susceptible to the antibiotic novobiocin. When agar plates are cultured with a novobiocin-susceptible organism and a novobiocin impregnated disk is placed on it, a large clearing around the disk will appear (Figure 7-72). Conversely, organisms resistant to novobiocin will produce a small zone or no zone at all, depending on several factors.

The factors affecting zone size are the susceptibility of the organism to novobiocin, the concentration of the inoculum, the concentration of diffuse antibiotic in the agar, and the temperature and duration of incubation. The rate and amount of diffusion of the antibiotic are standardized by using 5 μg novobiocin disks on 5% Sheep Blood Agar. The test organism concentration is controlled by diluting to 0.5 McFarland turbidity standard (Figure 19-3) immediately before inoculation. Incubation takes place at 35°C for 24 hours. An isolate producing a zone of 16 mm or less is considered novobiocin-resistant (R). A zone greater than 16 mm indicates susceptibility (S).

7-72 NOVOBIOCIN DISK TEST *Staphylococcus saprophyticus* (R) is on the left; *Staphylococcus epidermidis* (S) is on the right.

ONPG Test

● Purpose

The ONPG Test is used to differentiate late lactose fermenters from lactose nonfermenters in the family *Enterobacteriaceae*.

● Principle

In order for bacteria to ferment lactose, they must possess two enzymes: β-**galactoside permease**, a membrane-bound transport protein, and β-**galactosidase**, an intracellular enzyme that hydrolyzes the disaccharide into β-glucose and β-galactose (Figure 7-55).

Bacteria possessing both enzymes are active β-lactose fermenters. Bacteria that cannot produce β-galactosidase, even if their membranes contain β-galactoside permease, cannot ferment β-lactose. Bacteria that possess β-galactosidase but no β-galactoside permease may mutate and, over a period

of days or weeks, begin to produce the permease. Distinguishing these **late lactose fermenters** from non-fermenters is made possible by the compound *o*-nitrophenyl-β-D-galactopyranoside (ONPG).

When ONPG is made available to bacteria it freely enters the cells without the aid of a permease. Because of its similarity to β-lactose, it then can become the substrate for any β-galactosidase present. In the reaction that occurs ONPG is hydrolyzed to β-galactose and *o*-nitrophenol (ONP), which is yellow (Figures 7-73 and 7-74).

It should be noted that β-galactosidase is an **inducible enzyme**. That is, it is produced in response to the presence of an appropriate substrate. Therefore, organisms to be tested with ONPG are typically grown overnight in a lactose-rich medium to ensure they will be actively producing β-galactosidase, given that capability.

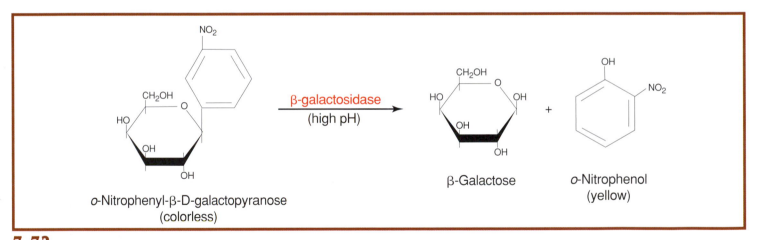

7-73 CONVERSION OF **ONPG** TO β-GALACTOSE AND *o*-NITROPHENYL BY β-GALACTOSIDASE

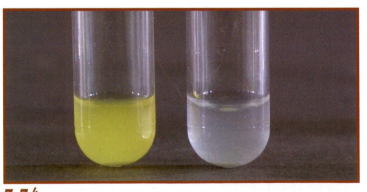

7-74 THE **ONPG** TEST *Escherichia coli* (+) is on the left and *Proteus vulgaris* (−) is on the right.

Optochin Susceptibility Test

● Purpose

The Optochin Test is used to presumptively differentiate *Streptococcus pneumoniae* from other α-hemolytic streptococci.

● Principle

Optochin is an antibiotic that interferes with ATPase activity and ATP production in susceptible bacteria. *Streptococcus pneumoniae* is the only streptococcus susceptible to small concentrations of the antibiotic optochin. Therefore, to eliminate the few streptococci which show susceptibility to large concentrations of the antibiotic, the optochin impregnated disks used in this procedure contain a scant 5 μg.

Three or four colonies of the organism to be tested are transferred and streaked on a Sheep Blood Agar plate in such a way as to produce confluent growth over approximately one half of the surface. The optochin impregnated disk is then placed in the center of the inoculum and the plate is incubated at 35°C for 24 hours in a candle jar or 5% to 7% CO_2.

The antibiotic will diffuse through the agar and inhibit growth of susceptible organisms in the area immediately surrounding the disk. This creates a clearing in the growth or **zone of inhibition** (Figure 7-75). A zone (14 mm in diameter surrounding a 6 mm disk or 16 mm surrounding a 10 mm disk) is considered presumptively positive identification of *Streptococcus pneumoniae*. Smaller zones indicate further testing is required.

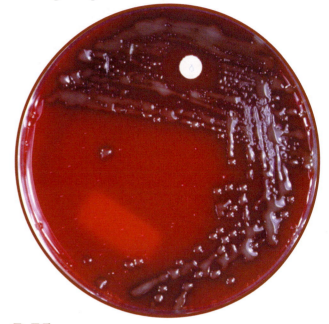

7-75 OPTOCHIN SUSCEPTIBILITY TEST The zone of inhibition surrounding the disk indicates susceptibility to optochin and presumptive identification of *Streptococcus pneumoniae*.

Oxidase Test

● Purpose

The Oxidase Test is used to identify bacteria containing the respiratory enzyme **cytochrome c oxidase**. Among its many uses is the presumptive identification of the oxidase-positive *Neisseria*. It also can be useful in differentiating the oxidase-negative *Enterobacteriaceae* from the oxidase-positive *Pseudomonadaceae*.

● Principle

Consider the life of a glucose molecule entering an aerobically respiring cell. It is first split (oxidized) in glycolysis where it is converted to two molecules of pyruvate and reduces two NAD (coenzyme) molecules to NADH $+H^+$. Then each of the pyruvate molecules becomes oxidized and converted to a two-carbon molecule called acetyl–CoA and one molecule of CO_2, which reduces another NAD to NADH. Then the Krebs cycle finishes the oxidation by producing two more molecules of CO_2 (per acetyl–CoA) and reduces three more NADs and one FAD to $FADH_2$.

As you can see, by this time the cell is becoming quite full of reduced coenzymes. Therefore, in order to continue oxidizing glucose, these coenzymes must be converted back to the oxidized state. This is the job of the electron transport chain (Figure 7-76).

Many aerobes, microaerophiles, facultative anaerobes, (and even some anaerobes) have ETCs. The functions of the ETC are to 1) transport electrons down a chain of molecules at lower energy levels (with increasingly positive reduction potentials) to the terminal electron acceptor—$\frac{1}{2}O_2$ in the case of an aerobic ETC and 2) generate a proton motive force by pumping H^+ out of the cell, thus creating an ionic imbalance that will drive the production of ATP by way of membrane ATPases. The protons pumped out of the cell come from the hydrogen atoms whose electrons are being transferred down the chain. Because only alternating ETC molecules are able to carry associated protons along with their electrons, the positively charged ions are expelled from the cell. **Flavoproteins, iron-sulfur proteins**, and **cytochromes** are important ETC molecules unable to donate protons.

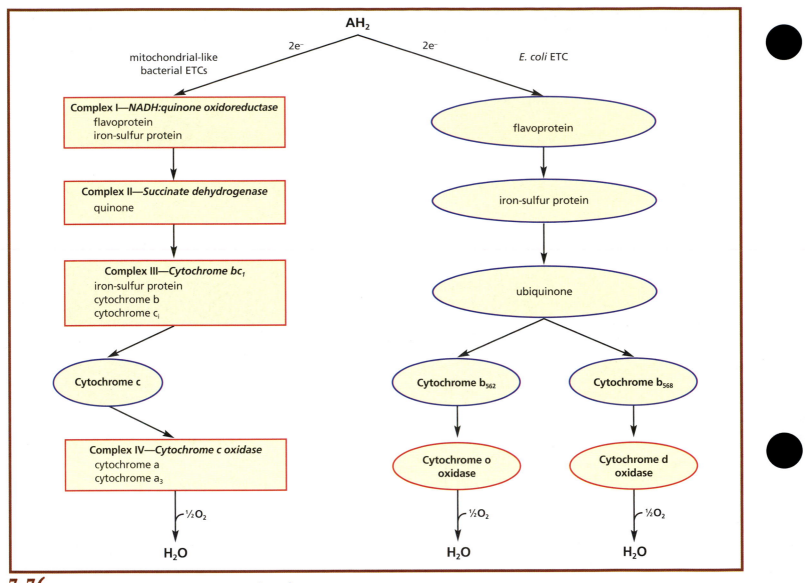

7-76 AEROBIC ELECTRON TRANSPORT CHAINS (ETCs) There are a variety of different bacterial aerobic electron transport chains. All begin with flavoproteins that pick up electrons from coenzymes, such as NADH or $FADH_2$ (represented by AH_2). Bacteria with chains that resemble the mitochondrial ETC in eukaryotes contain cytochrome c oxidase (Complex IV), which transfers electrons from cytochrome c to oxygen. These organisms give a positive result for the Oxidase Test. Other bacteria, such as members of the *Enterobacteriaceae*, are capable of aerobic respiration, but have a different terminal oxidase system and give a negative result for the Oxidase Test. The two paths shown on the right in the diagram are both found in *Escherichia coli*. The amount of available O_2 determines which pathway is most active. Enzymatic complexes and oxidases are outlined in red.

There are many different types of electron transport chains, but all share the characteristics listed above. Some organisms use more than one type of ETC depending on the availability of oxygen or other preferred terminal electron acceptor. *Escherichia coli*, for example, has two pathways for respiring aerobically and at least one for respiring anaerobically. Many bacteria have ETCs resembling mitochondrial ETCs in eukaryotes. These chains contain a series of four large enzymes broadly named Complexes I, II, III, and IV, each of which contains several molecules jointly able to transfer electrons and use the free energy released in the reactions. The last enzyme in the chain, Complex IV, is called cytochrome c oxidase because it makes the final

electron transfer of the chain from cytochrome c, residing in the periplasm, to oxygen inside the cell.

The Oxidase Test is designed to identify the presence of cytochrome c oxidase. It is able to do this because cytochrome c oxidase has the unique ability to not only oxidize cytochrome c, but to catalyze the *reduction* of cytochrome c by a **chromogenic reducing agent** called **tetramethyl-*p*-phenylenediamine**. Chromogenic reducing agents are chemicals that develop color as they become oxidized (Figure 7-77).

In the Oxidase Test, the reducing reagent is added directly to bacterial growth on solid media (Figure 7-78), or (more conveniently) a bacterial colony is transferred to paper

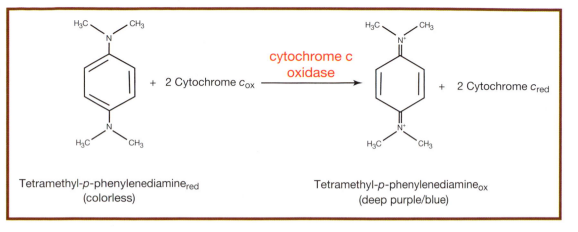

7-77 CHEMISTRY OF THE OXIDASE REACTION The oxidase enzyme shown is not involved directly in the indicator reaction as shown. Rather, it removes electrons from cytochrome c, making it available to react with the phenylenediamine reagent.

Tetramethyl-*p*-phenylenediamine$_{red}$
(colorless)

cytochrome c oxidase

Tetramethyl-*p*-phenylenediamine$_{ox}$
(deep purple/blue)

7-78 OXIDASE TEST ON BACTERIAL GROWTH A few drops of reagent on oxidase-positive bacteria will produce a purple-blue color immediately. Oxidase-negative organisms will not turn purple. The bacterium on the left is its natural color, not the color of an oxidase-negative organism.

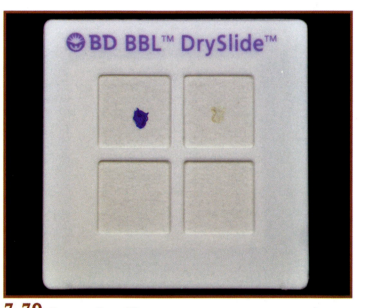

7-79 OXIDASE SLIDE TEST Positive results with this test should appear within 20 seconds. The dark blue is a positive result (left upper square). No color change is a negative result (right upper square).
(BBL™ DrySlide™ systems available from Becton Dickinson, Sparks, MD.)

saturated with the reagent (Figure 7-79). A dramatic color change occurs within seconds if the reducing agent becomes oxidized, thus indicating that cytochrome c oxidase is present. Lack of color change within the allotted time means that cytochrome c oxidase is not present and signifies a negative result.

Oxidation–Fermentation Test

● Purpose

The Oxidation-Fermentation (O–F) Test is used to differentiate bacteria based on their ability to oxidize or ferment specific sugars. It allows presumptive separation of the fermentative *Enterobacteriaceae* from the oxidative *Pseudomonas* and *Bordetella*, and the nonreactive *Alcaligenes* and *Moraxella*.

● Principle

The O–F Test is designed to differentiate bacteria on the basis of fermentative or oxidative metabolism of carbohydrates. In oxidation pathways a carbohydrate is directly oxidized to pyruvate and further converted to CO_2 and energy by way of the Krebs cycle and the electron transport chain, where an inorganic molecule such as oxygen is required to act as the final electron acceptor. Fermentation also converts carbohydrates to pyruvate, but uses it to produce one or more acids (as well as other compounds). Consequently, fermenters identified by this test acidify O-F medium to a greater extent than do oxidizers.

Hugh and Leifson's O–F medium includes a high sugar-to-peptone ratio to reduce the possibility that alkaline products from peptone utilization will neutralize weak acids produced by oxidation of the carbohydrate. Bromthymol blue dye, which is yellow at pH 6.0 and green at pH 7.1, is added as a pH indicator. A low agar concentration makes it a semi-solid medium that allows determination of motility.

The medium is prepared with glucose, lactose, sucrose, maltose, mannitol, or xylose and is not slanted. Two tubes of the specific sugar medium are stab-inoculated several times with the test organism. After inoculation, one tube is sealed with a layer of sterile mineral oil to promote anaerobic growth and fermentation. The other tube is left unsealed to allow aerobic growth and oxidation. (*Note:* Tubes of O–F medium are heated in boiling water and then cooled prior to inoculation. This removes free oxygen from the medium and ensures an anaerobic environment in all tubes. The tubes covered with oil will remain anaerobic, whereas the uncovered medium quickly will become aerobic as oxygen diffuses back in.)

Organisms able to ferment the carbohydrate or ferment *and* oxidize the carbohydrate will turn the sealed and unsealed media yellow throughout. Organisms that are able to oxidize only will turn the unsealed medium yellow (or partially yellow) and leave the sealed medium green or blue. Slow or weak fermenters will turn both tubes slightly yellow at the top. Organisms that are not able to metabolize the sugar will either produce no color change or turn the medium blue because of alkaline products from amino acid degradation. The results are summarized in Table 7-4 and shown in Figure 7-80.

TABLE 7-4 O–F Medium Results and Interpretations

TABLE OF RESULTS			
Sealed	**Unsealed**	**Interpretation**	**Symbol**
Green or blue	Any amount of yellow	Oxidation	O
Yellow throughout	Yellow throughout	Oxidation and fermentation or fermentation only	O–F or F
Slightly yellow at the top	Slightly yellow at the top	Oxidation and slow fermentation or slow fermentation only	O–F or F
Green or blue	Green or blue	No sugar metabolism; organism is nonsaccharolytic	N

7-80 OXIDATION–FERMENTATION TEST These pairs of tubes represent three possible results in the Oxidation–Fermentation (O–F) Test. Each pair contains one tube sealed with an overlay of mineral oil and one unsealed tube. The mineral oil creates an environment unsuitable for oxidation because it prevents diffusion of oxygen from the air into the medium. The result is that an organism capable of fermentation will turn both tubes yellow, whereas an organism capable only of oxidizing glucose will turn only the oxygen-containing portion of the unsealed medium yellow. An organism incapable of utilizing glucose by any means either will not change the color of the medium or will turn it blue-green as a result of alkaline products from protein degradation. Reading from left to right, the first pair of tubes on the left are uninoculated controls for color comparison. The second pair of tubes was inoculated with *Shigella flexneri*, an organism capable of both oxidative and fermentative utilization of glucose (O–F). Unfortunately, this determination cannot be made simply by visual examination, as the results of a fermentative organism (F) look exactly the same as an organism capable of both oxidation and fermentation (O–F). Therefore, when both tubes are yellow, the organism is assumed to be either (F) *or* (O–F). The third pair of tubes was inoculated with *Pseudomonas aeruginosa*, a glucose nonfermenter. This organism is capable only of oxidation. Note the yellowing only of the oxygenated portion of the unsealed tube. The fourth pair of tubes (right) was inoculated with *Alcaligenes faecalis*, an organism incapable of utilizing glucose. The blue color in the oxygenated portion of the unsealed tube suggests that the organism is both nonsaccharolytic (N) and a strict aerobe.

Phenylalanine Deaminase Test

● Purpose

The Phenylalanine Deaminase Test is used to differentiate the genera *Morganella*, *Proteus* and *Providencia* (phenylalanine deaminase-positive) from other members of the *Enterobacteriaceae* (phenylalanine deaminase-negative).

● Principle

Organisms that produce phenylalanine deaminase can be identified by their ability to remove the amine group (NH_2) from the amino acid phenylalanine. The reaction, as shown in Figure 7-81, requires oxygen and produces ammonia (NH_3) and phenylpyruvic acid. Deaminase activity is evidenced by the presence of phenylpyruvic acid.

Phenylalanine Agar provides a rich source of phenylalanine. A reagent containing ferric chloride ($FeCl_3$) is added to the medium after incubation. The normally colorless phenylpyruvic acid reacts with the ferric chloride and turns a dark green color almost immediately (Figure 7-82). Formation of green color indicates the presence of phenylpyruvic acid and, hence, the presence of phenylalanine deaminase. Yellow is negative (Figure 7-83).

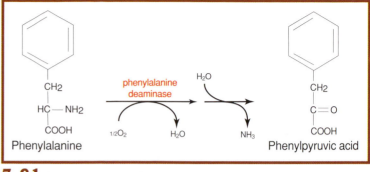

7-81 DEAMINATION OF PHENYLALANINE

Phenylpyruvic Acid + FeCl₃ ⟶ Green Color

7-82 INDICATOR REACTION Phenylpyruvic acid produced by positive organisms reacts with FeCl₃ to produce a green color. The test must be read immediately because the color may fade.

7-83 PHENYLALANINE DEAMINASE TEST
Note the color produced by the stream of ferric chloride in each tube. *Proteus mirabilis* (+) is on the left, an uninoculated control is in the middle, and *Escherichia coli* (−) is on the right.

PYR Test

● Purpose

The PYR Test is designed for presumptive identification of group A streptococci (*Streptococcus pyogenes*) and enterococci by determining the presence of the enzyme *L*-pyrrolidonyl arylamidase (PYR).

● Principle

Group A streptococci and enterococci produce the enzyme *L*-pyrrolidonyl arylamidase. This enzyme hydrolyzes the amide pyroglutamyl-β-naphthylamide to produce *L*-pyrrolidone and β-naphthylamine, both of which are colorless.

β-naphthylamine will react with *p*-dimethylaminocinnamaldehyde and form a red precipitate.

PYR may be performed as an 18-hour agar test, a four hour broth test or, as used in this example, a rapid disk test. In each case the medium (or disk) contains pyroglutamyl-β-naphthylamide (the PYR substrate) to which is added a heavy inoculum of the test organism. After the appropriate incubation or waiting period, a 0.01% *p*-dimethylamino-cinnamaldehyde solution is added. Formation of a deep red color within a few minutes is interpreted as PYR-positive. Yellow or orange is PYR-negative (Figure 7-84).

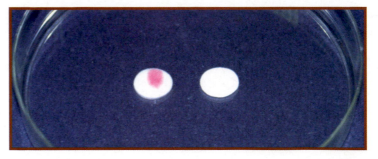

7-84 **PYR DISK TEST** The disk on the left was inoculated with *Streptococcus pyogenes* (PYR-positive); the disk on the right contains *Streptococcus agalactiae* (PYR–negative).

Starch Hydrolysis

● Purpose

Starch Agar originally was designed for cultivating *Neisseria*. It no longer is used for this, but with pH indicators, it is used to isolate and presumptively identify *Gardnerella vaginalis*. It aids in differentiating species of the genera *Corynebacterium, Clostridium, Bacillus, Bacteroides, Fusobacterium,* and *Enterococcus*, most of which have positive and negative species.

● Principle

Starch is a polysaccharide made up of α-D-glucose subunits. It exists in two forms—linear (amylose) and branched (amylopectin)—usually as a mixture with the branched configuration being predominant. The α-D-glucose molecules in both amylose and amylopectin are bonded by 1,4-α-glycosidic (acetal) linkages (Figure 7-85). The two forms differ in that amylopectin contains polysaccharide side chains connected

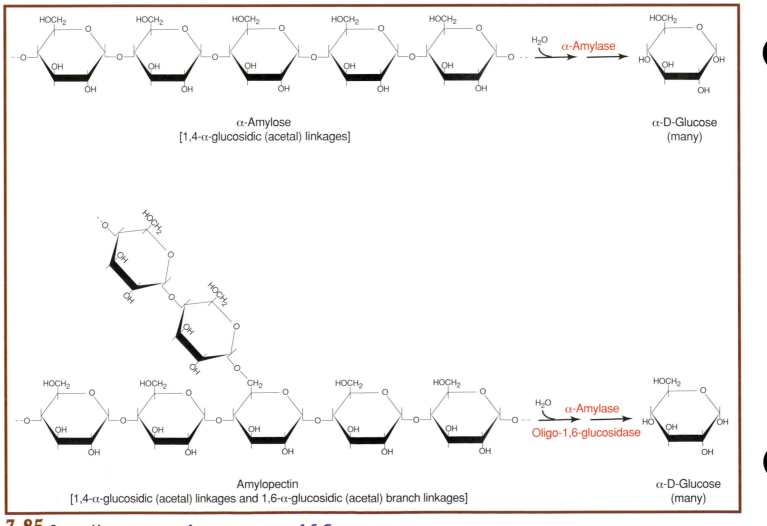

α-Amylose
[1,4-α-glucosidic (acetal) linkages]

α-D-Glucose
(many)

Amylopectin
[1,4-α-glucosidic (acetal) linkages and 1,6-α-glucosidic (acetal) branch linkages]

α-D-Glucose
(many)

7-85 STARCH HYDROLYSIS BY α-AMYLASE AND OLIGO-**1,6**-GLUCOSIDASE to approximately every 30th glucose in the main chain. These side chains are identical to the main chain except that the number 1 carbon of the first glucose in the side chain is bonded to carbon number 6 of the main chain glucose. The bond, therefore, is a 1,6-α-glycosidic linkage.

Starch is too large to pass through the bacterial cell membrane. Therefore, to be of metabolic value to the bacteria it must first be split into smaller fragments or individual glucose molecules. Organisms that produce and secrete the extracellular enzymes α-**amylase** and **oligo-1,6-glucosidase** are able to hydrolyze starch by breaking the glycosidic linkages between the sugar subunits. Although there usually are intermediate steps and additional enzymes utilized, the overall reaction is the complete hydrolysis of

the polysaccharide to its individual α-glucose subunits (Figure 7-86).

Starch agar is a simple plated medium of beef extract, soluble starch, and agar. When organisms that produce α-amylase and oligo-1,6-glucosidase are cultivated on starch agar they hydrolyze the starch in the area surrounding their growth. Because both the starch and its sugar subunits are soluble and virtually invisible in the medium, the reagent iodine is used to detect the presence or absence of starch in the vicinity around the bacterial growth. Iodine reacts with starch and produces a blue or dark brown color; therefore, any microbial starch hydrolysis will be revealed as a clear zone surrounding the growth (Figure 7-86).

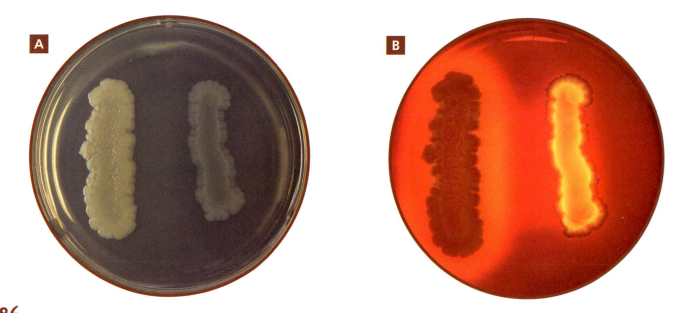

7-86 STARCH AGAR **A** *Bacillus subtilis* is on the left. *Escherichia coli* is on the right. Notice the wavy margin of *E. coli*. **B** After iodine has been added, the clearing in the medium around *B. subtilis* demonstrates a positive result for starch hydrolysis. *E. coli*, with no clearing, is negative. Note that the wavy margin of *E. coli* produced a lighter region around the growth that might be misinterpreted as clearing. To prevent reading a false positive, it is a good idea to establish the margin of growth for each tested organism prior to adding iodine.

Sulfur Reduction (SIM Medium)

● Purpose

The Sulfur Reduction Test is used to differentiate members of *Enterobacteriaceae*, especially the sulfur-reducing *Salmonella, Francisella,* and *Proteus* from the non-reducing *Morganella morganii* and *Providencia rettgeri.*

● Principle

The Sulfur Reduction Test, as it appears in this manual, is performed using SIM medium. SIM medium also tests for indole production (page 74) and motility (page 82). It

is a semi-solid medium that is formulated with casein and animal tissue as sources of amino acids, an iron-containing compound, and sulfur in the form of sodium thiosulfate.

Sulfur reduction to H_2S is an anaerobic activity and can be accomplished by bacteria in two different ways, depending on the enzymes present.

1. The enzyme **cysteine desulfurase** catalyzes the putrefaction of the amino acid cysteine to pyruvate (Figure 7-87).

2. The enzyme **thiosulfate reductase** catalyzes the reduction of sulfur (in the form of sulfate) at the end of the

anaerobic respiratory electron transport chain (Figure 7-88).

Both systems produce hydrogen sulfide gas (H_2S). When either reaction occurs in SIM medium, the H_2S produced combines with iron (ferrous ammonium sulfate in the medium) to form ferric sulfide (FeS), a black precipitate (Figure 7-90). Any blackening of the medium is an indication of sulfur reduction and a positive test. Absence of blackening in the medium indicates no sulfur reduction and a negative reaction (Figure 7-90).

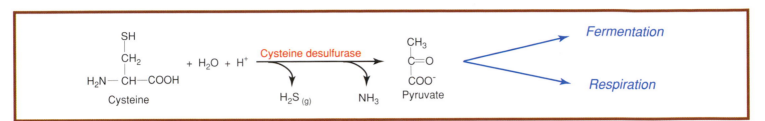

7-87 PUTREFACTION OF CYSTEINE Putrefaction involving cysteine desulfurase produces H_2S. The reaction is a mechanism for getting energy out of the amino acid cysteine.

$$3S_2O_3^= + 4H^+ + 4e^- \xrightarrow{\text{Thiosulfate reductase}} 2SO_3^= + 2H_2S_{(g)}$$

7-88 REDUCTION OF THIOSULFATE Anaerobic respiration with thiosulfate as the final electron acceptor also produces H_2S.

$$H_2S + FeSO_4 \longrightarrow H_2SO_4 + FeS_{(s)}$$

7-89 INDICATOR REACTION Hydrogen sulfide, a colorless gas, can be detected when it reacts with ferrous ammonium sulfate in the medium to produce the black precipitate ferric sulfide.

7-90 SULFUR REDUCTION IN SIM MEDIUM On the left is *Escherichia coli* (H_2S-negative); on the right is *Proteus mirabilis* (H_2S-positive).

SXT Susceptibility Test

● Purpose

The SXT (Sulfamethoxazole-Trimethoprim) Susceptibility Test is used to differentiate Groups A and B streptococci (SXT resistant) from other β-hemolytic streptococci (SXT susceptible). Used in conjunction with the Bacitracin Susceptibility Test (as in this example) it also differentiates Groups A and B streptococci from each other.

● Principle

When combined, Sulfamethoxazole and Trimethoprim act synergistically to disrupt bacterial folic acid metabolism.

SXT disks typically contain 23.75 µg of Sulfamethoxazole and 1.25 µg of Trimethoprim. When a disk is placed on the surface of a Sheep Blood Agar plate inoculated to produce confluent growth, a clearing will appear around the disk if the organism is susceptible (S) to the antibiotic mixture. Growth up to the edge of the disk indicates resistance (R).

The combination SXT and Bacitracin Susceptibility Test (page 58) is performed by placing one of each disk on the plate at least four centimeters apart (Figure 7-91). Any clearing around either disk is interpreted as susceptibility. Table 7-5 summarizes Bacitracin SXT susceptibilities of various streptococci.

7-91 BACITRACIN-SXT TEST This is a Bacitracin–SXT Susceptibility Test on a Sheep Blood Agar plate containing *Streptococcus pyogenes* (Group A). Bacitracin is on the left (S) and SXT (R) is on the right.

TABLE 7-5	Reactions of β-Hemolytic Streptococci to Bacitracin and SXT	
TABLE OF RESULTS		
Organism	**Bacitracin**	**SXT**
Group A	S	R
Group B	R	R
Groups C, F, and G	S or R	S

Triple Sugar Iron Agar

● Purpose

Triple Sugar Iron Agar (TSIA) is primarily used to differentiate members of *Enterobacteriaceae* and to differentiate them from other Gram-negative rods such as *Pseudomonas*.

● Principle

TSIA is a rich medium designed to differentiate bacteria on the basis of glucose fermentation, lactose fermentation, sucrose fermentation, and sulfur reduction. In addition to the three carbohydrates, it includes beef extract, yeast extract, and peptone as carbon and nitrogen sources, and sodium thiosulfate as a source of reducible sulfur. Phenol red is the pH indicator and the iron in ferrous sulfate is the hydrogen sulfide indicator.

The medium is prepared as a shallow agar slant with a deep butt, thereby providing both aerobic and anaerobic growth environments. It is inoculated by a stab in the agar butt followed by a fishtail streak of the slant. The incubation period is 18 to 24 hours for carbohydrate fermentation and up to 48 hours for hydrogen sulfide reactions. Many reactions in various combinations are possible (Figure 7-92 and Table 7-6).

When TSIA is inoculated with a glucose-only fermenter, acid products lower the pH and turn the entire medium yellow within a few hours. Because glucose is in short supply (0.1%), it will be exhausted within about 12 hours. As the glucose is used up, the organisms located in the aerobic region (slant) will begin to break down available amino acids, producing NH_3 and raising the pH. This process,

which takes 18 to 24 hours to complete, is called a **reversion** and only occurs in the slant because of the anaerobic conditions in the butt. Thus, a TSIA with a red slant and yellow butt after a 24-hour incubation period indicates that the organism ferments glucose but not lactose.

Organisms that are able to ferment glucose *and* lactose *and/or* sucrose also turn the medium yellow throughout. However, because the lactose and sucrose concentrations are ten times higher than that of glucose, greater acid production results and both slant and butt will remain yellow after 24 hours. Therefore, a TSIA with a yellow slant and butt at 24 hours indicates that the organism ferments glucose

7-92 TSI AGAR SLANTS From left to right: *Pseudomonas aeruginosa* (K/NC), uninoculated control, *Morganella morganii* (K/A, atypically not producing gas), *Escherichia coli*, (A/A, G) and *Proteus mirabilis* (K/A, H_2S).

TABLE 7-6

TSI Test Results and Interpretations

TABLE OF RESULTS		
Result	**Interpretation**	**Symbol**
Yellow slant/yellow butt	Glucose and lactose and/or sucrose fermentation with acid accumulation in slant and butt.	A/A
Red slant/yellow butt	Glucose fermentation with acid production. Proteins catabolized aerobically (in the slant) with alkaline products (reversion).	K/A
Red slant/red butt	No fermentation. Peptone catabolized aerobically and anaerobically with alkaline products. Not from *Enterobacteriaceae*.	K/K
Red slant/no change in butt	No fermentation. Peptone catabolized aerobically with alkaline products. Not from *Enterobacteriaceae*.	K/NC
No change in slant / no change in butt	Organism is growing slowly or not at all. Not from *Enterobacteriaceae*.	NC/NC
Black precipitate in the agar	Sulfur reduction. (An acid condition, from fermentation of glucose or lactose and/or sucrose, exists in the butt even if the yellow color is obscured by the black precipitate.)	H_2S
Cracks in or lifting of agar	Gas production.	G

and one or both of the other sugars. Gas produced by carbohydrate fermentation will appear as fissures in the medium or will lift the agar off the bottom of the tube.

Hydrogen sulfide (H_2S) may be produced by the reduction of thiosulfate in the medium or by the breakdown of cysteine in the peptone. Ferrous sulfate in the medium reacts with the H_2S to form a black precipitate, usually seen in the butt. Acid conditions must exist for thiosulfate reduction; therefore, black precipitate in the medium is an indication of sulfur reduction *and* fermentation. If the black precipitate obscures the color of the butt, the color of the slant determines which carbohydrates have been fermented (*i.e.*, red slant = glucose fermentation, yellow slant = glucose and lactose and/or sucrose fermentation).

An organism that does not ferment any of the carbohydrates but utilizes peptone and amino acids will alkalinize the medium and turn it red. If the organism can use the peptone aerobically and anaerobically, both the slant and butt will appear red. An obligate aerobe will turn only the slant red.

Timing is critical in reading TSIA results. An early reading could reveal yellow throughout the medium, leading one to conclude that the organism is a lactose or sucrose fermenter when it simply may not yet have exhausted the glucose. A reading after the lactose and sucrose have been depleted could reveal a yellow butt and red slant leading one to falsely conclude the organism is a glucose-only fermenter. Tubes that have been interpreted for carbohydrate fermentation and are negative for sulfur reduction can be re-incubated for 24 hours before H_2S determination. Refer to Table 7-6 for information on the correct symbols and method of reporting the various reactions.

Urease Tests

● Purpose

The Urease Test is used to differentiate organisms based on their ability to hydrolyze urea with the enzyme **urease**. Urinary tract pathogens from the genus *Proteus* may be distinguished from other enteric bacteria by their rapid urease activity.

● Principle

Urea is a product of decarboxylation of certain amino acids. It can be hydrolyzed to ammonia and carbon dioxide by bacteria containing the enzyme urease. Many enteric bacteria (and a few others) possess the ability to metabolize urea, but only members of *Proteus*, *Morganella*, and *Providencia* are considered rapid urease-positive organisms.

Urea Agar was formulated to differentiate rapid urease-positive organisms from slower urease-positive and urease-negative bacteria. It contains urea, peptone, potassium phosphate, glucose, phenol red, and agar Peptone and glucose provide essential nutrients for a broad range of bacteria. Potassium phosphate is a mild buffer used to resist alkalinization of the medium from peptone metabolism. Phenol red, which is yellow or orange below pH 8.4 and red or pink above, is included as an indicator.

Urea hydrolysis (Figure 7-93) to ammonia by urease-positive organisms will overcome the buffer in the medium and change it from orange to pink. The agar must be examined daily during incubation. Rapid urease-positive organisms will turn the entire slant pink within 24 hours. Weak positives may take several days (Table 7-7). Urease-negative organisms either produce no color change in the medium or turn it yellow from acid products (Figure 7-94).

Urea Broth differs from urea agar in two important ways. First, its only nutrient source is a trace (0.0001%) of yeast extract. Second, it contains buffers strong enough to inhibit alkalinization of the medium by all but the rapid urease-positive organisms mentioned above. Other organisms, even some that would ordinarily be able to metabolize urea, cannot survive the severe nutrient limitations or overcome the stronger buffers in urea broth. Pink color in the medium in less than 24 hours indicates a rapid urease-positive organism. Orange or yellow is negative (Figure 7-95).

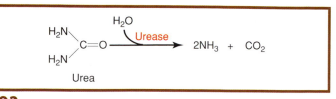
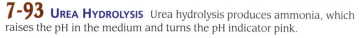

7-93 **UREA HYDROLYSIS** Urea hydrolysis produces ammonia, which raises the pH in the medium and turns the pH indicator pink.

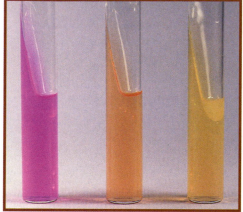

7-94 **UREASE AGAR TEST RESULTS** Urease agar tubes after a 24 hour incubation. *Morganella morganii* (urease-positive), a rapid urea splitter, is on the left and *Hafnia alvei* (urease-negative) is on the right. An uninoculated control is in the center.

7-95 **UREASE BROTH TEST RESULTS** Urease broth tubes with *Morganella morganii* (urease-positive) on the left and *Hafnia alvei* (urease-negative) on the right. An uninoculated control is in the center.

TABLE 7-7 — Urease Test Results and Interpretations

TABLE OF RESULTS			
AGAR			
Result			
24 Hours	**24 Hours to 6 Days**	**Interpretation**	**Symbol**
All pink		Rapid urea hydrolysis; strong urease production	+
Partially pink		Slow urea hydrolysis; weak urease production	w+
Orange or yellow	Partially pink	Slow urea hydrolysis; weak urease production	w+
Orange or yellow	Orange or yellow	No urea hydrolysis; urease is absent	–
BROTH			
Result			
24 Hours		**Interpretation**	**Symbol**
Pink		Rapid urea hydrolysis; strong urease production	+
Orange or yellow		No urea hydrolysis; organism does not produce urease or cannot live in broth	–

Voges-Proskauer Test

● Purpose

The Voges-Proskauer Test (VP) is a component of the IMViC battery of tests (*I*ndole, *M*ethyl Red, *V*oges-Proskauer, and *C*itrate) used to distinguish between members of the Family *Enterobacteriaceae* and differentiate them from other Gram-negative rods. It identifies organisms able to produce acetoin from the degradation of glucose during a **2,3-butanediol fermentation**.

● Principle

MR-VP Broth is the combination medium used for both Methyl Red (MR) and Voges-Proskauer (VP) tests. (Refer to page 82 for the MR test.) It is a simple solution containing only peptone, glucose, and a phosphate buffer. The peptone and glucose provide protein and a fermentable carbohydrate,

and the potassium phosphate resists pH changes in the medium.

The Voges-Proskauer test was designed for organisms that are able to ferment glucose, but quickly convert their acid products to acetoin and 2,3-butanediol (Figure 7-96 and Figure 7-97). Adding VP reagents to the medium after incubation oxidizes the **acetoin** (if present) to **diacetyl**, which in turn reacts with **guanidine nuclei** from peptone to produce a red color (Figure 7-98). A positive VP result, therefore, is red. No color change (or development of copper color) after the addition of reagents is negative. The copper color is a result of interactions between the reagents and should not be confused with the true red color of a positive result (Figure 7-98). Use of positive and negative controls for comparison is usually recommended.

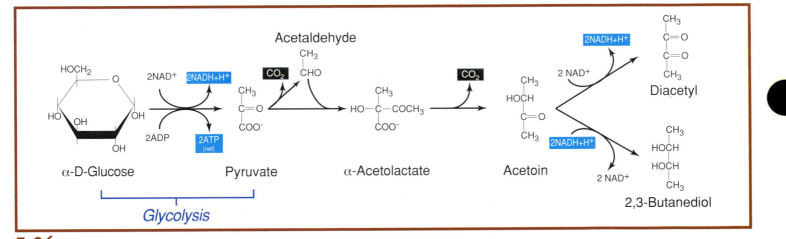

7-96 **2,3-BUTANEDIOL FERMENTATION** Acetoin is an intermediate in this fermentation. Reduction of acetoin by NADH leads to the end product 2,3-butanediol. Oxidation of acetoin produces diacetyl, as in the indicator reaction for the VP test.

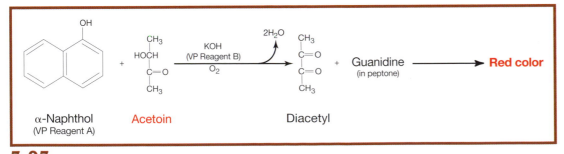

7-97 **INDICATOR REACTION OF VOGES-PROSKAUER TEST (VP)** Reagents A and B are added to VP broth after 48 hours of incubation. These reagents react with acetoin and oxidize it to diacetyl, which in turn reacts with guanidine (from the peptone in the medium) to produce a red color.

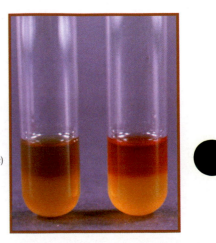

7-98 **THE VOGES-PROSKAUER TEST** *Escherichia coli* (VP-negative) is on the left and *Enterobacter aerogenes* (VP-positive) is on the right. The copper color at the top of the VP-negative tube is due to the reaction of KOH and α-naphthol and should not be confused with a positive result. Layering of the red color in positive tubes may or may not occur and is irrelevant to interpretation.

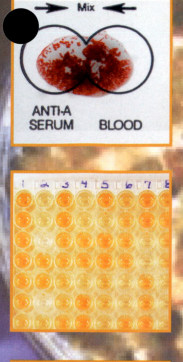

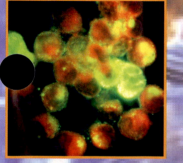

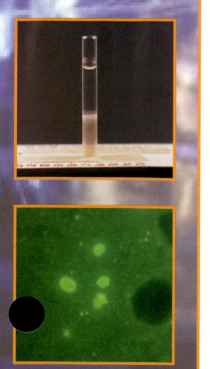

Serology

Precipitation Reactions

● Purpose

Precipitation reactions can be used to detect either the presence of antigen or antibody in a sample. They have mostly been replaced by more sensitive serological techniques for diagnosis, but are still useful to simply demonstrate serological reactions. Double-gel immunodiffusion is used to check samples for identical, related, or unrelated antigens.

● Principle

Soluble antigens may combine with **homologous antibodies** to produce a visible **precipitate**. Precipitate formation thus serves as evidence of antigen-antibody reaction and is considered a positive result.

Precipitation is produced because each antibody has (at least) two **antigen binding sites** and many antigens have multiple **epitopes** (sites for antibody binding). This results in the formation of a complex lattice of antibodies and antigens and produces the visible precipitate—a positive result. As shown in Figure 8-1, if either antibody or antigen is found in too high a concentration relative to the other, no visible precipitate will be formed even though both are present. **Optimum proportions** of antibody and antigen are necessary for precipitate formation and occur in the **zone of equivalence**.

Several styles of precipitation tests are used. The **precipitin ring test** is performed in a small test tube or capillary tube. Antiserum (containing antibodies homologous to the antigen being sought)

8-1 PRECIPITATION REACTIONS Precipitation occurs between soluble antigens and homologous antibodies where they are found in optimal proportions to produce a cross-linked lattice. Excess antigen or excess antibody prevent substantial cross-linking, so no lattice is formed and no visible precipitate is seen—even though both antigen and antibody are present. In this graph, antibody concentration is kept constant as antigen concentration is adjusted to demonstrate this phenomenon.

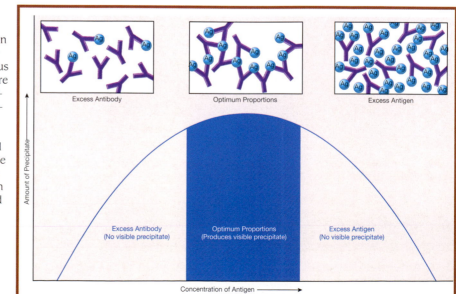

is placed in the bottom of the tube. The sample with the suspected antigen is layered on the surface of the antiserum in such a way that the two solutions have a sharp interface. As the two fluids diffuse into each other, precipitation occurs where optimum proportions of antibody and antigen are found (Figure 8-2). This test may also be run to test for antibody in a sample.

In its simplest form, **gel immunodiffusion** involves two wells formed in a saline agar plate. In one well is the antiserum; in the other is a sample of unknown antigen composition. The two diffuse out of their respective wells toward each other. If the sample has an antigen that will react with the antibody, then a precipitation line will form at the region of optimal proportions as their diffusion paths pass. If no precipitation line forms, the test is considered negative. That is, the sample has no antigen that will react with the antibodies. This procedure may also be used to identify the presence of antibody in a sample if a known antigen is used.

The diffusion path out of the well is not linear. Rather, it is radial in all directions. In a more complex form of immunodiffusion test, several wells are placed around a center well (Figure 8-3). Antiserum (which rarely contains only one kind of antibody) is placed in the center well. Samples of known or unknown antigen composition are put in the surrounding wells. Because diffusion out of the center well is radial, precipitation lines may form between the center well and any or all of the surrounding wells, depending on their antigen composition. The precipitation line pattern between neighboring wells is indicative of antigen relatedness in those wells (Figure 8-3). A single, smooth, curved precipitation line indicates the two antigens in neighboring wells are identical (**identity**). Two spurs indicate unrelated antigens (**nonidentity**) because two completely separate precipitation lines formed. A line with one spur indicates

the antigens are related, but not identical (**partial identity**), because two lines formed (Figure 8-4).

Antigens are molecules with a complex three-dimensional shape, like a protein or polysaccharide. Different parts of the antigen, called **epitopes** or **antigenic determinants**, can stimulate antibody production and, in turn, react specifically with those antibodies. So, a line of identity indicates the epitope(s) being tested are the same. Lines indicating partial identity actually demonstrate that some, but not all, epitopes being tested are the same.

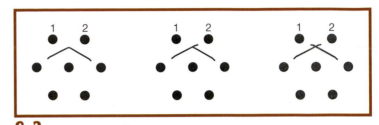

8-3 PRECIPITATION PATTERNS This diagram shows three possible precipitation patterns formed between the antibody in the center well and antigens in wells #1 and #2. The pattern on the left demonstrates identity between the antigens. This indicates that the antigens are identical (at least for the epitopes being tested). The pattern in the middle demonstrates partial identity, which means that the antigens are related but not identical (they share some epitopes). The pattern on the right shows nonidentity; the antigens are not related.

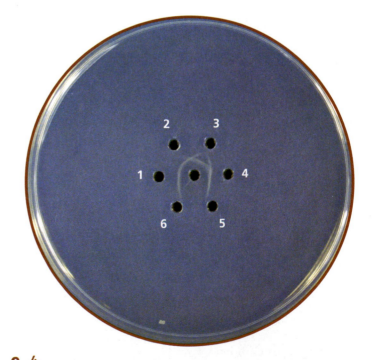

8-4 DOUBLE-GEL IMMUNODIFFUSION Antibodies are in the center well and antigens are in the outer wells. Precipitation lines without spurs formed between the central well and wells 1 and 2. They illustrate identity of the antigens in wells 1 and 2. The antigens in wells 2 and 3 illustrate nonidentity, as evidenced by the two spurs at their intersection. The lines formed between the central well and wells 3 and 4 illustrate partial identity. There is a shared epitope, but well 4 has an additional epitope absent in well 3, as evidenced by the single spur. No reaction occurred between the antibodies and antigens in wells 5 and 6.

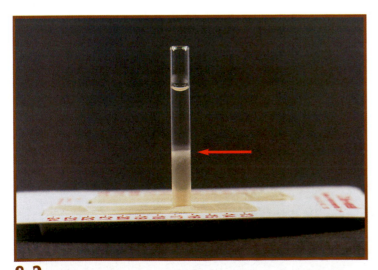

8-2 A POSITIVE PRECIPITIN RING TEST A sample of antigen has been layered over an antiserum. The white precipitation ring (**arrow**) formed at the site of optimal proportions of antibodies and antigens.

Agglutination Reactions

● Purpose

Agglutination reactions may be used to detect either the presence of antigen or antibody in a sample. Direct agglutination reactions are used to diagnose some diseases, determine if a patient has been exposed to a particular pathogen, and are involved in blood typing. Indirect agglutination is used in some pregnancy tests as well as in disease diagnosis.

● Principle

Particulate antigens (such as whole cells) may combine with homologous antibodies to form visible clumps called **agglutinates**. **Agglutination** thus serves as evidence of antigen–antibody reaction and is considered a positive result. Agglutination reactions are highly sensitive and may be used to detect either the presence of antigen or antibody in a sample.

There are many variations of agglutination tests (Figure 8-5). **Direct agglutination** relies on the combination of antibodies and naturally particulate antigens. **Indirect agglutination** relies on artificially constructed systems in which agglutination will occur. These involve coating particles (such as red blood cells—RBCs—or latex microspheres) with either antibody or antigen, depending on what is being sought in the sample. Addition of the homologous antigen or antibody will then result in clumping of the artificially constructed particles.

Slide agglutination (Figure 8-6) is an example of a direct agglutination test. Samples of antigen and antiserum are mixed on a microscope slide and allowed to react. Visible agglutinates indicate a positive result.

Hemagglutination is a general term applied to any agglutination test in which clumping of red blood cells indicates a positive reaction. Blood tests as well as a number of indirect diagnostic serological tests are hemagglutinations.

The most common form of blood typing detects the presence of **A** and/or **B antigens** on the surface of RBCs. A person's ABO blood type is genetically determined. An individual with type A blood has RBCs with the A antigen and produces anti-B antibodies. Conversely, an individual with type B blood has RBCs with the B antigen and produces anti-A antibodies. People with type AB blood have *both* A and B antigens on their RBCs and lack anti-A and anti-B antibodies. Type O individuals lack A and B antigens but produce *both* anti-A and anti-B antibodies.

ABO blood type is ascertained by adding a patient's blood to anti-A and anti-B antiserum and observing any signs of agglutination (Figure 8-7). Agglutination with anti-A antiserum indicates the presence of the A antigen and type A blood. Agglutination with anti-B antiserum indicates the presence of the B antigen and type B blood.

If both agglutinate, the individual has type AB blood; lack of agglutination occurs in individuals with type O blood.

A similar test is used to determine the presence or absence of the **Rh factor** (antigen). If clumping of the patient's blood occurs when mixed with anti-Rh antiserum (also known as anti-D), the patient is Rh positive (Figure 8-8).

Indirect hemagglutination may be used to detect the presence of either antigens or antibodies in a sample. In the example shown in Figure 8-9, sheep RBCs coated with *Treponema pallidum* (the causative agent of syphilis) antigen represent the particulate antigen. When added to antiserum containing anti-*Treponema pallidum* antibodies, agglutination occurs.

Another application of indirect agglutination is the Rapid Plasma Reagin Test (RPR). It is used for syphilis diagnosis (Figure 8-10).

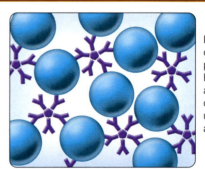

Direct agglutination occurs with naturally particulate antigens. Either antigen or antibody may be detected in a sample using this style of agglutination test.

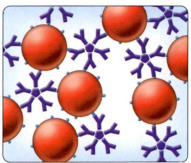

Detection of antibody in a sample can be done by indirect agglutination. A test solution is prepared by artificially attaching homologous antigen (light blue dots) to a particle such as red blood cells or latex beads (red spheres) and mixing with the sample suspected of containing the antibody (purple).

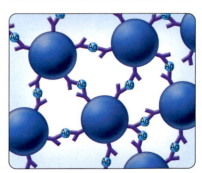

Another style of indirect agglutination detects antigen (light blue) in a sample. Antibodies (purple) are artificially attached to particles (dark blue), which are then mixed with the sample suspected of containing the antigen.

8-5 **DIRECT AND INDIRECT AGGLUTINATION TESTS** Direct agglutinations involve naturally particulate antigens. Indirect agglutination relies on attaching either the antigen or antibody to a particle, such as a latex bead or red blood cell.

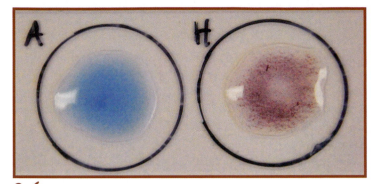

8-6 **SLIDE AGGLUTINATION** Agglutination of *Salmonella* H antigen with anti-H antiserum is shown on the right. Anti-H antiserum mixed with *Salmonella* O antigen is shown on the left. Serological variation of H (flagellar) and O (somatic lipopolysaccharide) antigens is an important diagnostic feature of *Salmonella* serovars.

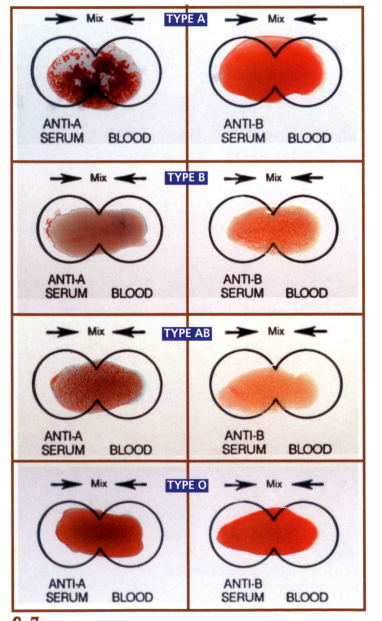

8-7 **ABO BLOOD GROUPS** Blood typing relies on agglutination of RBCs by Anti-A and/or Anti-B antisera. The blood types are as shown.

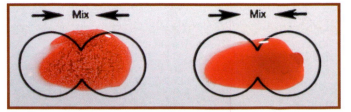

8-8 **RH BLOOD GROUPS** Rh blood type is determined by agglutination with anti-Rh (anti-D) antibody. Rh-positive blood is on the left, Rh-negative is on the right.

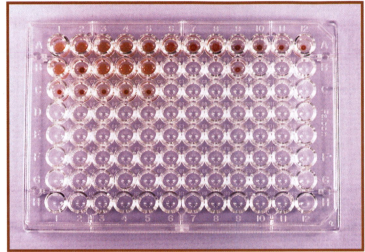

8-9 **INDIRECT HEMAGGLUTINATION TEST FOR SYPHILIS** Coating RBCs with *Treponema pallidum* antigens is the basis for this hemagglutination test. Because the antigens do not naturally cause agglutination, this test is an example of an indirect agglutination. The top row consists of serially diluted standards to act as positive (reactive) controls. A positive result is evidenced by a smooth mat of cells in the well (as in well A1). A negative result is a button of cells (as in well A12). Patient samples are in rows B and C. Patients B1, B3, B4, and B5 test positive for syphilis antibodies; patient B2 is negative. Samples in row C correspond to samples in row B and are negative (nonreactive) controls. In each case, the patient's serum is mixed with unsensitized RBCs to assure that agglutination (in Row B) is actually due to reaction with *Treponema* antibodies and not the RBCs themselves.

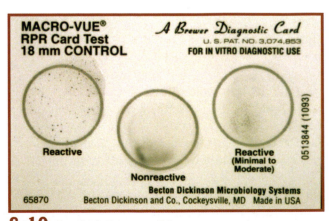

8-10 **THE RPR TEST FOR SYPHILIS** The Rapid Plasma Reagin (RPR) test for syphilis relies on antigen-coated particles agglutinating reagin (an antibody-like substance) present in an infected individual's plasma. Shown here is a control card that must be run with every set of tests.

Enzyme-Linked Immunosorbent Assay (ELISA)

● Purpose

An ELISA Test may be used to detect the presence and amount of either antigen or antibody in a sample. The indirect ELISA is used to screen patients for the presence of HIV antibodies, rubella virus antibodies, and others. The direct ELISA may be used to detect hormones (such as human chorionic gonadotropin [HCG] in some pregnancy tests and luteinizing hormone [LH] in ovulation tests), drugs, and viral and bacterial antigens.

● Principle

As with other serological tests, ELISAs can be used to detect antigen in a sample or antibody in a sample (Figure 8-11). All rely on a second antibody with an attached (**conjugated**) enzyme as an indicator of antigen–antibody reaction. It will be helpful to follow Figure 8-11 as you read the descriptions of different ELISAs in the following paragraphs.

The **direct ELISA** detects the presence of antigen in a sample. A microtiter well is first coated with homologous antibody specific to the antigen being sought. This is followed by coating the well with a blocking agent to prevent nonspecific binding of the following components to the well. The sample being assayed is added to the well. If the antigen is present, it will react with the antibody coating the well; if none is present, no reaction occurs. In this form of ELISA, the enzyme-linked (conjugate) antibody is also specific for the antigen being sought. When added to the well, it binds to the antigen, if present. After allowing time for the enzyme-linked antibody to react with the antigen, the well is washed to remove any unbound enzyme-linked antibody (which would produce a false positive when the substrate is added). Upon addition of substrate, a color change is evidence of the enzymatic conversion of substrate to its product, which indicates presence of the antigen.

The **indirect ELISA** detects the presence of antibody in a sample. In this style of test, the microtiter well is lined with antigen specific to the antibody being sought and a blocking agent. The sample being assayed is added to the well and, if the antibody is present, it will react with the antigen coating the well; if none is present, no reaction occurs. In this case, the enzyme-linked antibody is an *antihuman immunoglobin antibody*—its antigen is actually an antibody! When added to the well, it binds to the antibody in the sample, if present. As with the direct ELISA, unbound enzyme-linked antibody must be washed away to prevent a false positive result. Enzyme substrate is added and a color change indicates a positive test.

Figures 8-12 and 8-13 illustrate a quantitative form of indirect ELISA, *i.e.*, it is used to determine both the presence of antibody in a sample and the amount. Figure 8-14 illustrates a different version of the ELISA technique—a home pregnancy test—which screens for the presence of **human chorionic gonadotropin** found in pregnant women.

Direct ELISA method

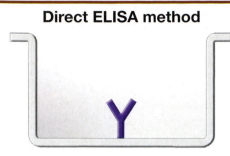

Step 1. The direct ELISA detects the presence of *antigen* in a sample. Antibody (antiserum) specific for the antigen is coated (adsorbed) onto the wall of a microtiter well.

Step 2. A blocking agent, such as gelatin or albumin, is added to coat the well's surface to prevent its interacting nonspecifically with any test reagents.

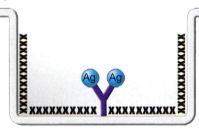

Step 3. The sample is added. If the *antigen* is present, it will bind to the antibody coating the well.

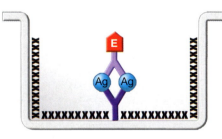

Step 4. A second antibody with an attached enzyme specific for the same antigen is added. Unbound enzyme-linked antibody is washed away.

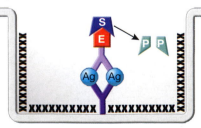

Step 5. Substrate for the enzyme is added. Conversion of substrate to product is evidenced by a color change. A color change means the sample has the antigen; no color change is a negative result.

Indirect ELISA method

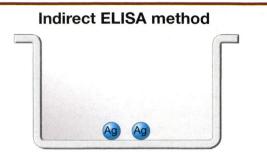

Step 1. The indirect ELISA detects the presence of *antibody* in a sample. The antigen specific for that antibody is coated (adsorbed) onto the wall of a microtiter well.

Step 2. A blocking agent, such as gelatin or albumin, is added to coat the well's surface to prevent its interacting nonspecifically with any test reagents.

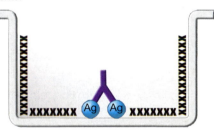

Step 3. The sample is added. If the *antibody* is present, it will bind to the antigen coating the well.

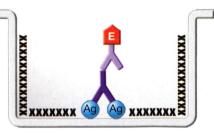

Step 4. An antihuman immunoglobin antibody with an attached enzyme is added. Unbound enzyme-linked antibody is washed away.

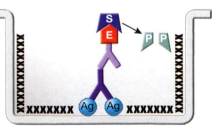

Step 5. Substrate for the enzyme is added. Conversion of substrate to product is evidenced by a color change. A color change means the sample has the antibody; no color change is a negative result.

8-11 **DIRECT AND INDIRECT ELISAS** A direct ELISA is used to identify antigen in a sample. An indirect ELISA identifies antibody in a sample.

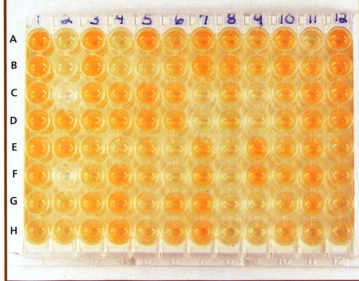

8-12 A Quantitative Indirect ELISA for HIV Antibodies In this ELISA, a dark yellow color indicates a negative reaction. The lighter the color, the higher the antibody titer. Color is read by a photometer, which is much more sensitive than the human eye (Figure 8-13) and results are fed into a computer. A variety of controls are also used. Serially diluted antibody samples of known concentration are in column 1, rows A through H and column 2, rows A through C. Absorbance values from these are used to develop a standard curve correlating antibody titer with absorbance. Patient samples are in the other wells. Each patient's antibody titer can then be determined by comparison with the standard curve.

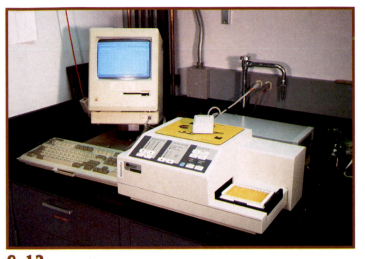

8-13 Microtiter Plate Reader This is the set-up for the ELISA illustrated in Figure 8-12. The photometer (plate reader) is in the foreground and the microtiter plate is visible on the photometer at the lower right. The plate is drawn into the photometer and absorbances in the wells are read and transmitted to the computer (visible in the background).

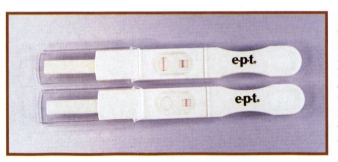

8-14 Membrane ELISA Fixing of antibodies to a membrane (rather than a microtiter dish well) and other advances have made ELISAs easier to perform and available to home consumers. Shown is a home pregnancy test. Human chorionic gonadotropin (HCG) is an antigen present only in pregnant women. A sample of urine is applied to the wick on the left of the test system. Two pink lines indicate a reaction of HCG with antibodies in the test system. A single line indicates absence of HCG in the urine (but is used as a positive control) and is interpreted as a negative result.

Fluorescent Antibody (FA) Technique

● Purpose

Like most serological tests, the fluorescent antibody (FA) technique can be used to identify the presence of either antigen or antibody in a sample. **Direct tests (DFA)** identify the presence of antigens; **indirect tests (IFA)** detect the presence of antibody in a sample. FAs are useful in diagnosing many viral infections as well as certain parasitic diseases.

● Principle

Fluorescent antibodies are labeled with **fluorescein isothiocyanate (FITC) dye**, which fluoresces when illuminated with UV light. In a DFA (Figure 8-15), a sample containing the suspected antigen is fixed to a microscope slide. The fluorescent antibody is added and allowed to react with the antigen. After rinsing to remove unbound antibody, the slide is viewed with a fluorescent microscope with a UV light source. If the suspected antigen is present, the labeled antibodies will have bound to it and will emit an apple green color (Figure 8-16).

IFAs (Figure 8-15) are used to detect antibodies in a sample. In this form of the test, the specific antigen is fixed to a microscope slide. Dilutions of the patient's sample are added to several slides and given time to react with the antigen. The FITC-labeled antibody is an anti-gamma globulin antibody, so if there is patient antibody bound to antigen

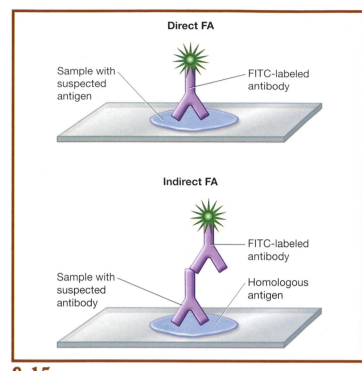

Direct FA

Sample with
suspected
antigen

FITC-labeled
antibody

Indirect FA

FITC-labeled
antibody

Sample with
suspected
antibody

Homologous
antigen

8-15 DIRECT AND INDIRECT FLUORESCENT ANTIBODY TECHNIQUES
The DFA and IFA are used to identify antigens and antibodies in a
sample, respectively.

on the slide, the fluorescent antibody will bind to it. After
rinsing to remove any unbound fluorescent antibodies, the
slide is viewed under a fluorescent microscope with a UV
light source. If the suspected antibody is present, the labeled
antibodies will fluoresce and appear apple green (Figures
8-17 and 10-6).

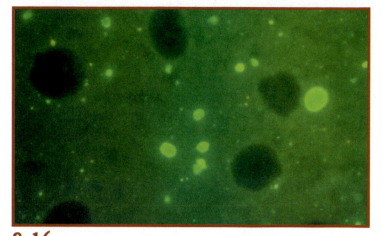

8-16 A FLUORESCENT MICROGRAPH OF A POSITIVE DFA FOR
RABIES VIRUS The fluorescent green color is due to anti-rabies virus
antibodies labeled with FITC dye bound to the virus in the specimen.

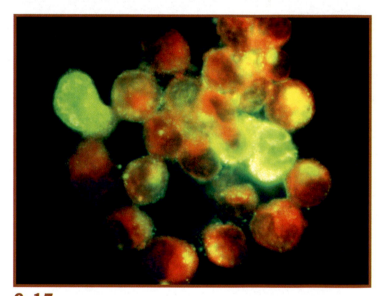

8-17 A POSITIVE IFA FOR INFLUENZA B VIRUS Infected cells
fluoresce an apple green color. Uninfected cells appear reddish due
to a second stain (Evans blue) in the preparation.

Western Blot Technique

● Purpose

Western blots are used to identify proteins in a sample.
(Similar techniques called the Southern blot and Northern
blot are used for identifying DNA and RNA in samples,
respectively.) This technique has applications in research,
especially with viruses, but its main clinical use is to identify
HIV antibodies in a patient's serum or plasma. Because it is
more expensive and requires greater skill than other serological tests, it is only used to confirm the results from
samples that are repeatedly positive for HIV antibodies
in preliminary ELISA screening.

● Principle

This test is used to check for specific antibodies in a sample,
so known antigens (proteins) are used. The procedure begins
with polyacrylamide gel electrophoresis (see Electrophoresis
on page 110) of the proteins to separate them by size and
charge. Then the bands of protein are transferred to a nitrocellulose membrane by the blotting technique. Simply, the gel
is sandwiched together with the membrane between layers
of absorbent material. The proteins are moved into the
membrane and remain fixed in the same position as the
original bands (but are not visible). The nitrocellulose is

8-18 HIV WESTERN BLOT
Shown is a sample lab sheet with the blotted nitrocellulose strips attached. This Western blot was used to detect anti-HIV antibodies in several patients' serum (identified only by a code number which we blacked out). Strips 1 and 2 are high positive and low positive controls, respectively. Strip 3 is a negative control. To be considered positive, the patient's strip must react equal to or greater than the low positive control. Of the strips shown, samples 4 and 6 were interpreted as positive (P), and samples 5, 7, and 8 were negative (N). The test may also produce indeterminate results (I). Unfortunately, the criteria for interpreting a positive differ slightly between different agencies, but all involve the presence of two or more bands (usually p24, gp41, and/or gp120/160).

HIV-1 WESTERN BLOT WORKSHEET

Organon Teknika Corporation · 100 AKZO Avenue · Durham, NC 27712

FACILITY: _____ DATE PERFORMED: 8-25 97
READ BY: _____ REVIEWED BY: _____ DATE: 8/26/97

KIT / TESTING INFORMATION

KIT MASTER LOT NO. M121601	NEGATIVE CONTROL 1115602 11/98	STRIP LOT NO. M0913601 3/98	CONJUGATE 1104602 11/97
KIT EXPIRATION DATE 11-97	LOW POSITIVE CONTROL 1011602 11/98	SAMPLE DILUENT 1127605 5/98	CHROMOGEN 1112602 11/97
PERFORMING TECHNOLOGIST	HIGH POSITIVE CONTROL 1101603 11/98	POWDERED MILK 1024601 4/98	

BAND EVALUATION: A - Absent I - Indeterminate P - Present
RESULTS: P - Positive I - Indeterminate N - Negative

(MOUNT THE WESTERN BLOT STRIPS HERE)

ORIGIN LINE

FORM VI-105-96

No.	SAMPLE ID	p18	p24	p31	gp41	p51	p55	p65	gp120	gp160	NOTES	RESULT
1	Hi Pos	P	P	P	P	P	I	P	P	P		P
2	Low Pos	P	P	P	P	P	A	P	I	P		P
3	Neg	A	A	A	A	A	A	A	A	A		N
4		A	P	P	P	A	A	P	I	P		P
5		A	P	A	A	A	A	A	A	A		I
6		A	P	P	P	A	A	P	I	P		P
7		A	P	A	I	A	A	A	A	A		I
8		A	P	A	I	A	A	A	A	A		I
9												
10												
11												
12												
13												
14												
15												
16												
17												
18												
19												
20												

then cut into strips, which are ready for use. (The manufacturer does the electrophoresis and blotting steps if a commercial kit is used.)

A tray with troughs is used to hold the strips so that several tests may be run simultaneously. After careful preparation, each sample (suspected of containing antibody) is applied to a strip and allowed to react for the prescribed time (usually 12 or 24 hours). This incubation allows any antibody in the sample to bind to the known antigens in the strip. After rinsing to remove unbound antibody, the strips are exposed to an anti-immunoglobin antibody, which is labeled with an enzyme or a fluorescent chemical. The strips are rinsed again to remove any unbound labeled antibody.

Visualization of the bands depends on the type of labeled antibody. If an enzyme is used, then substrate is added. If a fluorescent chemical is used, then the strip is observed under UV light. Comparing band patterns on each strip to positive and negative controls allows determination of whether the sample contains the relevant antibodies. Figures 8-18 and 8-19 show Western blot strips used in HIV screening. The HIV antigens on the strip are shown in Figure 8-20.

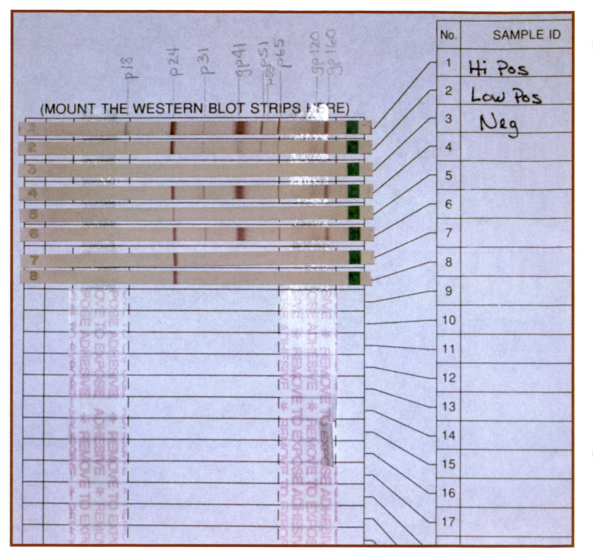

No.	SAMPLE ID
1	Hi Pos
2	Low Pos
3	Neg
4	
5	
6	
7	
8	
9	
10	
11	
12	
13	
14	
15	
16	
17	

8-19 **DETAIL OF HIV WESTERN BLOT STRIPS** These are the same strips as in Figure 8-18 to show the banding pattern more clearly. Above the strips are handwritten codes identifying each HIV protein blotted. The "p" and "gp" in each refers to protein and glycoprotein, respectively. The numbers are the molecular weight of each protein. Notice that the smaller proteins are at the left. During electrophoresis, smaller proteins migrate faster than bigger ones. Based on that, these proteins migrated from right to left.

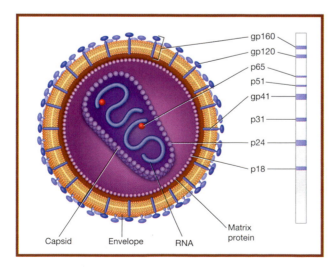

8-20 **SCHEMATIC DIAGRAM OF HIV** HIV is an enveloped retrovirus with virus-specific glycoproteins extending from it as spikes. The spikes are used for attachment to cells with the CD4 protein (such as Helper-T cells). There are also matrix and capsid proteins. Inside the capsid are two copies of its RNA with each attached to a reverse transcriptase enzyme. To the right is a drawing of a Western blot strip with each band labeled to indicate the HIV antigen to which it corresponds. The location of each band protein in the virus is also shown.

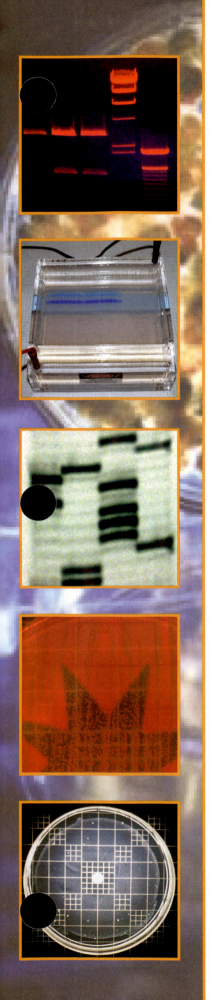

Molecular Techniques

DNA Extraction

● Purpose

DNA extraction is a starting point for many lab procedures, including DNA sequencing and cloning.

● Principle

DNA extraction from cells is surprisingly easy and occurs in three basic stages:

1 First, a detergent (*e.g.,* Sodium Dodecyl Sulfate—SDS) is used to lyse cells and release cellular contents, including DNA.

2 This is followed by a heating step (at approximately 65–70°C) that denatures protein (including DNases that would destroy the extracted DNA) and other cell components. Temperatures higher than 80°C will denature DNA, and this is undesirable. A protease may also be added to remove proteins (other techniques for purification may also be used).

3 Finally, the water-soluble DNA is precipitated in cold alcohol as a whitish, stringy mass (Figure 9-1).

After extraction, an ultraviolet spectrophotometer (Figure 9-2) can be used to estimate DNA concentration in the sample by measuring absorbance at 260 nm, the optimum wavelength for absorption by DNA. An absorbance of A_{260nm} of 1 corresponds to 50 μg/mL of double-stranded DNA (dsDNA). Reading absorbance at 280 nm and calculating the following ratio can determine purity of the sample:

$$\frac{Absorbance_{260nm}}{Absorbance_{280nm}}$$

If the sample is reasonably pure nucleic acid, then the ratio will be about 1.8 (between 1.65 and 1.85). Because protein absorbs maximally at 280 nm, a ratio of less than 1.6 is likely due to protein contamination. If purity is crucial, then the DNA extraction is repeated. If the ratio is greater than 2.0, the sample is diluted and read again.

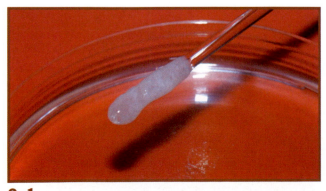

9-1 EUKARYOTIC DNA This onion DNA has been extracted and spooled onto a glass rod.

109

9-2 ULTRAVIOLET SPECTROPHOTOMETER **A** A UV spectrophotometer can be used to determine DNA concentration. A quartz cuvette is shown in the sample port (**arrow**). **B** This specimen has an A_{260nm} of 0.596 absorbance units. Since an A_{260nm} of 1.0 is equal to 50 µg/mL of dsDNA, this specimen has a concentration of 29.8 µg/mL. Absorbance also can be used to determine purity of the sample. A relatively pure DNA sample will have an A_{260nm}/A_{280nm} value of 1.8.

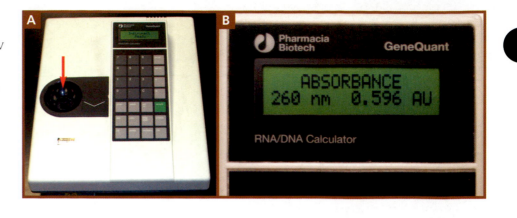

Electrophoresis

● Purpose

Electrophoresis is a technique in which molecules are separated by size and electrical charge in a gel. Once separated, the gel can be used in a number of ways. Protein or nucleic acid patterns can be compared for taxonomic or identification purposes. Separated molecules can be removed from the gel and used in biochemical studies. Other techniques, such as DNA fingerprinting and Southern, Western, and Northern blotting, begin with electrophoresis.

● Principle

Electrophoresis gels are typically prepared from **agarose** or **polyacrylamide**, depending on the molecules to be separated. Agarose is used for large DNA molecules and polyacrylamide is used for small DNA molecules and proteins. In preparation for the procedure the gel is cast as a thin slab containing tiny wells at one end and placed in a buffered solution to maintain proper electrolyte balance (Figure 9-3). Precast gels are also available. Samples to be examined (either nucleic acid or protein) are loaded into the different wells and electrodes are attached to create an electrical field in the gel.

Under the influence of the electrical field molecules in the samples migrate through the gel. Because of their negative charges, both proteins and DNA migrate toward the positive pole. The molecules travel different distances due to differences in size and electrical charge. At the end of the run, the gel is stained to show the location of the separated molecules as bands in each lane. **Coomassie blue** is commonly used for protein (Figure 9-4), whereas **ethidium bromide**, a fluorescent dye, can be used for nucleic acids (Figure 9-5). If the nucleic acid has been radioactively labeled, the gel can be placed on X-ray film. Radioactivity from the bands exposes the film, as in Figure 9-6, to produce an **autoradiograph**.

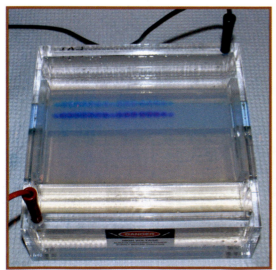

9-3 ELECTROPHORESIS GEL APPARATUS This agarose gel is being used to separate DNA fragments. The fragments are running toward the bottom of the photo. The blue dye is at the front and lets the operator know when to stop running the gel.

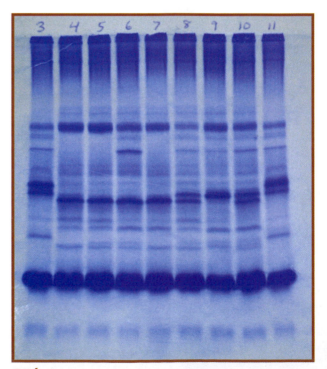

9-4 POLYACRYLAMIDE GEL ELECTROPHORESIS (PAGE) OF PROTEIN This polyacrylamide gel of serum proteins from several lemur species illustrates staining with Coomassie blue. Migration was from top to bottom.

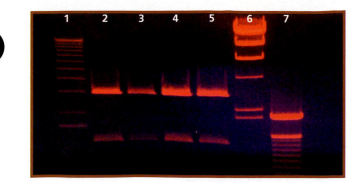

9-5 **ETHIDIUM BROMIDE STAIN OF A GEL** This agarose gel was used to separate DNA fragments and to determine their sizes. The first, sixth, and seventh lanes are DNA fragment samples of known sizes. The first lane forms a 1 Kilobase (Kb) "ladder" in which the slowest fragment is 12,216 bp (base pairs) in length and the fastest visible fragment is 1,636 bp. (Other smaller fragments are too faint to be seen in this gel.) In Lane 6, the fragments range in size from 23,130 bp to 2,027 bp. In Lane 7, the range is 2,072 bp to 100 bp. The distance migrated by the fragments of known size is then compared to those in the specimen samples found in lanes two through four to estimate their size.

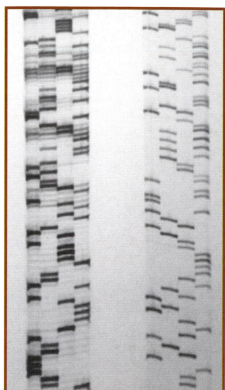

9-6 **AUTORADIOGRAPH OF DNA IN AN AGAROSE GEL** This shows a portion of an autoradiograph produced from a gel used in DNA sequencing. The radioactively labeled DNA fragments were separated by size under the influence of an electrical field. Migration of the samples was from top to bottom. The bands were visualized by placing the gel on X-ray film and allowing the radioactivity to expose it. The smaller, faster molecules are at the bottom of the autoradiograph.

Polymerase Chain Reaction

● Purpose

The polymerase chain reaction (PCR)[1] is a relatively simple and convenient method of **amplifying** (copying) even as little as one molecule of DNA. Once multiple copies of the DNA are made, they can be used in various ways ranging from research, diagnostics, and forensics.

● Principle

The **polymerase chain reaction (PCR)** is a technique conceived by the 1993 Chemistry Nobel Laureate Kary Mullis. This process is designed to make multiple copies of (amplify) a desired gene or other short DNA fragment. In the process, the double-stranded DNA sequence to be amplified (the **template**) is separated with heat and then replicated using free nucleotides, two commercially prepared **primers**, and a polymerase. The primers (short nucleic acid molecules) are selected to be complementary to positions on opposite strands of the DNA molecule. The points at which they attach flank the area to be replicated. DNA Polymerase is then able to attach the free nucleotides to complementary bases on the template and make the desired copy (Figure 9-7).

The PCR process involves 20 to 40 cycles of three different activities: **denaturation** (DNA strand separation),

annealing (of primers), and **extension** (DNA replication). In denaturation, the temperature of the reaction tube is raised to 92–96°C for one to a few minutes to separate the DNA strands. Following this, the temperature is lowered to 45–65°C, which allows the primers to anneal to their complementary sequences on opposite template strands. For the extension phase, the temperature is raised to 72°C, for a few seconds to a few minutes, to allow the polymerase to synthesize DNA complementary to the template (elongate primer). This process is performed automatically by a thermocycler programmed by the lab worker (Figure 9-8).

This completes the first cycle of amplification. The process then repeats itself, but this time there are four template strands to replicate and the result is eight strands of DNA (four dsDNA molecules). By continuing the process and using the products of one cycle as templates for the next cycle, the number of DNA target strands doubles each cycle and can be amplified a million-fold, all in a few hours. (For 20 cycles, each strand will be replicated $2^{20} = 1,048,576$ times!) As mentioned above, two primers are used in the reaction, but they must be added to the PCR reaction mixture in great excess to flood the mixture and promote primer-DNA annealing and to discourage DNA-DNA re-annealing. Other essential components of the mixture include sufficient quantities of free deoxyribonucleotides (dATP, dCTP, dTTP, and dGTP) needed for extension, buffers to

[1] PCR was conceived by Kary Mullis in 1983 and resulted in his being awarded the 1993 Nobel Prize in Chemistry.

maintain the appropriate pH, magnesium required by the polymerase, and other salts to create the proper osmotic balance. Because of the high temperatures required for the denaturation phase, the thermotolerant ***Taq*DNA polymerase**, isolated from the thermophile *Thermus aquaticus* (page 124), is used to catalyze the extension.

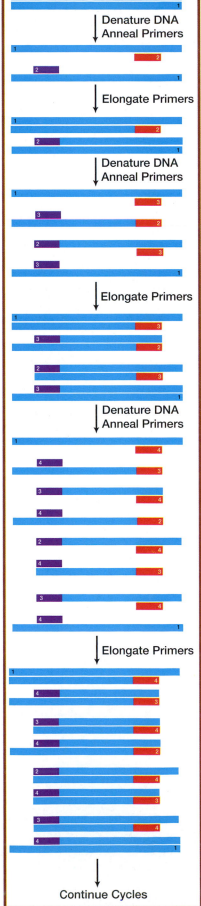

Denature DNA
Anneal Primers

Elongate Primers

Denature DNA
Anneal Primers

Elongate Primers

Denature DNA
Anneal Primers

Elongate Primers

Continue Cycles

9-7 Schematic Diagram of PCR Each PCR cycle doubles the amount of DNA in the sample. The numbers on the strands give generations of DNA. In this example, three replication cycles are shown, in which 2 original strands are amplified to a total of 16 strands.

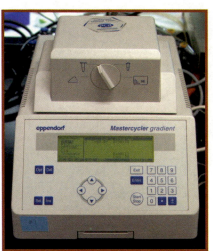

9-8 A Thermocycler Temperatures and durations of each phase can be programmed into the thermocycler to automate PCR.

DNA Sequencing

● Purpose

The key to unlocking the secrets of DNA function lies in determining its nucleotide sequence. Structural genes can be examined for normal sequence and mutations can be identified. Comparing DNA sequences has uncovered information about what defines certain nonstructural segments of DNA, such as promoters, operators, and introns. It is also useful in comparing relatedness between organisms by comparing similarity of homologous genes.

● Principle

In vivo DNA synthesis requires a template strand, a primer, DNA polymerase, and a pool of all four deoxyribonucleotide triphosphates[2] (dATP, dCTP, dTTP, and dGTP) (Figure 9-9A). The primer binds to the template, then DNA polymerase adds nucleotides to the 3′ hydroxyl of the primer (and each subsequent nucleotide as the chain grows) in the order determined by base pairing with the template strand. The new bond is between the 5′ phosphate of the next nucleotide and the 3′ hydroxyl of the replicated strand.

Frederick Sanger's **dideoxy method** of DNA sequencing involves *in vitro* synthesis of DNA strands complementary to the DNA template being sequenced. Multiple copies of the template, plus all four dNTPs, and radioactively or fluorescently labeled primers are added to four tubes. Then, each tube receives one ddNTP (Figure 9-9B); that is, one tube gets ddATP, another ddTTP, *etc. In vitro* replication is then allowed to occur in all four tubes (Figure 9-10). Since a ddNTP lacks the 3′ hydroxyl of a "normal" dNTP, the next

[2] Deoxyribonucleotides are incorporated into the growing DNA chain by removal of the two phosphates to produce the nucleotide structure as it is found in the DNA chain; that is, the sugar, phosphate, and nitrogenous base. (Removal of the two phosphates provides the energy required for DNA synthesis.) . The symbol dNTP is used to designate any of the four deoxyribonucleotides.

nucleotide in the sequence cannot be added and elongation of the DNA strand stops. If the proper ratio of the normal dNTP to ddNTP is used (about 10:1), then replicated DNA strands of all lengths ending with that ddNTP will be produced in each tube. Electrophoresis of these fragments separates them by size, with the smallest traveling the farthest. The sequence is then read directly from the autoradiogram (see Electrophoresis, page 110) beginning with the smallest fragment (which consists of the primer at the 5' end plus the first ddNTP) up through the slowest fragment (consisting of the 5' primer plus the entire length of the DNA strand being synthesized) (Figure 9-11). Note that the sequence given by this method is actually complementary to the DNA template.

This method has now been automated. Instead of labeling the primer, each of the four ddNTPs is labeled with a fluorescent molecule that produces a different color. In this method, all four ddNTPs can be mixed into one tube, since the fragments will be labeled with a different color depending on their terminating ddNTP. Electrophoresis is done in a tube through which a laser beam is passed. As each fragment migrates past the laser beam during electrophoresis, it emits the color appropriate to its ddNTP. The color is recorded and the nucleotide sequence is determined from the color sequence.

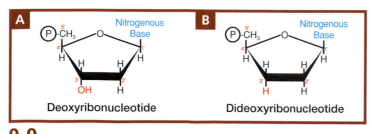

9-9 NUCLEOTIDE STRUCTURE A A deoxyribonucleotide as it is found in DNA consists of deoxyribose sugar, a phosphate, and one of four nitrogenous bases: thymine, adenine, cytosine, and guanine. Nucleotides are identified by the base they possess (dA, dC, dG, and dT). As added to the reaction mixture, this nucleotide would have three phosphates rather than just one. **B** A dideoxyribonucleotide differs only in the absence of a hydroxyl group at the 3' carbon. Since it is the 3'-OH that is used to connect adjacent nucleotides, incorporation of a dideoxyribonucleotide acts as a "cap" and prevents further elongation of the nucleotide chain.

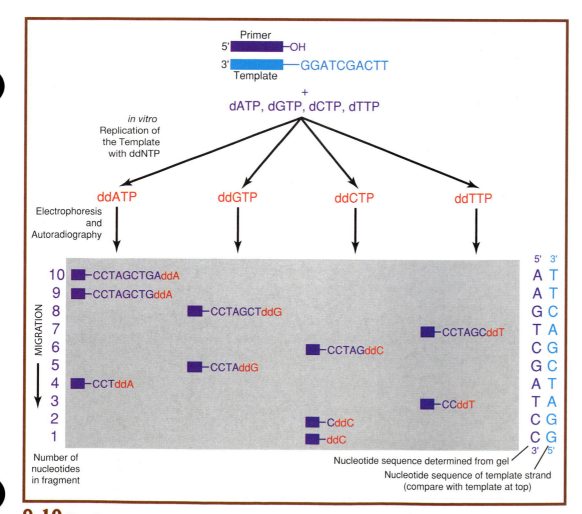

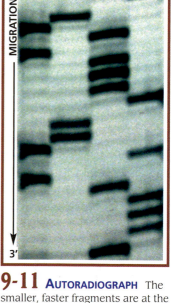

9-11 AUTORADIOGRAPH The smaller, faster fragments are at the bottom of this autoradiograph. The four lanes allow determination of nucleotide sequence, with the lanes containing (from left to right) fragments ending in ddA, ddG, ddC, and ddT nucleotides. The actual gel is much larger than this, but the nucleotide sequence in the region shown is: 5'CTGACACCCTGGAT-ACTTTC3', which corresponds to 3'GACTGTGGGACCTATGAAAG3' in the template strand.

9-10 THE SANGER DIDEOXY METHOD OF DNA SEQUENCING The Sanger method produces DNA fragments of all possible lengths due to chain termination by ddNTPs in their respective tubes. After electrophoresis of all samples, the band pattern is read to determine the DNA sequence *complementary* to that of the original DNA strand.

Ultraviolet Radiation Damage and Repair

● Purpose

Because ultraviolet radiation has a lethal effect on bacterial cells, it can be used as a sterilizing agent. However, its use is limited because it penetrates materials such as glass and plastic poorly. In addition, bacterial cells have mechanisms to repair UV damage.

● Principle

Ultraviolet radiation is part of the electromagnetic spectrum, but with shorter, higher energy wavelengths than visible light. Prolonged exposure can be lethal to cells because when DNA absorbs UV radiation at 254 nm, the energy is used to form new covalent bonds between adjacent pyrimidines: cytosine-cytosine, cytosine-thymine, or thymine-thymine. Collectively, these are known as pyrimidine dimers, with thymine dimers being the most common. These dimers distort the DNA molecule and interfere with DNA replication and transcription (Figure 9-12).

Many bacteria have mechanisms to repair such DNA damage. *Escherichia coli* performs **light repair** or **photoreactivation**, in which the repair enzyme, **DNA photolyase**, is activated by visible light (340–400 nm) and simply monomerizes the dimer by reversing the original reaction. A second *E. coli* repair mechanism, **excision repair** or **dark repair**, involves a number of enzymes (Figure 9-13). The thymine dimer distorts the sugar-phosphate backbone of the strand. This is detected by an **endonuclease** (UvrABC) that breaks two bonds—one eight nucleotides in the 5′ direction from the dimer, the other four nucleotides in the 3′ direction. A **helicase** (UvrD) removes the 13-nucleotide fragment

(including the dimer), leaving single stranded DNA. **DNA polymerase I** inserts the appropriate complementary nucleotides in a 5′ to 3′ direction to make the molecule double stranded again. Finally, **DNA ligase** closes the gap between the last nucleotide of the new segment and the first nucleotide of the old DNA, and the repair is complete. Both mechanisms are capable of repairing a small amount of damage,

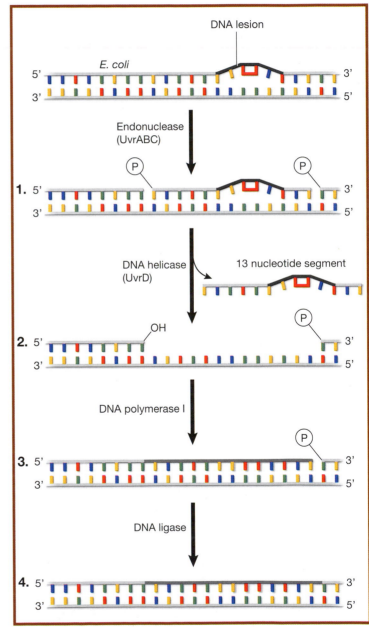

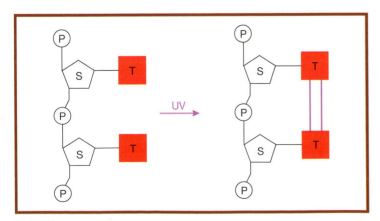

9-12 **A THYMINE DIMER IN ONE STRAND OF DNA** Thymine dimers form when DNA absorbs UV radiation with a wavelength of 254 nm. The energy is used to form two new covalent bonds between the thymines, resulting in distortion of the DNA strand. The enzyme DNA photolyase can break this bond to return the DNA to its normal shape and function. If it doesn't, and excision repair fails, the distortion interferes with DNA replication and transcription.

9-13 **EXCISION OR DARK REPAIR IN E. COLI** In the repair process, four enzymes are used: (**1**) An endonuclease (UvrABC) to break two covalent bonds in the sugar-phosphate backbone of the damaged strand, (**2**) a helicase (UvrD) to remove the nucleotides in the damaged segment, (**3**) DNA polymerase I to synthesize a new strand, and (**4**) DNA ligase to form a covalent bond between the new and the original strands.

but long and/or intense exposures to UV produce more damage than the cell can repair, thus making UV radiation lethal.

Figure 9-14 shows a sample plate inoculated with *Serratia marcescens* and exposed to UV radiation for 30 seconds. During exposure, this Petri dish lid was removed and a piece of posterboard with a star cut out of it was placed over the dish.

9-14 SAMPLE PLATE This nutrient agar plate was inoculated with *Serratia marcescens*. With the plate's lid off, the plate was covered with a posterboard mask with a star cut in it, and then exposed to UV radiation for 30 seconds. Incubation was for 24 hours in the dark at 25°C. Notice the different amounts of growth in the protected and unprotected areas of the plate. Colonies inside the pattern have undergone DNA repair, but most cells in that exposed region were killed. Regions of confluent growth were protected from irradiation by the mask.

Ames Test

● Purpose

Many substances that are mutagenic to bacteria are also carcinogenic to higher animals. The Ames Test is a rapid, inexpensive means of using specific bacteria to evaluate the mutagenic properties of potential carcinogens. There are many variations on the basic Ames Test that are used in specific applications.

● Principle

Bacteria that are able to enzymatically synthesize a particular necessary biochemical (such as an amino acid) are called **prototrophs** for that biochemical. If the bacterial strain can make the amino acid histidine, for instance, it is classified as a histidine prototroph. Bacteria that must be supplied with that biochemical (*e.g.*, histidine) are called (histidine) **auxotrophs.** Auxotrophs are typically created from prototrophs when a mutation occurs in the gene coding for an enzyme used in the pathway of the biochemical's synthesis.

The Ames Test employs mutant strains of *Salmonella typhimurium* that have lost their ability to synthesize histidine. One strain of histidine auxotrophs possesses a **frameshift mutation.** That is, they are missing one or have an extra nucleotide in the DNA sequence that would otherwise code for an enzyme necessary for histidine production. Other strains are **substitution mutants,** in which one nucleotide in the histidine gene has been replaced, resulting in a faulty gene product.

The Ames Test determines the ability of chemical agents to cause a reversal—a **back mutation**—of these auxotrophs to the original prototrophic state. In this test histidine auxotrophs are spread onto **minimal agar plates** that contain all nutrients for growth, but only a trace of histidine. **Complete agar** differs from minimal agar only in that it contains histidine.

When a filter paper disk saturated with a suspected mutagen is placed in the middle of an inoculated minimal agar plate, the substance will diffuse outward into the medium. If it is mutagenic, it will cause back mutation in some cells (converting them to histidine prototrophs) that freely grow into full-size colonies. (**Note:** histidine is initially included in the medium to allow the auxotrophs to grow for several generations and expose them to the effects of the mutagen. The unmutated auxotrophs typically exhibit faint growth, but do not develop into full-size colonies due to the rapid exhaustion of the histidine.)

Several variations of the Ames test are possible. This example uses two minimal agar plates and two complete agar plates (Figures 9-15 through 9-18). The complete medium contains all of the nutrients necessary for *Salmonella* growth. Each plate is inoculated with *Salmonella* histidine auxotrophs. One minimal agar plate and one complete agar plate each receive a filter paper disk saturated with the test substance. The second minimal agar plate and complete agar plate each receive a filter paper disk saturated with Dimethyl Sulfoxide, DMSO (a substance known to be nonmutagenic).

The minimal agar plate containing the test substance determines mutagenicity of the test substance. Only prototrophs will grow on minimal agar, so recovery of any colonies on the minimal agar inoculated with auxotrophs is indicative of back mutation. Depending on the strain used, the type of back mutation (either frameshift or base substitution) can also be determined. The minimal agar plate with DMSO serves as a control for the minimal agar/test substance plate by measuring the **spontaneous back mutations** (natural mutations that occur without the presence of a mutagen). In order for the test substance to be considered mutagenic, it must produce more back mutations than found on the control plate.

The purpose of the complete agar plate containing the test substance is a control to evaluate toxicity of the test substance. Creation of a **zone of inhibition** around the disk indicates toxicity. The more toxic the substance is, the larger the zone will be. If the substance is toxic, there may be no indication of mutagenicity because the cells are killed before they can back mutate. Finally, the complete agar plate containing DMSO serves as a control for comparison to the growth and zone of inhibition on the complete agar/test substance plate.

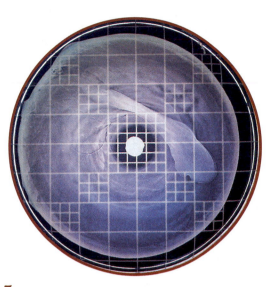

9-15 TESTING FOR TOXICITY Shown is a *Salmonella* histidine auxotroph grown on complete agar (containing histidine) and exposed to the test substance. The zone of inhibition around the paper disk indicates toxicity of the substance.

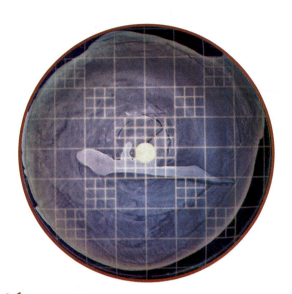

9-16 TOXICITY CONTROL The same *Salmonella* histidine auxotroph is grown on complete agar (containing histidine) and exposed to an inert substance (DMSO). This plate serves as a control for comparison of zone size with the plate in Figure 9-15. The absence of a zone around the disk indicates that neither the paper disk nor the DMSO is toxic or inhibitory and that the zone in Figure 9-15 is due to the test substance.

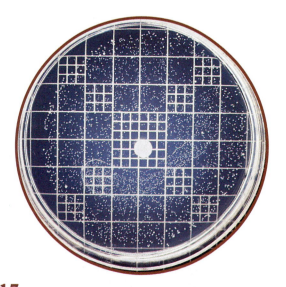

9-17 TESTING FOR MUTAGENICITY In this example, the same *Salmonella* histidine auxotroph is grown on histidine minimal agar and exposed to a suspected mutagen introduced onto the plate by the paper disk. A zone of inhibition is visible on this plate, but is not as well defined as on complete agar because the growth is not as dense. The number of colonies suggests that back mutations have occurred. However, it is not known at this time whether or not they are due to the effects of the test substance or to spontaneous mutation, so comparison must be made with the plate in Figure 9-18.

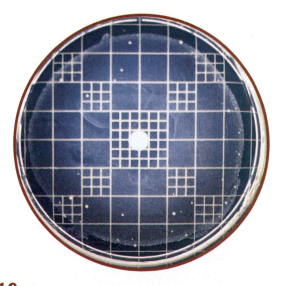

9-18 CONTROL FOR SPONTANEOUS MUTATIONS The same *Salmonella* histidine auxotroph is grown on histidine minimal agar and exposed to a known nonmutagen (DMSO). This plate is a control to demonstrate spontaneous mutation for comparison with the plate containing test substance shown in Figure 9-17. The faint background growth is due to the small amount of histidine in the medium necessary to promote initial growth.

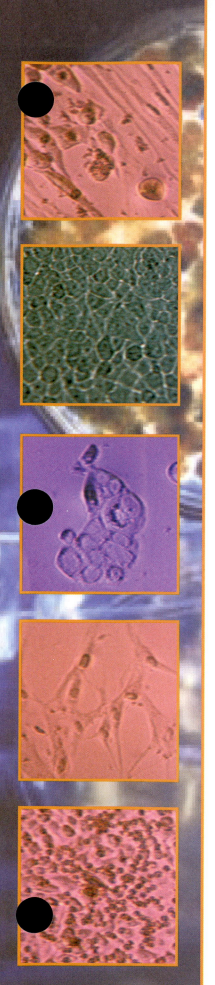

Viruses

Introduction to Viruses

In the opinion of most biologists viruses are not living. This is based primarily on the absence of two major characteristics associated with living things: viruses are not cellular and they have no metabolism. On the other hand, they do exhibit heredity and are made of biochemicals. Proteins form the structures and receptors of the virus particle (not cell!), and DNA *or RNA* (all cellular organisms use DNA) is the hereditary material. And, whereas cells always possess both DNA and RNA (for protein synthesis), viruses have only one or the other and use it as the genome. They are also very small, usually much smaller than bacteria. They are capable of making more of themselves (replication), but require a cellular host to do the work. As such, they are obligate intracellular parasites. And, unlike cells that remain intact when they reproduce, viruses disassemble during replication, then the progeny reassemble prior to release from the host—hence "viral replication" rather than "viral reproduction."

A virus particle consists minimally of a protein **capsid** surrounding its genome. The capsid is one of two basic geometric shapes and is composed of protein subunits called **capsomeres**. Some viruses have an **icosahedral** capsid with 20 triangular faces in which capsomeres combine to form the faces. Others have a rod shape, in which the capsomeres form a helix and the genome is threaded in the helical grooves (Figure 10-1). Many viruses that infect bacteria, called **bacteriophages** or simply **phages,** have a complex structure with a protein tail (Figures 10-2 and 10-3). It is not uncommon for the virus to possess enzymes, but they don't have many. Most enzymes that are required for replication are encoded in the genome and are made once inside the host cell. Others (typically viruses that infect animals) have an outer **envelope** composed of membrane obtained from the host cell upon release.

Viral replication involves the same basic stages, regardless of the host. These are: **attachment** to the host, **penetration** into the host,

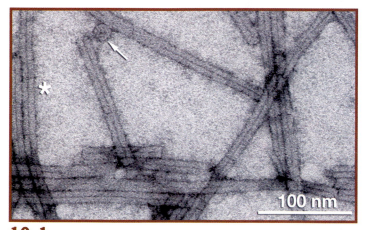

10-1 **TOBACCO MOSAIC VIRUS** TMV is the causative agent of tobacco mosaic disease. The virions are rod shaped and are composed of 2130 capsomeres arranged around a central canal (the dark line in each virion). Striations of the helix are faintly visible at the asterisk (*). These virions are approximately 400 nm long and 15 nm in diameter. Assembly of the TMV capsid involves addition of disk-like subassemblies consisting of two layers of 17 capsomeres each. These assume a "lock washer" shape when associated with the +ssRNA genome and integrate into the growing capsid. A disk (or at least a cross section) of a virion is indicated by the arrow.   Photograph by the author taken at the San Diego State University Electron Microscope Facility

117

uncoating of the genome, **genome replication** and **synthesis** of viral proteins, **assembly** of progeny, and **release**. Figure 10-4 illustrates the replicative cycle of bacteriophage T4.

The viral genome is either DNA or RNA. Further, some DNA viruses have double-stranded DNA (dsDNA), whereas others have single-stranded DNA (ssDNA), which does not exist in cells. RNA viruses can also have ssRNA or dsRNA. David Baltimore devised a viral taxonomy based on viral genome and the steps necessary to get information from the genome to messenger RNA. By convention, mRNA is considered to be "+" sense. A strand of DNA or RNA complementary to it is considered "−" sense. There are six categories.

1 **+ssRNA viruses**. The genome acts as messenger RNA. A −ssRNA molecule is synthesized from the +ssRNA and acts as the template for genome replication and mRNA synthesis. Examples are poliovirus, hepatitis A and C viruses, and West Nile virus.

2 **−ssRNA viruses**. These viruses synthesize +ssRNA from the genome that acts as mRNA and as a template for genome replication. Examples include rabies virus, Ebola virus, measles virus, mumps virus, and influenza A virus.

3 **dsRNA** viruses. The negative strand is used to produce +ssRNA that acts as mRNA. Both strands are used as templates for genome replication. Examples include rotavirus (gastroenteritis) and reovirus (mild respiratory and digestive symptoms).

4 **dsDNA viruses**. These viruses make mRNA and replicate their genomes just as cells do. Examples include herpes simplex viruses, variola virus (small pox), and human papillomaviruses (cervical cancer and genital warts).

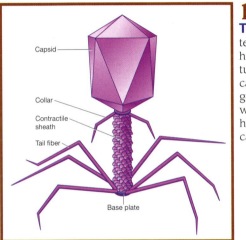

10-2 **DIAGRAM OF T4 COLIPHAGE** Bacteriophages frequently have a complex structure that includes the capsid containing the genome and a tail with many parts. T4 has an icosahedral capsid.

Capsid
Collar
Contractile sheath
Tail fiber
Base plate

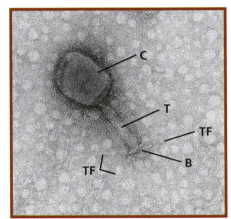

10-3 **T4 COLIPHAGE** This is a negative stain of one T4 phage particle. Shown are the capsid (**C**), tail (**T**), base plate (**B**), and tail fibers (**TF**). The length of this phage from base plate to tip of capsid is approximately 180 nm (0.18 μm).

Photo by author taken at the San Diego State University Electron Microscope Facility

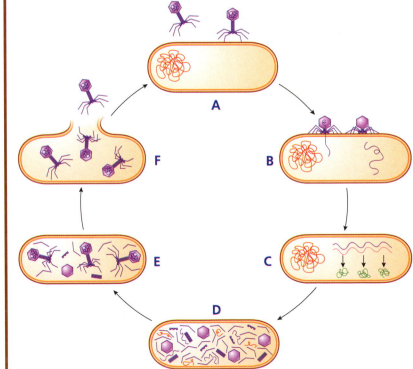

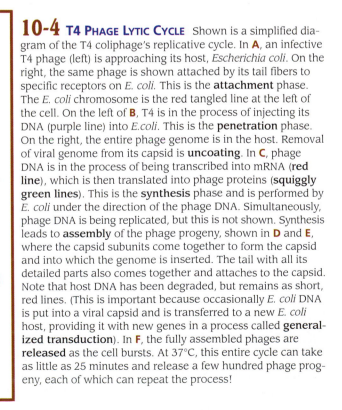

10-4 **T4 PHAGE LYTIC CYCLE** Shown is a simplified diagram of the T4 coliphage's replicative cycle. In **A**, an infective T4 phage (left) is approaching its host, *Escherichia coli*. On the right, the same phage is shown attached by its tail fibers to specific receptors on *E. coli*. This is the **attachment** phase. The *E. coli* chromosome is the red tangled line at the left of the cell. On the left of **B**, T4 is in the process of injecting its DNA (purple line) into *E. coli*. This is the **penetration** phase. On the right, the entire phage genome is in the host. Removal of viral genome from its capsid is **uncoating**. In **C**, phage DNA is in the process of being transcribed into mRNA (**red line**), which is then translated into phage proteins (**squiggly green lines**). This is the **synthesis** phase and is performed by *E. coli* under the direction of the phage DNA. Simultaneously, phage DNA is being replicated, but this is not shown. Synthesis leads to **assembly** of the phage progeny, shown in **D** and **E**, where the capsid subunits come together to form the capsid and into which the genome is inserted. The tail with all its detailed parts also comes together and attaches to the capsid. Note that host DNA has been degraded, but remains as short, red lines. (This is important because occasionally *E. coli* DNA is put into a viral capsid and is transferred to a new *E. coli* host, providing it with new genes in a process called **generalized transduction**). In **F**, the fully assembled phages are **released** as the cell bursts. At 37°C, this entire cycle can take as little as 25 minutes and release a few hundred phage progeny, each of which can repeat the process!

5 ssDNA viruses. These viruses must first replicate their genome to dsDNA, which is then used for transcription to mRNA. Normal DNA replication provides more ssDNA for the progeny genome. In most instances, only one "sense" of the ssDNA is packaged into the viral progeny, but there are exceptions where the progeny end up with one or the other. An example is human parvovirus B19 (which causes Fifth disease—a rash, seen mostly in children).

6 +ssRNA retroviruses. Retroviruses are capable of using an RNA template to make dsDNA, which is then incorporated into the host genome and becomes latent. When active, transcription produces +ssRNA, which can be used as mRNA or genome for the progeny. Examples include Human Immunodeficiency Viruses (HIV—causes AIDS) and Human T-lymphotrophic Viruses (HTLV—causes T-cell leukemia).

Human Immunodeficiency Virus (HIV)

HIV is the causative agent of AIDS (*Acquired Immune Deficiency Syndrome*). At first, only a single type of HIV was known, but in 1985, a second HIV was isolated. The two forms are now referred to as HIV-1 and HIV-2, respectively.

HIV-1 and HIV-2 (Figures 8-20, 10-5 and 10-6) are **retroviruses** (*Retroviridae*) and have the ability to perform **reverse transcription**; that is, they make DNA from an RNA template, a very unusual mechanism that characterizes the group. (In all other biological systems, RNA is made from a DNA template during **transcription**.) The enzyme **reverse transcriptase** catalyzes this process. Morphologically, a phospholipid envelope derived from the host cell membrane encloses the spherical capsid. Within it is a protein core surrounding two single stranded RNA molecules, each of which is associated with a molecule of reverse transcriptase. The HIV genome consists of only 9 genes. Glycoprotein spikes emerging from the envelope are involved in attachment to the host cell.

HIV infects cells with CD4 membrane receptors, normally used for antigen recognition, but used by HIV for attachment. A subpopulation of T cells, the T_4 helper cells, are most commonly infected and die as a result. Other cells, such as dendritic cells (a type of antigen presenting cell), macrophages, and monocytes may also be infected. After infection, the reverse transcriptase catalyzes the production of viral DNA (**provirus**), which integrates into the host chromosome and is the template for production of viral RNA and proteins. After assembly, new virions emerge from the host cell by budding and infect other cells. Latent infection in which no new virus is made is also a possible outcome of infection.

T_4 helper cells are essential to the normal operation of the immune system because they promote development of immune cells in both **humoral** and **cell-mediated responses.** Depletion of T_4 cells cripples the immune system and the patient becomes susceptible to infections by organisms not typically pathogenic to humans. Thus, AIDS is not a single

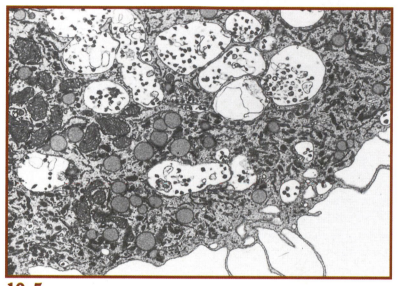

10-5 ELECTRON MICROGRAPH OF A MACROPHAGE FROM AN HIV INFECTED PERSON Vacuoles contain viral particles.

Photo courtesy of Dr. Rachel Schrier and Dr. Clayton Wiley

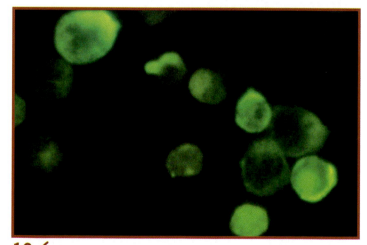

10-6 AN INDIRECT FLUORESCENT ANTIBODY (IFA) TEST POSITIVE FOR HIV The test system consists of HIV-infected cells attached to the glass slide. When patient serum or plasma is added, any anti-HIV antibodies bind to the infected cells. Subsequent addition of fluorescent anti-human immunoglobin antibodies results in binding to patient anti-HIV antibodies, if present. After washing away unbound fluorescent antibodies, the slide is observed under a UV microscope. A bright apple green color is a positive result.

disease, but rather a syndrome of diseases characteristic of patients with HIV infection.

HIV is transmitted via body fluids such as blood, breast milk, semen, and vaginal secretions. Infection can occur as a result of sexual intercourse with or blood transfusion from an infected individual. Infection may also occur across the placenta during pregnancy or via contaminated needles used for injection of intravenous drugs. An infected mother also may transmit it to a newborn during delivery or nursing. Casual social contact does not appear to be a route of infection.

According to United Nations 2008 Health Statistics[1], 33.4 million people globally are living with HIV infection. Most are in Subsaharan Africa.

_____

[1]http://www.unaids.org/en/KnowledgeCentre/HIVData/mapping_progress.asp

Viral Cytopathic Effects in Cell Culture

● Purpose

This procedure is used for *in vitro* identification of viruses. Presumptive identification of a virus in a specimen can be made by determining the host cell(s) in which it replicates, how quickly it causes damage, and the type of cytopathic effect (damage) it produces. Confirmation may be made using a specific serological test.

● Principle

Supplied with the appropriate nutrients and environment, viable virus host cells can be grown in a tube or flat bottle. This is a **cell culture** (Figure 10-7). Incubation is done in such a way that growth occurs only on one side. The cells divide and produce a characteristic monolayer on the container's inside surface.

Different media are used for cell culture at different stages. These are: **growth medium** and **maintenance medium**. Growth medium is used to begin a cell culture. When the cell layer is confluent or nearly so, the growth medium is replaced with maintenance medium. Both media are supplemented with amino acids, vitamins, and calf serum. To ensure that the serum is free of viral antibodies and certain infectious agents, only fetal, neonatal, or agammaglobulinemic calf serum is used. Antibiotics are also included to inhibit bacterial growth. The accumulation of carbon dioxide and the associated acidification of the medium is counteracted by a buffer. A pH indicator (such as phenol red) is used to monitor the effectiveness of the buffer.

A sample suspected of containing virus is introduced into the cell culture. Cultures are grown in an incubator and the tubes may be placed in a mechanical roller to keep the medium aerated (Figure 10-8). As they replicate in the cell culture, viruses inflict damage upon the host cells called a **cytopathic effect (CPE)**, which can be viewed under an inverted microscope (Figure 10-9). Depending on the virus and the host cell, CPEs will be evident after as little as 4 days to as much as four weeks. Most of the time, they start as small spots (**foci**) in the cell layer, then spread outwards. Common damage to the cells includes rounding (either small or large), a change in texture (either **granular** or **hyaline**—glassy), or formation of a **syncytium** (fusion of infected cells). Figures 10-10, 10-14, and 10-16 illustrate three cell types used in cell culture. Figures 10-11 through 10-13, Figure 10-15, and Figures 10-17 through 10-19 illustrate various CPEs in these three host cells.

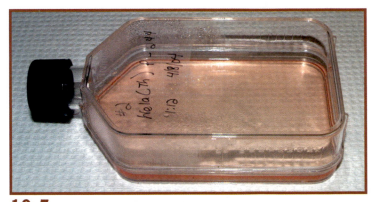

10-7 CELL CULTURE Viruses cannot be grown in bacteriological media (such as Nutrient Agar) because they require living host cells. So, the first challenge in propagating viruses is to grow their hosts in a tube or flat bottle to produce a cell culture. Shown is a culture of HeLa cells. HeLa is an established (continuous) cell line; that is, it has lasted more than 70 passages and continues to maintain its sensitivity to viral infection.

10-8 ROLLER DRUM Cultivation of some viruses (*e.g.,* respiratory viruses) requires aeration in order to more closely mimic their natural conditions. Incubation of the culture in a roller drum keeps the medium aerated. In this laboratory, all cell cultures are aerated.

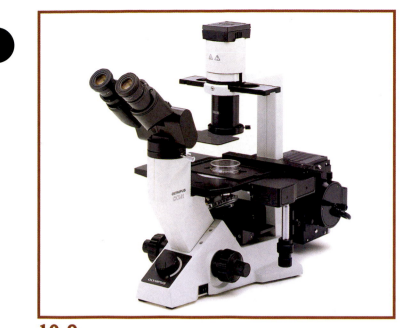

10-9 INVERTED MICROSCOPE Culture tubes and bottles are more easily viewed with an inverted microscope because the objective lenses are below the stage. This allows viewing of the cell monolayer without looking through the thickness of the flask or tube.

Photo courtesy of Olympus America Inc.

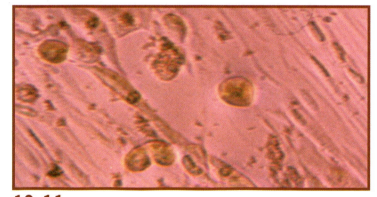

10-11 CYTOMEGALOVIRUS (CMV) CPE IN A CELL CULTURE OF MRC-5 CMV grows best in human fibroblasts, such as MRC-5. The infected fibroblasts form a row and are rounded and hyaline (glassy). CMV belongs to the *Herpesviridae* and, though common, its infections are usually asymptomatic.

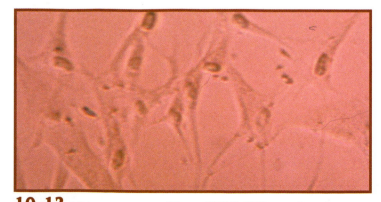

10-13 VARICELLA-ZOSTER VIRUS (VZV) CPE IN A CELL CULTURE OF MRC-5 Enlarged cells with odd shapes characterize the VZV CPE. Varicella-zoster belongs to the *Herpesviridae* and is responsible for producing chickenpox (varicella) and shingles (zoster).

10-10 NORMAL MRC-5 Normal MRC-5 is a cell line of human diploid fibroblasts. A cell line has a limited number (about 50) of passages (transfers) before it is no longer useful. MRC-5 is used for isolation of herpes simplex viruses (HSV), varicella-zoster viruses (VZV), cytomegaloviruses (CMV), adenoviruses, enteroviruses, respiratory syncytial viruses (RSV), and rhinoviruses.

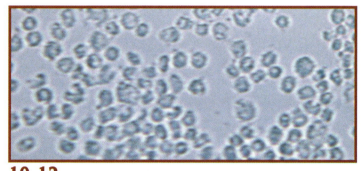

10-12 ENTEROVIRUS CPE IN A CELL CULTURE OF MRC-5 Enterovirus infected cells become small (pycnotic) and round. Most enterovirus infections are asymptomatic, but can result in acute diseases such as nonspecific febrile illness, aseptic meningitis, and poliomyelitis. Enteroviruses belong to the family *Picornaviridae* (pico-RNA-viridae—literally "small RNA viruses").

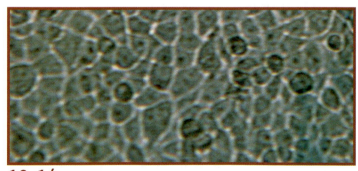

10-14 NORMAL HeLa CELLS IN CULTURE HeLa is an established cell line used for isolation of poxviruses, respiratory syncytial viruses (RSV), rhinoviruses, and enteroviruses.

10-15 RESPIRATORY SYNCYTIAL VIRUS (RSV) CPE RSV in HeLa cell culture produces characteristic syncytia of fused cells. RSV is responsible for lower respiratory tract infections, especially in infants.

10-16 NORMAL AFRICAN GREEN MONKEY KIDNEY (AGMK) CELL CULTURE This cell line is used for isolation of herpes simplex virus, varicella-zoster virus (VZV), mumps virus, and rubella virus, among others.

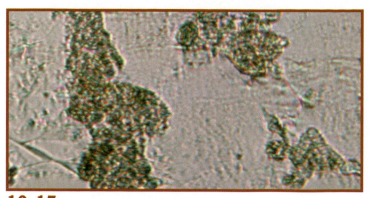

10-17 MEASLES VIRUS CPE IN AGMK CELL CULTURE Syncytia formation is the typical CPE for measles virus. Measles virus produces rubeola (also known as seven day measles). It is a –ssRNA virus and belongs to the family *Paramyxoviridae*.

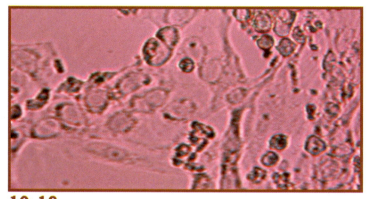

10-18 INFLUENZA A VIRUS CPE IN AGMK CELL CULTURE Cell degeneration and syncytia formation characterize the CPEs of influenza viruses. Influenza is an acute respiratory disease that may reach epidemic and pandemic proportions.

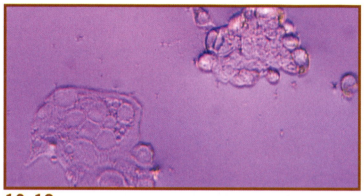

10-19 ADENOVIRUS CPE IN AGMK The typical CPE consists of rounded cells clustered like grapes. Adenoviruses cause a variety of upper and lower respiratory diseases, gastroenteritis, meningitis, and encephalitis, among others.

Hemadsorption in Cell Culture

● Purpose

Hemadsorption is used for presumptive identification of influenza, parainfluenza, and sometimes mumps virus, because these viruses do not produce much cytopathic effect (CPE) in cell culture. Confirmation is accomplished by serological tests.

● Principle

Infection with influenza, parainfluenza, or mumps virus results in viral glycoproteins being present in the infected cell's membrane. When these viruses emerge from the host, they carry the glycoproteins in their envelope (which is actually host cell membrane) and use them for attachment to and penetration of a new host. They also have the ability to **adsorb** (attach) to guinea pig RBCs. This property is exploited in the **hemadsorption test**.

Because influenza, parainfluenza, and mumps viruses often produce little or no CPE in cell culture, a hemadsorption test may be run. After incubation of the cell culture inoculated with the patient's sample, guinea pig RBCs are added to the medium. If the virus is present, the infected cells will have viral glycoproteins in their membranes, and the RBCs will adsorb to them (Figure 10-20).

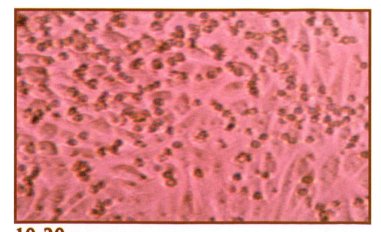

10-20 HEMADSORPTION TEST Shown is hemadsorption of guinea pig RBCs by human diploid fibrobast cells infected with parainfluenza virus. Notice that the RBCs (darker spots) are always associated with the fibroblast cells and are not in the spaces between cells.

Domain *Bacteria*

As you read these descriptions, refer to Figure 1-2 for an evolutionary perspective. By convention, most names of orders end with "-ales" and those of families end with "-aceae."

Phylum *Aquificae*

Aquificales is the only order in the phylum. Its genera are thought to reside on a very early branch of the *Bacterial* phylogenetic "tree." All are chemolithoautotrophic hyper-thermophiles. *Aquifex* (Figure 11-1) is able to grow at 95°C! Members of this phylum are autotrophs because they can perform the reverse Krebs cycle, in which CO_2 is added to the Krebs intermediates (**carbon fixation**) rather than being removed. Electron donors include H_2, S^0, or $S_2O_3^{2-}$; O_2 and NO_3^- are electron acceptors. Metabolic products from sulfur are sulfuric acid and H_2S; NO_3^- produces NO_2^- and N_2.

11-1 *Aquifex* **Habitat in Octopus Spring Runoff Channel** *Aquifex* forms pink streamers in the *hot* runoff channels (about 90°C!) of sulfur hot springs.   Photograph by Bob Lindstrom courtesy of the National Park Service

Phylum *Thermotogae*

Species of the order *Thermotogales* are Gram-negative rods with a distinctive outer sheath ("toga"), which loosely encloses the cell at both ends (Figure 11-2). All are anaerobic heterotrophs that produce acetate, CO_2, and H_2 (among other compounds) from glucose fermentation, and all reduce sulfur to H_2S. They are at least moderately thermophilic, but some are hyperthermophilic. This order, like *Aquificales*, appears to be an ancient branch within the Domain *Bacteria*.

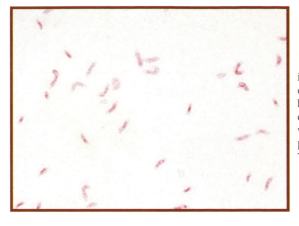

11-2 *THERMOTOGA MARITIMA* *T. maritima* was first isolated in a geothermal marine region in Italy. It grows over a temperature range of 55–90° C. Its genome has been sequenced and surprisingly, approximately one-quarter of its genes were obtained by lateral gene transfer with *Archaean* species. Cells are 0.6 μm wide by 1.5–11.0 μm long. Note the light, oval regions at the ends of cells. These are the "togas."

Phylum *"Deinococcus-Thermus"*

Deinococcus species (Figure 11-3) form either spherical or slightly elongated cells. Though they stain Gram-positive, their wall has a thin peptidoglycan layer *and* an outer membrane (as in Gram-negative cells). They are nonmotile, aerobic chemoheterotrophs, and may be mesophilic or thermophilic. Their genome consists of two different circular chromosomes in multiple copies (four copies each when the cells are not growing). They are noteworthy for their resistance to ionizing radiation due to an as-yet not understood DNA repair mechanism. They are able to withstand radiation doses many times that which is lethal to humans.

Thermus (Figure 11-4) is a genus of straight Gram-negative rods of variable length. They are aerobic respirers and are thermophilic (optimum temperature of about 70°C), preferring neutral and slightly alkaline hydrothermal regions. *Thermus aquaticus* is famous for its DNA Polymerase (*Taq*1), the enzyme that polymerizes DNA during synthesis. It is stable at high temperatures and is therefore useful in the polymerase chain reaction (PCR) technique of cloning DNA *in vitro* (page 111).

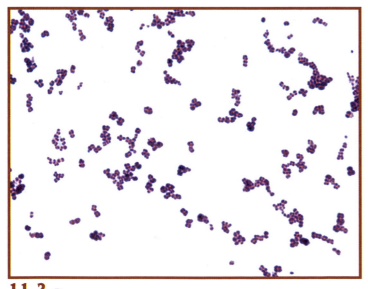

11-3 *DEINOCOCCUS* *Deinococcus* typically grows in pairs and tetrads (though sometimes as rods). Individual cells are up to 3.5 μm in diameter. This specimen was grown in culture and Gram stained.

11-4 *THERMUS AQUATICUS* HABITAT IN CISTERN SPRING, YELLOWSTONE NATIONAL PARK This hot spring reaches temperatures of 90°C. In its runoff channel (which cools as it becomes more removed from the spring), *T. aquaticus* thrives. It was in this and other Yellowstone hot springs that Dr. Thomas Brock and Dr. Hudson Freeze first discovered *T. aquaticus* in 1969.

Phylum *Chloroflexi*

Members of this phylum are filamentous rods with gliding motility. They can perform **anoxygenic photosynthesis** using bacteriochlorophyll *a* and other pigments, but don't use reduced sulfur as an electron source. They are primarily photoheterotrophic when growing anaerobically and chemoheterotrophic when growing aerobically. Most are thermophilic. *Chloroflexus* is the type genus (Figure 11-5). Cells are 0.5–1.0 μm wide and 2–6 μm long.

11-5 *Chloroflexus* **Habitat in Whirligig Geyser Runoff, Yellowstone National Park** *Chloroflexus* is the most studied member of the Chloroflexi. It stains Gram-negative, but lacks an outer membrane and, in fact, has a wall structure more consistent with Gram-positive cells. *Chloroflexus* can be found forming orange microbial mats in the runoff of low sulfur hot springs, often in association with cyanobacteria. Their preferred temperature is between 50 and 60°C. (The green algae at the left of the channel grow between 38 and 56°C, dramatically illustrating the varied habitats of Yellowstone's geological features and the variety of thermophilic organisms that reside in them.)

Phylum *Spirochaetes*

Spirochaetes are free living, symbiotic, or parasitic chemoheterotrophs. They are Gram-negative, flexible, tightly coiled rods. The cell wall, cell membrane, and cytoplasm constitute the **protoplasmic cylinder**, which is surrounded by the outer membrane or **outer sheath**. Between two and 100 **periplasmic flagella** are wound along the spiral cell in the space between the sheath and the protoplasmic cylinder.

One end of each flagellum is anchored to a pole of the protoplasmic cylinder, with an equal number attached at each end. The flagella can propel the cell forward, cause it to rotate on its axis, or flex. Aerobic, facultatively anaerobic, and anaerobic species are represented. Important genera include *Spirochaeta* (Figure 5-15), *Borrelia* (Figure 12-11), *Treponema* (Figure 12-68), and *Leptospira*.

Phylum *Cyanobacteria*

Cyanobacteria are easily seen without staining because of their combination of photosynthetic pigments, which confer on them a bluish-green color. In fact, they were formerly known as "blue-green algae." All are capable of oxygenic photosynthesis (oxygen is a waste product) and all are Gram-negative, though their peptidoglycan is thicker than most other Gram-negatives. When they are single-celled, they are about the size of bacteria. But when they are found in chains, called **trichomes**, they are easily visible at high dry magnification. Some trichomes have an extracellular **sheath**. Trichomes often have specialized cells, including **heterocysts**, which are nitrogen-fixing cells, and **akinetes**, which are resistant spores. Many trichomes are capable of gliding motility. Figures 11-6 to 11-13 illustrate some common forms and cyanobacterial variability. All micrographs are unstained wet mount preparations.

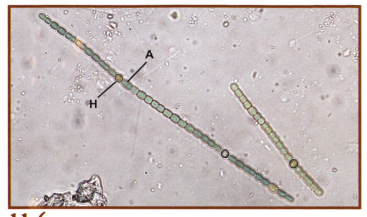

11-6 *ANABAENA* The trichomes of this gliding cyanobacterium may possess thick-walled spores called **akinetes** (**A**) and specialized, nitrogen-fixing cells called **heterocysts** (**H**). Trichomes are of variable lengths but are approximately 20 μm in width.

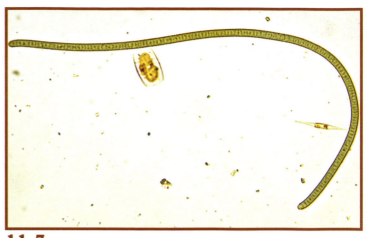

11-7 *OSCILLATORIA* Trichomes are formed from disc-shaped cells that are approximately 10 μm in width. Watch for gliding motility.

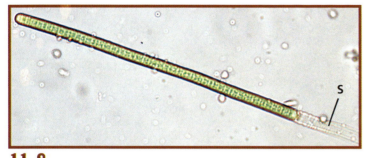

11-8 *LYNGBYA* *Lyngbya* trichomes have a sheath (**S**) that distinguish them from *Oscillatoria* (Figure 11-7). The trichomes are approximately 20 μm in width.

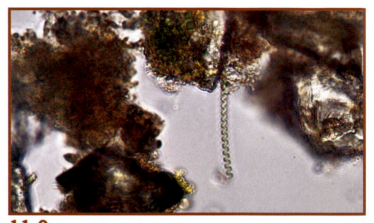

11-9 *SPIRULINA* *Spirulina* is perhaps the most distinctive cyanobacterium because of its helical shape. The width of the helix varies, but can obtain sizes up to 12 μm. This genus is sold in health food stores as a dietary supplement.

11-10 *NOSTOC* **A** This genus is easily identified macroscopically because of its globular colonies and thick, rubbery mucilage. **B** Trichomes are composed of spherical cells and form a tangled mass within the colony. Note the terminal spherical heterocysts. Trichomes are about 5 μm in width.

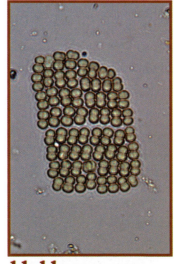

11-11 *MERISMOPEDIA* Cell division in two perpendicular directions produces the planar arrangement characteristic of this genus. The cells are enclosed in a mucilaginous sheath and are approximately 1–2 μm in diameter.

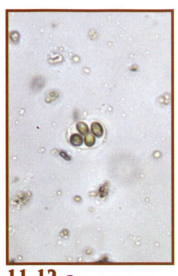

11-12 *GLOEOCAPSA* This cyanobacterium is distinctive because of its one, two, or four spherical cells held together within a layered sheath. Cells are 3–10 μm in diameter.

11-13 STROMATOLITES Stromatolites are made of layers of cyanobacteria, sediments, and minerals stacked upon one another. Fossil stromatolites have been dated to 3.5 billion years before the present. **A** These marine stromatolites are found at Shark Bay, Western Australia. They are in the 1 meter height range. **B** Hyperthermophilic stromatolites form in some runoff channels draining geothermal springs in Yellowstone National Park. These were found growing in the Mammoth Springs area and are only a few centimeters in height.

Photograph A courtesy of Ian and Todd Molloy, Crikey Adventure Tours

Phylum *Proteobacteria*

The largest and most diverse *Bacterial* phylum is the *Proteobacteria*. All are Gram-negative and show relationship based on 16s RNA comparison. Beyond that, they exhibit the gamut of aerotolerance, energy metabolism, and cell morphology categories. They also comprise the most commonly cultivated Gram-negative organisms of medical, industrial and general importance. The phylum is split into five classes: *Alphaproteobacteria*, *Betaproteobacteria*, *Gammaproteobacteria*, *Deltaproteobacteria*, and *Epsilonproteobacteria*. In the following, most groups are treated by order, but some physiological abilities span several classes and it is easier to cover these as a functional group rather than taxonomically.

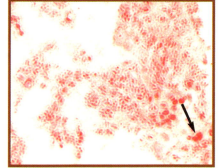

11-14 ACETOBACTER *Acetobacter* species are capable of oxidizing ethanol to acetic acid (acetate) during aerobic respiration. It further oxidizes the acetic acid to CO_2 and H_2O. In older cultures, involution forms can be observed. Some of these irregularly shaped cells are visible in this micrograph (**arrow**).

Alphaproteobacteria

Rhodospirillales

Rhodospirillaceae (type genus: *Rhodospirillum*) and Acetobacteraceae (type genus: *Acetobacter*) are the two families of this order.

● *Rhodospirillum* is a photoheterotroph and is covered in the purple nonsulfur bacteria (page 129).

● *Acetobacter* (Figure 11-14) and *Gluconobacter* (Figure 11-15) are two genera of "acetic acid bacteria." They are obligate aerobic respirers that oxidize ethanol to acetic acid. The former then oxidizes acetate to CO_2 and H_2O, whereas the latter does not.

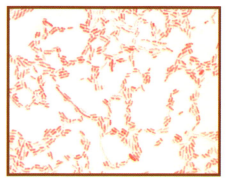

11-15 GLUCONOBACTER Like *Acetobacter*, *Gluconobacter* is capable of oxidizing ethanol, but it can't complete the oxidation to CO_2 and H_2O.

Rickettsiales

Members of this order are obligate intracellular parasites that include a vertebrate and an arthropod host in their life

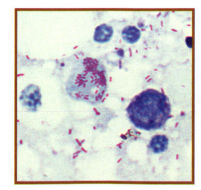

11-16 RICKETTSIA RICKETTSII This is a Giemenez stain of yolk sac infected with *Rickettsia rickettsii*. They must be grown in tissue culture because they are obligate intracellular parasites. The cells range in size from 0.2 by 0.5 µm to 0.3 by 2.0 µm.

Photo by Billie Ruth Bird (CDC), courtesy of the Public Health Image Library

cycles. Many are pathogenic. Important genera are *Rickettsia* (Figure 11-16) and *Ehrlichia*.

Caulobacterales

Caulobacter (Figure 11-17) is the type genus. Cells are vibrioid or elongated with tapered ends. An adhesive **stalk**, made from the cell wall and cytoplasmic membrane, emerges from one end. During division, the cell produces a daughter cell from the unattached end, which develops a flagellum and swims away after the cells separate. It eventually loses the flagellum, develops a stalk, and attaches to a surface. They are strict aerobic respirers found in freshwater, sewage, and bottled water!

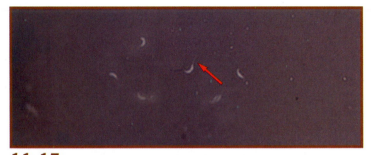

11-17 CAULOBACTER This micrograph is a negative stain of *Caulobacter* grown in pure culture. The cells are vibrioid; the stalk is faintly visible on some cells (**arrow**).

Betaproteobacteria
Neisseriales

Members of this order are typically single cocci or diplococci with adjacent sides flattened, though some are rods and spirals. They are Gram-negative (though may resist decolorization), chemoorganotrophic, oxidase positive, nonmotile, and aerobic or facultatively anaerobic. Representative genera include *Neisseria* (Figure 12-42), *Aquaspirillum*, and *Chromobacterium* (Figures 3-25 and 3-26).

Epsilonproteobacteria
Campylobacterales

The species of this order are Gram-negative, chemoorganotrophic, microaerophiles. Cell morphologies range from curved rods to S-shaped or helical rods. Most are motile and exhibit a corkscrew motion. Carbohydrates are not used as an energy source. *Campylobacter* (Figures 12-14 and 12-15) is the type genus and includes two pathogenic species: *C. jejuni* and *C. fetus*. The former causes gastroenteritis and abortion; the latter causes abortion in cattle and sheep.

Gammaproteobacteria
Pseudomonadales

The Pseudomonads are the "type" group for the *Proteobacteria*, meaning they are the ones against which the others

are compared for similarity. Pseudomonads are respiratory aerobic chemoorganotrophs and are either nonmotile or motile by polar or peritrichous flagella. Important genera are *Pseudomonas* (Figures 12-49 and 12-50) and *Azotobacter* (which is covered as a nitrogen-fixer on page 233 and is shown in Figure 19-29).

"Vibrionales"[1]

Vibrios are straight to curved rods that are motile by polar flagella. All are facultative anaerobes, capable of aerobic respiration and fermentation. Most are found in aquatic habitats and some are bioluminescent (Figure 19-21). Important genera are *Vibrio* with more than 40 species, and *Photobacterium*. Some *Vibrio* species are pathogenic (*e.g., V. cholerae*—Figures 12-69 and 12-70).

"Enterobacteriales"

This order comprises 42 genera. Their cells are straight rods, 0.3–1.0 μm wide by 1.0–6.0 μm long, and are motile by peritrichous flagella or nonmotile. They are chemoorganotrophs, capable of both aerobic respiration and fermentation, in which acid is produced from glucose. Most reduce NO_3^- to NO_2^- (page 83), are oxidase negative (page 87), and catalase positive (page 63). They also share a unique antigen (enterobacterial common antigen). Although the name "Enterobacteriales" literally means, "gut bacteria," their habitats also include soil, water, and plant material. Important genera include *Enterobacter*, *Citrobacter* (page 139), *Erwinia*, *Escherichia* (page 144), *Klebsiella* (Figure 11-18), *Proteus* (page 153), *Salmonella* (pages 155 and 156), *Shigella* (page 156), and *Yersinia* (page 163).

---

[1] Order names within quotation marks indicate that the order has no formal taxonomic standing.

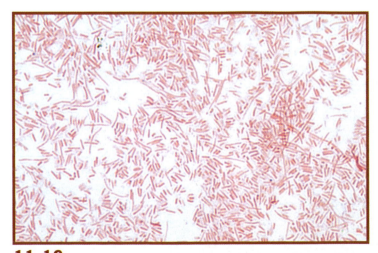

11-18 KLEBSIELLA MOBILIS (NÉE ENTEROBACTER AEROGENES) DNA-DNA hybridization studies show that *Enterobacter aerogenes* is more closely related to *Klebsiella* than to *Enterobacter cloacae*. As a result, *E. aerogenes* is now considered to be *Klebsiella mobilis*.

Nitrogen-Fixing Bacteria

Nitrogen-fixing bacteria are able to convert N_2 to ammonia. Some nitrogen-fixing bacteria (*e.g.*, *Rhizobium*, an *Alphaproteobacterium*) are symbionts of certain legumes and form nodules in their roots (Figures 19-26 though 19-28). Other nitrogen-fixing bacteria, such as *Azotobacter* (in the Pseudomonadales) are free-living in the soil (Figure 19-29). Most aquatic nitrogen fixation is performed by cyanobacteria, such as *Anabaena* (Figure 19-30)

Nitrifying Bacteria

Nitrification is the process of making nitrate (NO_3^-). Nitrifying bacteria are autotrophs and chemolithotrophs. Some nitrifiers use ammonium ion as an electron and energy source when it is oxidized to nitrite (NO_2^-); others then use the nitrite as an electron and energy source and oxidize it to nitrate. Organisms such as *Nitrosomonas* perform the ammonia oxidation. Ammonia-oxidizing bacteria are found in the *Betaproteobacteria* and *Gammaproteobacteria*. Nitrite-oxidizing organisms, such as *Nitrobacter*, continue the oxidation of nitrite to nitrate. Nitrite-oxidizers are found in the *Alphaproteobacteria*, *Gammaproteobacteria*, and *Deltaproteobacteria* (though the latter group is still in question).

Nitrosomonas (Figure 11-19) is a *Betaproteobacterium* that performs ammonia oxidation. Its cells range from spherical to rod-shaped, and may be seen as singles or short chains. The electron microscope reveals internal flattened membranous vesicles at the periphery of the cytoplasm that are involved in ATP production from ammonia oxidation. Some species can oxidize urea, producing CO_2 for autotrophic growth and NH_3 for ATP production—highly efficient! *Nitrosomonas* is most frequently isolated from aquatic habitats rich in ammonia, and occasionally from soil.

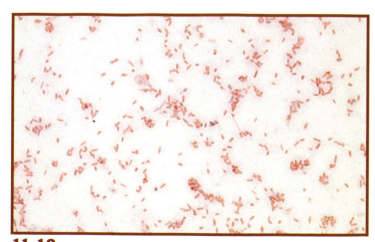

11-19 **NITROSOMONAS** *Nitrosomonas* is a genus of Gram-negative nitrifying bacteria found in seawater, brackish water, and freshwater, as well as soils. The cells are straight rods 0.7–1.5 μm wide by 1.5–2.4 μm long. They are aerobic chemoautotrophs that obtain energy by oxidizing ammonia to nitrite. This specimen was obtained from soil grown on an enrichment medium containing ammonia as the only nitrogen source.

Nitrobacter (Figure 11-19) is an *Alphaproteobacterium* that oxidizes NO_2^- to NO_3^-. Its cells are rods of various shapes (**pleomorphic**) that measure 0.5–0.9 μm wide by 1.0–2.0 μm long. The electron microscope reveals intracytoplasmic membranes organized at one pole of the cell and specialized regions for carbon-fixation called **carboxysomes**. Reproduction occurs via binary fission or budding. *Nitrobacter* species are capable of aerobic and anaerobic respiration.

Purple Nonsulfur *Bacteria*

Rhodospirillum (*Alphaproteobacteria*) is a freshwater photoheterotroph, but can live chemoorganotrophically in the dark and photoautotrophically with H_2 and sulfide as electron donors. Cells are curved rods to spirals (Figures 3-37 and 5-14) with internal photosynthetic membranes and bacteriochlorophyll *a*. Polar flagella provide motility.

Purple Sulfur *Bacteria*

The unifying feature of the purple sulfur bacteria is their ability to use H_2S as the electron donor for CO_2 reduction in photosynthesis. The S^0 resulting from H_2S oxidation is either stored as intracellular or extracellular granules. Because oxygen is not a product, these photoautotrophs are said to perform **anoxygenic photosynthesis** (as opposed to the oxygenic photosynthesis of cyanobacteria). The photosynthetic pigments bacteriochlorophyll *a* and carotenoids are embedded in the membranes of vesicles formed from infoldings of the cytoplasmic membrane. Purple sulfur bacteria are found in freshwater and marine mud and sediments illuminated by sunlight but lacking oxygen. All known species belong to the *Gammaproteobacteria*. The genera *Chromatium* and *Allochromatium* (Figure 19-33) belong to this group.

Green Sulfur *Bacteria* (Phylum *Chlorobi*)

The green sulfur bacteria constitute another group of anoxygenic phototrophs and also use H_2S as the electron donor. In addition to bacteriochlorophyll *a*, they possess a distinctive set of other bacteriochlorophylls, which are enclosed in membranous structures called **chlorosomes** that are located just to the interior of the cytoplasmic membrane. Another distinctive feature of these bacteria is that the chlorosome "membrane" does not have the usual phospholipid bilayer construction. Carbon fixation occurs by the reverse Krebs cycle. While found in similar habitats as the purple sulfur bacteria (*i.e.*, aquatic, anoxic, H_2S-rich mud), they are able to grow at deeper levels because the chlorosomes are extremely efficient at capturing the limited light. *Chlorobium* is the type genus of the phylum. A Winogradsky column with green sulfur bacterial growth is shown in Figure 11-20.

11-20 **Green Sulfur Bacteria** An accumulation of green sulfur bacteria is visible on the left side of this Winogradsky column.

Sulfur Oxidizing *Bacteria*

This *Bacterial* group is composed of chemolithotrophic organisms that get their energy by oxidizing reduced sulfur compounds, such as H_2S and S^0. They are also autotrophic. Examples include the genera *Beggiatoa* (Figures 19-32 and 19-34) and *Thiothrix* (both *Gammaproteobacteria*). They are distinctive because they form long filaments, move by gliding, and store sulfur granules in their cytoplasm. More information about sulfur oxidizing *Bacteria* can be found on pages 235 and 236.

Desulfovibrionales (*Deltaproteobacteria*)

Desulfovibrio is the type genus of the order. Its cells are curved (sometimes straight) motile rods. Metabolism is primarily respiratory, with sulfate as the final electron acceptor of the ETS being reduced to sulfide. Figure 19-35 shows a community of sulfur reducing bacteria recovered from anoxic mud.

Phylum *Firmicutes*

Members of this phylum are diverse and generally have a low $G+C\%$ (<50%). Most are Gram-positive, many of these with teichoic acids, but some genera are Gram-negative. Cell morphology ranges from cocci to rods of various shapes. Some produce endospores. The phylum includes aerobes, facultative anaerobes, and obligate anaerobes. Most are chemoorganotrophic mesophiles and neutrophiles.

Bacillales

Bacillaceae is the largest family (of the more than ten) within the order Bacillales, and *Bacillus* is by far the largest genus within the family. Species of *Bacillus* are rod-shaped and generally stain Gram-positive, at least when young. They form endospores (Figure 6-23) and are either aerobic or facultatively anaerobic. Most are soil organisms, though *B. anthracis* is a pathogen of cattle and humans (page 134). *B. mycoides* (Figure 3-9c) produces very distinctive colonies.

Listeriaceae

Listeriaceae comprises two genera, *Listeria* and *Brochothrix*, with the former being the larger of the two. *Listeria* (Figure 12-35) rods are short with blunt ends. They are aerobic or facultatively anaerobic, motile, but do not form endospores. *L. monocytogenes* is the causative agent of listeriosis.

Staphylococcaceae

Staphylococcus (Figures 5-24 and 12-57) is the largest genus of the four in *Staphylococcaceae*. They form characteristic grapelike clusters of spherical cells. No endospores are formed and they are usually catalase positive (page 63) and oxidase negative (page 87). Metabollically, they can ferment and aerobically respire, making them facultative anaerobes. *S. aureus* (page 157) and *S. epidermidis* (page 158) are normal inhabitants of the human body, but both are opportunistic pathogens.

Lactobacillales

This order comprises six families, of which only three will be addressed: *Lactobacillaceae*, *Streptococcaceae*, and *Enterococcaceae*.

The type genus of the *Lactobacillaceae* is *Lactobacillus* (Figure 11-21), whose cells range from long, slender rods to coccobacilli. They are Gram-positive, do not produce endospores, and are nutritionally fastidious. Lacking a cytochrome system, their metabolism is strictly fermentative with lactate being the primary end product. (Some species are **homofermentative**, meaning lactate is the sole end product of fermentation; others are **heterofermentative** and produce multiple end products.) They are found in the oral cavity, intestines, and vagina of mammals and are not considered to be pathogenic to healthy individuals. Some species are useful in making dairy products (*e.g.*, cheese and yogurt) whereas others are active in food spoilage.

The family *Streptococcaceae* is composed of species whose cells are spherical to ovoid and usually occur in pairs or chains. They are catalase negative (page 63) and produce lactic acid as the end product of fermentation. Often, elevated CO_2 in the environment is required for growth. Hemolytic reaction on blood agar (page 61) and serological testing for cell wall carbohydrates (for placement into one of the Lancefield groups—first established by Rebecca

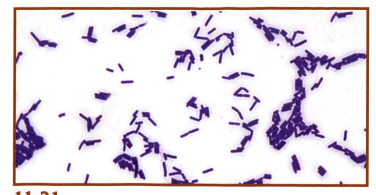

11-21 *LACTOBACILLUS PLANTARUM* *Lactobacillus* cells are Gram-positive, nonsporing rods of varying sizes (*L. plantarum* is among the largest, reaching lengths up to 8 μm). Metabolism is fermentative, with lactate comprising the majority of end products.

Lancefield in 1933) remain important characteristics in identifying *Streptococcus* species. *S. pneumoniae* (page 160) and *S. pyogenes* (page 161) are important human pathogens, but the majority of species are commensals of mucous membranes of warm-blooded animals. *Lactococcus*, once included in the genus *Streptococcus* because of morphological and metabolic similarities, was formed because there are many biochemical differences, including the Lancefield Group N antigen.

The family *Enterococcaceae* comprises four genera, but the type genus (and largest genus) is *Enterococcus* (Figure 11-22). Members of this genus are ovoid Gram-positive cocci usually arranged in pairs or short chains. Most perform

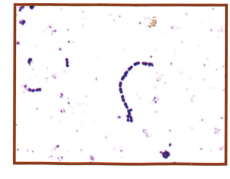

11-22 *ENTEROCOCCUS FAECIUM* Short chains of ovoid cocci are typical of the genus *Enterococcus*.

homofermentative metabolism with lactic acid being the primary end product. Catalase (page 63) is not produced. Most are resistant to 40% bile and hydrolyze esculin (page 60). At one time they were classified as Lancefield Group D *Streptococcus*, but more recently identified *Enterococcus* species do not demonstrate this antigen. Of the 30+ species, two are common human commensals (and opportunistic pathogens): *E. faecalis* and *E. faecium*.

Clostridiales

This order is large and diverse. We will focus on the type genus, *Clostridium* (Figure 11-23), which itself has 168 species! As a rule, clostridia are Gram-positive, obligately anaerobic, endospore-forming rods. They lack an electron transport chain and are thus fermentative. The fermentable substrate is often either carbohydrate(s) or amino acids, and the end products represent a wide range of organic compounds. Most are found in anaerobic regions of soil and mammalian digestive tracts. Five pathogenic species are covered beginning on page 140.

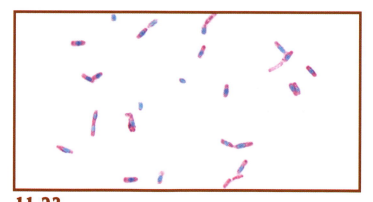

11-23 *CLOSTRIDIUM* Members of this genus are anaerobic, Gram-positive, endospore-forming rods. The spores often distend the cell, making the region look swollen. This is not the case in this micrograph of *C. sporogenes* grown in culture. See Figure 12-22 for a micrograph of *C. tetani* and its terminal spores causing a swelling of the cell.

Phylum *Actinobacteria*

Actinobacteria is a large and diverse phylum with a single order (Actinomycetales). Cells are typically Gram-positive rods with a high G+C%. Most are aerobes. They are found in soil and plant material, though there are some pathogens. Six families will be covered: *Corynebacteriaceae*, *Mycobacteriaceae*, *Micrococcaceae*, *Nocardiaceae*, *Propionibacteriaceae*, and *Streptomycetaceae*.

Cells of the family *Corynebacteriaceae* are irregularly-shaped rods that form "V" shapes as a result of "snapping division," where the adjoining wall between cells incompletely

separates (Figure 5-27). They are sometimes club-shaped (Figure 6-30). Metabolism is fermentative with acid, but no gas, being the end product. They are facultative anaerobes and are catalase positive (page 63). *Corynebacterium* species are found on mammalian mucous membranes. *C. diphtheriae* is a human pathogen (page 143).

A defining characteristic of the *Mycobacteriaceae* is that they are acid-fast at some point in their life cycle (page 49 and Figures 6-16 and 6-18) due to an abundance of waxy mycolic acid in their walls. They stain weakly Gram-positive because of the mycolic acid. *Mycobacterium* species are nutritionally nonfastidious, though *M. leprae* cannot be cultivated in standard bacteriological media because it is an intracellular parasite. Differentiation between *Mycobacterium* species relies, in part, on whether the isolate is a "slow grower" or a "fast grower," and whether it produces a carotenoid pigment in the light ("photochromogenic"), in the light or dark ("scotochromogenic") or not at all. Two important pathogens are *M. leprae* (Figure 12-37) and *M. tuberculosis* (Figure 12-38).

Micrococcus (Figure 11-24) is the type genus for the family *Micrococcaceae*. Its cells are cocci, ranging in diameter from 0.5–2 μm, and are often arranged into tetrads or irregular clusters. They are aerobic, respiratory chemoheterotrophs and are usually (weakly) oxidase and catalase positive (pages 87 and 63, respectively). They are found on human skin and in the soil. *Arthrobacter* is also in this family (Figure 11-25). Its cells are rods during exponential growth, but fragment to form cocci in stationary phase.

Propionibacterium is the type genus of the family *Propionibacteriaceae*. Cells are Gram-positive, pleomorphic rods that are often arranged in "V" or "Y" configurations. Metabolism is fermentative, with large amounts of propionic acid as the end product. They are aerotolerant to varying degrees. *Propionibacterium* is found in dairy products and is the primary fermenter in Swiss cheese production. They also inhabit human skin. *P. acnes* (Figure 11-26) is an example.

Species of *Nocardiaceae* produce branched filaments (hyphae) that cover and penetrate the growth surface. Aerial hyphae are also produced. *Nocardia* species are aerobic, weakly Gram-positive or Gram-variable, and partially acidfast. *Nocardia asteroides* (Figures 12-44 through 12-46) is a human pathogen.

Superficially, members of the family *Streptomycetaceae* have much in common with fungi, but they aren't considered fungi because they are prokaryotic. However, due to these similarities (and for historical reasons), fungal terminology is applied to them. Streptomycetes produce branching hyphae that intertwine to form a **mycelium**. As the mycelium ages, aerial hyphae emerge and produce reproductive spores at their tips. The type genus, *Streptomyces* (Figure 11-27), comprises 500 + species. They are Gram-positive obligate

aerobes with the ability to metabolize diverse carbon compound from their environment, which is frequently the soil. Many produce **geosmin**, a chemical responsible for the "earthy" fragrance of soil. The majority of *Streptomyces* species also produce antibiotics.

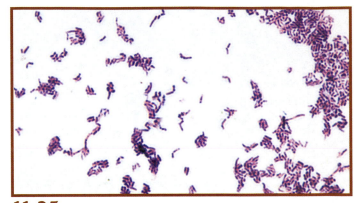

11-25 **ARTHROBACTER** Cells in the preparation made from *Arthrobacter* grown in culture demonstrate the angular arrangement from which their name is derived ("arthro" means "joint"). The slide was made during exponential growth of the culture, as evidenced by most cells being rod-shaped. As a culture enters stationary phase, the rods fragment and form coccid cells.

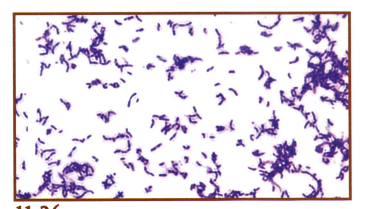

11-26 **PROPIONIBACTERIUM** This micrograph is of *Propionibacterium acnes* grown in culture. *P. acnes* is a commensal that lives in sebaceous glands (associated with hair follicles) and gets its energy from digesting the oily secretion. If the pore becomes blocked and ruptures, an infection can occur and produce a pimple.

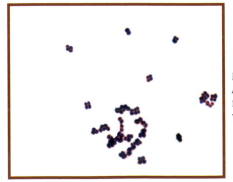

11-24 **MICROCOCCUS** Members of the genus *Micrococcus* frequently form tetrads. These cells were grown in culture.

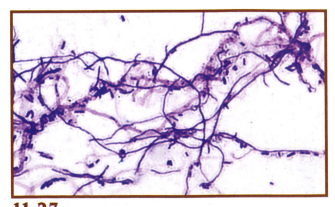

11-27 **STREPTOMYCES** This is a micrograph of *Streptomyces griseus* grown in culture. Note the branched hyphae and spores. The spores are approximately 1 μm in length.

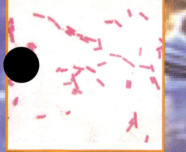

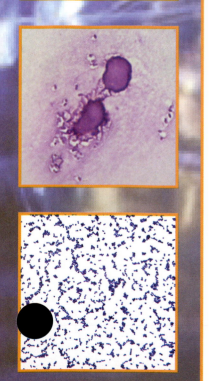

Bacterial Pathogens

Aeromonas hydrophila

Aeromonas hydrophila (Class *Gammaproteobacteria*) is a leech gut symbiont found in aquatic habitats worldwide. It causes infections by colonizing leech bite wounds, open trauma wounds, or by being ingested as a food or water contaminant. When ingested, it adheres to the intestinal mucous membrane and produces an **enterotoxin** that causes acute watery diarrhea. When introduced through a superficial wound, the organism may be contained locally or spread throughout surrounding tissue in a condition called cellulitis. Rarely, when introduced through an open wound (especially deep penetrating wounds) it can produce a gas gangrene-like infection called *A. hydrophila* myonecrosis. Both cellulitis and *A. hydrophila* myonecrosis can quickly lead to bacteremia and systemic toxicity. Mortality rates are high among leukemia, lymphoma, and otherwise immunosuppressed patients following sepsis.

Differential Characteristics

A. hydrophila is a motile, facultatively anaerobic Gram-negative rod (Figures 12-1 and 12-2). It ferments sucrose and mannitol, is positive for ONPG, indole, lysine decarboxylase, and esculin

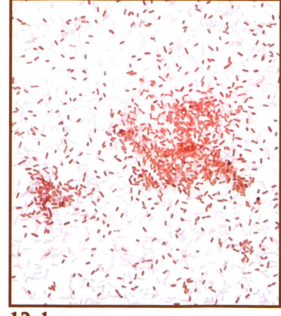

12-1 **GRAM STAIN OF AN *AEROMONAS HYDRO-PHILA* STOCK CULTURE** Cells can range in size from 1 μm or less wide and 1.0–3.5 μm long with rounded ends.

12-2 **AEROMONAS HYDROPHILA ON MACCONKEY AGAR** MacConkey Agar is typically used to identify coliforms—Gram-negative organisms that discolor the medium and produce pink colonies. *A. hydrophila* can be distinguished by its lack of color.

hydrolysis, and negative for ornithine decarboxylase. Diagnostic procedures include Gram stain, aerobic and anaerobic blood culture, stool culture, and wound culture. A positive oxidase result helps differentiate it from enterics.

Treatment

Administration of third generation cephalosporins, fluoro-quinolones, sulfamethoxazole, or trimethoprim.

Bacillus anthracis

Since the September 11, 2001 terrorist attack on the World Trade Center and the subsequent discovery of *Bacillus anthracis* spores in mail and other locations, this organism has received a great deal of attention. While that attention is important and necessary, "weaponized" bacteria or other microbes are not within the scope of this manual. When an organism is grown and processed as a biological weapon its effect on the population is dependent on innumerable variables such as strain, its current form and concentration, and all circumstances surrounding its distribution. Under such conditions the organism's virulence is, at the very least, unpredictable. Therefore, we discuss understood and observable characteristics of "wild-type" organisms and avoid speculating on the potential of man-made versions.

Bacillus anthracis (Phylum *Firmicutes*) causes anthrax in animals (mostly herbivores) and, more rarely, in humans. The intestinal tract of asymptomatic large animals is its principal habitat; however, *B. anthracis* spores have been known to remain viable in the soil for years. Three types of anthrax occur in humans: cutaneous anthrax, inhalation anthrax ("woolsorter's disease"), and gastrointestinal anthrax. The cutaneous and inhalation forms are most frequently the result of contact with spores carried in wool or goat hair; gastrointestinal disease usually results from the consumption of contaminated meat.

Two virulence factors account for the organism's pathogenicity: 1) a capsule which enables it to survive phagocytosis and disseminate via the bloodstream, and 2) secretion of three exotoxins—edema toxin, lethal toxin, and protective antigen. Protective antigen forms pores in the target cell's membrane, which allows entry of the other toxins. Edema toxin is responsible for the necrotic lesions (eschars) surrounded by large areas of swelling characteristic of cutaneous anthrax. Lethal toxin is a protease that interferes with cytokine production, neutrophil chemotaxis, and macrophage survival—all of which compromise the immune system and allow rapid multiplication of the pathogen. This is followed by entry into the blood, producing bacteremia, shock, and meningitis. [**Note:** Two plasmids—pOX1 and pOX2 are responsible for toxin and capsule production respectively. In addition, a product of pOX1 helps regulate capsule production by pOX2. Yet, surprisingly, organisms missing pOX1 are nearly as virulent as unaltered organisms, which suggests the possible presence of other undiscovered virulence factors.]

Differential Characteristics

B. anthracis is a facultatively anaerobic, nonmotile, encapsulated, endospore-forming, Gram-positive rod (Figures 12-3 and 12-4). It will not grow on phenylethyl alcohol blood agar, is catalase-positive, and gelatinase-negative.

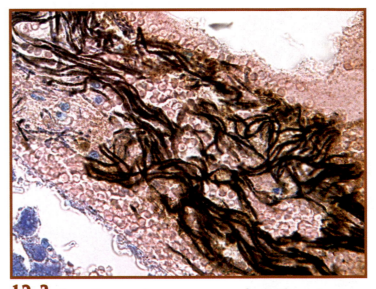

12-3 GRAM STAIN OF *BACILLUS ANTHRACIS* IN A MOUSE LIVER BLOOD VESSEL Cells resemble *Bacillus cereus* and are approximately 1 μm wide by 3.0–5.0 μm long.

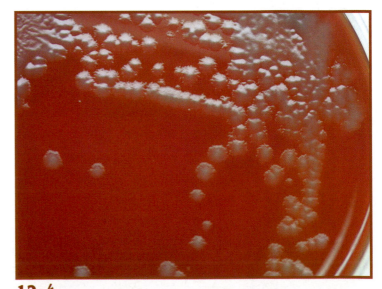

12-4 *BACILLUS ANTHRACIS* ON SHEEP BLOOD AGAR *B. anthracis* typically produces large, gray, rough-textured colonies on Sheep Blood Agar. It is nonhemolytic.

Diagnostic procedures include Gram stain, endospore stain, and aerobic culture.

Treatment

Penicillin is the traditional treatment for anthrax, although *B. anthracis* has demonstrated susceptibility to a broad variety of antibiotics. Recently however, the strains of *B. anthracis* isolated from victims of the bioterrorist attacks of 2001, although susceptible to penicillin and ampicillin, demonstrated *in vitro* resistance to several previously effective antibiotics. Even more significantly, the organisms were found to contain constitutive and inducible β-lactamases, which could lead to penicillin resistance. (See β-lactamase Test on page 59.) As a result, the CDC has advised against the use of penicillin or ampicillin. Today the recommended treatment is a sixty-day regimen of doxycycline or ciprofloxacin (intravenous in severe cases) combined with a second antibiotic.

Bacillus cereus

Bacillus cereus (Phylum *Firmicutes*) is the second of two principal pathogens in the *Bacillus* genus (see *B. anthracis*, page 134*)*. It is responsible for two types of food poisoning and severe ocular infections. The mechanism of ocular infection is not well understood, but may be caused by interaction of three toxins—necrotic toxin (heat-labile enterotoxin), cereolysin (a powerful hemolysin), and phospholipase C (a lecithinase). This rapidly destructive form of infection is common among intravenous drug users, immunosuppressed patients, and farmworkers following eye trauma. Food poisoning from *B. cereus* presents in two forms—emetic form and diarrheal form. The emetic form is caused by heat-stable enterotoxin, appears one to six hours after exposure, and typically lasts less than 24 hours. It most frequently appears in cooked rice that has not been properly refrigerated. The spores that survive the initial cooking germinate and multiply rapidly, releasing toxin that is not destroyed by further cooking. The diarrheal form, caused by heat-labile enterotoxin, appears approximately nine hours after exposure, and typically lasts 24 to 36 hours. Foods that cause the diarrheal form are meat, vegetables, and sauces.

Differential Characteristics

B. cereus is a motile, facultatively anaerobic, endospore-forming, Gram-positive rod (Figures 12-5 and 12-6). It produces acid from glucose, maltose, and salicin fermentation, and is lecithinase- and gelatinase-positive. Diagnostic procedures include Gram stain and aerobic culture.

Treatment

Gastrointestinal disorders are not typically treated with antibiotics. *B. cereus* is often resistant to β-lactam drugs such as penicillin and cephalosporin. The recommended treatment for ocular and other infections is vancomycin by itself or in combination with an aminoglycoside such as gentamicin, neomycin, or streptomycin.

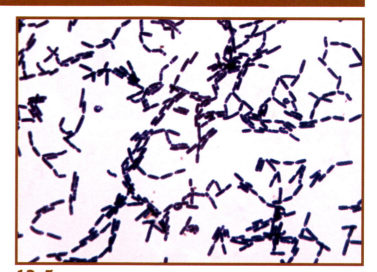

12-5 GRAM STAIN OF A *BACILLUS CEREUS* STOCK CULTURE Rods are approximately 1 μm wide by 3–5 μm long.

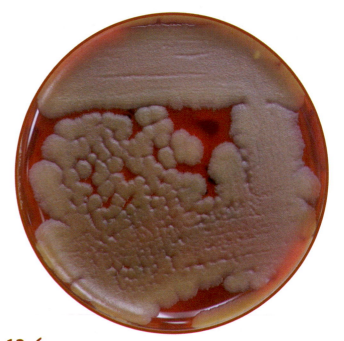

12-6 *BACILLUS CEREUS* ON SHEEP BLOOD AGAR Note the raised, dull, gray colony morphology compared to *B. anthracis* colonies in Figure 12-4.

Bacteroides fragilis

Several *Bacteroides* species (Phylum *Bacteroidetes*) reside in the human gastrointestinal tract and, to a lesser extent, in the female genital tract. Normal stool contains 10^{11} cells per gram, 1000 times greater than the facultative anaerobes! *Bacteroides fragilis* is responsible for the majority of intra-abdominal infections and is recovered from most other human infections. It causes intra-abdominal abscesses (peritonitis) and rarely lung abscesses. Intra-abdominal abscesses usually result after spillage of intestinal contents into the abdominal cavity from a ruptured appendix or a penetrating wound. Lung abscesses are usually a consequence of aspiration pneumonia and typically consist of a mixture of pathogens (polymicrobic) sometimes including *B. fragilis* and oral streptococci.

Differential Characteristics

B. fragilis is a pleomorphic, encapsulated, nonmotile, anaerobic, Gram-negative rod (Figures 12-7 and 12-8). It varies in size from 1.5 to 6 μm long. It does not ferment arabinose,

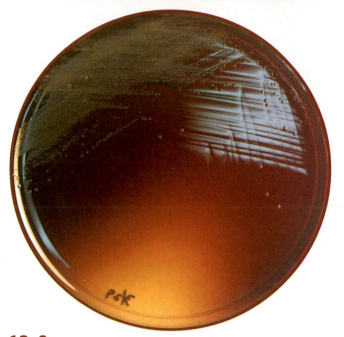

12-8 *BACTEROIDES FRAGILIS* GROWING ON BACTEROIDES BILE ESCULIN AGAR Note the darkening of the medium due to the reaction of esculin breakdown products with ferric ammonium citrate. For more information on Bile Esculin Agar, refer to Section 7.

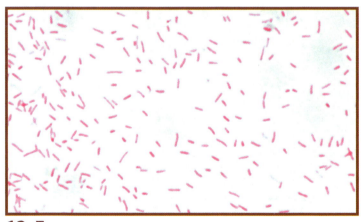

12-7 GRAM STAIN OF A *BACTEROIDES FRAGILIS* STOCK CULTURE Note the variable lengths (typically between 1.5 and 6 μm).

melezitose, or salicin, but grows well in the presence of 20% bile, is indole-negative, and catalase-positive (unusual for an anaerobe). Diagnostic procedures include Gram stain and anaerobic culture.

Treatment

Administration of metronidazole, clindamycin, ampicillin with sulbactam (a β-lactamase inhibitor), carbapenems, cefotetan, cefoxitin, piperacillin with tazobactam sodium, or ticarcillin with clavulanate potassium.

Bordetella pertussis

Bordetella pertussis (Class *Betaproteobacteria*) is the cause of the disease known as pertussis or "whooping cough," characterized by violent coughing, vomiting, and gasping for breath. It can infect anyone with no immunity or diminished immunity, but is most severe and communicable among infants less than one year of age. Humans are the exclusive host of this organism, and asymptomatic or unrecognized symptomatic adults are the likely reservoirs. This highly communicable organism infects greater than 90% of un-immunized people exposed. The bacteria enter the mouth or nasopharynx as aerosols then attach themselves to the respiratory cilia. Although the active disease caused by

B. pertussis appears to be a superficial infection, it secretes an array of virulence factors that destroy the underlying epithelial tissue and act to impair the body's natural defenses.

Differential Characteristics

B. pertussis is a small, nonmotile, obligately aerobic, Gram-negative coccobacillus (Figures 12-9 and 12-10). It is oxidase-positive, urease-negative, and nitrate-negative. Diagnostic procedures include polymerase chain reaction (PCR—page 111), direct fluorescent antibody (DFA—page 105), nasopharyngeal culture, and enzyme-linked immunosorbent assay (ELISA—page 103).

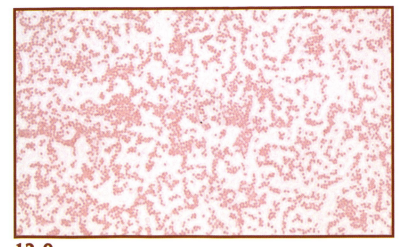

12-9 GRAM STAIN OF A *BORDETELLA PERTUSSIS* STOCK CULTURE These minute coccobacilli are usually arranged singly or in pairs and exhibit bipolar staining. They can range in size from 0.2–0.5 μm wide by 0.5–1.0 μm in length.

Treatment

Antibiotic treatment is primarily erythromycin, but also azithromycin, clarithromycin, tetracycline, sulfamethoxazole with trimethoprim, and chloramphenicol. But, the best treatment is immunization with 5 doses of pertussis vaccine—one at 2, 4, and 6 months of age, again at 15–18 months, and a final dose prior to entering school.

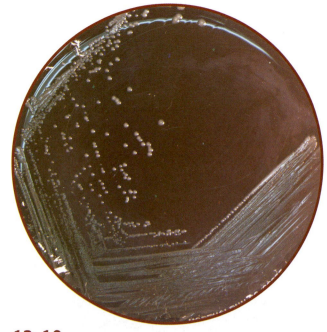

12-10 *BORDETELLA PERTUSSIS* GROWING ON REGAN-LOWE AGAR Regan-Lowe Agar is a selective medium designed to isolate *B. pertussis* and *B. parapertussis* from clinical specimens.

Borrelia burgdorferi

Borrelia burgdorferi (Phylum *Spirochaetes*) causes Lyme borreliosis, more commonly called Lyme disease because the first reported case occurred in 1977 in Lyme, Connecticut. *B. burgdorferi* was isolated in 1982 and thought to be the sole infective agent in the disease. Subsequent studies, however, have implicated at least 9 other *Borrelia* species.

Lyme disease is transmitted by two tick species from genus *Ixodes*—*I. dammini* and *I. pacificus*. It is estimated that from 30% to 75% of *I. dammini* carry the organism, which suggests why Lyme disease is the most common vector-borne illness in the United States. Disease carrying ticks reside most commonly in coastal wooded areas inhabited by white-footed mice and white-tailed deer. Nine states (California, Connecticut, Rhode Island, New Jersey, Pennsylvania, Minnesota, Wisconsin, Massachusetts, and New York) have reported 90% of all cases in the country.

Lyme borreliosis is characterized by three distinct stages: Stage 1. Localized, but expanding (erythema migrans), skin lesion accompanied by headache, fatigue, and malaise; Stage 2. Weeks to months later, the inflammation and pain become generalized with the possible development of

meningoencephalitis or myocarditis; Stage 3. After months or even years of latency the infection becomes chronic, producing severe headaches, muscle and joint pain, and secondary skin lesions.

Differential Characteristics

Borrelia burgdorferi is a motile, microaerophilic, Gram-negative, spirochete (Figure 12-11). The *B. burgdorferi* population in infected sites is low, so lab cultures are rarely positive. In their place, serological tests are used. An indirect enzyme-linked immunosorbent assay (ELISA—page 103), detects patient Igm and IgG targeting the spirochaete. A Western blot test (page 106) has higher specificity and is used to confirm positive ELISA tests. False negative ELISAs may result from a late rise in IgG just under half the patients and from the effect of antibiotic treatment.

Treatment

Administration of amoxicillin, deoxycycline, or cefuroxime.

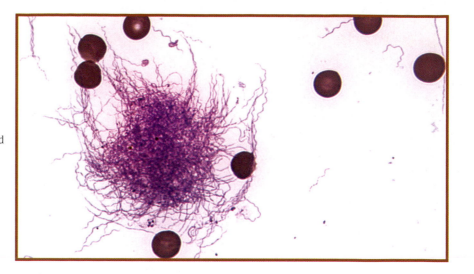

12-11 GIEMSA STAIN OF *BORRELIA BURGDORFERI* IN BLOOD   Although this organism is Gram-negative, it is best observed using Giemsa Stain. Note the red blood cells.

Brucella melitensis

Brucella melitensis (Class *Alphaproteobacteria*), the most virulent species of the genus *Brucella*, is a small, non-motile, aerobic, Gram-negative coccobacillus. Although most brucellae cause brucellosis (sometimes called undulant fever), *B. melitensis* is responsible for the most severe symptoms. Each of the infective agents of brucellosis has a domestic animal reservoir: *B. melitensis* (goats and sheep), *B. abortus* (cattle), *B. suis* (swine), and *B. canis* (dogs). Each organism has a different carrier, but all infect humans in three principal ways: ingestion, direct contact through abraded skin, or inhalation. The most common form in the United States is from ingestion of contaminated unpasteurized milk or other dairy products. *B. melitensis* resists the body's defense system because it is an intracellular parasite—it actually lives and multiplies inside macrophages. It travels throughout the body by way of the circulatory system, multiplying inside of and destroying host phagocytic cells, thus releasing more bacteria to continue the cycle. The result is granuloma formation and tissue destruction in the lymph nodes, bone marrow, kidneys, liver, and spleen.

Differential Characteristics

Brucella species can be preliminarily identified by cell and colony morphology, and growth characteristics in special *Brucella* media containing blood and antibiotics (Figures 12-12 and 12-13). Diagnostic procedures include *Brucella* blood culture, anaerobic culture, and Gram stain. A serum agglutination test (SAT—page 101) using *B. melitensis*-specific serum is used to confirm identification, as is an indirect ELISA (page 103).

Treatment

Administration of doxycycline in combination with rifampin or sulfamethoxazole and trimethoprim used in combination with rifampin.

12-12 GRAM STAIN OF A *BRUCELLA MELITENSIS* STOCK CULTURE   Cells are coccobacilli 0.5 μm wide by 0.6–1.7 μm long. Usually arranged singly, these poorly staining cells were counterstained for 5 minutes to darken the cells for photographic purposes.

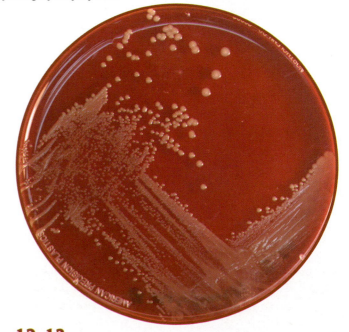

12-13 *BRUCELLA MELITENSIS* GROWING ON SHEEP BLOOD AGAR

Campylobacter jejuni

Campylobacter jejuni (Class *Epsilonproteobacteria*) is a common, worldwide human pathogen usually found in chickens, but also isolated from house pets, domestic animals, and waterfowl. It is estimated to cause more than 2 million cases of gastroenteritis each year in the United States. To put this number in perspective, *C. jejuni*-caused gastroenteritis is more common than that caused by *Salmonella* and *Shigella* combined!

Transmission of the disease is usually by ingestion of raw milk, undercooked poultry or meat, or contaminated water. Once inside the small intestine the organism corkscrews into the mucous layer, multiplies, and secretes a cholera-like enterotoxin that causes watery diarrhea. In most cases the infection is self-limiting and the diarrhea ends after a few days. Some strains, however, may secrete a cytotoxin that destroys local cells and causes bloody diarrhea. Dissemination by the bloodstream may result in salmonellosis-like enteritis and extraintestinal infection. In recent years, this organism has been implicated in a variety of infections including septic arthritis, meningitis, proctocolitis, spontaneous abortion, and Guillain-Barré syndrome, a degenerative nerve disorder.

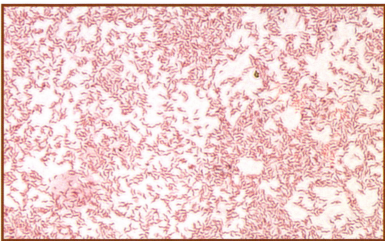

12-14 GRAM STAIN OF A *CAMPYLOBACTER JEJUNI* STOCK CULTURE Note the characteristic "S" and "gull wing" shapes of the paired organisms.

Differential Characteristics

C. jejuni is a motile, microaerophilic, capnophilic (requires 5% to 10% CO_2), nonsporing, Gram-negative helical or curved rod. Cells sometimes appear as "S" or "gull wing" shapes (Figure 12-14). It reduces nitrate to nitrite and hydrolyzes hippurate. Diagnostic procedures include aerobic and anaerobic blood culture, and stool culture (Figure 12-15).

Treatment

The infection typically resolves on its own, but the antibiotics azithromycin, ciprofloxacin, erythromycin, doxycycline, or fluoroquinolones may be used.

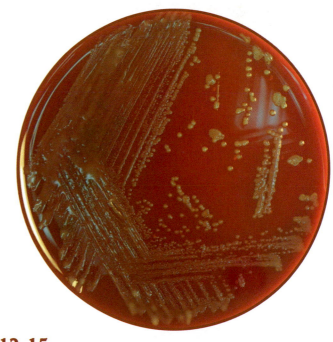

12-15 *CAMPYLOBACTER JEJUNI* ON SHEEP BLOOD AGAR

Citrobacter spp.

Species in the genus *Citrobacter* (Class *Gammaproteobacteria*) live almost exclusively in the human lower intestine. Unlike other members of the family *Enterobacteriaceae*, many of whom live freely outside a human host, presence of *Citrobacter* in the environment almost certainly suggests fecal contamination. *Citrobacter* species are potent opportunistic pathogens. They rarely cause disease in healthy people, but are significant agents of respiratory and urinary nosocomial infections, hospital-acquired bacteremia, and neonatal meningitis. Virulence factors include an enterotoxin and lipopolysaccharide outer membrane believed to mediate the "sepsis syndrome," including fever, leucopenia, and "disseminated intravascular coagulation." Sepsis involving *Citrobacter spp.* is usually polymicrobic whereas urinary infections and pneumonia tend to be monomicrobic, yielding pure cultures upon examination.

Differential Characteristics

Citrobacter spp. are motile, facultatively anaerobic Gram-negative rods (Figures 12-16 and 12-17). They ferment glucose and utilize citrate (often as the sole carbon source), are methyl red and catalase positive, and are Voges-Proskauer, oxidase, and lysine decarboxylase negative. Diagnostic procedures include Gram stain and aerobic culture.

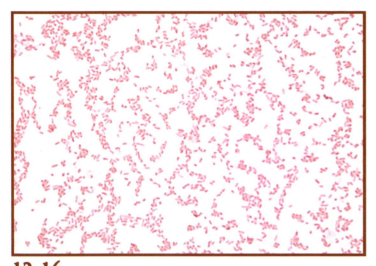

12-16 GRAM STAIN OF A *CITROBACTER KOSERI* STOCK CULTURE
These straight rods usually appear singly and are about 1 μm wide by 2.4 μm long.

12-17 *CITROBACTER KOSERI* ON SHEEP BLOOD AGAR

Treatment

Third generation cephalosporins, penicillins, imipenem with cilastatin, meropenem, or fluoroquinolones may be administered.

Clostridium botulinum

Clostridium botulinum (Phylum *Firmicutes*) is a spore forming anaerobe typically found in soil. Further, the spores are widely distributed in the environment. There are seven known strains—A, B, C, D, E, F, and G—each of which produces an antigenically distinct toxin. Neurotoxins A, B, E (and sometimes F)[1] cause botulism in humans. There are three types of botulism known to occur in humans—food-borne, infant, and wound. Although the word "botulism" has become almost synonymous with the food-borne illness, infant botulism actually occurs more frequently in the United States. Food-borne botulism most frequently occurs from ingesting insufficiently heated home-canned foods. Spores that remain viable in the undercooked food germinate and the resulting bacterial population flourishes in the anaerobic, nutrient-rich environment. Within a few hours to two days after ingestion the toxin travels, by way of the bloodstream, to cholinergic synapses where it irreversibly blocks release of acetylcholine. The result is "flaccid paralysis" (extreme weakness), usually beginning with cranial nerves (controlling facial muscles) and descending to the pharynx, neck, arms, and respiratory muscles, frequently resulting in respiratory failure and death. In infant botulism and wound botulism, bacterial colonization of the body occurs and *then* toxin is released. Once released, the toxin is absorbed into the bloodstream with progression and presentation of the disease similar to food-borne illness except that constipation is almost always an early sign of infant botulism. Fortunately, with proper treatment, infant botulism mortality is below 3%. It should be noted that food-borne botulism is easily preventable. Botulinum toxins (but not spores) are heat-labile and destroyed when boiled for at least 20 minutes.

Differential Characteristics

C. botulinum is a motile, anaerobic, endospore-forming, Gram-positive rod (Figure 12-18). Its spores are oval, sub-terminal, and distend the cell. Diagnostic procedures include toxin neutralization test in mice, isolation from feces (infant botulism), with cerebrospinal fluid analysis gas-liquid chromatography recommended for final identification.

[1] Type C produces bird disease, and type D infects other mammals.

Treatment

Botulinum Toxoid, Pentavalent Vaccine is an "investigational use" drug available as prophylaxis for people working with A, B, C, D, or E cultures. Trivalent anti-toxin (A, B, E) must be administered quickly to patients suspected of botulism intoxication.

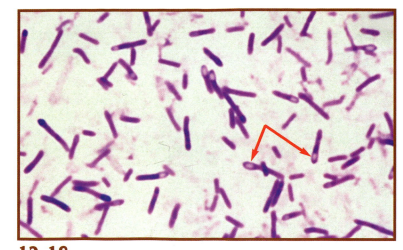

12-18 GRAM STAIN OF A *CLOSTRIDIUM BOTULINUM* STOCK CULTURE
Note the unstained oval subterminal endospores, which distend the cells (**arrows**). Cell sizes are highly variable between strains, ranging from about 0.5–2.0 µm wide by 3–20+ µm long!

Clostridium difficile

Clostridium difficile (Phylum *Firmicutes*) is a common pathogen found in water, soil, a variety of animal intestines, and the intestinal tracts of more than half of healthy human infants under one year of age. It is a strict anaerobe and can be killed by even brief exposure to oxygen. It produces highly resilient spores that are resistant to antibiotics and disinfectants and are virtually impossible to eliminate from the environment. It has been isolated from health-care workers, asymptomatic hospital patients, hospital bedding, sinks, toilet seats, and endoscopy equipment.

Many strains of the organism exist—some that produce toxins and other avirulent forms that do not. Most strains produce two toxins—A (an enterotoxin) and B (a cytopathic toxin). In humans, when the normal intestinal flora have been suppressed by antibiotic therapy, previously dormant intestinal *C. difficile* will proliferate, releasing toxins that may cause inflammation and necrosis of local cells. Nearly 90% of all *C. difficile*-caused diarrhea occurs in hospitals in one of the following forms: antibiotic-associated diarrhea (AAD), pseudomembranous colitis (PMC), or the more severe, antibiotic-associated colitis (AAC). Ampicillin, clindamycin, and fluoroquinolones are the major offenders. Rarely, *C. difficile* causes a severe form of "sepsis syndrome" that may require a variety of medical interventions including surgery.

Differential Characteristics

C. difficile is a motile, anaerobic, endospore-forming, Gram-positive rod (Figure 12-19). Diagnostic procedures include *Clostridium difficile* toxin assay, *Clostridium difficile* selective agar, and fecal leukocyte stain.

Treatment

Administration of medronidazole and vancoymcin.

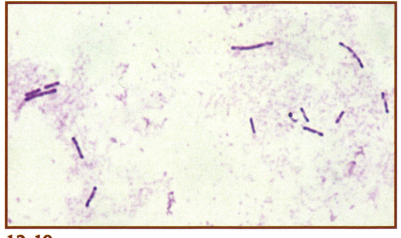

12-19 GRAM STAIN OF A *CLOSTRIDIUM DIFFICILE* STOCK CULTURE Although not easily seen in this micrograph, this organism does produce oval subterminal endospores. Cells can range in size from 0.5–1.9 µm wide by 3.0–17 µm long.

Clostridium perfringens

Clostridium perfringens (Phylum *Firmicutes*) is a very common spore-forming soil organism typically found living commensally in the gastrointestinal tract of humans and other mammals. The species has been divided into five types (A–E) based on the types of (or combinations of) toxins they produce. Type A produces alpha toxin, the lecithinase that causes the severe tissue damage associated with myonecrosis (gas gangrene) and fasciitis. It is also responsible for a type of gynecologic infection and anaerobic cellulitis. Gas gangrene, common in World War I because of the widespread soil contamination of battlefield wounds, is usually associated with traumatic wounds and crushing injuries, but also sometimes occurs after colon resections and septic abortions. The result is typically increased vascular permeability, hypotension, and shock. Death may occur within two days of onset of symptoms. Types B and C produce beta toxin that causes pigbel. Pigbel is a severe form of enteritis seen in New Guinea following feasts where large amounts of sweet potato and contaminated pork are eaten. Sweet potatoes contain protease inhibitors that prevent beta toxin degradation. The result is intense abdominal pain and bloody diarrhea sometimes accompanied by intestinal perforation. Types A, C, and D produce enterotoxin associated with the milder form of food poisoning. This heat-labile toxin is commonly found in contaminated meat or poultry and their products, such as gravies or stews. In much the same way as in *Bacillus cereus* food poisoning (page 135), *C. perfringens* spores that survive the heat during cooking germinate and produce enterotoxin when the conditions become favorable.

Differential Characteristics

Clostridium perfringens is a nonmotile, anaerobic, endospore-forming, Gram-positive rod (Figure 12-20). Although spores are produced by this organism, they are rarely seen in stained preparations. Diagnostic procedures include Gram stain, skin and muscle biopsy using direct or indirect fluorescent antibody (page 105), and anaerobic culture.

Treatment

Penicillin G, metronidazole, carbapenems or clindamycin may be used, but prompt administration of antitoxin is vital.

12-20 **GRAM STAIN OF *CLOSTRIDIUM PERFRINGENS*** Note the blunt ends of the cells and the absence of visible endospores because these cells were grown in culture. Cells can range in size from 0.6–2.4 µm wide by 1.3–19.0 µm long.

Clostridium septicum

Clostridium septicum (Phylum *Firmicutes*) causes a severe necrotic infection of the appendix and intestine. Infections are frequently accompanied by bacteremia and metastatic necrosis in other regions of the body. Although a high percentage of adults carry it asymptomatically in their appendices, its habitat has not been fully established. Entry to the bloodstream is believed to occur from this area. Although not completely understood, *C. septicum* is frequently associated with certain types of cancer. Patients with *C. septicum* bacteremia are also likely to be suffering from another underlying disease such as leukemia, lymphoma, or carcinoma of the large intestine. Because of this, mortality among patients with *C. septicum* bacteremia is greater than 65%.

Differential Characteristics

C. septicum is a motile, anaerobic, endospore-forming, Gram-positive rod (Figure 12-21). Diagnostic procedures include Gram stain and growth and hemolysis patterns on CDC Anaerobe Blood Agar or Phenylethyl Alcohol Blood Agar.

Treatment

Administration of β-lactam drugs such as penicillin and cephalosporins.

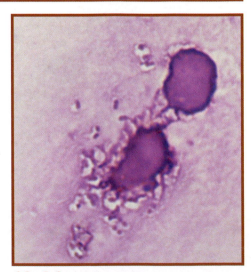

12-21 **_CLOSTRIDIUM SEPTICUM_ IN A HUMAN BLOOD SMEAR** Cells can range in size from 0.6–1.9 µm wide by 1.9–35 µm long.

Clostridium tetani

Clostridium tetani (Phylum *Firmicutes*) is an endospore-forming organism common in the soil and in a variety of animal intestinal tracts, including humans. It is the causative agent of tetanus, more commonly called "lockjaw" because of the difficulty chewing and swallowing characteristic of the disease's onset. In spite of the organism's ubiquity and the continued prevalence of disease in developing countries, tetanus has nearly been eradicated in the United States by tetanus toxoid vaccine. Tetanus is considered a strictly toxigenic disease because the local infection at the site of colonization is typically mild while the effect of released toxin is devastating. Typical transmission of disease is by entry of spores to a traumatic or puncture wound where they germinate, grow, and release the neurotoxin, tetanospasmin. Tetanospasmin is absorbed and transmitted by motor neurons to the central nervous system where it permanently binds to neurons and blocks the release of the inhibitory neurotransmitter γ-aminobutyric acid. The result is a descending severe muscle spasm that begins with facial muscles, neck muscles, and eventually chest muscles, which results in respiratory failure.

Note the comparison between the closely related *C. tetani* and *C. botulinum*. Botulinum toxin travels by way of the bloodstream to peripheral nerve synapses where it blocks release of acetylcholine, resulting in inability to contract muscles (flaccid paralysis); tetanospasmin travels within the nerve cells to central nervous system synapses where it blocks release of inhibitory γ-aminobutyric acid, resulting in the uninhibited or spastic contractions of tetanus.

Differential Characteristics

C. tetani is a motile, strictly-anaerobic, endospore-forming, Gram-positive rod (Figure 12-22). Diagnostic tests are typically not done. Patient immunization history is of greatest concern in suspected cases.

Treatment

Tetanus immune globulin used in conjunction with metronidazole or penicillin G.

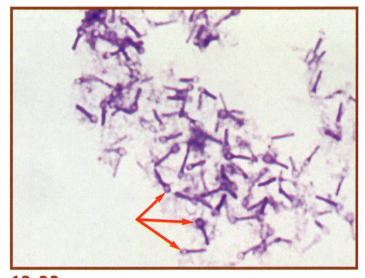

12-22 GRAM STAIN OF A *CLOSTRIDIUM TETANI* STOCK CULTURE
Note the round, terminal endospores (arrows). Occasionally the spores are oval or subterminal. Cells can range in size from 0.5–1.7 μm wide by 2.1–18.1 μm long.

Corynebacterium diphtheriae

Corynebacterium diphtheriae (Phylum *Actinobacteria*) is the toxigenic agent of diphtheria and cutaneous diphtheria. Although it can live for months in the environment, *C. diphtheriae* is transmitted most often from person to person in aerosol droplets. Once a leading cause of death in children, it is now a rare disease in the United States due to routine vaccinations with diphtheria toxoid. However, it still exists in some eastern European countries as well as developing countries. In recent years diphtheria has shifted from a primarily childhood disease to one affecting all ages including disproportionately high numbers of unimmunized poor people and intravenous drug users.

Diphtheria is characterized by two distinct syndromes: local respiratory infection and systemic poisoning from absorption of the cytotoxin produced at the local site. In the former, *C. diphtheriae* produces a thick membrane composed of bacteria, fibrin, immune cells, and dead cells, which obstructs the upper respiratory airway. In the latter, cell-killing toxin is dispersed throughout the body, frequently resulting in myocarditis and congestive heart failure. Cutaneous diphtheria is a result of bacterial entry through an open wound causing a local infection with similar systemic effects as the inhalation disease.

The exotoxin (*tox*) gene is introduced into *C. diphtheriae* by a lysogenic phage.[2] The toxin itself has three functional parts: a binding portion that attaches to heparin receptors on host nerve and heart cells, a translocation portion that moves the bound toxin to the inside of the cell, and an enzymatic portion that inactivates an essential component of protein synthesis.

[2] A lysogenic phage inserts its DNA genome into the host DNA and becomes part of its genome.

Differential Characteristics

C. diphtheriae is a nonmotile, nonsporing, Gram-positive rod (Figure 12-23). It produces acid from glucose and maltose fermentation, and no acid from sucrose. It is negative for urease, pyrazinamidase, and alkaline phosphatase. Diagnostic tests include throat culture.

Treatment

Penicillin G Procaine or erythromycin may be used.

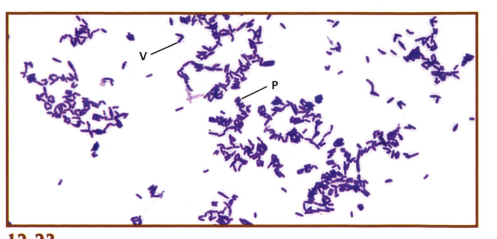

12-23 GRAM STAIN OF A *CORYNEBACTERIUM DIPHTHERIAE* STOCK CULTURE Note the club-shaped cells. *C. diphtheriae* frequently arranges itself in "V-shaped" pairs (**V**) or palisades (**P**). Cells can range in size from 1 μm or less wide by 1.0–8.0 μm long.

Escherichia coli

Escherichia coli (Class *Gammaproteobacteria*) is a member of the large family *Enterobacteriaceae*, the "Enterics." It inhabits the intestinal tract of humans and many other animals. Generally each type of animal host harbors a different strain of the organism. The strains most important to humans are those that inhabit us and those that live in the intestines of cattle.

Human *E. coli* is an opportunistic pathogen and in the right place at the right time may cause anything from mild stomach upset to diarrhea, urinary tract infections, sepsis, and meningitis. Strains of *E. coli* carried in cattle and contaminated beef are differentiated and named according to their virulence properties. These are: enteropathogenic *E. coli* (EPEC) that causes diarrhea in infants, enterotoxigenic *E. coli* (ETEC) that is responsible for infant diarrhea and traveler's diarrhea, enterohemorrhagic *E. coli* (EHEC) that is associated with hemorrhagic colitis and hemolytic uremic syndromes, entero-invasive *E. coli* (EIEC) that produces a shigellosis-like disease, and enteroaggregative *E. coli* (EAEC) that causes acute and chronic diarrhea. These strains are seen primarily in developing countries, but EHEC O157:H7 has been responsible for outbreaks of hemorrhagic colitis in the United States. Disease is almost always caused by ingestion of contaminated meat; however, person to person transmission has been reported.

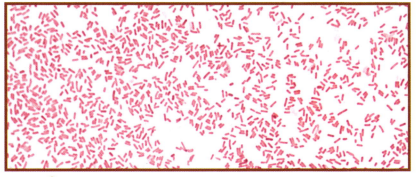

12-24 GRAM STAIN OF AN *ESCHERICHIA COLI* STOCK CULTURE The straight rods are usually arranged singly or in pairs. Cell sizes range from 1–1.5 μm wide to 2–6 μm long.

Differential Characteristics

All members of *Enterobacteriaceae* are oxidase-negative, Gram-negative, facultatively anaerobic rods that produce acid from glucose fermentation (Figures 12-24 and 12-25). Several commercial multiple test systems are available for the differentiation and identification of the individual species including

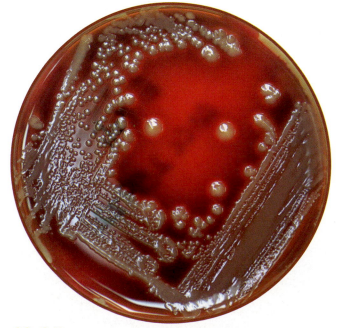

12-25 *ESCHERICHIA COLI* ON SHEEP BLOOD AGAR

Enterotube®II (page 70), API 20 E® (page 57), and BBL Crystal® (page 66). Diagnostic tests for identification of individual strains include Shiga toxin test (some strains of *E. coli* produce Shiga toxin or Shiga-like toxin very similar to that produced by *Shigella spp.*), and O157 and H7 serum agglutination tests (SAT—page 101).

Treatment

Cephalosporins, ampicillin, sulfamethoxazole are sometimes administered although there is evidence that EHEC disease is actually complicated by antibiotic use. Diarrhea is typically a self-limiting disease; therefore, fluid and electrolyte replacement therapy is the standard treatment.

Fusobacterium spp.

Fusobacterium species (Phylum *Fusobacteria*) are commonly encountered opportunistic pathogens normally found in the human mouth, as well as the urinary, gastrointestinal, and upper respiratory tracts. They are involved (usually in a mixture of organisms) in most dental infections and are very common agents in upper respiratory infections, including chronic sinusitis, aspiration pneumonia, lung abscesses, and brain abscesses. *Fusobacterium* has been shown to cause severe systemic infections in cancer patients following chemotherapy. The virulence of fusobacteria is largely due to endotoxins that evoke a vigorous immune reaction that can lead to toxic shock with widespread systemic collapse. Two species are of primary interest, *F. nucleatum* (Figure 12-26), which is involved in producing periodontal disease, and *F. necrophorum* (Figure 12-27), which can produce meningitis and thrombosis of the external jugular and cerebral veins.

Differential Characteristics

Fusobacterium nucleatum is a nonmotile, anaerobic, non-sporing, spindle-shaped, Gram-negative rod. It is indole-positive, does not grow on bile agar and does not ferment

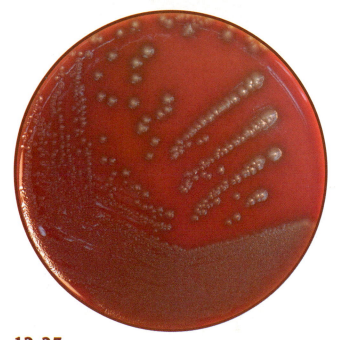

12-27 *FUSOBACTERIUM NECROPHORUM* GROWING ON CHOCOLATE AGAR   Note the flat, grayish-brown colonies.

mannitol, lactose, or rhamnose. It is negative for esculin hydrolysis, catalase, lecithinase, lipase, starch hydrolysis, milk proteolysis, DNase, and gelatinase. Butyrate is the major metabolic end product, which distinguishes it from most *Bacteroides* species.

Treatment

Some *Fusobacterium* species produce β-lactamase; therefore the use of penicillin is typically avoided or combined with β-lactamase inhibitors. Also useful are cefoxitin and imipenem.

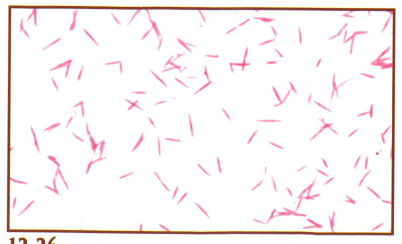

12-26 GRAM STAIN OF A *FUSOBACTERIUM NUCLEATUM* STOCK CULTURE
Note the long, thin spindle-shaped cells, ranging in length from 5–10 μm.

Haemophilus influenzae

Commensal strains of avirulent *Haemophilus influenzae* (Class *Gammaproteobacteria*) can be found in the nasopharynx of virtually everyone over the age of 3 months. Virulent strains also inhabit the upper respiratory tract but to a much lesser degree. Typically transmitted from person to person by aerosol droplets, it is an obligate human microorganism. It was given the name "*Haemophilus*" (blood loving) because it requires specific blood factors (V and X) to live (Figures 12-28 and 12-29). Of the six known capsular types (a–f), type b is the most pathogenic. The nonpathogenic forms are nonencapsulated and rarely cause disease. *Haemophilus influenzae* b was once the most common cause of bacterial meningitis in children; however, its epidemiologic impact has dramatically changed since the development and widespread use of vaccine in the 1990s. Still, it is the most common cause of bacterial meningitis in unvaccinated children, with as many as 700,000 deaths each year worldwide. Encapsulated forms of *H. influenzae* also cause epiglottitis, cellulitis, otitis, pneumonia, septicemia, and endocarditis.

Differential Characteristics

Haemophilus influenzae is a small, nonmotile, facultatively anaerobic, pleomorphic, Gram-negative rod (Figure 12-30). Taxonomically the species is divided into six serogroups (a–f) and/or eight biotypes (I–VIII). Serogroups are differentiated

based on capsule formation and biotypes are differentiated based on a battery of three tests—indole, urease, and ornithine decarboxylase. Each biotype demonstrates a unique combination of positive and negative results.

Treatment

Administration of third generation cephalosporins, chloramphenicol or fluoroquinolones for severe infection; though ampicillin may be used, up to 25% of *H. influenzae* b strains produce a β-lactamase (page 59).

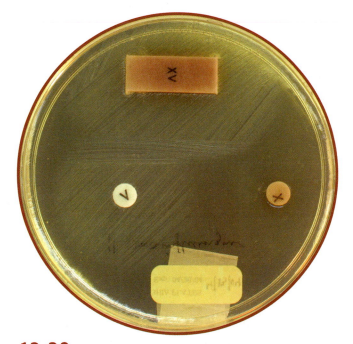

12-29 *HAEMOPHILUS PARAINFLUENZAE* DEMONSTRATING CHARACTERISTIC GROWTH IN THE X–V TEST *H. parainfluenzae* requires only V factor to survive. Note the growth surrounding both the V disc and X-V strip.

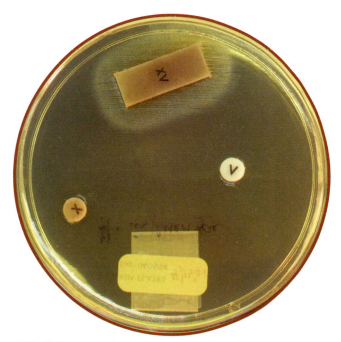

12-28 *HAEMOPHILUS INFLUENZAE* DEMONSTRATING CHARACTERISTIC REQUIREMENT OF BOTH X AND V BLOOD FACTORS Note the growth surrounding the strip containing both factors and absence of growth around the discs containing only X or V factor. X factor is hemin, V factor is NAD.

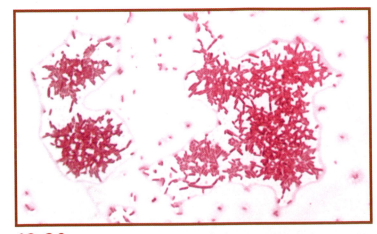

12-30 GRAM STAIN OF A *HAEMOPHILUS INFLUENZAE* STOCK CULTURE Note the various shapes and sizes of the cells (pleomorphism). Cells can range in size from about 0.5 μm wide by 0.5–3.0 μm long. *H. influenzae* b is also encapsulated.

Helicobacter pylori

Helicobacter pylori (Class *Gammaproteobacteria*) is associated with gastric ulcers, duodenal ulcers, nonulcer dyspepsia, and gastric carcinoma. *H. pylori* does not enter cells, but resides solely in the deepest parts of the mucous layer lining the gastric mucosa and epithelial cell surface. It causes inflammation by 1) blocking gastric acid production with inhibitory proteins, and 2) neutralizing acid with ammonia produced from urea hydrolysis. It avoids phagocytosis by producing superoxide dismutase and catalase. The host immune response to factors produced by *H. pylori* is responsible in part for the severity of the symptoms. The typical immune reaction includes secretion of interleukin-8, hypersecretion of gastric acid, and programmed epithelial cell death. Transmission is person-to-person.

Differential Characteristics

Helicobacter pylori is a motile, curved, spiral, or straight, slightly plump, Gram-negative rod (Figure 12-31). It is vigorously urease-positive, catalase-positive, and oxidase-positive. Diagnostic procedures include culture, direct antigen test, urease test, gastric biopsy, serology, and urea breath test.

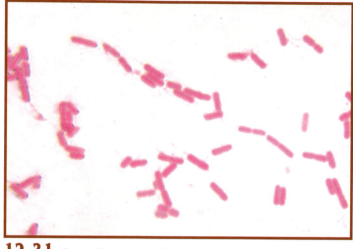

12-31 GRAM STAIN OF A *HELICOBACTER PYLORI* STOCK CULTURE Young cultures of *H. pylori* grown *in vitro* frequently stain Gram-positive. These cells are uncharacteristically straight. Most are curved or spiral-shaped. Cells range in size from 0.5 μm wide by 2.5–5 μm long.

Treatment

Administration of amoxicillin, tetracycline, metronidazole, or bismuth subsalicylate.

Klebsiella pneumoniae

Klebsiella pneumoniae (Class *Gammaproteobacteria*) is found in soil, water, grain, fruits, vegetables, and the intestinal tracts of a variety of animals including humans. It is harbored in the nasopharynx and oropharynx of humans and is frequently transmitted as aerosol droplets from person to person. *K. pneumoniae* is a very common nosocomial pathogen, but also causes community-acquired primary lobar pneumonia—a severe (frequently fatal) necrotizing infection. Nosocomial infections commonly caused by *K. pneumoniae* are pneumonia, urinary tract infections, bronchitis, surgical wound infections, biliary tract infections, and hospital associated bacteremia. The organism owes its virulence to endotoxin production and its ability to form a protective polysaccharide capsule. Over the last several years, plasmid-mediated antibiotic resistance in the species (in response to widespread antibiotic use) has complicated treatment efforts and necessitated antimicrobial susceptibility testing on specific isolates.

Differential Characteristics

K. pneumoniae is a nonmotile, encapsulated, facultatively anaerobic, Gram-negative rod (Figures 6-20, 12-32 and

12-33). *K. pneumoniae* is negative for indole, arginine and ornithine decarboxylase, and positive for lysine decarboxylase.

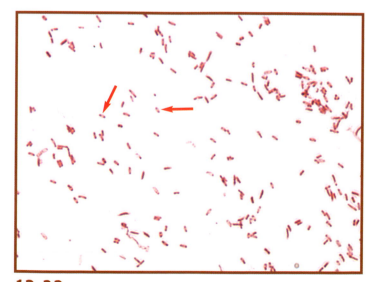

12-32 GRAM STAIN OF A *KLEBSIELLA PNEUMONIAE* STOCK CULTURE Cells range in size from 0.3–1.0 μm wide by 0.6–6.0 μm long. Note the bipolar staining (**arrows**).

Treatment

As mentioned above, plasmid-mediated antibiotic resistance has necessitated the use of antimicrobial susceptibility testing of individual isolates before selecting the most effective final treatment. Agents traditionally used are 1st, 2nd, and 3rd generation cephalosporins. Also used are penicillins, imipenem with cilastatin, aztreonam, fluoroquinolones, and meropenem.

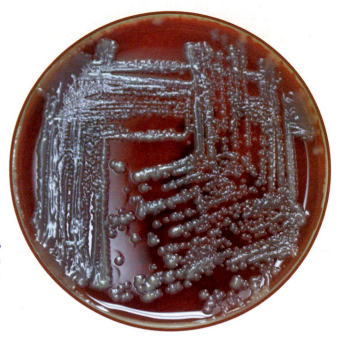

12-33 *KLEBSIELLA PNEUMONIAE* ON **SHEEP BLOOD AGAR** Note the mucoid appearance due to large polysaccharide capsules.

Legionella pneumophila

Legionella pneumophila (Class *Gammaproteobacteria*) is a comparatively "new" organism, having only been discovered following the outbreak of Legionnaires' disease in 1976. In the hotels and hospitals where outbreaks have occurred, the organism has been isolated from fresh water sources and various plumbing fixtures. Although recently discovered, *L. pneumophila* has been found in abundance in aquatic habitats worldwide, including chlorinated hot tubs. Interestingly, the organism survives in such harsh conditions because it is able to parasitize amoebae living in the water. *L. pneumophila* is not passed directly from person to person but is inhaled as aerosols from environmental sources. Legionellosis is the general heading used to include all of the diseases caused by this organism (*i.e.*, Legionnaires' disease— a pneumonia-like disease, Pontiac fever—a milder, short term flu-like illness, and a variety of other systemic infections). Although capable of surviving extracellularly, it is classified as an intracellular pathogen because of its ability to survive and multiply inside phagosomes of pulmonary macrophages. The multiplying bacteria eventually kill the macrophages, spread, and repeat the process. The number of *Legionella* associated infections reported in the United States annually is 1,500 to 1,800. The CDC estimates that 10,000 to 20,000 cases go unreported each year.

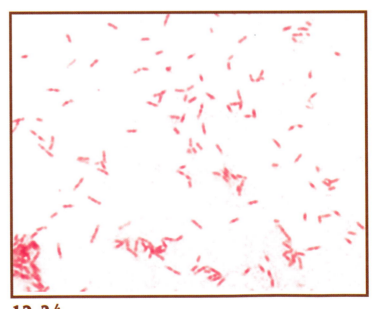

12-34 **GRAM STAIN OF A** *LEGIONELLA PNEUMOPHILA* **STOCK CULTURE** Cells can range in size from less than 1 μm wide by 2–20 μm long or more.

culture, *Legionella* antigen urine test, DNA probe, and polymerase chain reaction (PCR—page 111).

Treatment

Administration of azithromycin individually or combined with rifampin, erythromycin individually or combined with rifampin, clarithromycin, ciprofloxacin, or levofloxacin.

Differential Characteristics

L. pneumophila is a motile, nonsporing, aerobic, Gram-negative rod (Figure 12-34). Diagnostic procedures include

Listeria monocytogenes

Listeria monocytogenes (Phylum *Firmicutes*) is a very common soil saprophyte and vegetable matter decomposer, but it can also be found in red meat, poultry, fish, and the intestinal tract of many animals including humans. It is also a common contaminant of raw milk and cheeses. The organism gains entry to the body as a food-borne contaminant or through openings in the skin. After attaching to host epithelial cells, it induces phagocytosis. Once in the phagolysosome, it produces an enzyme that lyses the phagolysosome and releases the cells to the cytoplasm. The protein ActA on the cells' surface induces host cell actin to push them to the surface, where they enter protrusions called filopods. Filopods are subsequently phagocytized by adjacent epithelial cells and macrophages, and the process repeats in these new cells. This spreading mechanism protects *Listeria* from defenses such as complement and antibodies. *L. monocytogenes* primarily affects pregnant women and their fetuses, immunocompromised individuals, and the elderly, but has recently been associated with gastroenteritis in healthy adults. Listeriosis is the general heading used to include all diseases caused by the organism. In adults and elderly, meningitis is the most common form of listeriosis. In neonates, the disease takes one of two forms—early-onset and late-onset. Early-onset disease is acquired *in utero*, while late-onset infections occur at or soon after birth. Granulomatosis infantiseptica is the early-onset disease and is frequently fatal. Neonatal meningoencephalitis is the late-onset form. Bacteremia is the most common form of disease for immunocompromised individuals.

Differential Characteristics

L. monocytogenes is a small, motile, β-hemolytic, nonsporing, Gram-positive rod (Figure 12-35). It is catalase-positive, ferments glucose, trehalose and salicin, and hydrolyzes esculin (Figure 12-36). Diagnostic tests include Gram stain, cerebrospinal fluid (CSF) culture or analysis, aerobic and anaerobic blood culture, and lumbar puncture.

Treatment

Administration of ampicillin individually or combined with gentamicin, penicillin G individually or combined with gentamicin.

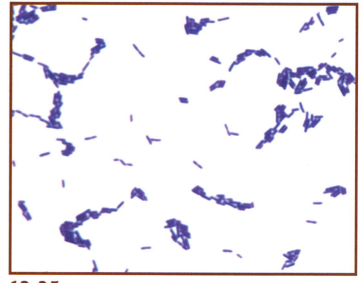

12-35 GRAM STAIN OF A *LISTERIA MONOCYTOGENES* STOCK CULTURE This organism typically appears as single cells, diplobacilli, chains, or clusters of parallel cells with blunt ends, all of which are visible in this micrograph. Sizes range from 0.5 μm wide to 1–2 μm long.

12-36 *LISTERIA MONOCYTOGENES* ON OXFORD MEDIUM Note the darkening of the medium due to esculin hydrolysis. See Bile Esculin Agar on page 60.

Mycobacterium leprae

Mycobacterium leprae (Phylum *Actinobacteria*) is the causative agent of leprosy—now rare in the United States, but still a serious problem in Asia and Africa. Although it can be cultivated in a few laboratory animals, it is believed to occur naturally only in humans and in the nine-banded armadillo of Texas and Louisiana. Like *Legionella* and *Listeria*, *M. leprae* is an intracellular parasite. Once ingested by a macrophage it survives by chemically suppressing the cell's defensive activity. Two distinctive forms of leprosy are known to occur—lepromatous leprosy and tuberculoid leprosy. In lepromatous leprosy, the more contagious form of disease, host immune response is suppressed, followed by rapid proliferation of the organism, severe disfigurement, and loss of nerve function. In tuberculoid leprosy, a vigorous host immune response results in the formation of granulomas on the face, trunk, and extremities. Several intermediate forms of the disease also exist. The mode of transmission is not well understood, however, a victim with the lepromatous form can shed billions of bacterial cells from the nose in a single day.

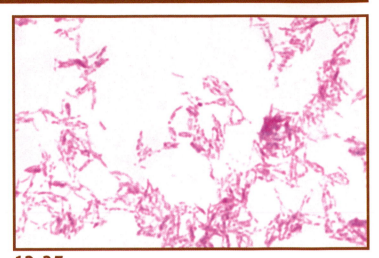

12-37 ACID-FAST STAIN OF A *MYCOBACTERIUM LEPRAE* STOCK CULTURE These rods can be straight or curved and are typically found in clusters.

Differential Characteristics

M. leprae is a nonmotile, anaerobic, acid-fast, nonsporing, weakly Gram-positive rod (Figure 12-37). *M. leprae* is uncultivable *in vitro*, therefore, standard biochemical tests are not useful in identifying it. Clinical diagnoses are based on characteristics of the disease, Gram and acid-fast staining, and biopsies from skin lesions or nasal secretions. A skin test using lepromin, an antigen extraction from lepromatous lesions is also available.

Treatment

The World Health Organization recommends multidrug therapy (MDT), which includes the drugs dapsone, rifampicin, and clofazimine. This approach has seen great success and the drugs are provided free of charge to leprosy patients worldwide.

Mycobacterium tuberculosis

Mycobacterium tuberculosis (Phylum *Actinobacteria*) is the pathogen responsible for tuberculosis. Humans are its principal host and reservoir, although it has been isolated from other primates. It can be passed directly from person-to-person or inhaled as droplet nuclei (bacteria carried on airborne particles). Two manifestations of the disease exist: primary tuberculosis and secondary tuberculosis. Primary tuberculosis, the condition produced upon initial exposure to the bacillus, is for most healthy individuals no more than a mild flu-like illness. In this initial stage, the bacteria enter the alveoli and are ingested by resident macrophages. They multiply intracellularly and spread to other areas of the lung, killing the macrophages in the process. Eventually, the host immune response kills most of the bacteria, but some remain alive inside small granulomas called tubercles. In otherwise healthy individuals, these tubercles usually remain intact for a lifetime, holding the bacteria in check. However, in immunocompromised individuals, the organism soon gets into the bloodstream and disseminates throughout the body. Secondary tuberculosis is the condition that occurs as the aging immune system weakens or is compromised by other factors. This condition, characterized by progressive, necrotic lung inflammation, is the form of tuberculosis most people associate with the disease.

Differential Characteristics

M. tuberculosis is a nonmotile, acid-fast, nonsporing, weakly Gram-positive rod (Figures 12-38 and 12-39). Diagnostic procedures include acid-fast stain, tuberculin skin test, lumbar puncture, sputum, biopsy or body fluid culture, and polymerase chain reaction (PCR—page 111).

Treatment

Administration of isoniazid and rifampin individually or combined, pyrazinamide, ethambutol, or streptomycin.

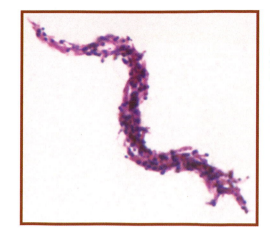

12-38 ACID-FAST STAIN OF A MYCOBACTERIUM TUBERCULOSIS STOCK CULTURE Note the characteristic cord-like orientation. Individual cells are approximately 0.4 µm wide by 3 µm long.

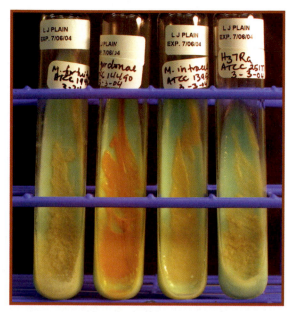

12-39 A COLLECTION OF MYCOBACTERIUM CULTURES ON LOWENSTEIN-JENSEN AGAR From left to right, *M. fortuitum*, *M. gordonae*, *M. intracellulus*, and a strain of *M. tuberculosis* (H37Ra). Note the friable (crumbly) growth texture of the *M. fortuitum* and *M. tuberculosis* cultures.

Neisseria gonorrhoeae

Neisseria gonorrhoeae (Class *Betaproteobacteria*) causes the exclusively human sexually transmitted disease (STD), gonorrhea. It attaches to urethral or vaginal columnar epithelial cells by Type IV pili and other surface proteins. The composition of these surface antigens is controlled genetically and can therefore change. Because of this, the organism is able to evade host antibodies that might otherwise attack it. Most infections caused by *N. gonorrhoeae* are confined to the lower reproductive area. However, if allowed to reach the bloodstream, certain strains of this organism that contain a surface antigen similar to that of red blood cells can evade host serum antibodies. When this occurs, disseminated gonococcal infection (DGI) is the result, frequently including dermatitis-arthritis-tenosynovitis syndrome and occasionally, endocarditis or meningitis. Other infections of this organism include endometritis, epididymitis, pelvic inflammatory disease (PID), proctitis, pharyngitis, conjunctivitis, peritonitis, and perihepatitis.

Differential Characteristics

N. gonorrhoeae is an aerobic, Gram-negative diplococcus that sometimes demonstrates "twitching motility." It produces acid only from glucose in the carbohydrate acidification test. Diagnostic procedures include Gram stain, nucleic acid probe, and genital culture (Figures 12-40 and 12-41).

Treatment

Resistance to penicillin G and tetracyclines has led to using ceftriaxone and azithromycin combined with doxycycline.

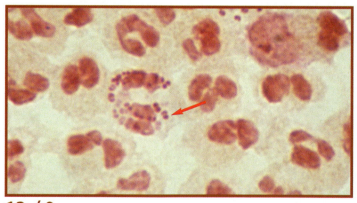

12-40 GRAM STAIN OF *NEISSERIA GONORRHOEAE* INSIDE TWO POLYMORPHONUCLEAR LEUKOCYTES Cells are typically seen as diplococci with adjacent sides flattened (**arrow**). Individual cells range in size from 0.6–1.9 µm in diameter.

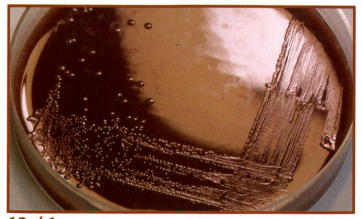

12-41 *NEISSERIA GONORRHOEAE* ON CHOCOLATE AGAR AFTER 48 HOURS INCUBATION *N. gonorrhoeae* typically forms smaller colonies than other members of the genus. Compare colony size with *N. meningitidis* in Figure 12-43.

Neisseria meningitidis

Neisseria meningitidis (Class *Betaproteobacteria*) is one of two human pathogens in the genus. It resides on mucous membranes of the nasopharynx, oropharynx, and the anogenital region. It does not remain viable for long outside the human body and must be transferred sexually or by direct contact with infected respiratory secretions. It causes meningococcemia and the accompanying meningococcal meningitis, a devastating disease primarily of children and young adults. The organism's virulence can be attributed to at least four factors: surface pili which help it attach to host mucous membranes, a heavy capsule which helps it survive and multiply inside phagocytes, a hemolysin which facilitates the destruction of red blood cells (RBCs), and in some strains, surface components similar to those of RBCs that fail to stimulate a serum antibody response. In most healthy individuals the organism produces a localized infection or no symptoms at all, but in the absence of an early antibody response, may result in fulminant sepsis and meningitis.

Differential Characteristics

N. meningitidis (Figures 12-42 and 12-43) is an aerobic, Gram-negative diplococcus that sometimes demonstrates "twitching motility." It produces acid from glucose and maltose in the carbohydrate acidification test. Diagnostic tests include cerebrospinal fluid (CSF) culture and latex agglutination test, Gram stain, and skin biopsy.

Treatment

Administration of penicillin G, 3rd generation cephalosporins, or chloramphenicol.

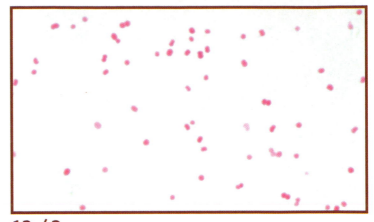

12-42 GRAM STAIN OF A *NEISSERIA MENINGITIDIS* STOCK CULTURE
Meningococci are usually seen as diplococci with adjacent sides flattened. Cells are about 1 μm in diameter.

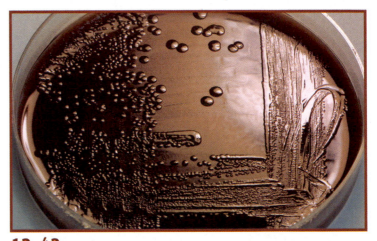

12-43 *NEISSERIA MENINGITIDIS* ON CHOCOLATE AGAR AFTER
48 HOURS INCUBATION Compare colony size with *N. gonorrhoeae* in Figure 12-41.

Nocardia asteroides

Nocardia asteroides (Phylum *Actinobacteria*) was once believed to be a fungus because of its ability to produce branching vegetative hyphae (Figures 12-44 through 12-46). However, its mycelia fragment into rod and coccus-like elements that contain no membrane-bound organelles. *N. asteroides* is found principally on vegetation and in the soil. It is the infective agent of nocardiosis. Although it occasionally affects healthy individuals, it is primarily an opportunistic pathogen of immunosuppressed patients following organ transplant or people whose immune systems have otherwise been compromised by AIDS, lymphoma, or corticosteroids. In the majority of cases, transmission is by inhalation of aerosol droplets leading to pulmonary nocardiosis (chronic pneumonia). Dissemination of the

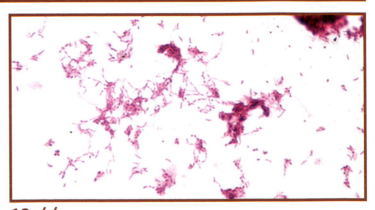

12-44 ACID-FAST STAIN OF A *NOCARDIA ASTEROIDES* STOCK
CULTURE Because *Nocardia* species are weakly acid-fast, decolorization is done with a lower concentration of acid-alcohol.

organism by the bloodstream typically leads to central nervous system nocardiosis (brain abscesses) and infection of virtually all organ systems. Other infections caused by *N. asteroides* include cellulitis with lymphocutaneous nodules, mycetoma (usually in the tropics), and keratitis.

Differential Characteristics

Norcardia asteroides is anaerobic, nonmotile, Gram-positive to Gram-variable, partially acid-fast rod. It is lysozyme-resistant and urease-positive. It reduces nitrate, does not hydrolyze casein, tyrosine, xanthine, hypoxanthine, gelatin, or starch, and does not produce acid from lactose, xylose, or arabinose. Diagnostic procedures include acid-fast stain and culture of the infected site.

Treatment

Trimethoprim-sulfamethoxazole is the treatment of choice.

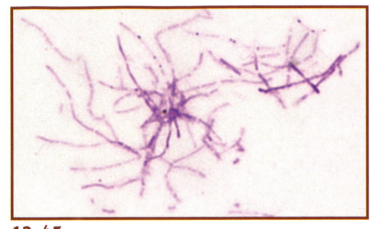

12-45 Gram Stain of an Old Culture of Nocardia asteroides Stock Culture The Gram reaction is weak due to mycolic acid in the cell walls. Note the beaded appearance of the branched filaments.

12-46 Nocardia asteroides on Sabouraud Dextrose Agar Note the fungus-like appearance due to aerial elements of the orange-pigmented mycelium.

Proteus mirabilis

Proteus mirabilis (Class *Betaproteobacteria*) is a normal inhabitant of the human intestinal tract and that of a variety of other animals. It is also common in soil and polluted water. *P. mirabilis*, like all *Proteus* species, has the ability to periodically migrate on the surface of plated agar media. This cycle of alternating migration and consolidation is due to a characteristic called "swarming motility" and produces a series of visible concentric rings (Figure 12-47). *P. mirabilis* is a common nosocomial pathogen isolated from septic wounds and urinary tract infections. Transmission is by direct contact with a carrier or other contaminated source. It is of particular importance as a urinary tract pathogen because of its ability to produce urease (page 96). Urease splits urea, thus creating an alkaline environment and promoting the formation of kidney stones. *Proteus* septicemia is a potential complication of urinary tract infections and can be fatal in weakened individuals.

Differential Characteristics

P. mirabilis is a straight, facultatively anaerobic, highly motile (swarming) Gram-negative rod (Figure 12-48). It is negative for indole, esculin hydrolysis, and lactose and salicin fermentation. It

12-47 Three Colonies of Proteus mirabilis on Sheep Blood Agar Note the characteristic swarming growth pattern.

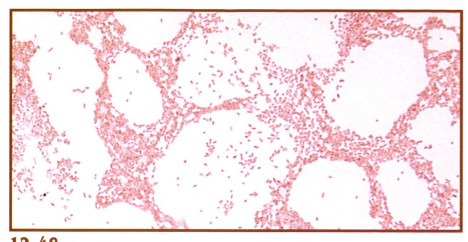

12-48 GRAM STAIN OF A *PROTEUS MIRABILIS* STOCK CULTURE Straight rods range in size from 0.4–0.8 μm wide by 1.0–3.0 μm long.

is positive for lipase and ornithine decarboxylase, and strongly positive for urease. Diagnostic procedures include Gram stain and culture of infected site.

Treatment

Administration of 1st, 2nd, or 3rd generation cephalosporins, carbapenems, fluoroquinolones, or extended spectrum penicillins.

Pseudomonas aeruginosa

Pseudomonas aeruginosa (Class *Gammaproteobacteria*) is an opportunistic pathogen ubiquitous in soil, water, and living or decaying plant material. It has also been isolated from hospital sinks and tubs, dialysis equipment, contact lens solution, aerators, irrigation fluids, hot tubs, ointments, insoles of shoes, and even in soaps and cleaning solutions. It is the most significant opportunistic pathogen of its genus and is an especially troublesome nosocomial agent because of its ability to survive eradication attempts. In addition, symptoms of *Pseudomonas* infections are problematic because they are virtually indistinguishable from those caused by *Enterobacteriaceae*, which tend to produce fewer fatalities. Transmission can be by ingestion, inhalation, or through openings in the skin. *P. aeruginosa* employs surface pili to attach to host cells and secretes an array of tissue-damaging enzymes. While healthy individuals are less frequently affected by the organism, immunosuppressed patients are susceptible to a variety of serious infections. Among the nosocomial infections caused by this organism are pneumonia, wound sepsis, bacteremia, and urinary tract infections. Other infections include: corneal ulcers, swimmer's ear, folliculitis (from contaminated swimming pools or hot tubs), and osteomyelitis of the calcaneus in children due to puncture wounds through the shoe.

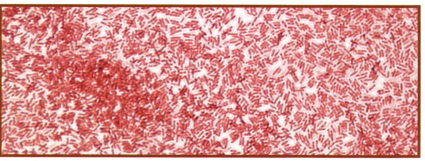

12-49 GRAM STAIN OF A *PSEUDOMONAS AERUGINOSA* STOCK CULTURE Cells are approximately 1 μm or less wide by 2–5 μm long.

12-50 *PSEUDOMONAS AERUGINOSA* ON SHEEP BLOOD AGAR
Note the greenish pigment, especially in the regions of heaviest growth.

Differential Characteristics

P. aeruginosa is an aerobic, motile, straight or slightly curved, Gram-negative rod that produces a green diffusible pigment when grown on solid media (Figures 12-49, 12-50, and 3-29). It does not ferment carbohydrates. It utilizes glucose oxidatively and does not utilize lactose or esculin. It reduces nitrate, is positive for oxidase and arginine decarboxylase, and negative for ONPG, urease, and lysine decarboxylase. Diagnostic procedures include Gram stain and appropriate-site culture.

Treatment

Administration of ceftazidime individually or combined with aminoglycosides, extended spectrum penicillins, cefepime, fluoroquinolones, or ciprofloxacin.

Salmonella enteritidis

Salmonella Enteritidis (Class *Gammaproteobacteria*)[3] typically resides in the gastrointestinal tract of humans and many other animals, including poultry, rodents, and wild birds. It is one of approximately 2,200 nontyphoidal *Salmonella* serotypes, all of which cause gastroenteritis in humans. The mechanisms described here for *S.* Enteritidis apply to those serotypes as well. Entry into the body is by ingestion of food or water contaminated with feces. *Salmonella spp.* are susceptible to acidic conditions and thus require a large number of organisms ($>10^6$) to infect a human with normal stomach acidity. Thus, the organism tends to favor hosts with low gastric acidity. Once through the hostile environment of the stomach, they are taken up by intestinal epithelial cells and are released into the underlying connective tissue where they begin to multiply. The mechanism by which diarrhea is induced is not fully understood, however, evidence suggests that it is due to the production of a cholera-like or Shiga-like toxin. *Salmonella* Enteritidis is not well suited for intracellular conditions, therefore, except in cases where the host immune system has been compromised, gastrointestinal infections are generally short-lived. Lacking an appropriate host immune response, however, dissemination of the organism may occur, resulting in widespread systemic infection.

Differential Characteristics

Salmonella Enteritidis is a straight, motile, facultatively anaerobic, nonsporing, Gram-negative rod (Figures 12-51 and 12-52). Diagnostic procedures include aerobic and anaerobic blood culture, bone marrow culture, and stool culture. It is methyl red and citrate positive, and negative for indole, VP, and lactose fermentation. Because the vast number of strains differ primarily in antigenic structure, serogrouping by a reference laboratory is necessary for final identification.

Treatment

In most cases of diarrheal disease, antibiotics are not necessary. However, in disseminated *Salmonella* infections, third generation cephalosporins, ampicillin, or sulfamethoxazole with trimethoprim are used.

[3] Abbreviated from *Salmonella enterica* serovar Enteritidis.

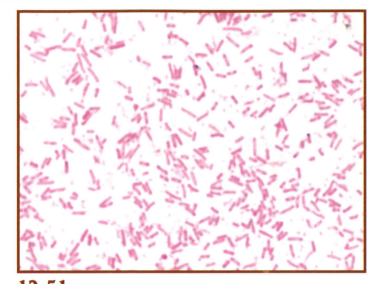

12-51 GRAM STAIN OF A *SALMONELLA* ENTERITIDIS STOCK CULTURE   The cells are straight rods ranging in size from 0.7–1.5 μm wide by 2.0–5.0 μm long.

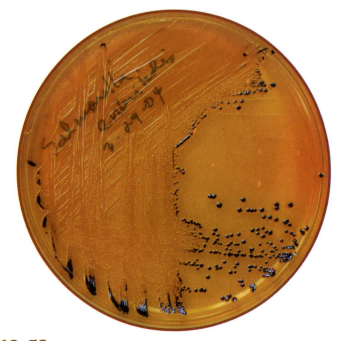

12-52 *SALMONELLA* ENTERITIDIS ON *SALMONELLA-SHIGELLA* (SS) AGAR   Compare to *Salmonella typhi* (Figure 12-54) and *Shigella flexneri* (Figure 12-56). Note the black colonies due to reaction of H_2S (from sulfur reduction) and ferric citrate in the medium. Also see page 16 for more information about SS Agar.

Salmonella typhi

Salmonella typhi (Class *Gammaproteobacteria*)[4] is the causative agent of typhoid fever in humans. The organism is typically transmitted by fecally contaminated food or water. As described in *Salmonella* Enteritidis on the previous page, *S. typhi* initially attacks epithelial cells of the small intestine, is ushered into the underlying connective tissue and regional lymph nodes, and begins to multiply. It then enters the bloodstream where it produces acute bacteremia and subsequently infects the liver, spleen, bone marrow, and eventually the kidneys and gallbladder. This phase, accompanied by high fever and sometimes diarrhea, is long lasting and continuous (up to 8 weeks in untreated cases). In a small percentage of patients ("carriers"), the organism is harbored asymptomatically in the gallbladder and sloughed in the feces for up to a year or more.

Differential Characteristics

S. typhi is a straight, motile, encapsulated, facultatively anaerobic, nonsporing, Gram-negative rod (Figures 12-53 and 12-54). Diagnostic procedures include aerobic and anaerobic blood culture,

---

[4] Abbreviated from *Salmonella enterica* subspecies *Enterica* serovar *Typhi*.

12-54 SALMONELLA TYPHI ON SALMONELLA-SHIGELLA AGAR Compare to *Salmonella* Enteritidis (Figure 12-52) and *Shigella flexneri* (Figure 12-56). Note the absence of black in the colonies due to weak (or lack of) sulfur reduction to H_2S.

12-53 GRAM STAIN OF A SALMONELLA TYPHI STOCK CULTURE The cells are straight rods ranging in size from 0.7–1.5 μm wide by 2.0–5.0 μm long.

bone marrow culture, and stool culture. *S. typhi* is MR positive and indole, VP, and citrate negative, and does not ferment lactose. Because the vast number of strains differ primarily in antigenic structure, serogrouping by a reference laboratory is necessary for final identification.

Treatment

Administration of third generation cephalosporins, ampicillin, sulfamethoxazole with trimethoprim, chloramphenicol, or ciprofloxacin

Shigella dysenteriae

Shigella dysenteriae (Class *Gammaproteobacteria*) is one of four *Shigella* species (*S. dysenteriae* [Figure 12-55], *S. flexneri* [Figure 12-56], *S. boydii*, and *S. sonnei*), all of which are responsible for bacillary dysentery (shigellosis) in humans and a few other primates. *S. dysenteriae* is endemic in Africa, Asia, and Latin America; *S. flexneri* and *S. sonnei* are found primarily in developed areas including the United States; and *S. boydii* is mostly restricted to India. The majority of cases occur in children under 10 years of age. Transmission is by direct person-to-person contact or ingestion of food or

water contaminated by human feces. It is highly communicable and virulent; it can cause illness with as few as 200 organisms, but more typically with 10^3 organisms. Although all species of *Shigella* cause the disease, *S. dysenteriae* alone produces the cell-killing Shiga exotoxin and is, therefore, responsible for the most severe symptoms. Unlike *Salmonella*, *Shigella* spp. are resistant to the stomach's acidic environment which accounts, in part, for the low infectious dose. Once in the intestine, they induce phagocytosis by host epithelial cells where they multiply and then spread in a

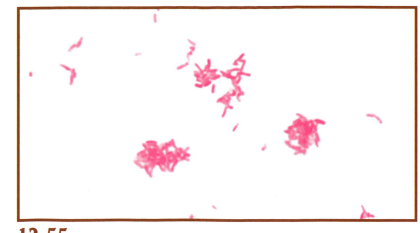

12-55 GRAM STAIN OF A *SHIGELLA DYSENTERIAE* STOCK CULTURE The cells are straight rods ranging in size from 0.7–1.0 μm wide by 1.0–3.0 μm long.

process that kills the cells and forms mucosal ulcerations. This process combined with an acute immune response is responsible for the purulent bloody diarrhea characteristic of the disease.

Differential Characteristics

S. dysenteriae is a straight, nonmotile, facultatively anaerobic, Gram-negative rod. It does not ferment lactose, mannitol, raffinose, sucrose, or xylose and is negative for ONPG and ornithine decarboxylase. Diagnostic procedures include fecal leukocyte stain and stool culture.

12-56 *SHIGELLA FLEXNERI* ON *SALMONELLA-SHIGELLA* **(SS)** AGAR Compare to *Salmonella* Enteritidis (Figure 12-52) and *Salmonella typhi* (Figure 12-54). Note the colorless colonies due to inability to ferment lactose or reduce sulfur—both included in the medium.

Treatment

Administration of ampicillin, sulfamethoxazole with trimethoprim, or ciprofloxacin.

Staphylococcus aureus

Staphylococcus aureus (Phylum *Firmicutes*) is a normal human inhabitant, most commonly found in the nose, but also known to inhabit the skin and vagina. It is a common nosocomial pathogen that causes toxic shock syndrome, food poisoning, scalded skin syndrome, and abscesses virtually anywhere in the body. Factors that increase its virulence include: antiphagocytic proteins, lipase production (which aids entry through the skin), coagulase (which enhances the formation of abscesses), enterotoxins (which induce vomiting and diarrhea), and exotoxins (which destroy polymorphonuclear leukocytes, aid necrosis, and produce fever, chills, shock, and rash). *S. aureus* is transmitted by direct human-to-human contact, aerosols, or environmental factors. It is a robust organism that resists cleaning solutions and antimicrobial agents, and can survive for weeks in the environment.

is positive for the slide coagulase test (bound coagulase), the tube coagulase test (free coagulase), and DNAse. It can grow in media containing up to 10% NaCl. Diagnostic procedures include Gram stain, appropriate-site aerobic culture, and teichoic acid antibody test.

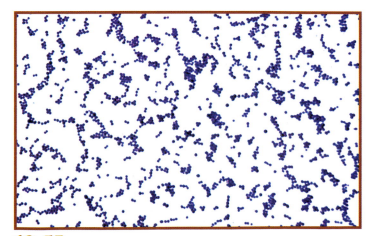

12-57 GRAM STAIN OF A *STAPHYLOCOCCUS AUREUS* STOCK CULTURE Note the characteristic grape-like clusters. Cells are approximately 0.5–1.0 in diameter.

Differential Characteristics

S. aureus is a nonmotile, facultatively anaerobic, β-hemolytic, Gram-positive coccus (Figures 12-57 and 12-58). *S. aureus*

Treatment

Possible effective antibiotics are too numerous to mention here. Since *S. aureus* has shown a remarkable ability to resist most antibiotics (*e.g.*, Methicillin-resistant *Staphylococcus aureus*—MRSA), susceptibility testing (page 223) is recommended for each isolate.

12-58 *STAPHYLOCOCCUS AUREUS* ON SHEEP BLOOD AGAR
Note the β-hemolysis. Note also the absence of yellow color in the colonies, typical of *S. aureus* growth on Nutrient Agar. Compare with *S. epidermidis* colonies in Figure 12-60.

Staphylococcus epidermidis

Staphylococcus epidermidis (Phylum *Firmicutes*) is a normal inhabitant of human skin that has become a significant opportunistic nosocomial pathogen. It is the most common coagulase-negative *Staphylococcus* encountered clinically. Most strains produce a slime layer that may enable them to attach to certain hospital apparati used in invasive procedures, thereby gaining entry to the body. Infections originating at the site of prosthetic implantation are frequently caused by *S. epidermidis*. Due to multiple antibiotic resistance and the generally weakened condition of a convalescing patient, disseminated *S. epidermidis* infection can be quite severe and is frequently fatal.

Differential Characteristics

S. epidermidis is a nonmotile, facultatively anaerobic, non-hemolytic, Gram-positive coccus (Figures 12-59 and 12-60). It ferments maltose but does not ferment sucrose, xylose, or trehalose. It is positive for alkaline phosphatase production and negative for coagulase and DNase. Diagnostic procedures include Gram stain and appropriate-site aerobic culture.

Treatment

Like *S. aureus*, *S. epidermidis* has demonstrated an ability to resist certain antibiotics. Susceptibility testing (page 223) is recommended for individual isolates.

12-60 *STAPHYLOCOCCUS EPIDERMIDIS* ON SHEEP BLOOD AGAR Note the small white colonies and absence of hemolysis. Compare with *S. aureus* colonies in Figure 12-58.

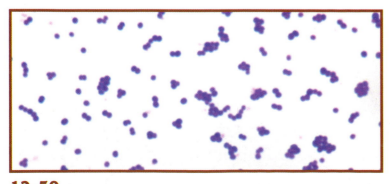

12-59 GRAM STAIN OF A *STAPHYLOCOCCUS EPIDERMIDIS* STOCK CULTURE Cells are approximately 0.8–1.0 μm in diameter.

Streptococcus agalactiae

Known also as group B streptococci, strains of *Streptococcus agalactiae* (Phylum *Firmicutes*) are the major cause of neonatal meningitis in the United States. The reservoir for this organism is believed to be the intestinal tracts of humans and animals, but it is often found in the vagina of pregnant women. The organism is typically acquired by the infant *in utero* through a damaged membrane, from the birth canal during childbirth, or from contact with contaminants after birth. Its virulence is attributable to a polysaccharide capsule which allows it to survive phagocytosis, multiply, and eventually spread by way of the bloodstream. Disseminated disease also causes pneumonia and septic shock, especially in the elderly and immunocompromised populations.

Differential Characteristics

S. agalactiae is a β-hemolytic or nonhemolytic, nonmotile, encapsulated, facultatively anaerobic, Gram-positive coccus (Figures 12-61 and 12-62). It is positive for the CAMP test and sodium hippurae hydrolysis, negative for Voges-Proskauer and PYR, and is bacitracin and SXT-resistant. Diagnostic procedures include appropriate-site aerobic culture and group B *Streptococcus* antigen test.

Treatment

Administration of penicillin G, amoxicillin, ampicillin, 1st generation cephalosporins, erythromycin, or vancomycin.

12-62 *STREPTOCOCCUS AGALACTIAE* (GROUP B STREPTOCOCCI) ON SHEEP BLOOD AGAR Note the β-hemolysis (some strains are nonhemolytic).

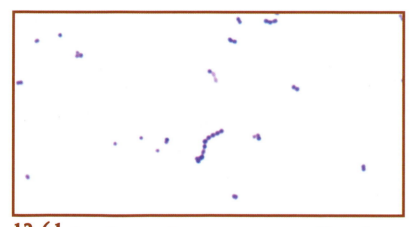

12-61 GRAM STAIN OF A *STREPTOCOCCUS AGALACTIAE* (GROUP B STREPTOCOCCI) STOCK CULTURE Spherical or ovoid cells 0.6–1.2 μm in diameter are usually seen as pairs or in chains.

Streptococcus mutans

Streptococcus mutans (Phylum *Firmicutes*) is one member of the streptococcal group known as the "mutans" group. The mutans group is one of five groups in the "viridans group," which also includes the "anginosus group," "bovis group," "mitis group," and "salivarius group." All viridans streptococci are either α-hemolytic or nonhemolytic, Gram-positive cocci typically found in the mouth, upper respiratory tract, and urogenital tract of humans.

Members of the mutans group are the most common cause of subacute endocarditis in patients with existing heart valve problems or prosthetic heart valves. They are also responsible for bacteremia following dental or urogenital invasive procedures, and in immunosuppressed patients undergoing chemotherapy and bone marrow transplantation. Clinically, the most common encounter with oral streptococci is in the dentist's chair. Several of these organisms are capable of hydrolyzing sucrose and forming dental plaque, which in turn provides the anaerobic environment ideal for fermentation. Acid produced by this fermentation and that of certain *Lactobacilli* erodes the tooth enamel and is responsible for the formation of dental caries (see Snyder Test on page 237).

Differential Characteristics

S. mutans is an α-hemolytic or nonhemolytic, nonmotile, facultatively anaerobic, Gram-positive coccus (Figure 12-63) and is resistant to optochin (page 87). Species identification is usually not clinically necessary for the α-hemolytic and nonhemolytic streptococci. The various groups can be differentiated from other groups based on their reactions in six biochemical tests: arginine hydrolysis, esculin hydrolysis, urease, Voges-Proskauer, and acid production from mannitol and sorbitol fermentation. Diagnostic procedures include Gram stain and appropriate-site aerobic culture.

Treatment

Administration of penicillin G, vancomycin, or 1st generation cephalosporins.

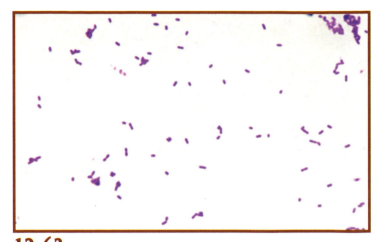

12-63 **GRAM STAIN OF A *STREPTOCOCCUS MUTANS* STOCK CULTURE** Ovoid cells usually appear in short chains and range in diameter from 0.5–0.75 µm.

Streptococcus pneumoniae

Streptococcus pneumoniae (Phylum *Firmicutes*) is estimated to be carried asymptomatically by up to 75% of the human population. Children and adults with children are the principal carriers. It is a significant cause of community-acquired bacterial pneumonia and meningitis in adults. The organism typically colonizes the nasopharynx where it either is eliminated from the body, spreads to the lungs and develops into pneumonia, or is harbored asymptomatically for up to several months. Transmission is usually by direct contact with a carrier or contaminated aerosols. At least 80 different serotypes of *S. pneumoniae* exist and are defined antigenically by their capsules, which are their primary virulence factor. Some serotypes are more virulent than others due to their ability to avoid phagocytosis by host cells and the degree to which they stimulate antibody production. In the lungs the organism stimulates a vigorous immune response marked by copious fluid production. In the majority of infections, the invading organisms are cleared with no long term effects. However, if complicated by bacteremia, meningitis and other secondary infections are the likely result.

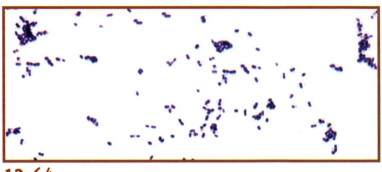

12-64 **GRAM STAIN OF A *STREPTOCOCCUS PNEUMONIAE* STOCK CULTURE** Specimens from sputum samples are typically seen as singles or in pairs and the cells are often elongated (lancet-shaped). They range in diameter from 0.5–1.25 µm.

Differential Characteristics

S. pneumoniae is an α-hemolytic, nonmotile, encapsulated, facultatively anaerobic, Gram-positive coccus (Figures 12-64 and 12-65). It is negative for arginine hydrolysis, esculin hydrolysis, and acid production from mannitol and sorbitol. It is also urease and Voges-Proskauer negative and susceptible to optochin. Diagnostic procedures include Gram stain, appropriate-site aerobic culture, and rapid *Streptococcus* antigen test.

Treatment

As with the staphylococci, drug resistance is an issue with *Streptococcus* and requires isolate susceptibility testing (page 223).

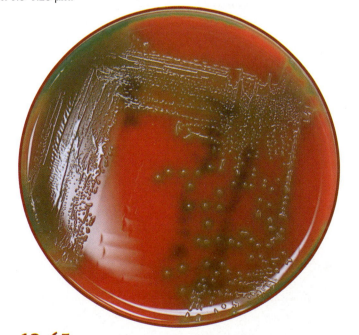

12-65 **STREPTOCOCCUS PNEUMONIAE ON SHEEP BLOOD AGAR** Note the greenish color characteristic of α-hemolysis.

Streptococcus pyogenes

Streptococcus pyogenes (Phylum *Firmicutes*), the principal member of the group A streptococci (β-hemolytic streptococci), is responsible for a variety of severe infections. It is responsible for streptococcal pharyngitis ("strep throat"), impetigo, middle ear infections, mastoiditis, and an array of infections resulting from hematogenic dissemination of the organism, including glomerulonephritis and acute rheumatic fever (ARF). The human nose, throat, and skin are reservoirs for *S. pyogenes*. It is transmitted by direct person-to-person contact or by contaminated aerosols. A variety of virulence factors allow it to attach to epithelial cells and also help it avoid phagocytosis. Once attached to the host cells, it releases several toxins that elicit a vigorous inflammatory response, resulting in severe local inflammation sometimes accompanied by tissue necrosis. Once thought to be waning after the discovery of antibiotics, group A streptococci have made a comeback over the last 20 + years. Since outbreaks of ARF in 1985 there have been reports of other infections including postpartum endomyometritis (puerpural fever), necrotizing fasciitis ("flesh eating"), and toxic shock-like syndrome (TSLS), which is very similar to staphylococcal toxic shock syndrome.

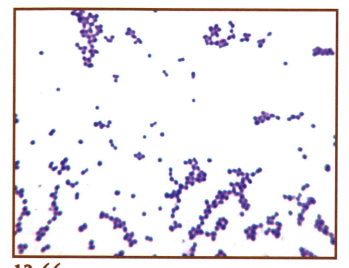

12-66 GRAM STAIN OF A *STREPTOCOCCUS PYOGENES* STOCK CULTURE Specimens isolated from patients are usually seen in pairs and short chains.

Differential Characteristics

S. pyogenes is a β-hemolytic, nonmotile, encapsulated, facultatively anaerobic, Gram-positive coccus (Figures 12-66 and 12-67). It ferments lactose, salicin, and trehalose but not inulin, mannitol, raffinose, fibose, or sorbitol. It hydrolyzes arginine and PYR, but not hippurate. Alkaline phosphatase is produced, but acetoin and α-galactosidase are not. It is susceptible to bacitracin. Diagnostic procedures include throat culture for β-hemolysis (large zones, approximately 1 cm), Gram stain, appropriate-site aerobic culture, serum antideoxyribonuclease-B titer, serum antistreptolysin-O titer, group A streptococcus antigen test, and streptozyme test.

Treatment

Administration of penicillin G, erythromycin, vancomycin, or 1st generation cephalosporins.

12-67 *STREPTOCOCCUS PYOGENES* ON SHEEP BLOOD AGAR Note the extensive β-hemolysis.

Treponema pallidum

Treponema pallidum (Phylum *Spirochaetes*) is an exclusively human pathogen and the infective agent of syphilis. It is primarily a sexually transmitted disease (STD), however, intravenous drug use has broadened the epidemic. Although easily treated with penicillin, the number of congenital syphilis cases (where the organism crosses the placenta and infects the fetus) has also increased dramatically. The organism enters the body through mucous membranes, abrasions, or fissures in the epithelia. Some of the organisms attach to host epithelial cells and multiply, while others are carried to lymph nodes where they enter the bloodstream and disseminate throughout the body. The disease develops in three distinct stages: primary, secondary, and tertiary syphilis. Primary syphilis lasts about two to six weeks and is characterized by the formation of a local lesion called a "chancre." Hematogenic dissemination to all body regions (including the CNS) takes place in this stage. An asymptomatic period lasting up to six months follows. Secondary syphilis is characterized by formation of lesions in the liver, lymph nodes, muscles, and skin. A latent (asymptomatic) period follows the secondary phase and lasts anywhere from five years to several decades. Tertiary syphilis, the final stage of the disease, is characterized by the destruction of neural and cardiovascular tissue and the formation of tumors throughout the body.

12-68 SILVER STAIN OF *TREPONEMA PALLIDUM* (CENTER) IN ANIMAL TISSUE   This spirochete demonstrates "corkscrew motility" by means of periplasmic flagella. Cells range in size from 0.2 μm wide by 5–15 μm long.

microscopic examination of the patient's sample is useful. Following that, serological tests, such as immunofluorescence and rapid plasma reagin tests (Figure 8-10), have proven to be effective methods of determining the presence of *T. pallidum*. Biochemical tests are not done because the organism does not grow well outside the host.

Differential Characteristics

T. pallidum is a motile, microaerophilic, Gram-negative corkscrew-shaped rod (Figure 12-68). Initially, darkfield

Treatment

Administration of penicillin G benzathine, penicillin G procaine, or doxycycline.

Vibrio cholerae

Vibrio cholerae (Class *Gammaproteobacteria*) strains are typed according to their cell wall composition (O antigen). Although there are 139 serotypes of this species, only two (the O1 serogroup) have been responsible for the seven cholera pandemics since 1817 including the current one. The strains have been somewhat arbitrarily divided into the O1 *V. cholerae* and the non-O1 *V. cholerae* to distinguish the cholera-causing organisms from the rest. In 1992, however, a new strain appeared in Madras, India and quickly spread throughout India, Bangladesh, and Southeast Asia. This new strain, called serogroup O139, is believed by some to be the etiologic agent of the eighth cholera pandemic. Although immunity to O1 strains does not confer immunity to O139, the diseases caused are indistinguishable. The organism enters the body by the fecal-oral route, frequently by way of undercooked contaminated seafood. A large

inoculum (10^{10} cells in water) is required to infect healthy individuals because sufficient numbers of bacteria must survive the stomach's acidity and reach the small intestine to cause disease. The infectious dose is considerably smaller if ingested with food. Once in the small intestine, the organism attaches to the mucosal layer and secretes cholera toxin. The toxin begins a cascade of reactions that ultimately alter electrolyte levels and stimulate a vigorous outpouring of fluids into the intestinal lumen. The result is the characteristic "watery" or "secretory diarrhea," which is frequently fatal within a few hours. Because the infection is self-limiting, fluid and electrolyte replacement is standard treatment.

Differential characteristics

V. cholerae is a motile, facultatively anaerobic, salt-tolerant, Gram-negative straight or curved rod (Figures 12-69 and

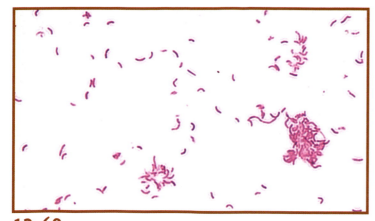

12-69 GRAM STAIN OF A *VIBRIO CHOLERAE* STOCK CULTURE
Note the slight curvature of the rods. Rods range in length from 2–4 µm.

12-70). Diagnostic procedures include fecal leukocyte stain, dark field or phase contrast microscopic examination of fecal material, and stool culture. It can be further identified using various ELISA (page 103) techniques to identify cholera toxin.

Treatment

Administration of sulfamethoxazole with trimethoprim, tetracycline, or doxycycline.

12-70 *VIBRIO CHOLERAE* ON THIOSULFATE CITRATE BILE SALTS SUCROSE (TCBS) AGAR TCBS Agar is a selective medium used for isolation of *V. cholerae* and *V. parahaemolyticus* from clinical and environmental specimens. Refer to Section 2 for more information on TCBS Agar.

Yersinia pestis

Yersinia pestis (Class *Gammaproteobacteria*) has been responsible for dozens of plague epidemics and pandemics over the last several hundred years, one of which took the lives of 25 million Europeans in the fourteenth century. Existing on every continent except Australia, its habitat is any of a variety of small animals, including rats, ground squirrels, rabbits, mice, and prairie dogs. In urban outbreaks, rats are the principal carriers. *Y. pestis* produces several antiphagocytic factors that enable it to survive and multiply both intracellularly and extracellularly. It also produces exotoxins and endotoxins which are believed to be responsible for acute inflammation and necrosis. The organism is most commonly transmitted by fleas, but can be inhaled as droplet nuclei, resulting in pneumonic plague (with a nearly 100% mortality). Fleas ingest the organism when feeding on infected animal blood and pass it to another animal during a subsequent blood meal. *Y. pestis* produces a coagulase that clots the blood inside the flea's stomach. When the flea attempts to feed again, it regurgitates the coagulated material and contaminated blood back into the bite wound. If the bacteria are deposited directly into the bloodstream by the

flea (usually in children), septicemic plague is the likely outcome. The most common form of the disease is bubonic plague, characterized by severe inflammation and hemorrhagic necrosis of the inguinal or axillary lymph nodes called "bubos." This is an extremely serious disease with a very high mortality rate (approaching 50%) when untreated.

Differential Characteristics

Y. pestis is a nonmotile, facultatively anaerobic, Gram-negative rod or coccobacillus (Figures 12-71 and 12-72). It forms an envelope (not a capsule) when grown at 37°C. *Y. pestis* is negative for indole production and ornithine decarboxylase. It does not ferment sucrose, rhamnose, or cellobiose. Diagnostic procedures include aerobic and anaerobic blood culture and appropriate-site aerobic culture.

Treatment

Administration of streptomycin, gentamicin, tetracycline, doxycyline, or chloramphenicol.

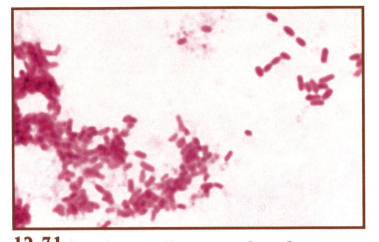

12-71 GRAM STAIN OF A *YERSINIA PESTIS* STOCK CULTURE This organism is typically seen as straight rods or coccobacilli ranging in size from 0.5–0.8 μm wide by 1–3 μm long.

12-72 *YERSINIA PESTIS* ON SHEEP BLOOD AGAR Note the characteristic "fried egg" appearance.

Photo by Larry Stauffer, Oregon State Public Health Laboratory.
(Courtesy of CDC Public Health Image Library)

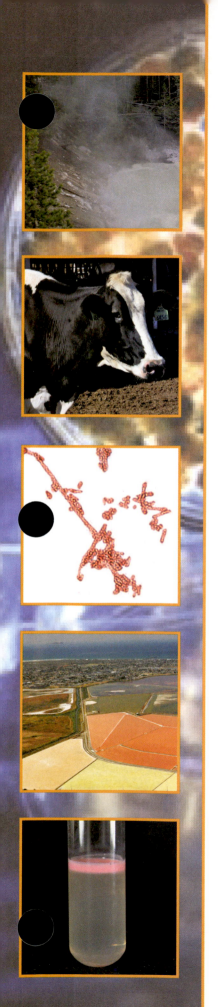

Domain *Archaea*

At one time, *Archaeans* were classified in the Kingdom Monera along with *Bacteria*. Molecular evidence, however, has led to the realization that *Archaeans* and *Bacteria* have very little in common beyond being small prokaryotes—hence, their removal from Monera and placement into different domains.[1] Refer to Table 1-1, page 2 for a comparison of the three domains.

One physiological characteristic of *Archaea* is that frequently they are **extremophiles**. That is, they live in environments that are very hot, very acidic, or very salty. At the present, two phyla are recognized: **Crenarchaeota** and **Euryarchaeota**.

---

[1] Consider the implications: Placing *Archaea* and *Bacteria* into different domains means they have less in common with each other than earthworms, amoebas, sunflowers, mushrooms, humans, and all *Eukaryans* do!

Crenarchaeota

Members of *Crenarchaeota* are morphologically diverse (including unusual disk-shaped cells!), Gram-negative, acidophilic, obligate thermophiles. They are metabolically diverse with chemolithotrophic (a majority metabolize sulfur) and chemoheterotrophic species. Aerotolerance groups include aerobes, facultative anaerobes, and obligate anaerobes. In spite of this metabolic diversity within the phylum, nucleotide comparisons indicate that this is a natural, therefore valid, grouping. Figure 13-1 shows the habitat of *Sulfolobus*, a species in one of the three orders in the phylum.

13-1 *SULFOLOBUS* IN SULFUR CAULDRON, YELLOWSTONE NATIONAL PARK This geologic feature of Yellowstone National Park produces copious amounts of H_2S gas. *Sulfolobus* uses the H_2S as an energy source and oxidizes it to sulfuric acid (H_2SO_4), lowering the pH of its environment to 2 or less. The high acidity breaks down rock and soil to produce the muddy conditions seen in the photo. The steam you see rising from the cauldron is due to its high temperature. *Sulfolobus* species grow between 65°C and 85°C. Although *Sulfolobus* is primarily a chemolithoautotroph, it also can grow heterotrophically.

Euryarchaeota

Seven classes comprise *Euryarchaeota*. These are characterized in Table 13-1. Our emphasis will be on the methanogens and halophiles.

Methanogens obtain energy from the oxidation of H_2 gas, formate ($CHCOO^-$), or a few other simple organic compounds. The electrons and hydrogens from the oxidation are used to reduce CO_2 to methane (CH_4). The ability to make methane is the basis for their name: methanogens. They are found in anaerobic mud of freshwater environments (where they produce "swamp gas"), sludge digesters, and in the rumen of cattle (Figure 13-2).

Halobacterium is a genus of extreme halophiles. Representatives include aerobes and facultative anaerobes, motile and nonmotile forms, and cell morphologies of rods, cocci, flat triangles and discs, and sheets of flat squares (Figure 13-3)! While some can survive and grow at a salinity of 1.5M NaCl, most require salt in the 3.5–4.5M range. They are able to survive at such high environmental osmotic pressures because they concentrate KCl intracellularly to achieve osmotic balance. While enzymes of nonhalophiles are denatured by high intracellular salinity, those of halophiles are actually more stable at higher osmotic pressures and are denatured at lower ones. The same is true of their ribosomes.

Pigments play a major role in *Halobacterium* survival (Figure 13-4). Metabolism is chemoheterotrophic (aerobic respiration), but in the absence of oxygen some species can become phototrophic because of the membrane-bound pigment, **bacteriorhodopsin**. Absorption of light by this pigment generates a proton gradient—the pigment acts as light receptor *and* proton pump—and the resulting proton motive force is used to phosphorylate ADP to ATP. It is unclear if these organisms can live photoautotrophically, but

13-2 **METHANOGENS IN COW RUMENS** Methanogens are found in the anaerobic digestive tracts of ruminants, such as cows. According to the EPA, the gut flora of ruminants is responsible for the production of 80 million metric tons of methane (a greenhouse gas) globally! This cow is a resident of the Van Ommering Dairy Farm in Lakeside, CA. The Van Ommering farm uses methane produced by its herd to generate electricity that supplies the farm's energy needs, thereby reducing greenhouse emissions and providing them with their own energy source—a win-win situation!

they certainly are capable of photoheterotrophic growth. **Halorhodopsin**, a second membrane-bound pigment, is used by probably all halophilic cells to pump chloride ions inward (to increase KCl, as mentioned previously). Other pigments are involved in phototactic responses. Some species produce **gas vacuoles** that assist in floatation. Figure 13-5 shows a culture of *Halobacterium* with gas vacuoles. These are also visible in Figure 13-3.

TABLE 13-1 Brief Characterizations of the Seven Classes of *Euryarchaeota*

Class	Characteristics
Methanobacteria	Gram-positive with pseudomurein wall; obligate anaerobes that oxidize H_2, using CO_2 as the electron acceptor to form CH_4; do not catabolize carbohydrates, protein, or most other organic compounds (exceptions are methanol, secondary alcohols, formate, and CO).
Methanococci	Obligate anaerobes with proteinaceous cell wall; most oxidize H_2, formate, or alcohols with concurrent reduction of CO_2 to CH_4.
Halobacteria	Extreme halophiles.
Thermoplasmata	Aerobic (or facultative), thermoacidophilic heterotrophs.
Thermococci	Obligately anaerobic, hyperthermophilic heterotrophs; reduce S^0 to H_2S in anaerobic respiration.
Archaeoglobi	Obligately anaerobic, hyperthermophilic heterotrophs; S^0 inhibits growth; sulfate, sulfite, thiosulfate, and nitrate are used as final electron acceptors in anaerobic respiration.
Methanopyri	Chemoautotrophic by forming CH_4 from H_2 and CO_2; won't grow below 85°C.

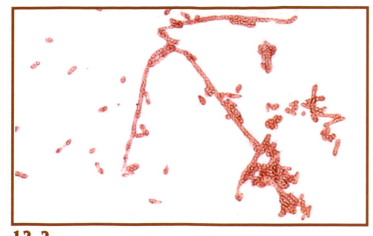

13-3 *HALOBACTERIUM* **GROWN IN CULTURE** Cells are pleomorphic rods that vary in different media and temperatures. Note the gas vacuoles in the cells.

13-4 **A SALTERN IN SAN DIEGO BAY** Salterns are low pools of saltwater used in the harvesting of salt. As water evaporates, the saltwater becomes saltier and saltier, until only salt remains. This can then be purified and sold. The colors in the pools are the result of differently pigmented communities of halophilic microorganisms that are associated with different salinities as the pools dry out.

13-5 *HALOBACTERIUM* **CULTURE** The pink layer at the top is where *Halobacterium* is growing. Due to their gas vacuoles, cells float to the surface.

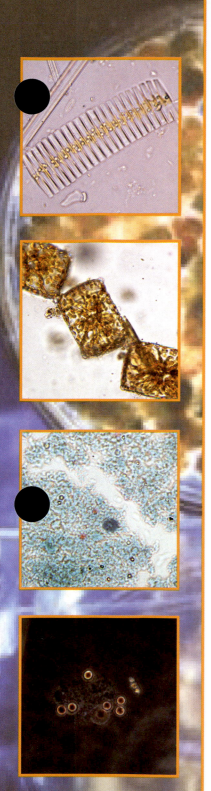

Domain *Eukarya:* Simple Eukaryotes

Simple, microbial eukaryotes are found in five major groupings: Excavata, Chromalveolata, Rhizaria, Archaeplastida, and Unikonta. Archaeplastida also includes true plants and Unikonta includes animals. Plants and animals will not be covered, as they don't fit within the traditional boundaries of microbiology.

Group Excavata

This group obtains its name from the presence in many members of a feeding groove *excavated* from one side of the cell. Among the major groups of Excavata are **parabasalids** (Figure 14-1), **diplomonads** (Figure 14-2), **kinetoplastids** (Figure 14-3), and **euglenids** (Figure 14-4).

- One uniting feature of parabasalids is the presence of a **parabasal body** associated with the Golgi complex. Parabasalids also possess **hydrogenosomes**, organelles that perhaps have evolved multiple times, but some are thought to be degenerated mitochondria. These organelles earn their name from their ability to make ATP anaerobically with H_2 as a waste product. Other parabasalid features include flagella, a longitudinal aggregation of microtubules called an **axostyle**, and an undulating membrane. For more information about *Trichomonas* as a pathogen, see page 194.

- Diplomonads are unicellular flagellates with two, large nuclei (visible in this specimen). At one time diplomonads were thought to lack mitochondria, but more

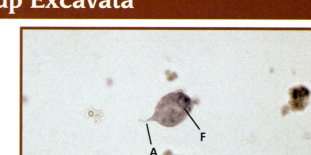

14-1 *TRICHOMONAS HOMINIS*, A PARABASALID Note the prominent posterior axostyle (**A**). A couple of flagella (**F**) are faintly visible at the anterior of the cell.

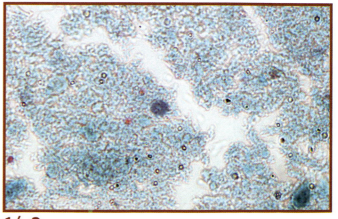

14-2 THE DIPLOMONAD *GIARDIA LAMBLIA* SHOWN IN A FECAL SMEAR (TRICHROME STAIN) This is a *Giardia* cyst, as evidenced by the three visible (there are actually four) nuclei. The trophozoite stage has the two nuclei typical of diplomonads.

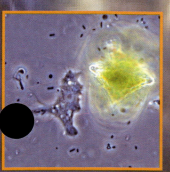

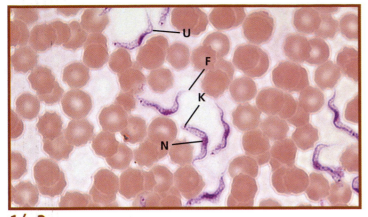

14-3 THE KINETOPLASTID *TRYPANOSOMA* IN A BLOOD SMEAR
Note the following features: nucleus (**N**), undulating membrane (**U**), kinetoplast (**K**), and flagellum (**F**).

14-4 *EUGLENA* *Euglena* is a large genus of mixotrophic flagellates. Most species have chloroplasts (**C**), which are discoid in this specimen. A red "eyespot" is located in the colorless anterior of the cell. The single flagellum also emerges from the anterior.

recent evidence shows they have degenerated into **mitosomes** that lack the electron transport chain and are thus nonfunctional in generating ATP for the cell. Instead, diplomonads use cytoplasmic biochemical pathways, such as glycolysis. For more information on *Giardia* as a pathogen, see page 193.

● The presence of a DNA mass within their single mito-chondrion, called a **kinetoplast**, is a unifying feature of kinetoplastids. As with euglenids, they have a distinctive **crystalline rod** within their flagella. Many are free living,

but *Trypanosoma* is a parasite that causes sleeping sickness in humans. For more information on *Trypanosoma* as a pathogen, see pages 195 and 196.

● **Euglenids** (Figure 14-4) are green, photosynthetic protists when light is available, but they are capable of heterotrophy when light is not (making them **mixotrophic**). One or two flagella are present and emerge from an invagination of the anterior (forward) cytoplasmic membrane. Flagella possess a crystalline rod similar to those of kinetoplastids. A red photoreceptor called an **eyespot** at the cell's anterior is another distinctive feature.

Group Chromalveolata

The chromalveolates may or may not be a **monophyletic group** (that is, descended from a single, common ancestor with chromalveolate traits); the jury is still out on that question. However, there is evidence to suggest that early in their evolution they underwent **secondary endosymbiosis** by engulfing a red alga. Many **extant** (living) species of chromalveolates have functional plastids that clearly resemble red algae, whereas others possess reduced plastids that also resemble red algae. Some have no plastids, but have red algal plastid DNA in their genome. Still others show no evidence of a red algal connection. A mystery is there for the solving if you choose to engage it! The major groups of chromalveolates are the **alveolates**, **stramenopiles** (Heterokontophyta), and **haptophytes**.

● The alveolates possess cytoplasmic membranous sacs (**alveoli**) near the cytoplasmic membrane. It has been speculated that the alveoli are somehow involved in maintaining osmotic balance, but their function is not known for certain. There are three main groups of alveolates: **dinoflagellates**, **apicomplexans**, and **ciliates**.

Dinoflagellates (Figure 14-5) are typically unicellular and autotrophic. Most have two flagella: one protruding from the cell and the other positioned in a groove encircling the cell. Most dinoflagellates are mixotrophic, though strictly autotrophic and heterotrophic species are known.

Apicomplexans, such as *Plasmodium* (Figure 14-6), are animal parasites, but retain a remnant of a plastid. Life cycles are complex, usually involving more than one host. The name "apicomplexa" derives from a complex of organelles at the

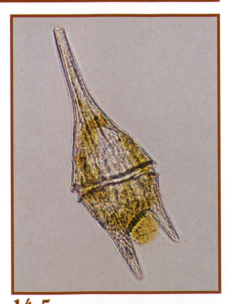

14-5 THE DINOFLAGELLATE *CERATIUM*
Ceratium is easily identified by the "horns" protruding from the cell wall. Note the groove at the cell's center that encases the circular flagellum. This specimen is a marine species.

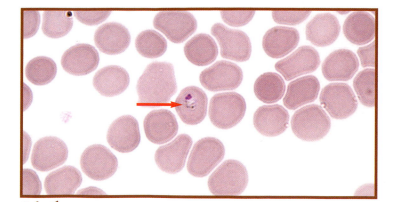

14-6 *PLASMODIUM,* AN APICOMPLEXAN, SHOWN IN A BLOOD SMEAR A *Plasmodium* **trophozoite** (**arrow**) has infected this red blood cell. Over the course of a *Plasmodium* infection, the parasite assumes many forms. This is the **ring stage**. A second ring stage is visible in the upper left of the field.

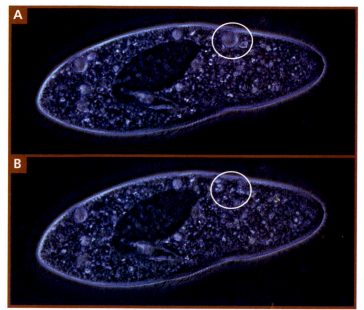

14-7 THE CILIATE *PARAMECIUM* **A** Notice in this phase contrast micrograph the prominent cilia covering the entire cell surface and the oral groove (which is barely visible at the bottom of the cell). Also notice the round, light area indicated by the **circle**. This is a **contractile vacuole** that constantly pumps water out of the cell to keep it from bursting. **B** Notice that the contractile vacuole has disappeared in this photomicrograph taken seconds after the one in **A**.

cell's apex, which are used in penetrating host cells. For more information about *Plasmodium,* see pages 197–199.

Ciliates are characterized by their possession of numerous cilia over the cell's entire surface or localized in specific regions. They are heterotrophs and use the cilia for feeding as well as locomotion. There are both marine and freshwater species (Figures 14-7 through 14-9).

● Stramenopiles (Heterokontophyta) are soil, marine, and freshwater autotrophs and heterotrophs. They are characterized by having a flagellum with "hairs" made of a basal attachment, a hollow shaft, and glycoprotein filaments split into three parts at the ends. A second smooth flagellum is often present. There are four groups of stramenopiles: **oomycetes** or **water molds** (Figures 14-10 and 14-11), which are colorless and heterotrophic, **diatoms** (Figures 14-12 through 14-19), the **golden algae,** and the **brown algae,** all of which are photosynthetic. These latter two groups are not covered here.

Many water molds (oomycetes) produce filaments of multinucleate cells, a feature similar to fungi. But, molecular evidence shows that they are not closely

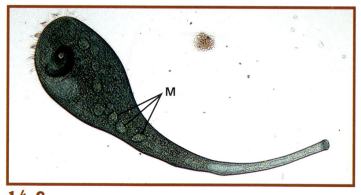

14-8 THE CILIATE *STENTOR* Its trumpet shape, size (up to 2 mm), and beaded macronucleus (**M**) make *Stentor* an easy ciliate to identify. It is covered with cilia, some of which surround its "mouth" (the white spot inside the dark coiled region at the left). This species is naturally green; this is not a stained specimen.

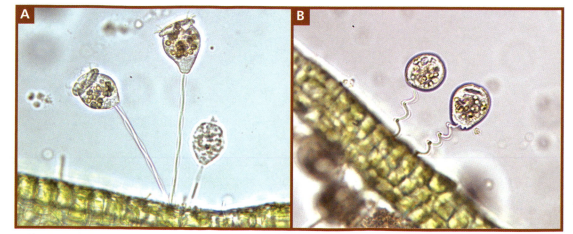

14-9 THE CILIATE *VORTICELLA*
A *Vorticella* is a genus of stalked, inverted bell-shaped ciliates. A crown of cilia surround the oral groove and are involved in feeding. **B** *Vorticella* is capable of retraction when the stalk coils. If you find a *Vorticella,* spend some time watching it until it recoils. It's worth the wait (which shouldn't be more than a minute).

related to the fungi. They have lost their plastids and are now primarily saprophytes (decomposers) or parasites. The water mold Genera *Allomyces* and *Saprolegna* are shown in Figures 14-10 and 14-11.

Diatoms, or **bacillariophytes**, are photosynthetic unicellular eukaryotes (Figures 14-12 to 14-19). Notice the distinctive golden brown color from the pigment **fucoxanthin** located in the **chromoplasts**, which may be of variable shape. Oil droplets are also frequently visible. Cell shapes are either round (**centric**) or bilaterally symmetrical and elongated (**pennate**). The cell wall is made of silica embedded in an organic matrix and consists of two halves, with one half overlapping the other in the same way the lid of a Petri dish overlaps its base. The combination of both halves is called a **frustule**. (Often,

diatoms can be identified from the frustules of deceased cells.) Some pennate diatoms are motile and have a central, longitudinal line called a **raphe**.

● Haptophytes are unicellular algae with two smooth flagella. They are distinguished by the presence of a **haptonema** extending from the cytoplasm between the two flagella. It is composed of layers of membranes surrounding seven microtubules, so is fundamentally different in structure from flagella, which have the 9+2 arrangement of microtubules within (9 pairs surrounding two single microtubules). The haptonema is a feeding structure that gathers food particles and delivers them to a food vacuole at the posterior of the cell. Many haptophytes have calcified scales called **coccoliths**. Figure 14-20 shows the haptophyte *Coccolithophora*.

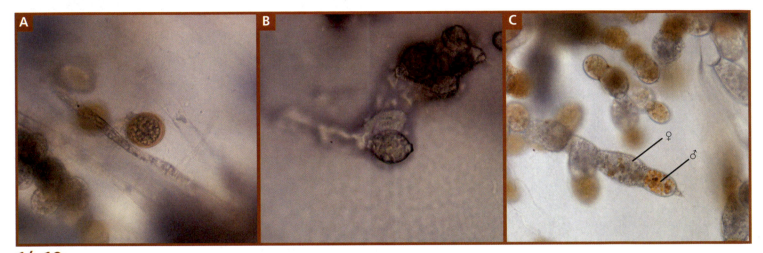

14-10 *ALLOMYCES, A REPRESENTATIVE WATER MOLD GROWN IN CULTURE* *Allomyces* is a soil **saprophyte** (decomposer). It exhibits alternation of generations, with a diploid filamentous phase (**sporophyte**) that produces **meiospores** by meiosis, which develop into a filamentous haploid phase (**gametophyte**) that produces male and female gametes by mitosis. In addition, the sporophyte is also capable of producing diploid meiospores that develop into another sporophyte. **A** Shown is a thick-walled meiosporangium. **B** This is a mitosporangium. The exit pore for the mitospores is at the right. **C** Gametophyte branches with male and female gametangia. In *Allomyces*, male gametangia (♂) are golden in color, whereas female gametangia (♀) are colorless.

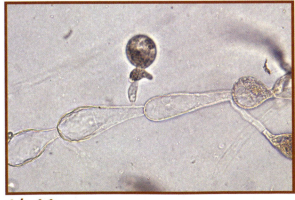

14-11 **WET MOUNT OF** *SAPROLEGNIA* *Saprolegnia* is another water mold. A diploid filament is shown, with the globular **oogonium** and the diploid, irregularly shaped **antheridium**. When an antheridium contacts an oogonium, meiosis occurs in both to produce eggs and haploid male nuclei. The male nuclei migrate into the oogonium where fertilization occurs. *Saprolegna* is a fish parasite.

14-12 *ARACHNOIDISCUS, A CENTRIC DIATOM* Note the radial symmetry, the golden chromoplasts, and the minute pores in the frustule. This is a marine species.

14-13 *NAVICULA, A PENNATE DIATOM* All of the many species of *Navicula* are shaped like a cigar or a boat. Cells are identifiable by prominent transverse lines converging on the central open space. A longitudinal line is also present.

14-14 *TABELLARIA* This distinctive diatom forms zigzag colonies. Note the golden brown chloroplasts.

14-15 *BACILLARIA* Members of this genus glide with individual cells sliding over one another. In this colony, the top cells are in the process of gliding to the right over the lower cells.

14-16 *GYROSIGMA* All species of this genus have sigmoid shaped cells. Note the golden brown chloroplasts at the edge and two prominent oil droplets.

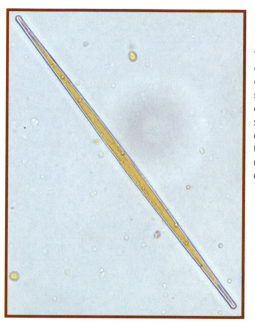

14-17 *SYNEDRA* These diatoms are distinctive because of their long, needle-shaped cells. They occur singly or sometimes in groups of cells attached at their ends, radiating outward like spokes of a wheel.

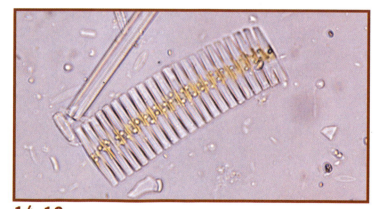

14-18 *FRAGILLARIA* These rectangular cells form ribbons with cells attached side-by-side. Note the golden brown chloroplast and oil droplets.

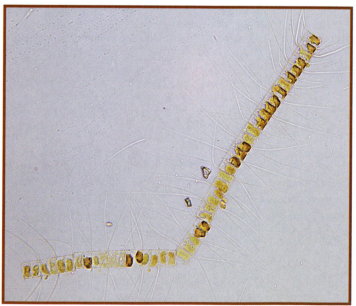

14-19 *CHAETOCEROS* This large, marine genus of beautiful diatoms is cosmopolitan in distribution.

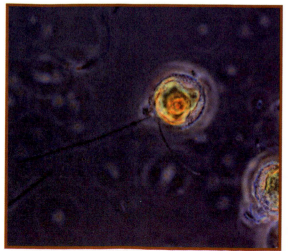

14-20 A HAPTOPHYTE (*COCCOLITHOPHORA*) GROWN IN CULTURE Note the two discoid golden chloroplasts, the two smooth flagella, and the scales on the cell's surface.

Group Rhizaria

Rhizarians are amoeboid unicells. Unlike the amoebas described below, whose **pseudopods** (cellular extensions used in moving and feeding) are blunt or lobate, rhizarians have long, thin pseudopods ("false feet"). Most rhizarians are covered with an inorganic shell called a **test**. There are two main rhizarian groups: **foraminferans** (Figure 14-21) and **radiolarians** (Figure 14-22).

● Foraminiferans have threadlike pseudopods extending from their multichambered, calcium

carbonate test. All foraminifera are marine and mostly occur in coastal waters. Though heterotrophy is the rule, some forams host endosymbiotic algae and are thus able to live autotrophically.

● Radiolarians are marine heterotrophs with silica cell walls. Their tests are radially symmetrical with spines.

14-22 A Radiolarian Test
This is the radially symmetrical test of an unidentified radiolarian. Radiolarian cell walls are made of silica.

14-21 A Foraminiferan Test Shown is a test from one species of the common genus *Elphidium*.
A The entire *Elphidium* test. **B** A detail of the same test showing pores through which pseudopodia extend in life.

Group Archaeplastida

There is strong evidence that the Archaeplastida are descended from an ancestral protist that engulfed a cyanobacterial endosymbiont, which eventually evolved into the chloroplasts of **red algae** (**Rhodophyta**), **green algae** (**Chlorophyta**), and land plants.

● Red algae are mostly marine and have complex life cycles. They possess the photosynthetic pigments chlorophylls *a* and *d*, as well as the accessory pigment **phycoerythrin**. All red algae lack flagella. Most rhodophytes are macroalgae and are not in the domain of microbiology, but *Porphyridium* (Figure 14-23) is among the few exceptions.

● Green algae (**Chlorophyta**) grow as single cells, colonies, and branched or unbranched filaments (Figures 14-24

to 14-31). All possess chlorophyll *a* and *b* in chloroplasts of various shapes, which are responsible for their green color. Many also exhibit **pyrenoids** in the chloroplasts where photosynthetic products are stored. If present, flagella are paired and of equal length. Cell walls typically are made of **cellulose**. The majority of chlorophytes live in freshwater, but there are marine and terrestrial species as well.

● **Charophyceans** (Figures 14-32 to 14-34) comprise a second, diverse group of Chlorophyta. Their distinctions are complex and often not visible to the casual light microscopist. Because of shared characters in flagellar structure, cellulose synthesis, mitosis, and certain enzymes, it is thought charophyceans and green plants are derived from a common ancestor.

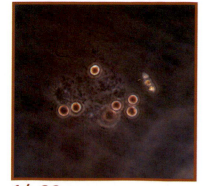

14-23 *PORPHYRIDIUM* **(PHASE CONTRAST, WET MOUNT)** Cells of the unicellular red alga *Porphyridium* measure approximately 5 μm in diameter. They are motile and exhibit positive **phototaxis** by secreting mucilage behind themselves that propels them toward the light.

14-24 *CHLAMYDOMONAS* This unicellular green alga has two flagella and a single, cup-shaped chloroplast. A red-orange stigma is found within the chloroplast and is involved in phototaxis. Cells are approximately 30 μm long and 20 μm wide.

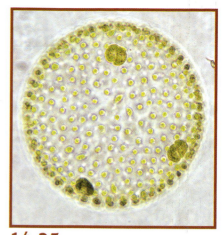

14-25 *VOLVOX* This is a colonial green alga made of cells similar in shape to *Chlamydomonas*. Daughter colonies form asexually from special cells in the parent colony. Release of each daughter colony involves its eversion as it exits through an enzymatically-produced pore. Mature colonies can reach a size visible to the naked eye.

14-26 *OEDOGONIUM* **A** *Oedogonium* is a large chlorophyte genus composed of unbranched filaments. Division of cells within the filament results in its elongation and produces distinctive **division scars** (**arrows**). **B** The cylindrical cells of this filament are interrupted by two oogonia (eggs).

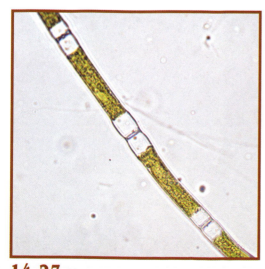

14-27 *ULOTHRIX* *Ulothrix* is another unbranched, filamentous chlorophyte. Its chloroplasts are found near the cell wall and form either a complete or incomplete ring around the cytoplasm. Prominent pyrenoids are usually present.

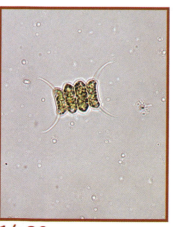

14-28 *SCENEDESMUS* This common chlorophyte consists of 4 or 8 cells joined along their edges. Cells range from 30–40 μm across.

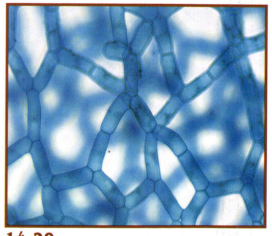

14-29 *HYDRODICTYON* The cells of this green alga form open connections with 4 (sometimes more) of its neighbors to produce a complex network of multinucleate cells. This explains its common name: the "water net." Cells may reach 1cm in length and each contains a single chloroplast with numerous pyrenoids. This specimen is from a culture.

14-30 *PEDIASTRUM* The colonies of *Pediastrum* are angular and star-like, and the surface cells often contain bristles that are thought to be used for buoyancy. The cell number and arrangement are constant for each species. Each cell has the potential to produce a colony of the same number and arrangement of cells as the parent colony!

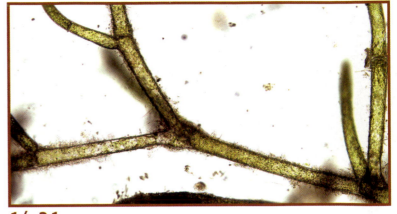

14-31 *CLADOPHORA* *Cladophora* is a branched chlorophyte with elongated cells. The single chloroplast has numerous pyrenoids and may look like a network of unconnected pieces.

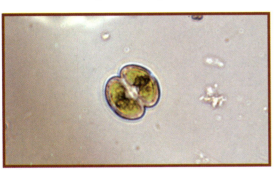

14-32 *COSMARIUM* *Cosmarium* is a desmid, which are characterized by paired "semicells." In this species of *Cosmarium* (one of over 1000!) two chloroplasts—one at each end—are present in each cell.

14-33 *CLOSTERIUM* Seen here are two *Closterium* individuals. *Closterium* is another desmid composed of two cells, but lacks the distinct constriction typical of most desmids. Vacuoles are present at the outer ends of the cells.

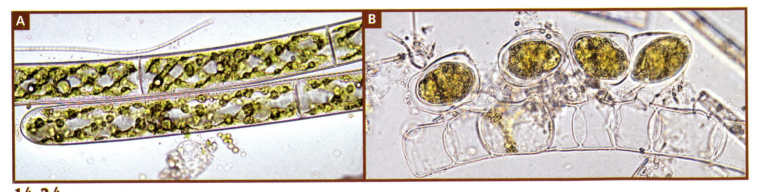

14-34 *SPIROGYRA* **A** *Spirogyra* is a well-known filamentous charophyte because of its distinctive spiral chloroplast. Note the numerous pyrenoids. The nucleus is located in the center of the cell and is obscured by the chloroplast. **B** Sexual reproduction occurs as two parallel filaments form conjugation tubes, through which one cell (a gamete) moves to join a cell (gamete) of the other filament, resulting in a zygote. This type of conjugation has happened in four cells in this micrograph. Each zygote undergoes meiosis and each resulting cell is capable of developing into a new filament.

Group Unikonta

Unikonta, comprising **amoebozoans, fungi,** and animals, is the last major eukaryotic group. **Lichens** are also covered in this section because of their relationship with fungi.

Amoebozoans

Amoebozoans are characterized by producing lobe-shaped pseudopodia (as compared to the thread-like pseudopodia of foraminiferans and radiolarians). Pseudopods perform the dual function of feeding and locomotion. Amoebozoans include **gymnamoebas, entamoebas,** and **slime molds.**

Gymnamoebas include the "classical" amoebas (Figure 14-35). Most are predatory heterotrophs, and there are marine, freshwater, and soil representatives. The cytoplasm is differentiated into a central portion (**endoplasm**) and the portion just beneath the cytoplasmic membrane (**ectoplasm**). Microfilaments in the ectoplasm produce **cytoplasmic streaming,** which is responsible for pseudopod formation.

Entamoebas are parasitic heterotrophs (Figure 14-36). They live in the guts of vertebrates and invertebrates. Important identification features are the presence and location of condensed peripheral and central chromatin. The latter is called the **karyosome.** For more information on *Entamoeba* as a pathogen, see pages 200–201.

Slime molds are divided into **cellular slime molds** and **plasmodial slime molds.** At some point in the life cycle, all slime molds produce sporangia that liberate reproductive spores. This feature at one time was thought to indicate relationship with fungi, but this has not been borne out by molecular evidence. The vegetative stage of a plasmodial slime mold is usually a brightly colored **plasmodium** (Figure 14-37) that engages in feeding by phagocytosis as the pseudopodia push their way through soil and decaying organic material. The unique feature of the plasmodium is that it is a single, giant cell easily visible to the naked eye (reaching sizes of several centimeters). Within the plasmodium are multiple diploid nuclei. Nutrients and oxygen are distributed by cytoplasmic streaming. When nutrients become limiting or the plasmodium begins to dry out, haploid spores are produced. When conditions become favorable again, spores germinate to produce flagellated swarm cells or amoeboid cells which act as gametes in fertilization to reestablish the diploid state. The zygote then undergoes mitosis without cytokinesis to produce a new plasmodium.

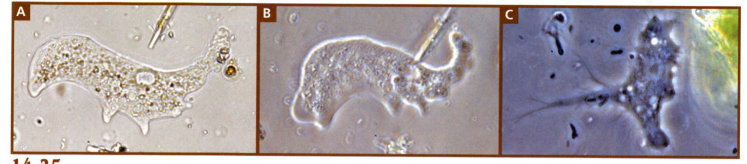

14-35 **AMOEBA** Cells with flowing cytoplasm and a constantly changing shape are likely to be amoebas. They move and capture prey by extending pseudopods outward. **A** This bright field micrograph clearly illustrates the difference between the cytoplasm at the periphery of the cell (ectoplasm) with that in the interior (endoplasm). The nucleus is visible as are numerous food vacuoles (the golden spots—probably an indication of this individual's food preferences!) **B** This is the same amoeba viewed with phase contrast only one or two seconds after the previous micrograph (notice that the shape is basically the same and the diatom at the top has moved only a short distance). Phase contrast produces a different texture to the image. Compare the ectoplasm, endoplasm, and nucleus with the bright field image. **C** This is a totally different amoeba, interesting for its ornate pseudopods.

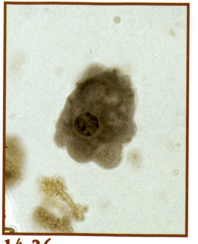

14-36 *ENTAMOEBA* **IN A FECAL SMEAR (IRON HEMATOXYLIN STAIN)** Note the lobed pseudopods and the condensed chromatin in the center (the karyosome) and the periphery of the nucleus.

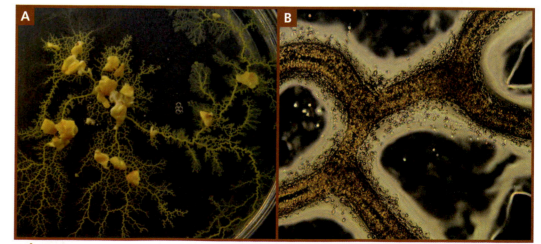

14-37 *PHYSARIUM,* **A PLASMODIAL SLIME MOLD** **A** Shown is a *Physarium* plasmodium growing on a water agar plate. The nutrients are supplied by oat flakes (the lumps in the photo) and the plasmodium has spread over the agar surface "in search" of more food. *Physarium* is a typical plasmodial slime mold in that it is brightly colored. **B** This is the same plasmodium viewed under low power. When the photograph was snapped, the central portion of each plasmodial strand was streaming to the left (meaning back toward the older portions).

Cellular slime molds (Figure 14-38) exist as haploid, single-celled feeding amoebas. When food becomes limiting, the individual amoebas begin to aggregate and form a motile, multicellular **slug**. When migration is complete, the slug becomes vertically oriented to form a stalked fruiting body. Cells of the stalk produce cellulose to support the head, which is formed by cells from the rear of the slug that migrate upward. Head cells differentiate into asexual spores that will germinate into amoebas once conditions are favorable again. A sexual cycle occurs when two amoebas fuse to make a diploid zygote, which then begins to consume other amoebas and then encysts within a cellulose wall. Prior to germination, the diploid nucleus undergoes meiosis to produce haploid nuclei, which are distributed to new amoebas that enter the asexual cycle.

Fungi

Fungi are nonmotile eukaryotes. Their cell wall is usually made of the polysaccharide chitin, not cellulose as in plants. Unlike animals (that ingest then digest their food), fungi are **absorptive heterotrophs**. That is, they secrete exoenzymes into the environment, then absorb the digested nutrients. Most are **saprophytes** that decompose dead organic matter, but some are **parasites** of plants, animals, or humans (Section 15).

Fungi are informally divided into unicellular **yeasts** (Figure 14-39) and filamentous **molds** (Figure 14-40) based on their overall appearance. **Dimorphic fungi** have both mold and yeast life cycle stages. Filamentous fungi that produce fleshy reproductive structures—mushrooms, puffballs, and shelf fungi—are referred to as **macrofungi** (Figure 14-41), even though the majority of the fungus is filamentous and hidden underground or within decaying matter.

Individual fungal filaments are called **hyphae**; collectively they form a **mycelium**. The hyphae are darkly pigmented in **dematiaceous fungi** and unpigmented in **hyaline** or **moniliaceous fungi** (Figure 14-42). Hyphae may be **septate**, in which there are walls separating adjacent cells, or **nonseptate** if walls are absent (Figure 14-43).

Fungal life cycles are usually complex, involving both sexual and asexual forms of reproduction. Gametes are

14-38 **DICTYOSTELIUM, A CELLULAR SLIME MOLD** **A** Shown is a portion of an aggregating *Dictyostelium* slug. Notice the regular shape of the cells, which is very unlike the irregular shapes of the amoebas when acting as individuals. The blurry part in the lower left is the base of a growing stalk. **B** This is the head of an immature fruiting body. **C** A mature fruiting body of *Dictyostelium*.

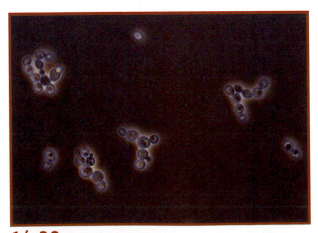

14-39 **YEAST** This is a wet mount of the brewer's yeast, *Saccharomyces cerevisiae*, viewed with a phase contrast microscope. Notice the small buds forming on some cells.

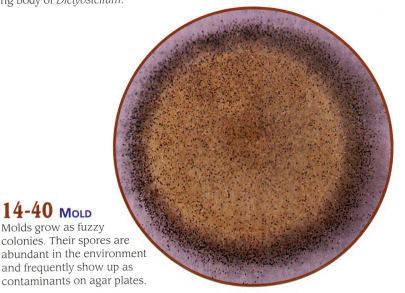

14-40 **MOLD** Molds grow as fuzzy colonies. Their spores are abundant in the environment and frequently show up as contaminants on agar plates.

14-41 MACROFUNGUS This mushroom is the fruiting body from a mycelium that is busily engaged in decomposing the redwood log below.

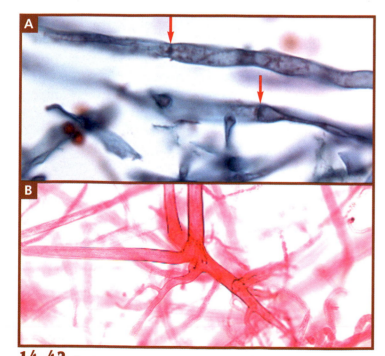

14-42 HYALINE HYPHAE This tangled mass of hyphae belongs to the bread mold, *Rhizopus*. They are hyaline because they lack pigment. The black spots are sporangia.

14-43 SEPTATE AND NONSEPTATE HYPHAE A The hyphae of *Aspergillus* are septate. Note the crosswalls (**arrows**) dividing cells. B *Rhizopus* provides an example of nonseptate hyphae.

produced by **gametangia** and spores are produced by a variety of **sporangia**. Typically, the only diploid cell in the fungal life cycle is the zygote, which undergoes meiosis to produce haploid spores characteristic of the fungal group (see the following paragraph). Various asexual spores may also be produced during the life cycle of many fungi. If they form at the ends of hyphae, they are called **conidia**. Other asexual spores are **blastospores**, which are produced by budding, and **arthrospores**, which are produced when a hypha breaks. **Chlamydospores** (**chlamydoconidia**) are formed at the end of some hyphae and are a resting stage.

Formal taxonomic categories are based primarily on the pattern of sexual spore production and presence of cross walls in the hyphae. Members of the **Class Zygomycetes** are terrestrial, have nonseptate hyphae, and produce nonmotile **sporangiospores** and **zygospores**. Members of the **Class Ascomycetes** produce a sac (an **ascus**) in which the zygote undergoes meiosis to produce haploid **ascospores**. Ascomycete hyphae are septate. Members of the **Class Basidiomycetes** have septate hyphae and produce a **basidium** during sexual reproduction that undergoes meiosis to produce four **basidiospores** attached to its surface.

Saccharomyces cerevisiae is an ascomycete used in production of bread, wine, and beer, but is not an important human pathogen. It does not form a mycelium, but rather produces a colony similar to bacteria (Figure 14-44). The vegetative cells (**blastoconidia**) are generally oval to round in shape and asexual reproduction occurs by budding (Figure 14-45). Short **pseudohyphae** are sometimes produced when the budding cells fail to separate. Meiosis produces one to four ascospores within the vegetative cell, which acts as the ascus (Figure 14-46). Ascospores may fuse to form another generation of diploid vegetative cells or they may be released to produce a population of haploid cells that are indistinguishable from diploid cells. Haploid cells of opposite mating types may also combine to create a diploid cell.

Microscopic examination, and biochemical and antibiotic sensitivity tests are used in identification. Asci stain

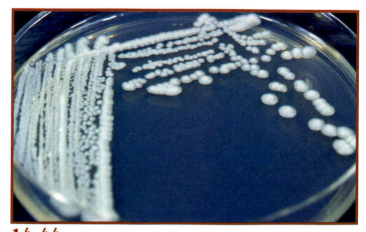

14-44 SACCHAROMYCES CEREVISIAE COLONIES Note the appearance is similar to a typical bacterial colony, not fuzzy like mold colonies.

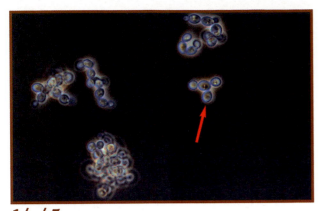

14-45 WET MOUNT OF *SACCHAROMYCES CEREVISIAE* VEGETATIVE CELLS (CRYSTAL VIOLET STAIN) Note the budding cell (blastoconidium) in the center of field (**arrow**).

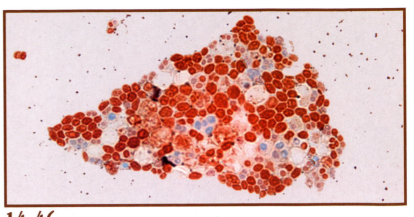

14-46 *SACCHAROMYCES CEREVISIAE* ASCOSPORES One to four ascospores are produced in the original cell (acting as an ascus) by meiosis. In this specimen, the vegetative cells are blue and the ascospores are red.

14-47 *RHIZOPUS STOLONIFER* Black asexual sporangia of this bread mold have begun to form, giving the growth a "salt and pepper" appearance.

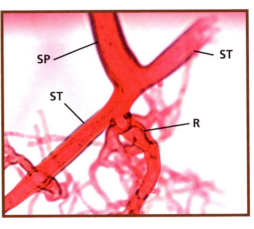

14-48 *RHIZOPUS* RHIZOIDS Anchoring root-like rhizoids (**R**) form at the junction of each sporangiophore (**SP**) and the stolon (**ST**). Note the absence of septa.

Gram-negative whereas the vegetative cells are Gram-positive. The asci and ascospores stain pink in a Kinyoun acid-fast stain, whereas the vegetative cells stain blue.

Rhizopus species are fast growing zygomycetes that produce white or grayish cottony growth. The mycelium becomes darker with age as sporangia are produced, giving it a "salt and pepper" appearance (Figure 14-47). Microscopically, *Rhizopus* species produce broad (10 μm), hyaline, and usually nonseptate surface and aerial hyphae. Anchoring **rhizoids** (Figure 14-48) are produced where the surface hyphae (**stolons**) join the bases of the long, unbranched **sporangiophores**.

The *Rhizopus* life cycle (Figure 14-49) includes sexual and asexual phases. Asexual **sporangiospores** are produced by large, circular sporangia (Figures 14-50 and 14-51) borne at the ends of long, nonseptate, elevated sporangiophores. A hemispherical **columella** supports the sporangium. The spores develop into hyphae identical to those that produced them. On occasion, sexual reproduction occurs when hyphae of different mating types (designated + and − strains) make

contact. Initially, **progametangia** (Figure 14-52) extend from each hypha. Upon contact, a septum separates the end of each progametangium into a gamete (Figure 14-53). The walls between the two gametangia dissolve and a thick-walled **zygospore** develops (Figures 14-54 and 14-55). Fusion of nuclei occurs within the zygospore and produces one or more diploid nuclei, or **zygotes**. After a dormant period, meiosis of the zygotes occurs. The zygospore then germinates and produces a sporangium similar to asexual sporangia. Haploid spores are released and develop into new hyphae, completing the life cycle.

Rhizopus species are common contaminants. *R. stolonifer* is the common bread mold. *R. oryzae* and *R. arrhizus* are responsible for producing zygomycosis, a condition found most frequently in diabetics and immunocompromised patients. Inhalation of spores may lead to hypersensitivity reactions in the respiratory system. Entry into the blood leads to rapid spreading of the organism, occlusion of blood vessels, and necrosis of tissues.

Pilobolus is another genus of zygomycetes, with the unusual ability to aim and shoot its sporangia (Figure 14-56), which form at the tips of sporangiophores. The **subsporangial vesicle** acts as a lens and orients itself so that the sporangium is aimed at a light source. Using a burst of water from the subsporangial vesicle, spores are released a meter or

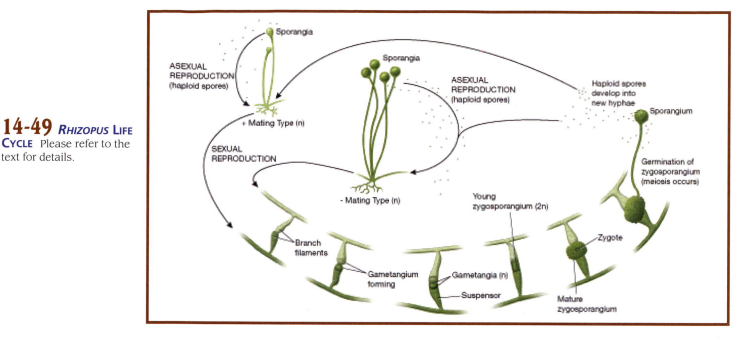

14-49 *RHIZOPUS* **LIFE CYCLE** Please refer to the text for details.

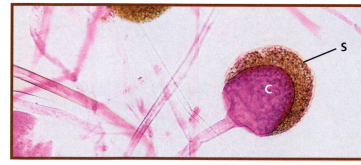

14-50 *RHIZOPUS* **SPORANGIOPHORES**
The sporangium is found at the end of a long, unbranched, and nonseptate sporangiophore. The haploid asexual sporangiospores (**S**) cover the surface of the columella (**C**), which has a flattened base.

14-51 *RHIZOPUS* **COLUMELLA** Note the umbrella-shaped columella that remains after the sporangium has released its spores.

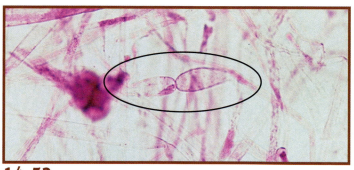

14-52 *RHIZOPUS* **PROGAMETANGIA** Progametangia from different hyphae are shown in the center of the field. Contact between the progametangia results in each forming a gamete.

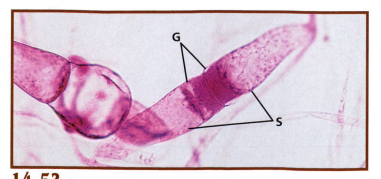

14-53 *RHIZOPUS* **GAMETANGIA AND SUSPENSORS** Gametangia (**G**) and suspensors (**S**) are shown in the center of the field. Gametangia contain haploid nuclei from each mating type.

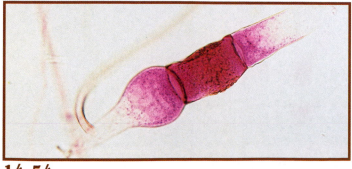

14-54 **YOUNG** *RHIZOPUS* **ZYGOSPORE** The zygospore forms when the cytoplasm from the two mating strains fuse (**plasmogamy**).

14-55 MATURE *RHIZOPUS* ZYGOSPORE Haploid nuclei from each strain fuse within the zygospore (**karyogamy**) to produce many diploid nuclei. Meiosis of each occurs to produce numerous haploid spores.

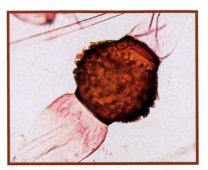

14-56 *PILOLOBUS* CULTURE These *Pilolobus* sporangiophores are oriented vertically because they were incubated in the dark. Had there been a directional light source, they would have been oriented toward it. Spores are in the black cap; the clear, swollen area beneath them is the subsporangial vesicle. The culture was raised on Rabbit Dung Agar; the brown object is a rabbit pellet.

more toward the light with the "intent" of shooting them toward vegetation that will be ingested by an animal. Spores are distributed in the animals' feces, and the cycle repeats.

Lichens

Lichens are an amalgam of two organisms living in a mutualistic symbiosis. One partner, the **mycobiont**, is a fungus. The other partner, the **photobiont**, is either a cyanobacterium or a green alga (or sometimes both are present). Most mycobionts

are ascomycetes and worldwide, approximately 20% of fungi participate in forming lichens. Photobionts are limited to a few dozen genera.

The association between mycobiont and photobiont favors both. In fact, frequently the lichenized fungus can survive in places where the individuals cannot. The photobiont photosynthesizes and produces organic compounds from CO_2 and water. If it is a cyanobacterium, it may also be capable of nitrogen fixation. In turn, the mycobiont benefits from the productivity of its partner and provides it with moisture and protection.

Lichens reproduce asexually by fragmentation of the thallus and by producing propagules containing both the mycobiont and photobiont. Sexual reproduction also occurs, but the mechanisms are varied and poorly understood. It appears that the sexually reproducing fungus must obtain a new photobiont partner each generation, thus emphasizing the continuity of the fungus and validating the convention of naming lichens after the mycobiont.

The lichen body (**thallus**) can usually be categorized into one of three types: **foliose** (leafy), **fruticose** (shrubby), and **crustose** (crusty). Examples are shown in Figures 14-57 through Figure 14-59.

14-57 A FOLIOSE LICHEN This foliose lichen was found in a public park in Oregon. Note the leafy appearance of the thallus.

14-58 A FRUTICOSE LICHEN This stringy lichen was provisionally identified as *Ramalina menziesii*. Note the delicate network of thallus strands. It was photographed in Northern California.

14-59 A CRUSTOSE LICHEN This crustose lichen was provisionally identified as *Caloplaca marina*. It was found high in the intertidal zone of a rocky shore in Oregon.

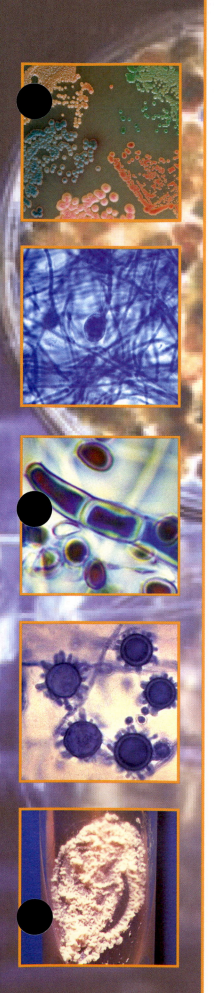

Fungi of Clinical Importance

This section is a brief treatment of fungal pathogens. For an introduction to fungi in general, please refer to page 178 in Section 14.

Yeasts of Medical Importance

Candida albicans

Candida albicans (Figures 15-1 through 15-3) is part of the normal respiratory, gastrointestinal, and female urogenital tract floras. Under the proper circumstances, it may flourish and produce pathological conditions, such as thrush in the oral cavity, vulvovaginitis of the female genitals, and cutaneous candidiasis of the skin. Systemic candidiasis may follow infection of the lungs, bronchi, or kidneys. Entry into the blood may result in endocarditis. Individuals most susceptible to *Candida* infections are diabetics, those with immuno-deficiency (*e.g.*, AIDS), catheterized patients, and individuals taking antimicrobial medications. Budding results in chains of cells called **pseudohyphae** that produce clusters of round, asexual blastoconidia at the cell junctions. Large, round, thick-walled **chlamydospores** form at the ends of pseudohyphae. Presumptive identification of *C. albicans* can be made from a positive germ tube test (Figure 15-4).

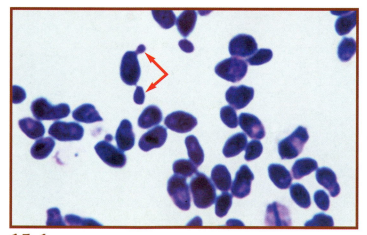

15-1 *CANDIDA ALBICANS* **VEGETATIVE CELLS** Note the oval shape, nuclei, and budding cells (**arrow**).

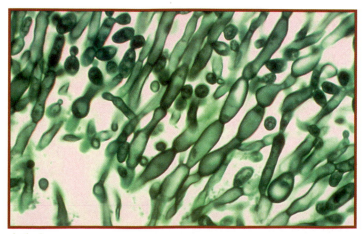

15-2 *CANDIDA ALBICANS* **PSEUDOHYPHAE** Note the constrictions between cells.

15-3 **CANDIDA ALBICANS COLONIES ON CHROMAGAR CANDIDA** CHROMagar *Candida* is a commercial differential medium for isolation and presumptive identification of clinically important yeasts. The colonies are (clockwise from top) *C. albicans* (green), *C. glabrata* (dark pink), *C. krusei* (pink and velvety), and *C. tropicalis* (blue/purple). The beige growth at the top left is *Trichosporon beigeli*.
Photograph courtesy of CHROMagar, Paris, France

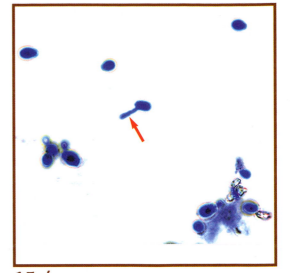

15-4 **CANDIDA ALBICANS GERM TUBE TEST** Presence of germ tubes (**arrow**) allows presumptive identification of *C. albicans*.

Cryptococcus neoformans

Cryptococcus neoformans causes cryptococcosis and is the only known serious human pathogen of the genus. It is an encapsulated, nonfermenting, aerobic yeast (Figure 15-5) often found in soil mixed with accumulated bird (pigeon) droppings that enrich it with nitrogen. Urban sites where pigeons roost may also harbor the organism in the dried feces. Infection by *C. neoformans* from inhalation leads to pneumonia and then meningitis. Cryptococcosis, at one time a disease of poultry workers, is increasing in incidence and is among the more common opportunistic infections of AIDS patients. Due to the capsule, colonies of *C. neoformans* are shiny, cream-colored, and mucoid (Figure 15-6). Identification is made by direct microscopic examination and biochemical tests.

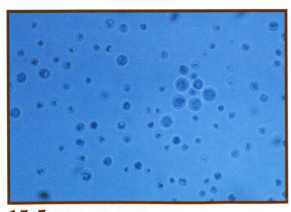

15-5 **CRYPTOCOCCUS NEOFORMANS (LACTOPHENOL BLUE STAIN)** *C. neoformans* is characterized by spherical, encapsulated cells that range in size from 2–15 μm. The capsule is faintly visible in this preparation.

15-6 **CRYPTOCOCCUS NEOFORMANS COLONIES** The colonies are mucoid due to the encapsulated yeast cells.
Photograph courtesy of CDC Public Health Image Library

Pneumocystis jirovecii

Pneumocystis jirovecii (formerly *P. carinii*) is an opportunistic pathogen whose taxonomy and natural history has been difficult to work out due to the inability to grow it outside of its mammalian host. Comparison of ribosomal RNA and genome sequencing has led to the conclusion that *Pneumocystis*, long classified as a protozoan, is more closely related to certain ascomycete yeasts. Its protozoan roots are still evident, however, in the terminology associated with it. *Pneumocystis* exists as a **trophozoite** (trophic stage) and a multinucleate **cyst** (spore case) (Figure 15-7). Asexual reproduction is by fission of the trophozoite, not budding as in most yeast. Its sexual phase is thought to resemble yeast-like conjugation to form a zygote that produces four spores by meiosis. These then undergo mitosis to produce a cyst with eight spores.

Most people become seropositive for *Pneumocystis* in childhood and humans—even immunocompetent individuals—are the apparent reservoirs for the organism. Transmission is through the air, with the primary infection occurring in the lungs. Infection produces pneumocystis pneumonia (PCP) in AIDS patients and immunosuppressed

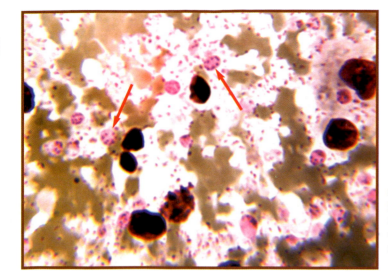

individuals, and interstitial plasma cell pneumonitis in malnourished infants. Identification is made by direct examination of the cyst (usually) using immunofluorescence. Co-trimoxazole is given to immunocompromised patients whose CD4 (T-helper) cell counts are less than $200/mm^3$.

15-7 *SECTION OF PNEUMOCYSTIS JIROVECII CYST IN AN INFECTED LUNG (PERIODIC ACID SCHIFF STAIN)* Zygotic meiosis followed by a mitotic division of each spore results in a mature cyst with eight spores (**arrows**). Once released, the spores become trophozoites.

Monomorphic Molds

Dermatophytes

The dermatophytes include *Epidermophyton, Microsporum,* and *Trichophyton,* related genera of fungi that infect keratinized tissues of mammals—epidermis, nails, and hair. They produce a group of conditions known as "tinea" or "ringworm." The latter name comes from their growth pattern in which the infection spreads outwards from the center of initial infection. The actively growing cells are at the edge of the growth, whereas healing tissue is toward the middle, thus giving the impression of a worm at the lesion's periphery. Various forms of tinea are recognized based on body location: tinea capitis occurs on the head, tinea corporis occurs on the face and trunk, tinea cruris occurs on the groin, tinea unguium occurs on the nails, and tinea pedis occurs on the feet (producing a condition known as "athlete's foot").

Dermatophytes may infect more than one body region and often produce similar symptoms, so they are considered together here. Inflammation of infected tissue due to fungal antigens is the primary symptom and is often manifested as scaling, discoloration, and itching. Transmission is through contact with infected skin or contaminated items, such as towels, clothing, combs, or bedding.

Identification generally involves consideration of the tissue infected (as some are fairly specific), examination of the infection, and microscopic examination of patient samples and/or cultures. Tissues infected with *Microsporum* fluoresce when illuminated with a **Wood's lamp** (an ultraviolet light source) whereas *Epidermophyton* and *Trichophyton* do not produce fluorescence. Large **macroconidia** and smaller **microconidia** are especially useful microscopic characteristics used in differentiating species.

Epidermophyton

Epidermophyton floccosum is the only pathogen in the genus. It invades the dead, keratinized tissues of skin and nails, but not hair, and is highly contagious. In culture, colonies have an olive-green to khaki central portion with an orange periphery (Figure 15-8). Older cultures become overgrown with a white aerial mycelium.

Microscopically, characteristic macroconidia can be observed arising from conidiophores either singly or in clusters of two or three. These are septate with one to five cells, and club shaped with thin, smooth walls (Figure 15-9). Microconidia are absent.

15-8 *EPIDERMOPHYTON FLOCCOSUM COLONY ON SABOURAUD DEXTROSE AGAR* Notice the khaki color is somewhat obscured by the white aerial mycelium.

Photograph by Dr. Lucille K. Georg, courtesy of CDC Public Health Image Laboratory

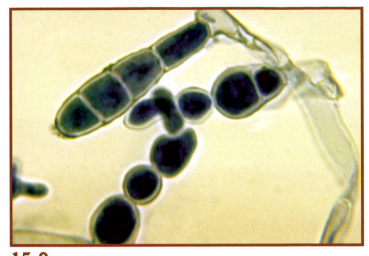

15-9 *EPIDERMOPHYTON FLOCCOSUM* **MACROCONIDIA** Note the hyphae with characteristic club-shaped, septate macroconidia with thin, smooth walls. They range in size from 5–10 μm wide by 20–65 μm long.
Photograph by Dr. Libero Ajello, courtesy of CDC Public Health Image Laboratory

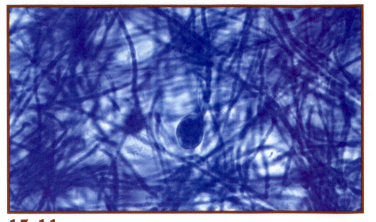

15-11 *MICROSPORUM AUDOUINII* **CHLAMYDOCONIDIUM (LACTO-PHENOL COTTON BLUE STAIN)** When grown in culture, *M. audouinii* often produces terminal chlamydoconidia, which contain resistant resting cells.

Microsporum

Terminal, septate macroconidia with thick, rough walls characterize the genus *Microsporum*. Microconidia may be present, but are not common. Chlamydoconidia, a resting stage, are produced by some species. Hyphae are septate and either branched or unbranched.

M. audouinii was at one time responsible for scalp ringworm epidemics in children. It rarely infects adults. Colonies are gray to tan with a light orange reverse (Figure 15-10). Unlike other species in the genus, *M. audouinii* rarely produces macroconidia or microconidia. Pointed chlamydoconidia may be seen (Figure 15-11).

M. gypseum (Figure 15-10) infects humans less frequently than *M. adouinii*. Colonies are variously colored, ranging from tan to reddish brown and often developing a white border or white center. Thin walled and rough macroconidia with no more than 6 cells are abundant (Figure 15-12). Club-shaped microconidia may also be observed.

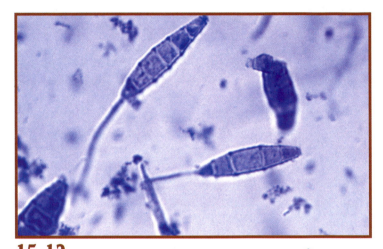

15-12 **MACROCONIDIA OF** *MICROSPORUM GYPSEUM* **(LACTO-PHENOL COTTON BLUE STAIN)** *M. gypseum* typically has fewer than six cells in each macroconidium. Note the rough surface. Macroconidia range in size from 8–16 μm wide by 22–60 μm long.

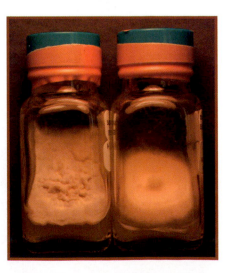

15-10 *MICROSPORUM* **COLONIES** On the left is *M. gypseum. M. audouinii* is on the right.

Trichophyton spp.

Trichophyton species (Figures 15-13 through 15-15) are the most important dermatophytes causing infection in adults. They are responsible for most cases of tinea pedis and tinea unguium, and occasionally tinea corporis and tinea capitis. Macroconidia are rare, but are located at the ends of hyphae and are club-shaped, smooth, thin-walled and septate with up to ten cells. Spherical microconidia are more common. An *in vitro* hair perforation test is used to distinguish *T. mentagrophytes* from other members of the genus (except *T. terrestre* and some *T. tonsurans*) (Figure 15-16).

15-13
TRICHOPHYTON MENTAGROPHYTES
The colonies are granular, whitish to tan, and may form concentric rings. Generally, no conidiation is observed.
Photograph by Dr. Libero Ajello, courtesy of CDC Public Health Image Laboratory

15-14
TRICHOPHYTON MENTAGROPHYTES REVERSE This is the same colony as shown in Figure 15-13, but viewed from below.
Photograph by Dr. Libero Ajello, courtesy of CDC Public Health Image Laboratory

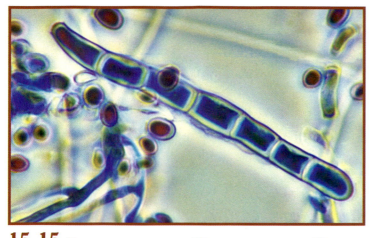

15-15 TRICHOPHYTON RUBRUM MACROCONIDIUM AND MICRO-CONIDIA (LACTOPHENOL COTTON BLUE STAIN) The macroconidia of *T. rubrum* are cigar-shaped, have smooth, thin walls and between three and eight cells. They range in size from 4–8 μm wide by 40–60 μm long. The microconidia are teardrop in shape and are borne in clusters.
Photograph by Dr. Libero Ajello, courtesy of CDC Public Health Image Laboratory

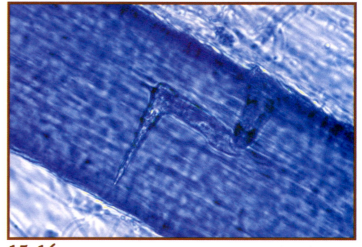

15-16 HAIR PERFORATION TEST (LACTOPHENOL COTTON BLUE STAIN) *Trichophyton mentagrophytes* infection can be diagnosed by a hair perforation test. Note the indentation in the hair.

Aspergillus

The genus *Aspergillus* is characterized by green to yellow or brown granular colonies with a white edge (Figure 15-17). One species, *A. niger*, produces distinctive black colonies (Figure 15-18). Vegetative hyphae are hyaline (unpigmented) and septate. The *Aspergillus* fruiting body is distinctive, with chains of conidia arising from one (uniseriate) or two (biseriate) rows of **phialides** attached to a swollen **vesicle** at the end of an unbranched conidiophore (Figure 15-19). The conidiophore grows from a foot cell in the vegetative hypha (Figure 15-20). Fruiting body structure and size, and conidia color are useful in species identification.

A. fumigatus and other species are opportunistic pathogens that cause aspergillosis, an umbrella term covering many diseases. One form of pulmonary aspergillosis (referred to as "fungus ball") involves colonization of the bronchial tree or tissues damaged by tuberculosis. Allergic

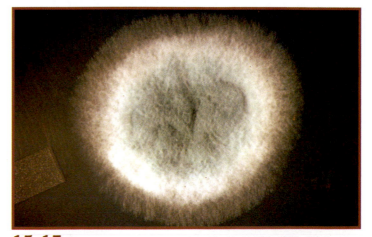

15-17 ASPERGILLUS FUMIGATUS COLONY ON SABOURAUD DEXTROSE AGAR Note the rugose topography and green, granular appearance with a white margin. The reverse is white. Although a common cause of aspergillosis, normally healthy people are not at great risk from *A. fumigatus* infection.

15-18 *ASPERGILLUS NIGER* COLONY ON SABOURAUD DEXTROSE AGAR *A. niger* produces distinctive black colonies. This colony was grown 7 days at 25°C.

aspergillosis may occur in individuals who are in frequent contact with the spores and become sensitized to them. Subsequent contact produces symptoms similar to asthma. Invasive aspergillosis is the most severe form. It results in necrotizing pneumonia and may spread to other organs.

Some species of *Aspergillus* are of commercial importance. Fermentation of soybeans by *A. oryzae* produces soy paste. Soy sauce is produced by fermenting soybeans with a mixture of *A. oryzae* and *A. soyae*. *Aspergillus* is also used in commercial production of citric acid.

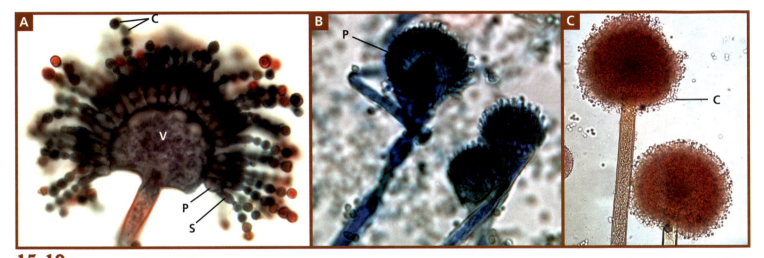

15-19 *ASPERGILLUS* CONIDIAL HEADS A Shown is a section of an *A. niger* conidiophore. The conidia (**C**), primary (**P**) and secondary (**S**) phialides, and vesicle (**V**) are visible. This is a biseriate conidium. **B** The *A. fumigatus* conidial head is uniseriate with just a single row of phialides (**P**). The conidia are mostly absent due to handling during slide preparation. **C** Shown is a whole mount of an *A. niger* conidiophore. Note the chains of conidia (**C**) are shorter than in Figure 15-19A due to handling during slide preparation. The vesicle (**V**) is visible, but the phialides are not distinct.

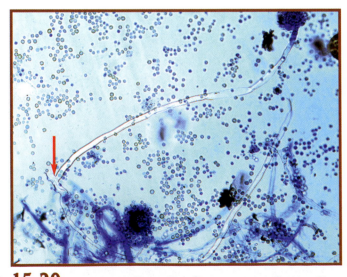

15-20 *ASPERGILLUS* FOOT CELL (LACTOPHENOL COTTON BLUE STAIN) Sporangiophores emerge from a foot cell with the shape of an inverted "T" (**arrow**). This is a wet mount of *A. flavus*. Notice all the conidia in the field.

Coccidioides immitis

Coccidioides immitis causes coccidioidomycosis ("Valley fever"), a lung disease associated with desert regions of the southwestern United States, northern Mexico, and parts of Central and South America. Most infections are asymptomatic and self-limiting, but in some individuals symptoms are influenza-like and may include hypersensitivity reactions. Rarely, the disease becomes disseminated and then may be lethal. It is the most frequent cause of laboratory-acquired fungal infections, so extreme care must be taken when handling it.

The mold form consists of branched, septate, hyaline hyphae. Barrel-shaped **arthroconidia** develop separated by thin-walled **disjunctor cells**. When the disjunctor cells die, the arthroconidia become separated (Figure 15-21). Infection occurs when these become airborne and are inhaled. Once in the host, arthroconidia develop into thick-walled

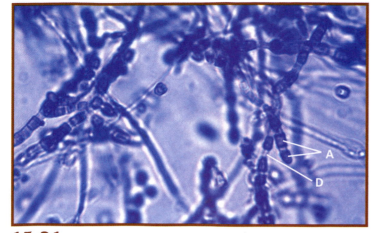

15-21 *COCCIDIOIDES IMMITIS* **ARTHROCONIDIA (LACTOPHENOL COTTON BLUE STAIN)** Typically, the barrel-shaped arthroconidia (**A**) are separated by thinner walled disjunctor cells (**D**). Arthroconidia range in size from 3–4 μm wide by 3–6 μm long.

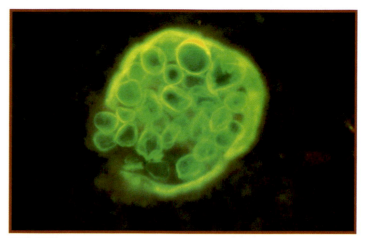

15-22 *COCCIDIOIDES IMMITIS* **SPHERULE (FLUORESCENT ANTIBODY STAIN)** Presence of *C. immitis* spherules in patient specimens is useful in coccidioidomycosis diagnosis. Spherules range in size from 10–80 μm in diameter. Specimens examined range from sputum and other pulmonary samples, to urine, blood, and cerebrospinal fluid.
Photograph courtesy of CDC Public Health Image Library

spherules containing endospores (not to be confused with bacterial endospores), which may in turn develop into spherules upon release (Figure 15-22). In culture, arthroconidia develop into hyphae.

C. immitis colonies are white and wooly, but may develop a variety of colors with age. The yeast form does not grow on standard culture media.

Colony morphology, hyphae with alternating barrel-shaped arthroconidia and disjunctor cells, and direct examination of patient samples for the presence of spherules are used in identifying *C. immitis*. DNA probes are also used in identification.

Fonsecaea

Fonsecaea pedrosoi is a dematiaceous fungus that causes chromoblastomycosis, a disease of skin and subcutaneous tissues, particularly in the lower extremities. It has a worldwide distribution, but is more common in tropical and subtropical regions. Colonies are olive green to black with a velvety texture and a black reverse (Figure 15-23). The branched and septate hyphae have dark cell walls due to the pigment melanin. The dark conidia are borne on septate conidiophores in four basic patterns (Figure 15-24). At least two of these must be seen to identify the isolate as *F. pedrosoi*.

15-23 *FONSECAEA PEDROSOI* **COLONY** This dematiaceous fungus is the primary cause of chromoblastomycosis.

15-24 *FONSECAEA PEDROSOI* **CONIDIA (LACTOPHENOL COTTON BLUE STAIN)** There is great variation in *F. pedrosoi* conidia formation, and at least two different ones must be seen to identify a specimen as *Fonsecaea*. Hyphae are septate and branched. Conidia range in size from 1.5–3.0 μm wide by 2.5–6.0 μm long.
Photograph courtesy of CDC Public Health Image Library

Penicillium

Members of the genus *Penicillium* produce distinctive green, powdery, radially furrowed colonies with a white apron (Figure 15-25) and a light colored reverse surface. The hyphae are septate and thin. Distinctive *Penicillium* fruiting bodies, consisting of **metulae, phialides,** and chains of spherical conidia, are located at the ends of branched or unbranched **conidiophores** (Figure 15-26).

  Penicillium is best known for its production of the antibiotic penicillin, but it is also a common contaminant. One pathogen, *P. marneffei*, is endemic to Asia and is responsible for disseminated opportunistic infections of the lungs, liver, and skin in immunosuppressed and immuno-compromised patients. It is thermally dimorphic, producing a typical velvety colony with a distinctive red pigment at 25°C but converting to a yeast form at 35°C. Other species of *Penicillium* are of commercial importance for fermentations used in cheese production. Examples include *P. roquefortii* (Roquefort cheese) and *P. camembertii* (Camembert and Brie cheeses).

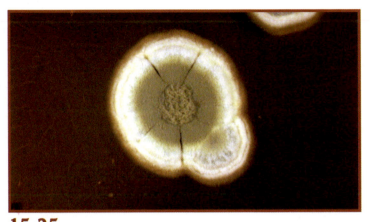

15-25 PENICILLIUM NOTATUM COLONY ON SABOURAUD DEXTROSE AGAR The green, granular surface with radial furrows and a white apron are typical of the genus.

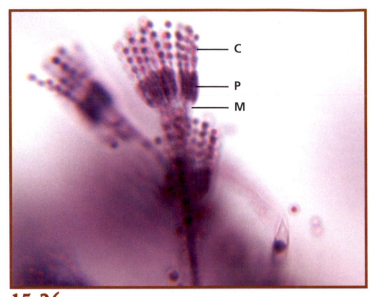

15-26 PENICILLIUM CONIDIOPHORE *Penicillium* species produce a characteristic brush-shaped conidiophore (penicillus). Metulae (**M**), phialides (**P**), and chains of spherical conidia (**C**) are visible.

Dimorphic Molds

Blastomyces dermatitidis

Blastomyces dermatitidis is a dimorphic soil fungus with a mold and yeast phase. The mold form produces character-istic oval or pear-shaped, single-celled conidia at the tips of conidiophores arising from the septate hyphae (Figure 15-27). The yeast form consists of single cells that bud from a wide base.

  B. dermatitidis is found in damp, alkaline soils rich in organic material of the Great Lakes, upper Mississippi River, and southeastern regions of the United States. Pulmonary infection due to inhalation of conidia from disturbed soil results in the disease blastomycosis. Colony morphology (Figure 15-28) varies depending on the medium, but the mold often has a white to brownish cobweb appearance. Identification is made through direct examination, tissue samples showing the typical yeast cells, serological methods, or a DNA probe.

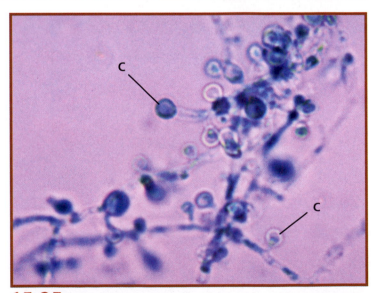

15-27 *BLASTOMYCES DERMATITIDIS* CONIDIA (LACTOPHENOL COTTON BLUE STAIN) This micrograph shows the septate hyphae and the characteristic thick-walled, lollipop-shaped, unicellular conidia (**C**). Conidia range from 2–10 μm in diameter.

Photograph courtesy of CDC Public Health Image Library

15-28 BLASTOMYCES DERMATITIDIS YEAST COLONIES ON LOWENSTEIN-JENSEN AGAR

B. dermatitidis is a thermally dimorphic fungus, producing yeast-like colonies at 35°C and mold-like growth at 25°C. It is typically grown on Sabouraud Dextrose Agar or Brain Heart Infusion Agar.

Photograph by Dr. William Kaplan, courtesy of CDC Public Health Image Laboratory

15-29 HISTOPLASMA CAPSULATUM GROWN ON SABOURAUD DEXTROSE AGAR

H. capsulatum is a slow-growing dimorphic fungus. It is mold-like at 25°C and is a yeast at 37°C. There is great variation in colony morphology depending on medium, temperature, and age.

Photograph by Dr. Lenore Haley, courtesy of CDC Public Health Image Laboratory

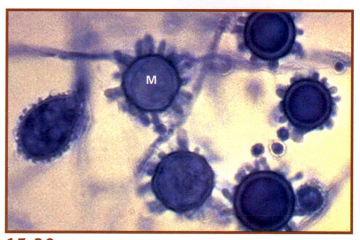

15-30 TUBERCULATE MACROCONIDIA OF HISTOPLASMA CAPSULATUM (LACTOPHENOL COTTON BLUE STAIN)
Hyphae of *H. capsulatum* showing the distinctive rough (tuberculate) macroconidia (**M**).

Photograph courtesy of CDC Public Health Image Library

Histoplasma capsulatum

Histoplasma capsulatum (Figure 15-29) is found in the Midwestern and southern United States where soil or buildings have accumulated bird or bat droppings. Alveolar macrophages phagocytize inhaled microconidia which then spread throughout the reticuloendothelial system. Most infections are asymptomatic or produce a flu-like set of symptoms that are self-limiting. In immunocompromised individuals, a potentially fatal disseminated histoplasmosis may occur.

Colonies are slow growing and highly variable in appearance depending on incubation temperature and medium used. The yeast form grows at 25°C whereas the mold form is seen at 37°C. Hyphae are slender, hyaline, and septate. Macroconidia are more or less spherical and contain a single cell. They develop tubercles as they age (Figure 15-30). Microconidia are borne on short conidiophores or may be found directly on the hyphae. Yeast cells are similar to *Candida* in shape and budding pattern (Figure 15-31).

Tentative identification may be made from observation of macroconidia covered with tubercles arising from the hyphae or by seeing the yeast form inside macrophages and other cells. Positive identification is now done with a DNA probe or serological techniques.

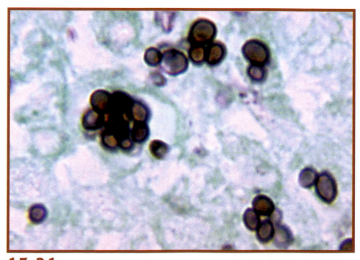

15-31 HISTOPLASMA CAPSULATUM YEAST FORM (METHENAMINE SILVER STAIN)
Note the budding cells and resemblance to Candida.

Photograph by Dr. Libero Ajello, courtesy of CDC Public Health Image Laboratory

Paracoccidioides brasiliensis

Paracoccidioides brasiliensis is a dimorphic fungus (Figure 15-32) that is a yeast at 37°C and a mold at 25°C. It is found in acidic soil of humid regions of South America, Central America, and southern Mexico. It is transmitted by airborne routes and is very infectious. Pulmonary paracocci-dioidomycosis may result in immunocompromised or mal-nourished individuals who inhale the organism. Subclinical infections are the rule for persons with normal immune systems. Secondary infections involving the spread of the organism occur in some cases.

Identification is made by converting the mold to the yeast form. The yeast has a characteristic appearance, with buds arising from around the mother cell (Figure 15-33). Buds are typically attached by a thin stalk.

15-32 YEAST PHASE OF *PARACOCCIDIOIDES BRASILIENSIS* At 37°C, *P. brasiliensis* grows as a yeast with wrinkled, whitish colonies. It is slow growing and mold-like with a variety of morphologies at 25°C.
Photograph by Dr. Lenore Haley, courtesy of CDC Public Health Image Laboratory

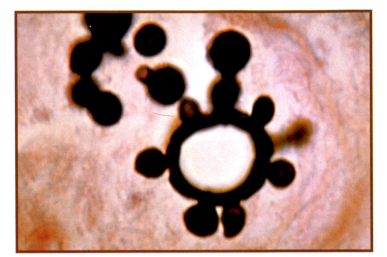

15-33 *PARACOCCIDIODES BRASILIENSIS* YEAST FORM The budding of the yeast form produces a characteristic "mariner's wheel." Buds are thick walled and about 10 µm in diameter.
Photograph courtesy of CDC Public Health Image Library

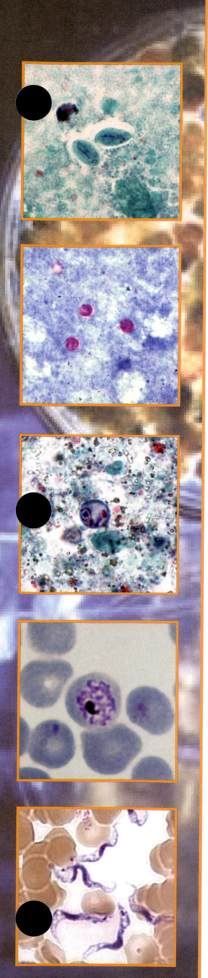

Protozoans of Clinical Importance

Group Excavata

Giardia lamblia

Giardiasis is caused by *Giardia lamblia* (also known as *Giardia intestinalis*), a diplomonad (page 169). It is most frequently seen in the duodenum as a heart-shaped vegetative trophozoite (Figure 16-1) with four pairs of flagella and a sucking disc that allows it to resist gut peristalsis. Multinucleate cysts lacking flagella (Figures 16-2 and 14-2) are formed as the organism passes through the colon. Cysts are shed in the feces and may produce infection of a new host upon ingestion. Transmission typically involves fecally contaminated water or food, but direct fecal-oral contact transmission is also possible.

The organism attaches to epithelial cells, but does not penetrate to deeper tissues. Most infections are asymptomatic. Chronic diarrhea, dehydration, abdominal pain, and other symptoms may occur if the infection produces a large enough population to involve a significant surface area of the small intestine. Diagnosis is made by identifying trophozoites or cysts in stool specimens. Serological tests are also available to detect *Giardia* antigens.

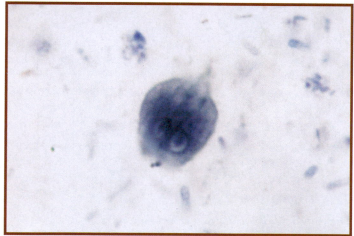

16-1 *GIARDIA LAMBLIA* TROPHOZOITE (IRON HEMATOXYLIN STAIN)
Trophozoites have a long, tapering posterior end and range in size from 9–21 μm by 5–15 μm. There are two nuclei with small karyosomes. Two median bodies are visible, but the four pairs of flagella are not.

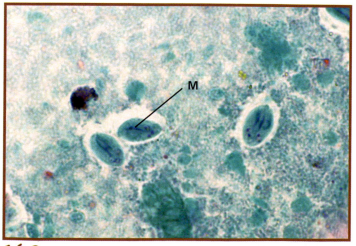

16-2 *GIARDIA LAMBLIA* CYST (TRICHROME STAIN) Giardia cysts are smaller than trophozoites (8–12 μm by 7–10 μm), but the four nuclei with eccentric karyosomes and the median bodies (**M**) are still visible.

Dientamoeba fragilis

At one time, *Dientamoeba fragilis* was considered to be an amoeba, but cytological evidence suggests it is better classified as a parabasalid (page 169). Only the trophozoite (Figure 16-3) is known; no cyst form has been identified. The trophozoite lives primarily in the cecum where it feeds on the bacterial and yeast flora as well as cellular debris. It is found in approximately 4% of humans and is being identified in stool samples more frequently. Typical symptoms include diarrhea, abdominal pain, and fatigue. The mode of transmission is unclear, but there is evidence supporting the idea that *D. fragilis* is transmitted in the eggs of parasitic helminths, such as *Enterobius vermicularis* and *Ascaris*.

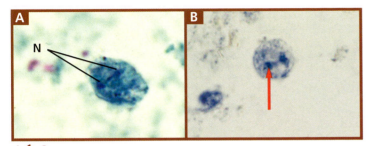

16-3 *DIENTAMOEBA FRAGILIS* TROPHOZOITES (IRON HEMATOXYLIN STAIN) Trophozoites are 5–12 μm in diameter. Most cells have two nuclei (**N**), but many have only one. The nucleus contains a single karyosome and the nuclear membrane is indistinct. The cytoplasm is often vacuolated. **A** A typical trophozoite. **B** A trophozoite with a fragmented karyosome (**arrow**).

Trichomonas vaginalis

Trichomonas vaginalis (Figure 16-4), a parabasalid (page 169), is the causative agent of trichomoniasis (vulvovaginitis) in humans. It has four anterior flagella and an **undulating membrane**.

Trichomoniasis may affect both sexes, but is more common in females. *T. vaginalis* causes inflammation of genitourinary mucosal surfaces—typically the vagina, vulva, and cervix in females and the urethra, prostate, and seminal vesicles in males. Most infections are asymptomatic or mild. There may be some erosion of surface tissues and a discharge associated with infection. The degree of infection is affected by host factors, especially the bacterial flora present and the pH of the mucosal surfaces. Transmission typically is by sexual intercourse.

The morphologically similar nonpathogenic

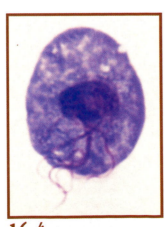

16-4 *TRICHOMONAS VAGINALIS* The trophozoite is the only stage of the Trichomonas life cycle. Several flagella are visible. Cells range in size from 5–15 μm wide by 7–23 μm long.

Trichomonas tenax and *T. hominis* are residents of the oral cavity and intestines, respectively.

Naegleria fowleri

Naegleria fowleri is a free-living soil and water microbe with an amoeboid stage (Figure 16-5), a cyst stage, and a flagellated stage. Under the proper conditions, it also is a facultative parasite that causes primary amebic meningoencephalitis (PAM). Infection is most prevalent in children and young adults. It probably occurs when the individual forces contaminated water containing the protozoan up the nasal passages (as in diving). The organisms travel up the olfactory nerves into the cranial vault where they multiply and digest the olfactory bulbs and cerebral cortex. Symptoms occur about a week after infection and include fever, severe headache, and coma. Death occurs within about a week from the onset of symptoms.

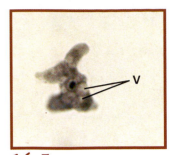

16-5 *NAEGLERIA FOWLERI* TROPHOZOITE FROM CULTURE (IRON HEMATOXYLIN STAIN) Trophozoites are between 10–35 μm in size. Notice the large karyosome within the nucleus and the lobed pseudopods. Vacuoles (**V**) are also visible in the cytoplasm.

Leishmania donovani

Leishmania donovani, a kinetoplastid (page 170), actually represents a number of geographically separate species and subspecies that are difficult to distinguish morphologically. All produce visceral leishmaniasis or kala-azar, a disease found in tropical and subtropical regions. The pathogen exists as a nonflagellated **amastigote** (Figure 16-6) in the mammalian host (humans, dogs, and rodents) and as an infective, motile **promastigote** in the sand fly vector (Figure 16-7). They are introduced into the mammalian host by sand fly bites. Distribution of the disease is associated with distribution of the appropriate sand fly vector.

Upon introduction into the host by the sand fly, the organism is phagocytized by macrophages and converts to the amastigote stage. Mitotic divisions result in filling of

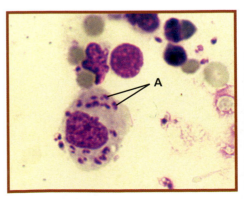

16-6 *LEISHMANIA DONOVANI* AMASTIGOTES IN SPLEEN TISSUE Amastigotes (**A**) are 3–5 μm in size and multiply within phagocytic cells by binary fission. Amastigotes are also known as Leishman-Donovan (L-D) bodies.

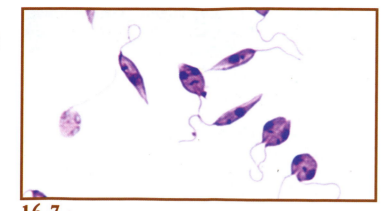

16-7 *LEISHMANIA DONOVANI* **PROMASTIGOTES, THE INFECTIVE STAGE, OBTAINED FROM A CULTURE** Notice the anterior flagellum, the kinetosome at its base, and the nucleus. The two cells at the lower right are dividing.

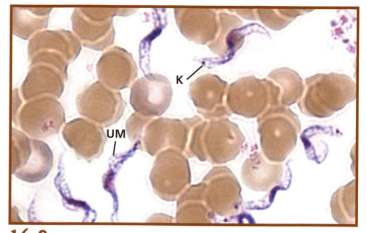

16-8 *TRYPANOSOMA BRUCEI* **TRYPOMASTIGOTES IN A BLOOD SMEAR** The central nucleus, posterior kinetoplast (**K**), and undulating membrane (**UM**) are visible. Cells range in size from 1.5–3.5 μm wide by 14–33 μm long.

the macrophage, which bursts and releases the parasites. Phagocytosis by other macrophages follows and the process repeats. In this way, the organism spreads through much of the reticuloendothelial system, including lymph nodes, liver, spleen, and bone marrow. Kala-azar is a progressive disease and is fatal if untreated.

Amastigotes in an infected host may be ingested by a sand fly during a blood meal. Once inside the sand fly, they develop into promastigotes and multiply. They eventually occupy the fly's buccal cavity where they can be transmitted to a new mammalian host during a subsequent blood meal. Transmission requires the vector and does not occur by direct contact.

Leishmania tropica and *L. major* (both subgenus *Leishmania*) in the Old World, and *L. mexicana* (subgenus *Leishmania*) and *L. braziliensis* (subgenus *Viannia*) in the New World cause cutaneous leishmaniasis, an infection of skin and oral, nasal and pharyngeal mucous membranes. In all cases, infection involves macrophages in the affected region. Unlike *L. donovani*, all four may be transmitted by direct contact with lesions or by sand fly bites.

Trypanosoma brucei

Trypanosoma brucei (Figure 16-8), a kinetoplastid (page 170), is a complex of flagellated microbes divided into subspecies: *T. brucei brucei* (which is nonpathogenic), and *T. brucei gambiense* and *T. brucei rhodesiense*, which produce African trypanosomiasis, also known as African sleeping sickness. The organisms are very similar morphologically, but differ in geographic range and disease progress. West African trypanosomiasis (caused by *T. brucei gambiense*) is generally a mild, chronic disease that may last for years, whereas East African trypanosomiasis (caused by *T. brucei rhodesiense*) is more acute and results in death within a year. Modern molecular methods that compare proteins, RNA, and DNA, are used to differentiate between them.

Trypanosomes have a complex life cycle. One stage of the life cycle, the **epimastigote**, multiplies in an intermediate host, the tsetse fly (genus *Glossina*). The infective **trypomastigote** stage is then transmitted to the human host through tsetse fly bites. Once introduced, trypomastigotes multiply and produce a chancre at the site of the bite. They enter the lymphatic system and spread through the blood, ultimately to the heart and brain. Immune response to the pathogen is hampered by the trypanosome's ability to change surface antigens faster than the immune system can produce appropriate antibodies. This antigenic variation also makes development of a vaccine unlikely. Diagnosis is made from clinical symptoms and identification of the trypomastigote in patient specimens (*e.g.*, blood, CSF, and chancre aspirate). An ELISA (page 103) and indirect agglutination test (page 101) also have been developed to detect trypanosome antigens in patient samples.

Progressive symptoms include headache, fever, and anemia, followed by symptoms characteristic of the infected sites. The sleeping sickness symptoms—sleepiness, emaciation, and unconsciousness—begin when the central nervous system becomes infected. Depending on the infecting strain, the disease may last for months or years, but mortality rate is high. Death results from heart failure, meningitis, or severe debility of some other organ(s).

The infective cycle is complete when an infected individual (humans, cattle, and some wild animals are reservoirs) is bitten by a tsetse fly, which ingests the organism during its blood meal. It becomes infective for its lifespan.

Trypanosoma cruzi

Trypanosoma cruzi (Figure 16-9) causes American trypanosomiasis (Chagas' disease). Cone-nosed ("kissing") bugs are the insect vector. They transmit the infective trypomastigote during a blood meal through their feces. Scratching introduces the organism into the bite wound or conjunctiva. A

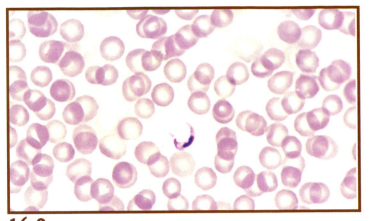

16-9 TRYPANOSOMA CRUZI IN A BLOOD SMEAR The nucleus, kinetoplast, and undulating membrane are visible. Cells in blood smears are about 20 μm long and assume a "C" or "V" shape, as seen here.

local lesion (chagoma) forms at the entry site and is accompanied by fever. Spreading occurs via lymphatics (producing lymphadenitis) and trypomastigotes may be found in the blood within a couple of weeks. Trypanosomes then become localized in reticuloendothelial cells of the spleen, liver, and bone marrow where they become **amastigotes** and multiply intracellularly. Infected individuals may infect the cone-nosed bugs during a subsequent blood meal.

American trypanosomiasis occurs in South and Central America. It may be fatal, mild, or asymptomatic in adults. It is especially severe in children who often introduce the trypanosome through the conjunctiva, leading to edema of the eyelids and face of the affected side. The disease may spread to the central nervous system or to the heart, causing severe myocarditis.

Group Chromalveolata

Babesia microti

Babesia microti, an apicomplexan (page 170), is a blood parasite found in the northeastern United States and other parts of the world. Mice (genus *Peromyscus*) are the main reservoir and the parasite is introduced into human hosts by a bite from an infected tick (*Ixodes dammini*). The parasites then infect RBCs and resemble young *Plasmodium* trophozoites (Figure 16-10). Symptoms of babesiosis, which are not easily distinguished from other diseases, appear in non-splenectomized individuals after about a week and include malaise, fever, and generalized aches and pains. Other species may be responsible for producing a fulminant hemolytic disease of immunosuppressed or splenectomized patients. Diagnosis is by detection of parasites in the blood.

Cryptosporidium parvum

Cryptosporidium parvum is an apicomplexan (page 170) parasite of intestinal microvilli and causes cryptosporidiosis. Infection of immunocompetent individuals is usually self-limiting, but infection of immunocompromised patients results in a long-term disease characterized by profuse, watery diarrhea. Infective **oocysts** containing **sporozoites** (Figure 16-11) are passed in the feces, so transmission is by fecal-oral contact. Infection may also occur through contact with infected animals. Diagnosis is made by finding acid-fast oocysts in feces.

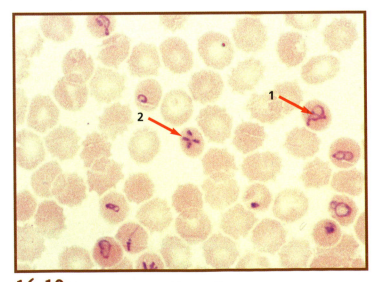

16-10 BABESIA MICROTI IN HUMAN ERYTHROCYTES The ring forms resemble *Plasmodium falciparum* (**arrow 1**), but are more variable in size, never pigmented, and occasionally form a cross-like tetrad (**arrow 2**).

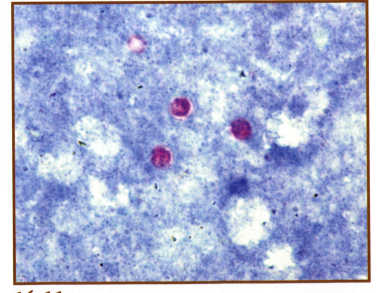

16-11 CRYPTOSPORIDIUM PARVUM OOCYSTS FROM A HUMAN FECAL SAMPLE (MODIFIED ACID-FAST STAIN) Oocysts contain sporozoites (not visible) and are the infective stage. They are typically about 5 μm in diameter.

Plasmodium spp.

Plasmodia are apicomplexan parasites (page 170) with a complex life cycle, part of which is in various vertebrate tissues, while the other part involves an insect. In humans, the tissues are the liver and red blood cells, while the insect vector is the female *Anopheles* mosquito. A generalized life cycle is shown in Figure 16-12. Diagnostic life cycle stages for the various species are shown in Figures 16-13 to 16-20.

There are four species of *Plasmodium* that cause malaria in humans. These are *P. vivax* (benign tertian malaria), *P. malariae* (quartan malaria), *P. falciparum* (malignant tertian malaria), and *P. ovale* (ovale malaria). The life cycles are similar for each species as is the progress of the disease, so *P. falciparum* will be discussed as an example, with unique aspects of the others mentioned.

The **sporozoite** stage of the pathogen is introduced into a human host during a bite from an infected female *Anopheles* mosquito. Sporozoites then infect liver cells

and produce the asexual **merozoite** stage. Merozoites are released from lysed liver cells, enter the blood, and infect erythrocytes. (Reinfection of the liver occurs at this stage in all but *P. falciparum* infections.) Once in RBCs, merozoites enter a cyclic pattern of reproduction in which more merozoites are released from the red cells synchronously every 48 hours (hence *tertian*—every third day—malaria). These events are tied to the symptoms of malaria. A chill, nausea, vomiting, and headache are symptoms that correspond to rupture of the RBCs. A spiking fever ensues and is followed by a period of sweating. It is during this latter phase that the parasites reinfect RBCs, and the cycle repeats.

The sexual phase of the life cycle begins when certain merozoites enter erythrocytes and differentiate into male or female **gametocytes**. The sexual life cycle continues when gametocytes are ingested by a female *Anopheles* mosquito during a blood meal. Fertilization occurs and the zygote eventually develops into a cyst within the mosquito's gut

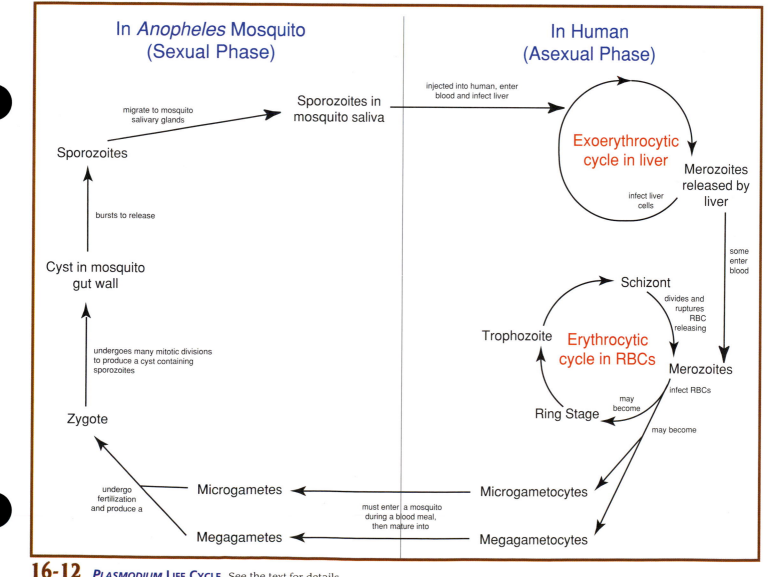

16-12 **PLASMODIUM LIFE CYCLE** See the text for details.

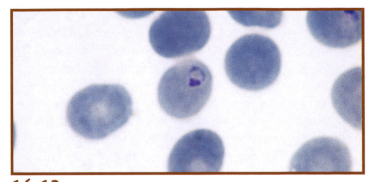

16-13 *PLASMODIUM FALCIPARUM* RING STAGE IN A RED BLOOD CELL The ring stage is a young trophozoite. Note the chromatin dots in the nucleus.

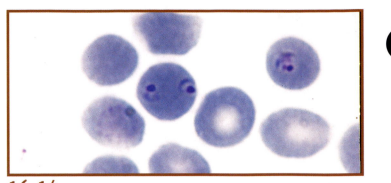

16-14 *PLASMODIUM FALCIPARUM* Double Infection of an RBC. This is commonly seen in *P. falciparum* infections.

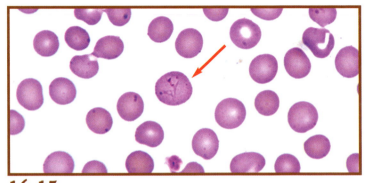

16-15 ERYTHROCYTE INFECTED WITH *PLASMODIUM VIVAX* The parasite is in the ring stage, and the RBC (**arrow**) exhibits characteristic cytoplasmic Schüffner's dots. Schüffner's dots are also seen in RBCs infected with *P. ovale*.

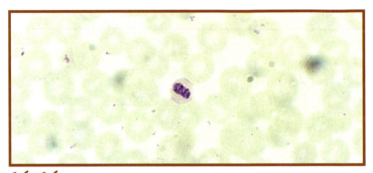

16-16 A BAND TROPHOZOITE OF *PLASMODIUM MALARIAE* Older trophpzoites of *P. malariae* may elongate to form a band.

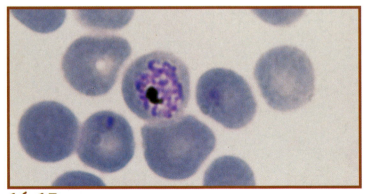

16-17 *PLASMODIUM FALCIPARUM* DEVELOPING SCHIZONT IN A RED BLOOD CELL These are usually not seen in peripheral blood smears since they reside in visceral capillaries.

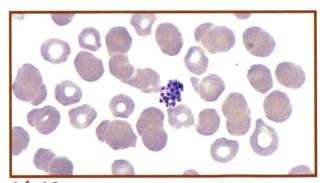

16-18 A MATURE *PLASMODIUM VIVAX* SCHIZONT COMPOSED OF APPROXIMATELY 16 MEROZOITES More than 12 merozoites distinguishes *P. vivax* from *P. malariae* and *P. ovale*, which both typically have eight, but up to 12. *P. falciparum* may have up to 24 merozoites, but they are not typically seen in peripheral blood smears and so are not confused with *P. vivax*.

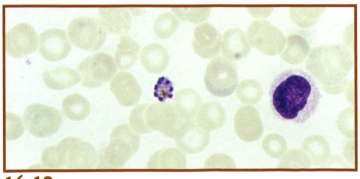

16-19 *PLASMODIUM MALARIAE* SCHIZONT The schizont has 8 merozoites in a distinctive rosette arrangement.

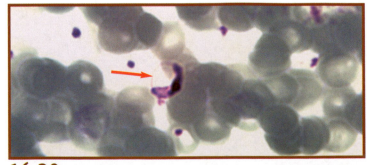

16-20 *PLASMODIUM FALCIPARUM* GAMETOCYTE IN AN ERYTHROCYTE Differentiation between microgametocytes and megagametocytes is difficult in this species. The erythrocyte membrane is visible around the gametocyte (**arrow**).

wall. After many divisions, the cyst releases sporozoites, some of which enter the mosquito's salivary glands ready to be transmitted back to the human host.

Most malarial infections eventually are cleared, but not before the patient has developed anemia and has suffered permanent damage to the spleen and liver. The most severe infections involve *P. falciparum*. Erythrocytes infected by *P. falciparum* develop abnormal projections that cause them to adhere to the lining of small blood vessels. This can lead to obstruction of the vessels, thrombosis, or local ischemia, which account for many of the fatal complications of this type of malaria—including liver, kidney, and brain damage.

Treatment includes antimalarial drugs and, in severe cases, blood replacement. Prevention is a better alternative and targets the mosquito vector. Draining standing water, which serves as a mosquito breeding site, use of insect repellant (Deet), mosquito NETS, and minimizing exposed skin reduce the chance of infection.

Toxoplasma gondii

Like other apicomplexans (page 170), *Toxoplasma gondii* (Figure 16-21) has sexual and asexual phases in its life cycle. The sexual phase occurs in the lining of cat intestines where **oocysts** are produced and shed in the feces. Each oocyst undergoes division and contains 8 **sporozoites**. If ingested by another cat, the sexual cycle may be repeated as the sporozoites produce **gametocytes,** which in turn produce gametes. If ingested by another animal host (including humans) the oocyst germinates in the duodenum and releases the sporozoites. Sporozoites enter the blood and infect other tissues where they become trophozoites, which continue to divide and spread the infection to lymph nodes and other parts of the reticuloendothelial system. Trophozoites ingested by a cat eating an infected animal develop into gametocytes in the cat's intestines. Gametes are formed, fertilization produces an oocyst, and the life cycle is completed.

Infection via ingestion of the oocyst typically is not serious. The patient may notice fatigue or muscle aches. The more serious form of the disease involves infection of a fetus across the placenta from an infected mother. This type of infection may result in stillbirth, liver damage, or brain damage. AIDS patients may also suffer fatal complications from infection.

Diagnosis is made by using molecular probes, a variety of serological tests, and by examining histologic preparations.

Balantidium coli

Balantidium coli, a ciliate (page 171) is the causative agent of balantidiasis and exists in two forms: a vegetative trophozoite (Figure 16-22) and a cyst (Figure 16-23). Laboratory diagnosis is made by identification of either the cyst or trophozoite in feces, with the latter being more commonly found.

The trophozoite is highly motile due to the cilia and has a macro- and a micronucleus. Cysts in sewage-contaminated water are the infective form. Trophozoites may cause ulcerations of the colon mucosa, but not to the extent produced

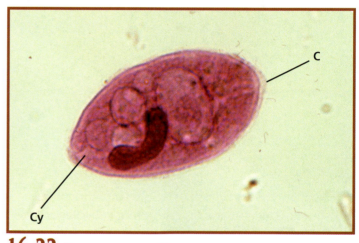

16-22 *BALANTIDIUM COLI* TROPHOZOITE Trophozoites are oval in shape and have dimensions of 50–100 μm long by 40–70 μm wide. Cilia (C) cover the cell surface. Internally, the macronucleus is prominent; the adjacent micronucleus is not. An anterior cytostome (Cy) is usually visible.

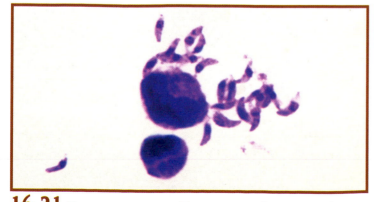

16-21 *TOXOPLASMA GONDII* TROPHOZOITES (TACHYZOITES) Notice the bow-shaped cells and the prominent nuclei.

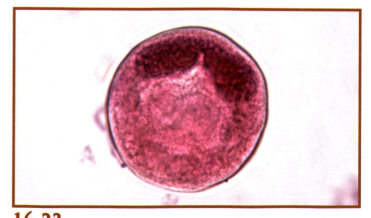

16-23 *BALANTIDIUM COLI* CYST Cysts are usually spherical and have a diameter in the range of 50–75 μm. There is a cyst wall and the cilia are absent. As in the trophozoite, the macronucleus is prominent, but the micronucleus may not be.

by *Entamoeba histolytica*. Symptoms of acute infection are bloody and mucoid feces. Diarrhea alternating with constipation may occur in chronic infections. Most infections are probably asymptomatic.

Blastocystis hominis

Blastocystis hominis is a heterokont (page 171) commensal microbe that occupies the large intestine of up to 20% of the population. In most cases, patients with *B. hominis* show no symptoms, but in some it appears responsible for symptoms such as fever, nausea, diarrhea, and abdominal cramps. The fecal-oral route of transmission is responsible for its spread. Identification is made by finding the central body form (Figure 16-24) in a stool sample and by detecting antibodies with ELISA (page 103) or fluorescent antibody tests (page 105).

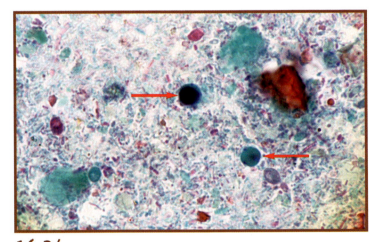

16-24 **BLASTOCYSTIS HOMINIS TROPHOZOITES (TRICHROME STAIN)** Trophozoites vary greatly in size over the range of 6–40 µm. A large central body surrounded by several small nuclei is distinctive of the trophozoite. Staining properties also may vary, as shown in these two specimens (**arrows**).

Chilomastix mesnili

Chilomastix mesnili is a heterokont (page 171) most commonly found in warmer climates, but can be found most anywhere. It exists as a trophozoite and a cyst (Figures 16-25 and 16-26). Both may be found in stool samples and are used in identifying infection by this nonpathogen. It typically lives in the cecum and large intestine as a commensal, but may be indicative of infection by other parasites. Infection occurs through ingestion of cysts.

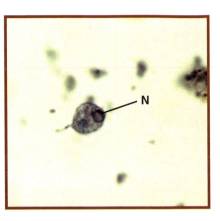

16-25 **CHILOMASTIX MESNILI TROPHOZOITE (IRON HEMATOXYLIN STAIN)** Trophozoites are elongated with a tapering posterior and a blunt anterior end that holds the nucleus (**N**). The dimensions are 6–20 µm long by 5–7 µm wide. There are four flagella: three at the anterior end (which may be difficult to see) and one associated with the prominent cytostome.

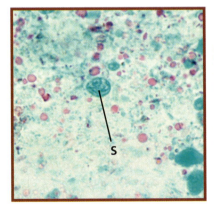

16-26 **CHILOMASTIX MESNILI CYST (TRICHROME STAIN)** Cysts are lemon-shaped, often with an anterior knob, and are 6–10 µm long. The nucleus may be difficult to see. A distinctive "shepherd's crook" (**S**) associated with the cytostome is also visible.

Group Unikonta

Entamoeba histolytica

Entamoeba histolytica, an amoebozoan (page 176), is the causative agent of amoebic dysentery (amebiasis), a disease most common in areas with poor sanitation. Identification is made by finding either trophozoites (Figure 16-27) or cysts (Figure 16-28) in a stool sample. The diagnostic features of each are described in the captions.

Infection occurs when a human host ingests cysts, either through fecal-oral contact or more typically, contaminated food or water. Cysts (but not trophozoites) are able to withstand the acidic environment of the stomach. Upon entering the less acidic small intestine, the cysts undergo

excystation. Mitosis produces eight small trophozoites from each cyst.

The trophozoites parasitize the mucosa and submucosa of the colon causing ulcerations. They feed on red blood cells and bacteria. The extent of damage determines whether the disease is acute, chronic, or asymptomatic. In the most severe cases, infection may extend to other organs, especially the liver, lungs, or brain. Abdominal pain, diarrhea, blood and mucus in feces, nausea, vomiting, and hepatitis are among the symptoms of amebic dysentery.

Initially uninucleate, mitosis produces the mature quadranucleate cyst. These are shed in the feces and are infective. They may also persist in the original host resulting in an **asymptomatic carrier**—a major source of contamination and infection.

Other members of the genus *Entamoeba* deserve mention here. *Entamoeba hartmanni* resembles *E. histolytica*, but is nonpathogenic and has smaller trophozoites and cysts. *Entamoeba coli* is a fairly common, nonpathogenic intestinal commensal that must be differentiated from *E. histolytica* in stool samples. Its characteristic features are given in the captions to Figures 16-29 and 16-30. *Entamoeba dispar* comprises nonpathogenic strains of *E. histolytica* and is morphologically indistinguishable from it. Molecular methods, such as protein electrophoresis, and rRNA and DNA comparisons, are used for identification.

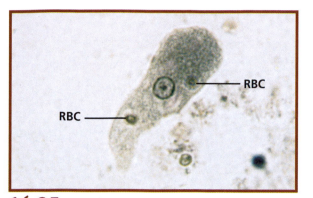

16-27 *ENTAMOEBA HISTOLYTICA* **TROPHOZOITE (IRON HEMATOXYLIN STAIN)** Trophozoites range in size from 12–60 μm. Notice the small, central karyosome, the beaded chromatin at the nucleus' margin, the ingested red blood cells (**RBC**), and the finely granular cytoplasm. Compare with an *Entamoeba coli* trophozoite in Figure 16-29.

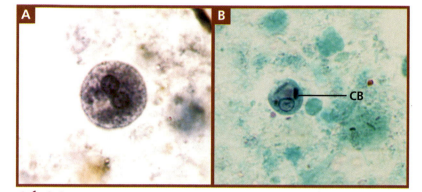

16-28 *ENTAMOEBA HISTOLYTICA* **CYSTS** **A** Cysts are spherical with a diameter of 10–20 μm. Two of the four nuclei are visible; other nuclear characteristics are as in the trophozoite. Compare with an *Entamoeba coli* cyst in Figure 16-30 (iron hematoxylin stain). **B** *E. histolytica* cyst (trichrome stain) with cytoplasmic chromatoidal bars (**CB**). These are found in approximately 10% of the cysts, have blunt ends, and are composed of ribonucleoprotein.

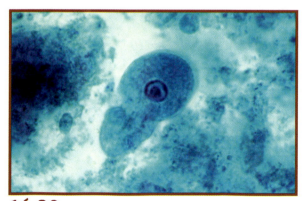

16-29 *ENTAMOEBA COLI* **TROPHOZOITE (TRICHROME STAIN)** Trophozoites have a size range of 15–50 μm. Notice the relatively large and eccentrically positioned karyosome, the unclumped chromatin at the nucleus' periphery, and the vacuolated cytoplasm lacking ingested RBCs. The usually nonpathogenic *E. coli* must be distinguished from the potentially pathogenic *E. histolytica*, so compare with Figure 16-27.

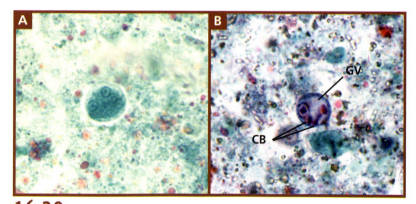

16-30 *ENTAMOEBA COLI* **CYSTS** Cysts are typically spherical and are between 10–35 μm in diameter. They contain 8, or sometimes 16 nuclei. This makes differentiation from *E. histolytica* cysts simpler, because they never have more than 4 nuclei. **A** Five nuclei are visible in this specimen (trichrome stain). **B** Chromatoidal bars (**CB**) and a large glycogen vacuole (**GV**) characteristic of immature cysts are visible in this specimen (trichrome stain).

Endolimax nana

Endolimax nana is a fairly common commensal amoebozoan (page 176) that resides mainly in the cecum of humans. It exists as a trophozoite and cyst (Figures 16-31 and 16-32) and its life cycle resembles that of *Entamoeba histolytica*. Infection occurs by ingestion of cysts in fecally contaminated food or water. Identification is made by finding the trophozoites and/or cysts in stool samples.

Iodamoeba bütschlii

Iodamoeba bütschlii is less commonly found in humans than other amoebozoans, *Entamoeba coli* or *Endolimax nana*, but when present, it lives in the cecum and feeds on the other resident organisms. Transmission is by fecal contamination, but it is nonpathogenic. Laboratory diagnosis is done by identifying trophozoites and/or cysts (Figures 16-33 and 16-34) in stool specimens. Distinguishing characteristics are given in the captions.

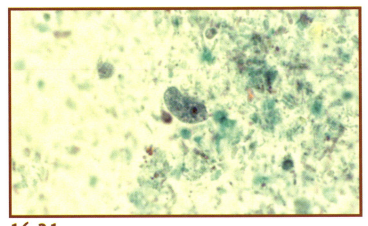

16-31 *ENDOLIMAX NANA* TROPHOZOITE (TRICHROME STAIN) Trophozoites are small, with a size range of 6–15 μm. Notice the large karyosome filling the majority of the nuclear space as well as the absence of peripheral chromatin.

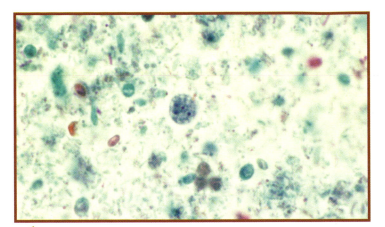

16-32 *ENDOLIMAX NANA* CYST (TRICHROME STAIN) *E. nana* cysts range in size from 5–14 μm. There are typically four nuclei, with each having the distinctive large karyosome.

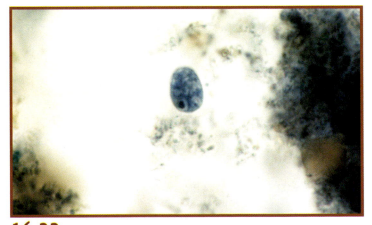

16-33 *IODAMOEBA BÜTSCHLII* TROPHOZOITE (IRON HEMATOXYLIN STAIN) *I. bütschlii* trophozoites are 6–15 μm in size. The nucleus has a large karyosome, but lacks peripheral chromatin. On occasion, fine karyosome strands may be observed radiating outward from the karyosome to the nuclear membrane.

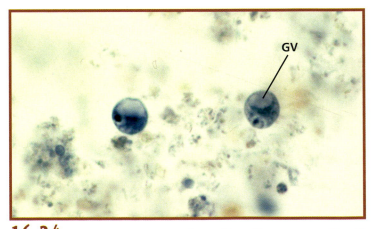

16-34 *IODAMOEBA BÜTSCHLII* CYSTS (IRON HEMATOXYLIN STAIN) Cysts of *I. bütschlii* range in size from 6–15 μm. The single nucleus has a large karyosome and no peripheral chromatin. A glycogen vacuole (**GV**) is typically found in these cysts.

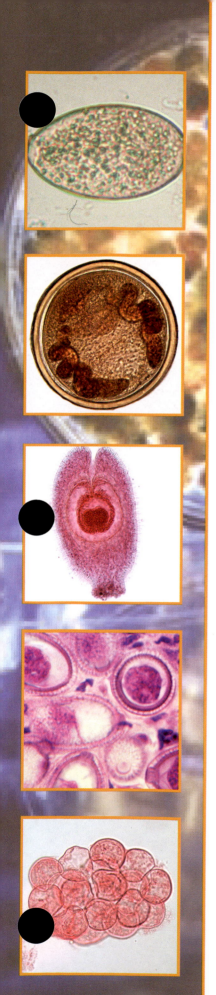

Parasitic Helminths

A study of helminths is appropriate to the microbiology lab because clinical specimens may contain microscopic evidence of helminth infection. The three major groups of parasitic worms encountered in lab situations are trematodes (flukes), cestodes (tapeworms), and nematodes (round worms). Life cycles of the parasitic worms are often complex, sometimes involving several hosts, and are beyond the scope of this book. Emphasis here is on a brief background and clinically important diagnostic features of each worm.

Trematode Parasites Found in Clinical Specimens

Clonorchis (Opisthorchis) sinensis

C. *sinensis* is the oriental liver fluke (Figure 17-1) and causes clonorchiasis, a liver disease. It is a common parasite of people living in Japan, Korea, Vietnam, China, and Taiwan and is becoming more common in the United States with the influx of Southeast Asian immigrants. Infection typically occurs when undercooked infected fish is ingested. The adults migrate to the liver bile ducts and begin laying eggs in approximately one month. Degree of damage to the bile duct epithelium and surrounding liver tissue corresponds with the number of worms and the duration of infection. Diagnosis is made by identifying the characteristic eggs in feces (Figure 17-2).

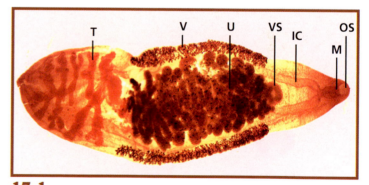

17-1 CLONORCHIS SINENSIS ADULT Adults range in size from 1–2.5 cm. Visible in this specimen are the oral sucker (**OS**), mouth (**M**), intestinal ceca (**IC**), ventral sucker (**VS**), uterus (**U**), vitellaria (**V**), and testis (**T**).

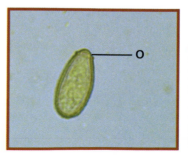

17-2 CLONORCHIS SINENSIS EGG IN A FECAL SPECIMEN (D'ANTONI'S IODINE STAIN) The eggs are thick shelled and between 27 and 35 μm long. There is a distinctive operculum (**O**) (positioned to give the appearance of shoulders) and often a knob at the aboperular end (not visible in this specimen).

Fasciola hepatica

F. hepatica (Figure 17-3) is a liver fluke commonly associated with domestic sheep and cattle. Human infection results when juvenile worms attached to aquatic vegetation are ingested. Penetration of the intestine and subsequently the liver by metacercaria leads the juveniles to the bile ducts where they develop into adults. Migration by the juveniles damages the liver; adults damage the bile ducts, gall bladder, and liver, resulting in cirrhosis, jaundice, or in severe cases, abscesses. Diagnosis is made by identification of eggs in feces (Figure 17-4).

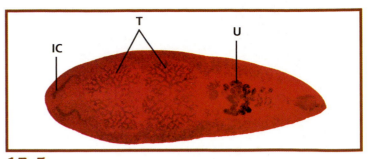

17-5 FASCIOLOPSIS BUSKI ADULT Adults are up to 7.5 cm long and 2 cm wide. The unbranched intestinal ceca (**IC**), uterus (**U**), and highly branched testes (**T**) are visible in this preparation. *F. buski* lacks the anterior conical region of *Fasciola hepatica*.

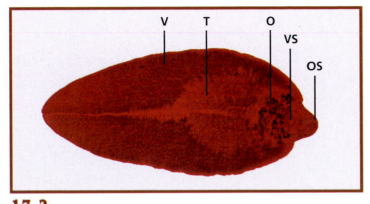

17-3 FASCIOLA HEPATICA ADULT Adults are leaf shaped with a conical anterior end. They are about 3 cm long by 1 cm in width. In this specimen, the oral sucker (**OS**), ventral sucker (**VS**), ovary (**O**), testis (**T**), and vitellaria (**V**) are visible.

17-6 FASCIOLOPSIS BUSKI EGG IN A FECAL SPECIMEN (D'ANTONI'S IODINE STAIN) These eggs are very similar to those of *Fasciola hepatica*, but are smooth on the abopercular end. They range in size from 130–140 µm long by 80–85 µm wide. Note the prominent operculum (**O**).

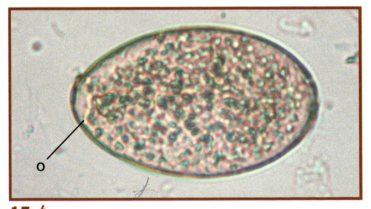

17-4 FASCIOLA HEPATICA EGG IN A FECAL SPECIMEN (D'ANTONI'S IODINE STAIN) The large eggs (130–150 µm long by 60–90 µm wide) are unembryonated in fecal samples and have an inconspicuous operculum (**O**). These eggs are difficult to distinguish from *Fasciolopsis buski*.

Fasciolopsis buski

F. buski (Figure 17-5) is common in central and southeast Asia where it infects humans and pigs. Its life cycle is similar to *Fasciola hepatica,* but differs in that its site of infection is the small intestine, not the liver. Consequences of infection include inflammation of the intestinal wall and obstruction of the gut if the worms are numerous. Chronic infections lead to ulceration, bleeding, diarrhea, and abscesses of the intestinal wall. Metabolites from the worm may sensitize the

host, which may cause death. Diagnosis is made by identification of the eggs (up to 25,000 per day per worm!) in fecal samples (Figure 17-6).

Paragonimus westermani

P. westermani (Figure 17-7) is a lung fluke and one of several species to cause paragonimiasis, a disease mostly found in Asia, Africa, and South America. *P. westermani* is primarily a parasite of carnivores, but humans (omnivores) may get infected when eating undercooked crabs or crayfish infected with the cysts containing juveniles (Figure 17-8). Ingested juveniles (metacercaria) excyst in the duodenum and travel to the abdominal wall. After several days, they resume their journey and find their way to the bronchioles where the adults mature. Eggs (Figure 17-9) are released in approximately two to three months and are diagnostic of infection. They may be recovered in sputum, lung fluids, or feces. Consequences of lung infection are a local inflammatory response followed by possible ulceration. Symptoms include cough with discolored or bloody sputum and difficulty breathing. These cases are rarely fatal, but may last a couple of decades. Occasionally, the wandering juveniles end up in other tissues, such as the brain or spinal cord, which can cause paralysis or death.

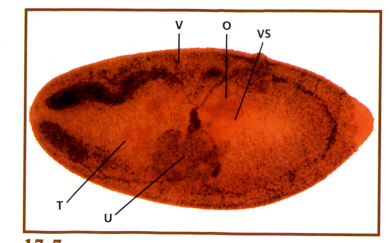

17-7 PARAGONIMUS WESTERMANI ADULT Adults are up to 1.2 cm long, 0.6 cm wide, and 0.5 cm thick. Visible in this specimen are the ventral sucker (**VS**), ovary (**O**), uterus (**U**), testis (**T**), and vitellaria (**V**).

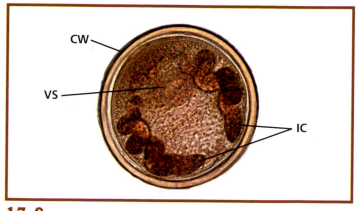

17-8 PARAGONIMUS WESTERMANI CYST The cyst stage, which is found in crabs or crayfish, contains a living metacercaria. Once the vertebrate host eats the crab or crayfish, the juvenile fluke is released from the cyst where it begins its migration from the intestines to the lungs. Prominent in this cyst are the ventral sucker (**VS**), intestinal ceca (**IC**), and thick cyst wall (**CW**).

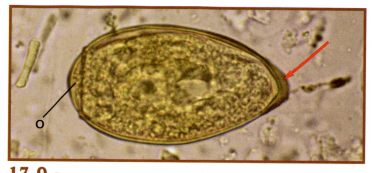

17-9 PARAGONIMUS WESTERMANI EGG IN A FECAL SPECIMEN (D'ANTONI'S IODINE STAIN) *P. westermani* eggs are ovoid and range in size from 80–120 μm long by 45–70 μm wide. They have an operculum (**O**) and the shell is especially thick at the abopercular end (**arrow**). They are unembryonated when seen in feces.

Schistosoma haematobium

S. haematobium is an African and Middle Eastern blood fluke that causes urinary schistosomiasis. Infection occurs via contact with fecally contaminated water containing **cercariae** which penetrate the skin, enter circulation, and continue development in the liver. No metacercaria stage is seen. After about three weeks in the liver, adult worms, which have separate sexes, colonize the veins associated with the urinary bladder and begin to lay eggs (Figure 17-10).

Some eggs pass through the wall of the vein and then the bladder to be passed out in urine, but a majority of them become trapped in the wall and initiate a build-up of fibrous tissue as well as an immune response. Symptoms of the disease include hematuria and painful urination. There is also a high probability of developing bladder cancer. If there is a high parasite load and the infection is chronic, other parts of the genitourinary system may become involved. Diagnosis is by finding eggs in urine or feces.

Schistosoma japonicum

S. japonicum is a Southeast Asian blood fluke. It has a life cycle similar to *S. haematobium*, but the adults reside in veins of the small intestine. Adults produce eggs (Figure 17-11) that penetrate the intestine and pass out with the feces. Presence of eggs in the feces indicates infection. Some patients are asymptomatic, whereas others have bloody diarrhea, abdominal pain, and lethargy. In some cases, eggs reach the brain and the infection may be fatal.

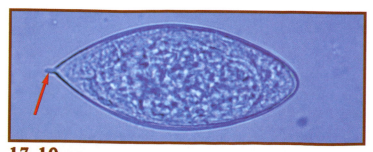

17-10 SCHISTOSOMA HAEMATOBIUM EGG IN A URINE SPECIMEN *S. haematobium* eggs are large (112–170 μm long by 40–70 μm wide), thin-shelled, and lack an operculum. There is a distinctive terminal spine (**arrow**). Each egg contains a larva called a miracidium.

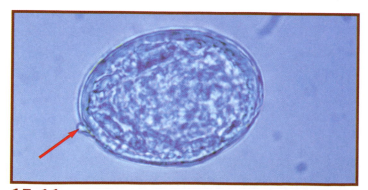

17-11 SCHISTOSOMA JAPONICUM EGG IN A FECAL SPECIMEN *S. japonicum* eggs are thin-shelled and lack an operculum. They range in size from 70–100 μm long by 55–65 μm wide. There may be a small spine (**arrow**) visible near one end. Each egg contains a larva called a miracidium.

Schistosoma mansoni

S. mansoni (Figure 17-12) is found in Brazil, some Caribbean islands, Africa, and parts of the Middle East. It has a life cycle similar to *S. haematobium*, but the adults reside in the veins of the hepatic portal system. Eggs (Figures 17-13 and 17-14) from the adults penetrate the intestinal wall and are passed out with the feces. Presence of eggs in the feces indicates infection. Symptoms are similar to those produced by *S. japonicum* infection.

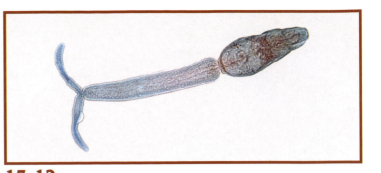

17-12 *Schistosoma mansoni* Cercaria Schistosome cercariae have a forked tail and penetrate the human host directly. There is no metacercaria stage, which is unusual among trematodes.

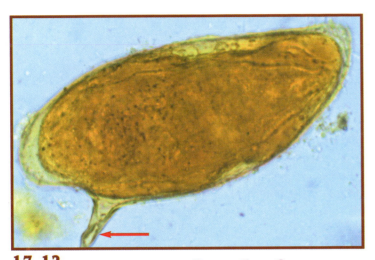

17-13 *Schistosoma mansoni* Egg in a Fecal Specimen (D'Antoni's Iodine Stain) *S. mansoni* eggs are large (114–175 μm long by 45–70 μm wide) and contain a larva called a miracidium. They are thin-shelled, lack an operculum, and have a distinctive lateral spine (**arrow**).

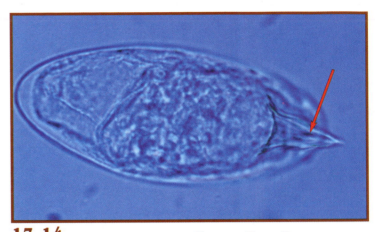

17-14 *Schistosoma mansoni* Egg in a Fecal Specimen The lateral spine may be oriented in such a way as to be difficult to see. In this specimen, the spine (**arrow**) is above the egg and the egg may be misidentified as *S. haematobium*.

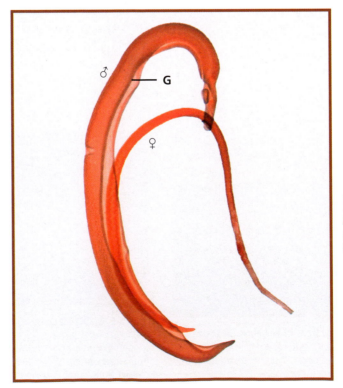

17-15 *Schistosoma mansoni* Adults The male is larger and has a gynecophoric groove (**G**) in which the slender female resides during mating.

Cestode Parasites Found in Clinical Specimens

Diphyllobothrium latum

D. latum is the broad fish tapeworm. It is found in Northern Europe, and the Great Lakes and west coast regions of North America. The closely related *D. ursi* is responsible for infection in northeastern North America. *D. latum* juveniles infect the muscle of fish-eating carnivores, which pass the infection on when they are eaten raw or are undercooked. Adults develop in the carnivore's intestine and begin egg production between one and two weeks later. Infection may result in no symptoms or mild symptoms, such as diarrhea, nausea, abdominal pain, and weakness. In heavy infections, mechanical blockage of the intestine may occur. Rarely, infection results in pernicious anemia due to the worm's uptake of vitamin B_{12}. Diagnosis is commonly made by finding the eggs (Figure 17-16) or more rarely proglottids (Figure 17-17) in feces. Adults may reach a length of 9 m with more than 4,000 proglottids!

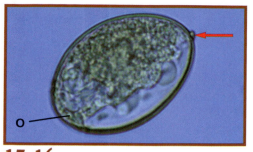

17-16 **DIPHYLLOBOTHRIUM LATUM EGG IN A FECAL SPECIMEN (D'ANTONI'S IODINE STAIN)** The eggs are unembryonated when passed in feces and have an operculum (**O**). A knob (**arrow**) is often present at the abopercular end. Their dimensions are 58–75 μm long by 44–50 μm wide.

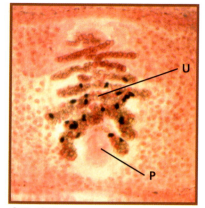

17-17 **DIPHYLLOBOTHRIUM LATUM PROGLOTTID** Proglottids are typically wider than long and contain a rosette-shaped uterus (**U**) opening to a midventral pore (**P**). *D. latum* is hermaphroditic, but the testes are obscured by the abundant vitellaria (**V**) (yolk glands) in this specimen.

Dipylidium caninum

D. caninum (Figure 17-18) is a common parasite of dogs and cats. Human infection usually occurs in children. The adult worms reside in dog or cat intestines and release proglottids (Figure 17-19) containing egg packets that migrate out of the anus. When these dry, they look like rice grains. Larval fleas may eat the eggs and become infected. If a dog, cat, or child ingests one of these fleas, the life cycle is completed in the new host. Infection may be asymptomatic or produce mild abdominal discomfort, loss of appetite, and indigestion. Diagnosis is made by identifying the egg packets (Figure 17-20).

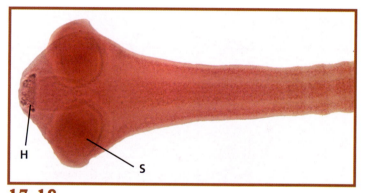

17-18 **DIPYLIDIUM CANINUM SCOLEX** Adult worms may reach a length of 50 cm with a width of 3 mm. The scolex has four suckers (**S**) and a retractable rostellum with rows of hooks (**H**).

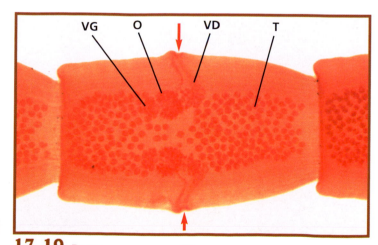

17-19 **DIPYLIDIUM CANINUM PROGLOTTID** Visible are the testes (**T**), vasa deferentia (**VD**), ovaries (**O**), and vitelline glands (**VG**). The reproductive openings (**arrows**) on each side of the proglottid give this worm its common name—the "double-pored tapeworm."

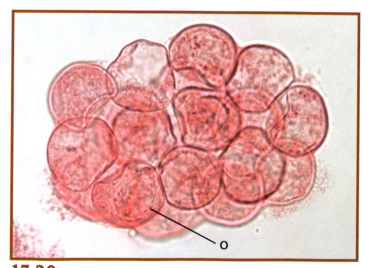

17-20 **DIPYLIDIUM CANINUM EGG PACKET** Each *D. caninum* egg packet is composed of 5–15 eggs, each with an onchosphere (**O**). The onchosphere (larva) contains six hooklets.

Echinococcus granulosus

The definitive host of *E. granulosus* (Figure 17-21) is a carnivore, but the life cycle requires an intermediate host, usually an herbivorous mammal. Humans involved in raising domesticated herbivores (*e.g.*, sheep with their associated dogs) are most susceptible as intermediate hosts and develop hydatid disease. Ingestion of a juvenile *E. granulosus* leads to development of a **hydatid cyst** in the lung, liver, or other organ, a process that may take many years. The cyst (Figure 17-22) has a thick wall and develops many protoscolices within (Figure 17-23). The protoscolices, if ingested, are infective to the definitive host. Symptoms depend on the location and size of the hydatid cyst, which interferes with normal organ function. Due to sensitization by the parasite's antigens, release of fluid from the cyst can result in anaphylactic shock of the host. Diagnosis is made by detection of the cyst by ultrasound or X-ray.

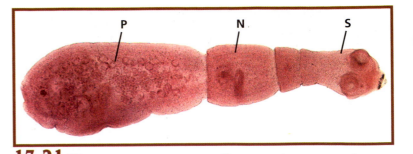

17-21 *Echinococcus granulosus* **Adult** Adult worms are about 0.5 cm in length. There is a scolex (**S**) with a ring of hooks, a neck (**N**), and one proglottid (**P**) that contains up to 1,500 eggs.

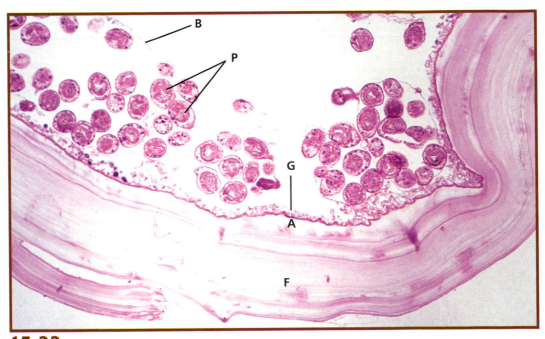

17-22 **Section of an** *Echinococcus granulosus* **Cyst in Lung Tissue** The cyst wall consists of a fibrous layer of host tissue (**F**), an acellular layer (**A**), and a germinal epithelium (**G**) that gives rise to stalked brood capsules (**B**). Brood capsules produce many *E. granulosus* protoscolices (**P**).

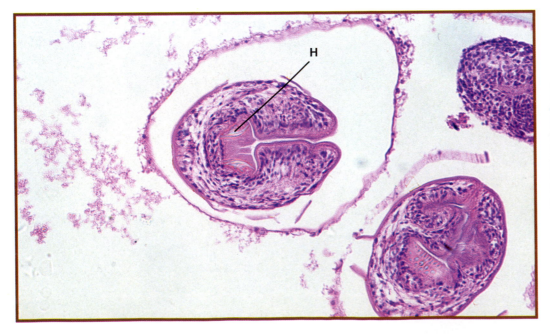

17-23 **Longitudinal Section of an** *Echinococcus granulosus* **Protoscolex** The protoscolex contains an invaginated scolex with hooks (**H**). Upon ingestion by the host, the protoscolex evaginates and produces an infectious scolex that attaches to the intestinal wall, matures, and produces eggs.

Hymenolepis diminuta

H. diminuta is a tapeworm that has various arthropods as its intermediate hosts and rodents as the definitive hosts. Humans may also be infected via ingestion of arthropods infected with the **cysticercoid** (Figure 17-24). The adult worms develop in and attach to the intestinal mucosa, with one host harboring numerous worms. They release eggs (Figure 17-25), which exit with the feces and are useful in diagnosis. Proglottids are rarely found in feces and are not of diagnostic value. Many infections are asymptomatic, but some result in mild abdominal discomfort and digestive upset.

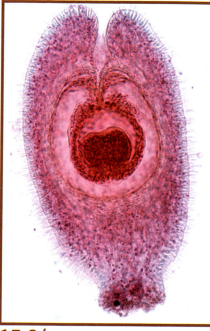

17-24 HYMENOLEPIS DIMINUTA CYS-TICERCOID The larval cysticercoid stage is found in arthropods of various sorts. Rodents are the definitive host, but if ingested by humans, the cysticercoid can develop in the intestines. Eating grain containing infected beetles is a common mode of infection.

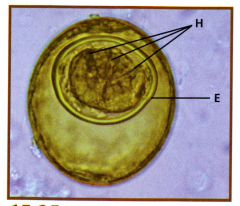

17-25 HYMENOLEPIS DIMINUTA EGG IN FECES (D'ANTONI'S IODINE STAIN) The spherical, thick-shelled eggs of *H. diminuta* range in size from 70–85 µm long by 60–80 µm wide. The embryo (E) is centrally positioned separate from the wall. Three pairs of hooks (H) are also present.

Hymenolepis (Vampirolepis) nana

H. nana (Figures 17-26 and 17-27) is the dwarf tapeworm and is the most common cestode parasite of humans in the world. When eggs (Figure 17-28) are ingested, the oncospheres develop into juveniles in the lymphatics of intestinal villi. These juveniles are then released into the lumen within a week and attach to the intestinal mucosa to mature into adults. Infection may involve hundreds of worms, yet symptoms are usually mild: diarrhea, nausea, loss of appetite, or abdominal pain. Eggs may reinfect the same host or pass out with the feces to infect a new host. Eggs in the feces are used for identification, but proglottids are not as they are rarely passed.

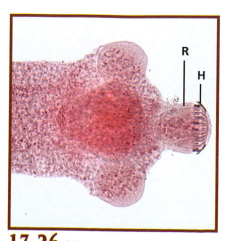

17-26 HYMENOLEPIS NANA SCOLEX Adults gain a length of up to 10 cm, but are only 1 mm in width. The rostellum (R) is armed with up to 30 hooks (H).

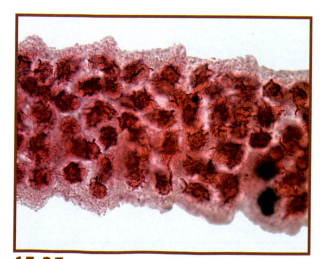

17-27 HYMENOLEPIS NANA PROGLOTTIDS *H. nana* is hermaphroditic, but in this specimen, the numerous testes obscure most other structures.

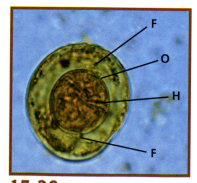

17-28 HYMENOLEPIS NANA EGG IN FECES (D'ANTONI'S IODINE STAIN) The *H. nana* egg resembles the egg of *H. diminuta*, but it is smaller (30–47 µm in diameter) and has a thinner shell. The oncosphere (O) is separated from the shell and contains six hooks (H). Another distinguishing feature is the presence of between four and eight filaments (F) arising from either end of the oncosphere.

Taenia spp.

Two taeniid worms are important human pathogens. These are *Taenia saginata* (*Taeniarhynchus saginatus*)—the beef tapeworm—and *Taenia solium*—the pork tapeworm.

T. saginata infects humans who eat undercooked beef containing juvenile worms. In the presence of bile salts, the juvenile develops into an adult and begins producing gravid proglottids within a few weeks. Symptoms of infection are usually mild nausea, diarrhea, abdominal pain, and headache. Diagnosis to species is impossible with only the eggs (Figure 17-29); specific identification requires a scolex or gravid proglottid (Figures 17-30 and 17-31).

The *T. solium* life cycle is similar to *T. saginata*, but the host is pork, not beef, so human infection occurs when undercooked pork is eaten. If eggs are ingested, a juvenile form called a **cysticercus** develops. Cysticerci (Figure 17-32) may be found in any tissue, especially subcutaneous connective tissues, eyes, brain, heart, liver, lungs, and coelom. Symptoms of cysticercosis depend on the tissue infected, but mostly they are not severe. However, death of a cysticercus can produce a rapidly fatal inflammatory response. As with *T. saginata*, diagnosis to species is impossible with only the eggs; specific identification requires a scolex or gravid proglottid (Figures 17-33 and 17-34).

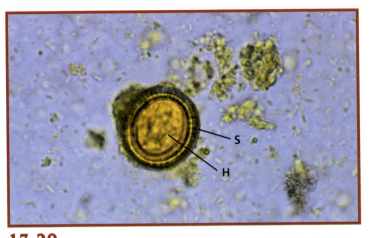

17-29 *Taenia* **Egg in Feces** Taeniid eggs are distinctive looking enough to identify to genus, but not distinctive enough to speciate. Eggs are spherical and approximately 40 μm in diameter with a striated shell (**S**). The oncosphere contains six hooks (**H**).

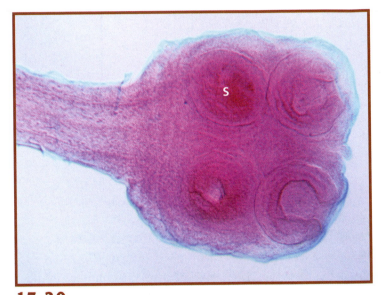

17-30 *Taenia saginata* **Scolex** The *T. saginata* scolex has four suckers (**S**) and no hooks.

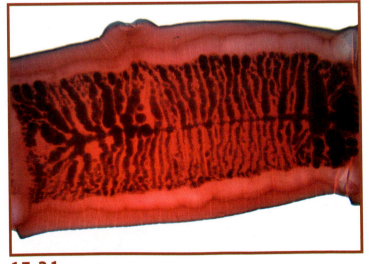

17-31 *Taenia saginata* **Proglottid** The uterus of *T. saginata* proglottids consists of a central portion with 15–20 lateral branches (compare to the *T. solium* uterus in Figure 17-34).

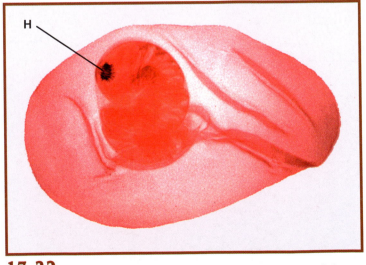

17-32 *Taenia* **Cysticercus** The cysticercus (cysticercus cellulosae) consists of a bladder with the head and hooks (**H**) invaginated.

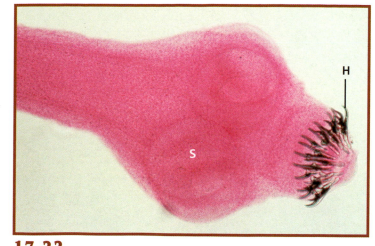

17-33 *TAENIA SOLIUM SCOLEX* The *T. solium* scolex has two rings of hooks (**H**) and four suckers (**S**).

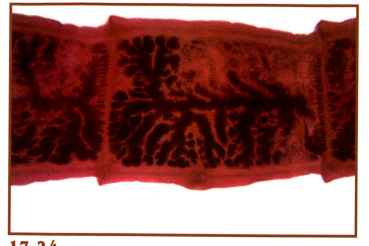

17-34 *TAENIA SOLIUM PROGLOTTID* The uterus of *T. solium* proglottids consists of a central portion with 7–13 lateral branches (compare to the *T. saginata* uterus in Figure 17-31).

Nematode Parasites Found in Clinical Specimens

Ascaris lumbricoides

A. lumbricoides (Figures 17-35 and 17-36) is a large nematode—females may reach a length of 49 cm! Human infection occurs when eggs in fecally contaminated soil or food are ingested. Juveniles emerge in the intestine, penetrate its wall, and then migrate to the lungs and other tissues. After a period of development in the lungs, the juveniles move up the respiratory tree to the esophagus and are swallowed again. Adults then reside in the small intestine and produce eggs (Figures 17-37 and 17-38). Infection may result in inflammation in organs other than the lungs where juvenile worms settled incorrectly. *Ascaris* pneumonia occurs in heavy infections due to the lung damage caused by the juveniles. If secondary bacterial infections occur, the pneumonia can be fatal. Blockage of the intestines and malnutrition also are possible in heavy infections. Lastly, under certain conditions, worms can wander to other body locations and cause damage or blockage. Identification of an *Ascaris* infection is made by observing the eggs in feces.

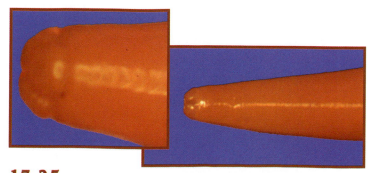

17-35 *ASCARIS LUMBRICOIDES ANTERIOR* *A. lumbricoides* has a cylindrical shape with three prominent mouth parts (see inset).

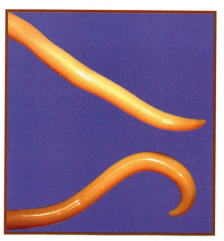

17-36 *ASCARIS LUMBRICOIDES ADULT WORMS* *A. lumbricoides* males (bottom) are shorter than females (top) (up to 31 cm vs. 35 cm) and have a curved posterior.

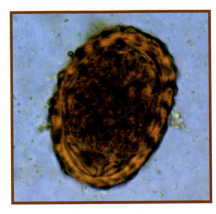

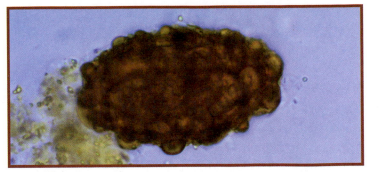

17-37 **Fertile *Ascaris* *lumbricoides* Egg in Feces (D'Antoni's Iodine Stain)** Fertile *A. lumbricoides* eggs are 55–75 μm long by 35–50 μm wide and are embryonated. Their surface is covered by small bumps called mammillations.

17-38 **Infertile *Ascaris lumbricoides* Egg in Feces (D'Antoni's Iodine Stain)** Infertile eggs are longer (up to 90 μm) than fertile eggs. There is no embryo inside.

Capillaria hepatica

C. hepatica is mostly a rodent parasite, but human infections do occur. Infection results when food or soil contaminated with eggs is ingested. Juveniles emerge in the small intestine and migrate to the liver where development into adults occurs. Eggs (Figure 17-39) are deposited in the liver, but cannot develop there. For further development, a predator must eat the infected host's liver. The eggs pass through the predator's gut and are deposited in the soil with the feces. The main symptom of infection is hepatitis with eosinophilia, but other symptoms of liver dysfunction may be present. Identification is made by liver biopsy or postmortem examinations.

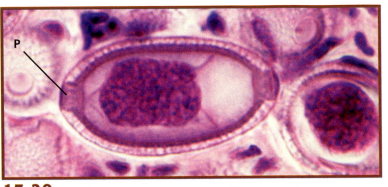

17-39 **Section of *Capillaria hepatica* Eggs in the Liver** *C. hepatica* eggs are 51–67 μm long by 30–35 μm wide and have "plugs" (**P**) at either end. These are only passed in the feces if an infected liver has been eaten, but still must be distinguished from the similar eggs of *Trichuris trichiura* which has much more prominent plugs at each end.

Enterobius vermicularis

E. vermicularis (Figure 17-40) is the human pinworm. It is found worldwide and is especially prevalent among people in institutions because conditions favor fecal-oral transmission of the parasite. Bedding, clothing, and the fingers (from scratching) become contaminated and may be involved in transmission. Poor sanitary habits of children make them especially prone to infecting others. Inhalation of eggs (Figure 17-41) carried on air currents is another mode of transmission. After ingestion (or inhalation), eggs hatch in the duodenum and mature in the large intestine where the adults reside. Adult females emerge from the anus at night to lay between 4,600 and 16,000 eggs in the perianal region. About one-third of pinworm infections are asymptomatic. The other two-thirds usually do not produce serious symptoms. Diagnosis is made by identifying the eggs. Since the eggs are laid externally, they are rarely found in feces. Instead, they are collected on cellophane tape from the perianal region and examined microscopically.

17-40 ***Enterobius vermicularis* Adult Female** Female pinworms are about 1 cm long and have a pointed tail (**T**) from which this group derives its common name. Males are about half that size and have a hooked tail.

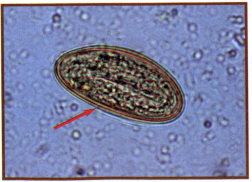

17-41 ***Enterobius vermicularis* Egg (D'Antoni's Iodine Stain)** The eggs of *E. vermicularis* are 50–60 μm long by 20–40 μm wide with one side flattened (**arrow**). They are usually embryonated in typical preparations.

Hookworms (*Ancylostoma duodenale and Necator americanus*)

The hookworms *A. duodenale* (Figures 17-42 and 17-43) and *N. americanus* (Figure 17-44) have very similar morphologies and life cycles, and the eggs are indistinguishable, so they are considered together here. Infection occurs when juveniles penetrate the skin, enter the blood, and travel to the lungs. They penetrate the respiratory membrane and are carried up and out of the lungs by ciliary action to the pharynx, where they are swallowed. When they reach the small intestine, they attach and mature into adults that feed on blood and tissues of the host. Adults are rarely seen as they remain attached to the intestinal mucosa. Eggs (Figure 17-45) are passed in the feces and are diagnostic of infection. The severity of hookworm disease symptoms is related to the parasite load, and most infections are asymptomatic. As a rule, severe symptoms of bloody diarrhea and iron deficiency anemia are only seen in heavy acute or chronic infections.

17-42 ANTERIOR OF *ANCYLOSTOMA DUODENALE* *A. duodenale* head showing the mouth and thick-walled esophagus. The bend in the head gives this group its common name—hookworm. In the inset, the chitinous teeth (**arrow**) are visible (compare with Figure 17-44).

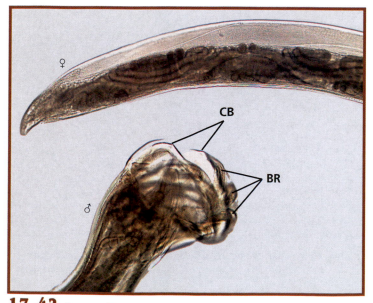

17-43 SEXUAL DIMORPHISM IN *ANCYLOSTOMA DUODENALE*
Males have a copulatory bursa (**CB**) at the posterior end; females do not. The arrangement of the bursal rays (**BR**) is helpful in identification.

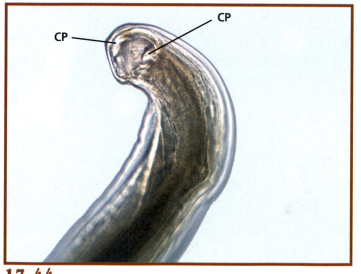

17-44 NECATOR AMERICANUS HEAD This detail of *N. americanus* shows the cutting plates (**CP**) that help to differentiate it from *Ancylostoma duodenale* (compare with Figure 17-42). Also notice the hooked head.

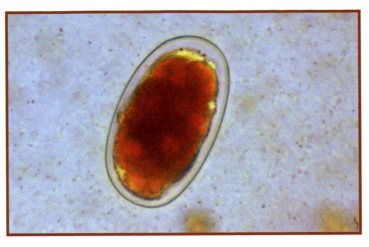

17-45 HOOKWORM EGG IN FECES (D'ANTONI'S IODINE STAIN) Hookworm eggs are 55–75 µm long by 36–40 µm wide. They have a thin shell and contain a developing embryo (seen here at about the 16 cell stage) that is separated from the shell when seen in fecal samples.

Onchocerca volvulus

O. volvulus is found in Africa, Mexico, and parts of South and Central America. It causes onchocerciasis ("river blindness") and is transmitted through bites of infected black flies (*Simulium spp.*). Juveniles enter the tissues and develop into adults in about a year. Adults then reside in subcutaneous tissues and become surrounded by a collagenous capsule (Figure 17-46). Microfilariae (Figure 17-47) develop and may be picked up by a black fly when feeding to complete the cycle. Damage due to the adult worm is negligible, at worst forming a nodule. The microfilariae are more troublesome. Dead microfilariae may cause dermatitis followed by a thickening, cracking, and depigmentation of the skin. Living microfilariae may infect the eyes, die, and stimulate an immune response. Sclerosing keratitis, which results in blindness, is one consequence of chronic eye inflammation. Diagnosis is by demonstration of microfilariae in skin snips.

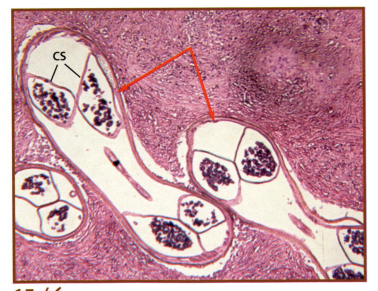

17-46 SECTION OF ADULT *ONCHOCERCA VOLVULUS* IN NODULES The adult worms are highly coiled within fibrous nodules (**arrows**) beneath the skin. Some worm cross-sections are labeled (**CS**).

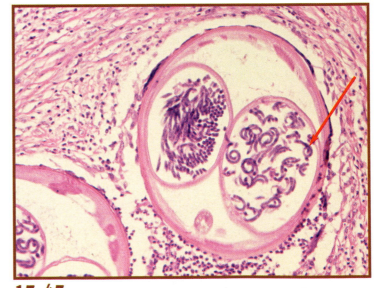

17-47 SECTION OF ADULT *ONCHOCERCA VOLVULUS* SHOWING DEVELOPING MICROFILARIAE Microfilariae are indicated by the **arrow**. They are 220–360 µm long.

Strongyloides stercoralis

S. stercoralis is the intestinal threadworm. Infection occurs as infective juveniles from fecally contaminated soil penetrate the skin. The juveniles then migrate to the lungs and develop into parthenogenetic females that migrate to the pharynx, are swallowed, and then burrow into the intestinal mucosa. Each day they release a few dozen eggs that develop into juveniles (Figure 17-48) before they are passed in the feces. These juveniles may become infective or may follow a developmental path that produces free-living adults. These adults eventually produce more infective juveniles and the cycle is completed. Symptoms of infection may be itching or secondary bacterial infection at the site of entry by the infective juveniles, a cough, burning of the chest during the pulmonary phase, and abdominal pain and perhaps septicemia during the intestinal phase. Diagnosis is by finding rhabditiform larvae in fresh fecal samples.

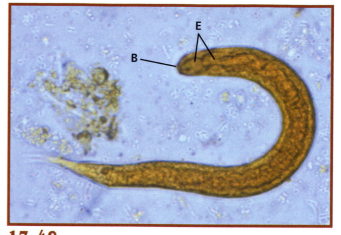

17-48 *STRONGYLOIDES STERCORALIS* **RHABDITIFORM LARVA IN FECES (D'ANTONI'S IODINE STAIN)** These larvae may be distinguished from hookworm larvae (which are rarely in feces) by their short buccal cavity (**B**). The name "rhabditiform" refers to the esophagus (**E**) shape, which has a constriction within it.

Trichinella spiralis

T. spiralis produces trichinosis, a disease of carnivorous mammals. Infection occurs when undercooked meat (*e.g.,* pork) containing infective juveniles in **nurse cells** is eaten. These juveniles emerge from their nurse cells and enter the intestinal mucosa. Between two and three days later, the juveniles have developed into mature adults that burrow within rows of the intestinal epithelial cells. Juveniles emerge from the females and are distributed throughout the body. When they are in skeletal muscle, they enter the muscle

fibers and each induces the formation of a nurse cell (Figures 17-49 and 17-50). In as little as four weeks, these juveniles become infective. Humans, unless they are eaten, are a dead-end host for this parasite. Symptoms of infection are many and varied because the juveniles migrate throughout the body. Some consequences of infection are pneumonia, meningitis, deafness, and nephritis. Death may occur due to heart, respiratory, or kidney failure, but most infections are subclinical. Diagnosis is by muscle biopsy.

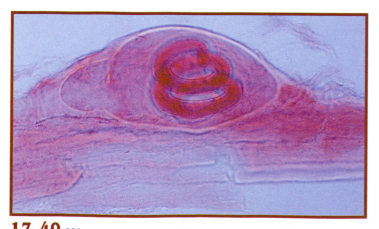

17-49 **WHOLE MOUNT OF A** *TRICHINELLA SPIRALIS* **LARVA IN SKELETAL MUSCLE** The spiral juvenile and its nurse cell are visible in this preparation.

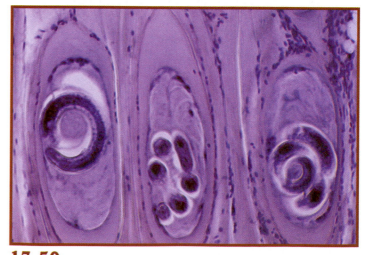

17-50 **SECTION OF** *TRICHINELLA SPIRALIS* **LARVAE IN SKELETAL MUSCLE** Each larva has entered a different skeletal muscle cell and converted it into a nurse cell that sustains it with nourishment.

Trichuris trichiura

The whipworm *T. trichiura* is a parasite of the large intestine and is often associated with *Ascaris* infections. Infection occurs through ingestion of eggs in fecally contaminated soil or plants. The juveniles then emerge and penetrate the mucosa of the large intestine. As they grow, their posterior projects into the lumen while the anterior remains buried in the mucosa and feeds on cell contents and blood. The adult females (Figure 17-51) release up to 20,000 eggs a day (Figure 17-52), which pass out with the feces and are diagnostic of infection; adult worms are rarely seen. Most infections are asymptomatic. With heavy worm burdens (more than 100), dysentery, anemia, and slowed growth and cognitive development are common.

17-51 ADULT FEMALE *TRICHURIS TRICHIURA* Adults are about 5 cm in length, with females being slightly longer than males. The blunt posterior end is indicative of females. The long, thin anterior portion remains embedded in the intestinal mucosa and feeds.

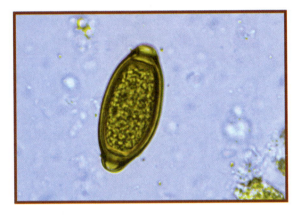

17-52 *TRICHURIS TRICHIURA* EGG IN FECES (D'ANTONI'S IODINE STAIN) The barrel-shaped eggs of *T. trichiura* have distinctive plugs at either end. They are 50–55 μm in length by 22–24 μm wide.

Wuchereria bancrofti

W. bancrofti is a filarial worm that causes lymphatic filariasis. Infection occurs from the bite of a mosquito harboring infective juveniles. Upon injection into the host, the worms migrate into the large lymphatic vessels of the lower body and mature. Adults are found in coiled bunches and the females release microfilariae (Figure 17-53) by the thousands. Microfilariae enter the blood and circulate there, often with a daily periodicity—most abundant at night when the mosquito vector is active and hidden away in lung capillaries during the day when it is not. Some infections are asymptomatic, whereas others result in acute inflammation of lymphatics associated with fever, chills, tenderness, and toxemia. In the most serious cases, obstruction of lymphatic vessels occurs and results in elephantiasis, a disease caused by accumulation of lymph fluid in the tissues, an accumulation of fibrous connective tissue, and a thickening of the skin. Diagnosis of infection is made by identifying microfilariae in blood smears.

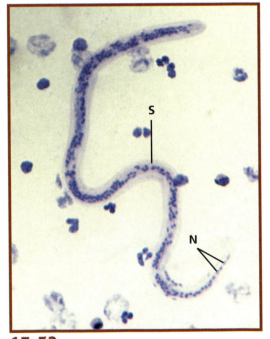

17-53 *WUCHERERIA BANCROFTI* MICROFILARIA IN A BLOOD SAMPLE The microfilariae of *W. bancrofti* can be distinguished from others in the blood by the sheath (**S**) and the single column of nuclei (**N**) not extending to the tip of the tail.

Quantitative Microbiology

Standard Plate Count (Viable Count)

● Purpose

The viable count is one method of determining the density of a microbial population. It provides an estimate of actual *living* cells in the sample.

● Principle

The standard plate count is a procedure that allows microbiologists to estimate the population density in a liquid sample by plating a very dilute portion of that sample and counting the number of colonies it produces. The inoculum that is transferred to the plate contains a *known* proportion of the original sample because it is the product of a **serial dilution**.

As shown in Figure 18-1, a serial dilution is simply a series of controlled transfers down a line of **dilution blanks** (tubes containing a known volume of sterile diluent—water, saline, or buffer). The series begins with a sample containing an unknown concentration (density) of cells and ends with a very dilute mixture containing only a few cells. Each dilution blank in the series receives a known volume from the mixture in the previous tube and delivers a known volume to the next, typically reducing the cell density by 1/10 or 1/100 at each step.

For example, if the original sample in Figure 18-1 contains 1,000,000 cells/mL, following the first transfer, the 1/100 dilution (0.1 mL into 9.9 mL) in dilution tube 1 would contain 10,000 cells/mL. In the second dilution (tube 2), the 1/100 dilution would reduce it further to 100 cells/mL. Because the cell density of the original sample is not known at this time, only the dilutions (without mL units) are recorded on the dilution tubes. By convention, dilutions are expressed in scientific notation. Therefore, a 1/10 dilution is written as 10^{-1} and a 1/100 dilution is written as 10^{-2}.

A known volume of appropriate dilutions (depending on the *estimated* cell density of the original sample) is then spread onto agar plates to produce at least one **countable plate**. A countable plate is one that contains between 30 and 300 colonies (Figure 18-2). A count lower than 30 colonies is considered statistically unreliable and greater than 300 is typically too many to be viewed as individual colonies. A colony counter (Figure 18-3) with a magnifying lens is useful if the colonies are small.

In examining Figure 18-1, you can see that the first transfer in the series is a simple dilution, but that all successive transfers are compound dilutions. Both types of dilutions can be calculated using the following formula,

$$V_1 D_1 = V_2 D_2$$

where V_1 and D_1 are the volume and dilution of the concentrated broth, respectively, while V_2 and D_2 are the volume and dilution of the completed dilution. Undiluted samples are always expressed as 1.

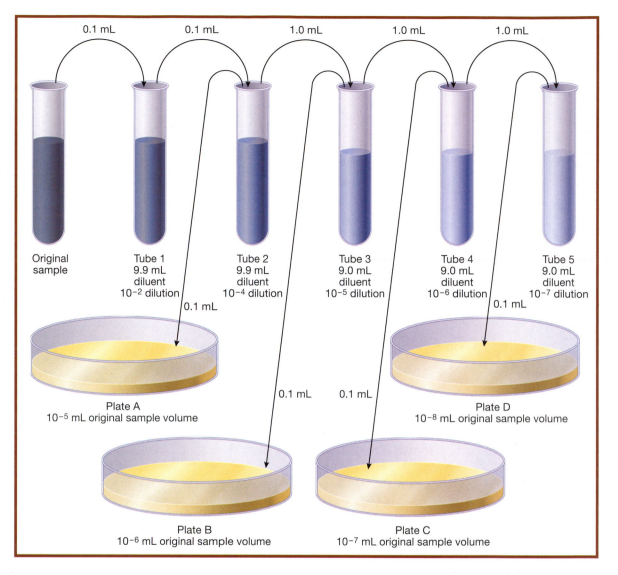

18-1 SERIAL DILUTION

This is a sample dilution scheme. The dilution assigned to each tube (written below the tube) represents the proportion of original sample inside that tube. For example, if the dilution is 10^{-4}, the proportion of original sample inside the tube would be 1/10000th of the total volume. When 0.1 mL of that solution is transferred to a plate, the volume of sample in the plate is 0.1 mL $\times 10^{-4} = 10^{-5}$ mL.

0.1 mL   0.1 mL   1.0 mL   1.0 mL   1.0 mL

Original sample

Tube 1
9.9 mL diluent
10^{-2} dilution

Tube 2
9.9 mL diluent
10^{-4} dilution

Tube 3
9.0 mL diluent
10^{-5} dilution

Tube 4
9.0 mL diluent
10^{-6} dilution

Tube 5
9.0 mL diluent
10^{-7} dilution

0.1 mL

0.1 mL

0.1 mL   0.1 mL

0.1 mL

Plate A
10^{-5} mL original sample volume

Plate D
10^{-8} mL original sample volume

Plate B
10^{-6} mL original sample volume

Plate C
10^{-7} mL original sample volume

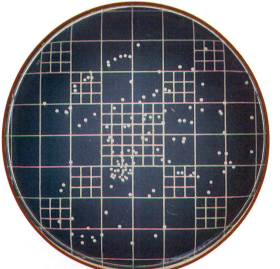

18-2 COUNTABLE PLATE

A countable plate has between 30 and 300 colonies. Therefore, this plate with approximately 130 colonies is countable and can be used to calculate cell density in the original sample. Plates with fewer than 30 colonies are TFTC ("too few to count"). Plates with more than 300 colonies are TMTC ("too many to count").

Therefore, to calculate the dilution of a 1 mL sample transferred to 9 mL of diluent, the permuted formula would be used as follows.

$$D_2 = \frac{V_1 D_1}{V_2} = \frac{1.0 \text{ mL} \times 1}{10 \text{ mL}} = \frac{1}{10} = 10^{-1}$$

As mentioned above, compound dilutions are calculated using the same formula. However, because D_1 in compound dilutions no longer represents undiluted sample, but rather a fraction of the original density, it must be represented as something less than 1 (*i.e.*, 10^{-1}, 10^{-2}, *etc.*) For example, if 1 mL of the 10^{-1} dilution from the last example were transferred to 9 mL of diluent, it would become a 10^{-2} dilution as follows.[1]

$$D_2 = \frac{V_1 D_1}{V_2} = \frac{1.0 \text{ mL} \times 10^{-1}}{10 \text{ mL}} = 10^{-1} \times 10^{-1} = 10^{-2}$$

[1] Permutations of this formula work with all necessary dilution calculations. For calculations involving unconventional volumes or dilutions, the formula is essential, but for simple ten-fold or hundred-fold dilutions like the ones described here, the final compounded dilution in a series can be calculated simply by multiplying each of the simple dilutions by each other. For example, a series of three 10^{-1} dilutions would yield a final dilution of 10^{-3} ($10^{-1} \times 10^{-1} \times 10^{-1} = 10^{-3}$). Three 10^{-2} dilutions would yield a final dilution of 10^{-6} ($10^{-2} \times 10^{-2} \times 10^{-2} = 10^{-6}$). We encourage you to use whatever means is best for you. In time you will be doing the calculations in your head.

18-3 COLONY COUNTER The magnifying lens and grid (Figure 18-2) make colony counting easier. Counted colonies are either punched with an inoculating needle (as in the photo) or marked on the Petri dish base with a pen to ensure all colonies are counted and none are counted twice. A hand tally counter (seen in the left hand) is used to ensure that distractions don't cause the microbiologist to lose track of the counted colonies.

Spreading a known volume of this dilution onto an agar plate and counting the colonies that develop would give you all the information you need to calculate the original cell density (OCD). Below is the basic formula for this calculation.

$$OCD = \frac{CFU}{D \times V}$$

CFU (colony forming units) is actually the number of colonies that develop on the plate. CFU is the preferred term because colonies could develop from single cells or from groups of cells, depending on the typical cellular arrangement of the organism. *D* is the dilution as written on the dilution tube from which the inoculum comes. *V* is the volume transferred to the plate. (**Note:** The volume is included in the formula because densities are expressed in CFU/mL, therefore a 0.1 mL inoculation—which would contain 1/10th as many cells as 1 mL—must be accounted for.)

As you can see in the formula, the volume of *original sample* being transferred to a plate is the product of the *volume transferred* and the *dilution* of the tube from which it came. Therefore 0.1 mL transferred from 10^{-2} dilution contains only 10^{-3} mL of the original sample (0.1 mL $\times$ 10^{-2}). The convention among microbiologists is to condense D and V in the formula into "Original sample volume" (expressed in mL). The formula thus becomes,

$$OCD = \frac{CFU}{Original\ sample\ volume}$$

The sample volume is written on the plate at the time of inoculation. Following a period of incubation, the plates are examined, colonies are counted on the countable plates, and calculation is a simple division problem. Suppose, for example, you inoculated a plate with 0.1 mL of a 10^{-5} dilution. This plate now contains 10^{-6} mL of original sample. Suppose, too, that after incubation you count 37 colonies on this plate. Calculation would be as follows:

$$OCD = \frac{CFU}{Sample\ volume} = \frac{37\ CFU}{10^{-6}\ mL} = 3.7 \times 10^{7}\ CFU/mL$$

Direct Count (Petroff-Hausser)

● Purpose

The direct count method is used to determine bacterial cell density in a sample.

● Principle

Microbial direct counts, like plate counts, take a small portion of a sample and use the data gathered from it to calculate the overall population cell density. This is made possible with a device called a **Petroff-Hausser counting chamber.** The Petroff-Hausser counting chamber is very much like a microscope slide with a 0.02 mm deep chamber or "well" in the center containing an etched grid (Figure 18-4). The grid is one square millimeter and consists of 25 large squares, each of which contains 16 small squares, making a total of 400 small squares. Figures 18-5 and 18-6 illustrate the counting grid.

When the well is covered with a cover glass and filled with a suspension of cells, the volume of liquid above each small square is 5×10^{-8} mL. This may seem like an extremely small volume, but the space above each small square is large enough to hold about 50,000 average-size cocci! Fortunately, dilution procedures prevent this scenario from occurring and cell counting is easily done using the microscope.

Original cell density (OCD) is determined by counting the cells found in a predetermined group of small squares and

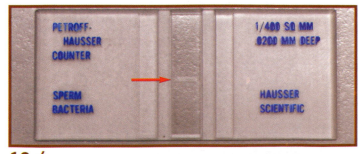

18-4 PETROFF-HAUSSER COUNTING CHAMBER The Petroff-Hausser counting chamber is a device used for the direct counting of bacterial cells. Bacterial suspension is drawn by capillary action from a pipette into the chamber enclosed by a coverslip. The cells are then counted against the grid of small squares in the center of the chamber. The horizontal lines of the grid are faintly visible at the **arrow**.

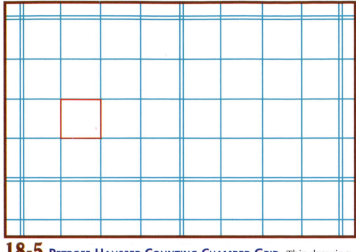

18-5 PETROFF-HAUSSER COUNTING CHAMBER GRID This drawing shows a portion of the Petroff-Hausser counting chamber grid. The smallest squares are the ones referred to in the formula. The volume above a small square is 5×10^{-8} mL. When cells land on a line, count them with the square below or to the right.

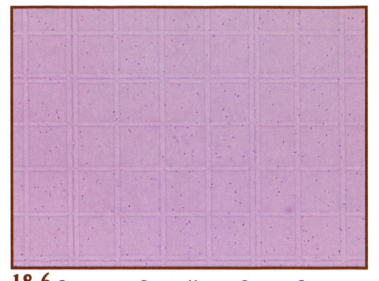

18-6 ORGANISM IN A PETROFF-HAUSSER COUNTING CHAMBER This is a 10^{-4} dilution of *Vibrio natriegens* on the grid. Can you determine the original cell density?

dividing by the number of squares counted multiplied by the dilution[1] and the volume of sample above one small square.

The following is a standard formula for calculating original cell density in a direct count.

$$OCD = \frac{\text{Cells counted}}{(\text{Squares})(\text{Dilution})(\text{Volume})}$$

To maintain accuracy, some experts recommend a minimum overall count of 600 cells in one or more samples

---
[1] Dilutions are calculated using the following formula.

$$D_2 = \frac{V_1 D_1}{V_2}$$

D_2 is the new dilution to be determined. V_1 is the volume of sample being diluted. D_1 is the dilution of the sample before adding diluent (undiluted samples have a dilution factor of 1). V_2 is the new combined volume of sample and diluent after the dilution is completed.

taken from a single population. Optimum density for counting is between 5 and 15 cells per small square.

If, for example, 200 cells from a sample with a dilution of 10^{-2} were counted in 16 squares (remembering that the volume above a single small square is 5×10^{-8} mL), the cell density in the original sample would be calculated as follows:

$$OCD = \frac{\text{Cells counted}}{(\text{Squares}) (\text{Dilution}) (\text{Volume})}$$

$$OCD = \frac{200 \text{ cells}}{(16)(10^{-2})(5 \times 10^{-8} \text{ mL})}$$

$$OCD = 2.5 \times 10^{10} \text{ cells/mL}$$

The advantages of direct counting are that it is fast, easy to do, and relatively inexpensive. The major disadvantage is that living as well as dead cells are counted.

Plaque Assay for Determination of Phage Titer

● Purpose

This technique is used to determine the concentration of viral particles in a sample. Samples taken over a period of time can be used to construct a viral growth curve.

● Principle

Viruses that attack bacteria are called **bacteriophages,** or simply **phages** (Figures 18-7, 10-2, and 10-3). Some viruses attach to the bacterial cell wall and inject viral DNA into the bacterial cytoplasm. The viral **genome** then commands

the cell to produce more viral DNA and viral proteins, which are used for the assembly of more phages. Once assembly is complete, the cell lyses and releases the phages, which then attack other bacterial cells and begin the replicative cycle all over again. This process, called the **lytic cycle,** is shown in Figure 10-4.

Lysis of bacterial cells growing in a lawn on an agar plate produces a clearing that can be viewed with the naked eye. These clearings are called **plaques**. In the plaque assay, a sample of bacteriophage (generally diluted by means of a serial dilution) is added to a plate inoculated

18-7 T4 COLIPHAGE

This is a negative stain of two T4 phage particles. Shown are the capsid (**C**), tail (**T**), and base plate (**B**). Tail fibers are visible only as broken pieces in the background. The length of this phage from base plate to tip of capsid is approximately 180 nm (0.18 μm).

Photo by author taken at the San Diego State University Electron Microscope Facility

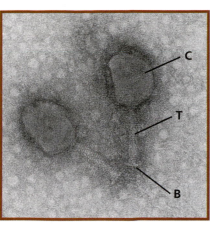

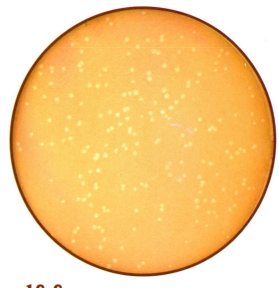

18-8 COUNTABLE PLATE
This plaque assay plate has between 30 and 300 plaques; therefore, it is "countable."

with enough bacterial **host** to produce a lawn of growth. After incubation, the number of plaques formed can be used to calculate the original phage **titer** (density).

Plaque assay technique is similar to the standard plate count in that it employs a serial dilution to produce countable plates needed for later calculations. (**Note:** Refer to Standard Plate Count, pages 217–219, as needed for a description of serial dilutions and calculations.) One key difference is that the plaque assay is done using the **pour-plate technique,** in which bacterial cells and viruses are first added to molten agar and then poured into the plate.

In this procedure, diluted phage is added directly to a small amount of *E. coli* culture (its host) and allowed a 15-minute **preadsorption period** to attach to the bacterial cells. Then this phage–host mixture is added to a tube of **soft agar**, mixed, and poured onto prepared Nutrient Agar plates as an **agar overlay**. The consistency of the solidified soft agar is sufficient to immobilize the bacteria while allowing the smaller bacteriophages to diffuse short distances and infect surrounding cells. During incubation, the *E. coli* produces a lawn of growth on the plate in which plaques appear where contiguous cells have been lysed by the virus (Figure 18-8).

The procedure for counting plaques is the same as that for the standard plate count. To be statistically reliable, countable plates must have between 30 and 300 plaques. Calculating phage titer (original phage density) uses the same formula as other plate counts except that PFU (plaque forming unit) instead of CFU (colony forming unit) becomes the numerator in the equation. Phage titer, therefore, is expressed in PFU/mL and the formula is written as follows:

$$\text{Phage titer} = \frac{\text{PFU}}{\text{Volume plated} \times \text{Dilution}}$$

As with the standard plate count, it is customary to condense *volume plated* and *dilution* into *original sample volume*. The formula then becomes:

$$\text{Phage titer} = \frac{\text{PFU}}{\text{Original sample volume}}$$

The original sample volume is written on the plate at the time of inoculation. Following a period of incubation, the plates are examined, plaques are counted on the countable plates, and calculation is a simple division problem.

Suppose, for example, you inoculated a plate with 0.1 mL of a 10^{-4} phage dilution mixed with a few mL *E. coli* broth culture. (Remember, you are calculating the *phage density*; the *E. coli* has nothing to do with the calculations.) This plate now contains 10^{-5} mL of original phage sample. If you subsequently counted 45 plaques on the plate, calculation would be as follows:

$$\text{Original phage density} = \frac{45\ \text{PFU}}{10^{-5}\ \text{mL}} = 4.5 \times 10^6\ \text{PFU/mL}$$

Urine Streak—Semiquantitative Method

● Purpose

Urine culture is a common method of detecting and quantifying bacteria responsible for urinary tract infections. It frequently is combined with selective media for specific identification of members of *Enterobacteriaceae* or *Streptococcus*.

● Principle

Urine culture is a semiquantitative CFU (colony-forming unit) counting method that quickly produces countable plates without a serial dilution. The instrument used in this procedure is a volumetric loop, calibrated to hold 0.001 mL or 0.01 mL of sample. Urine culture procedures using volumetric loops are useful in situations where a rapid diagnosis is essential and approximations ($\pm 10^2$ CFU/mL) are sufficient to choose a course of action. Volumetric loops are useful substitutes for serial dilutions in situations where population density is not likely to exceed 10^5 CFU/mL.

In this standard procedure, a loopful of urine is carefully transferred to a Blood Agar plate. The initial inoculation is a single streak across the diameter of the agar plate. Then the plate is turned 90° and (without flaming the loop) streaked again, this time across the original line in a zigzag pattern to evenly disperse the bacteria over the entire plate (Figure 18-9). Following a period of incubation, the resulting colonies are counted and population density, usually referred to as "original cell density," or OCD, is calculated (Figures 18-10 and 18-11).

OCD is recorded in "colony forming units," or CFU per milliliter (CFU/mL). CFU/mL is determined by dividing the number of colonies on the plate by the volume of the loop. For example, if 75 colonies are counted on a plate inoculated with a 0.001 mL loop, the calculation would be as follows:

$$OCD = \frac{CFU}{\text{loop volume}}$$

$$OCD = \frac{75 \text{ CFU}}{0.001 \text{ mL}}$$

$$OCD = 7.5 \times 10^4 \text{ CFU/mL}$$

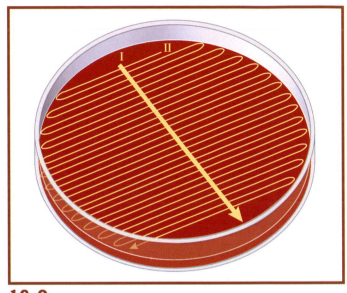

18-9 SEMIQUANTITATIVE STREAK METHOD Streak 1 is a simple streak line across the diameter of the plate. Streak 2 is a tight streak across Streak 1 to cover the entire plate. The loop is not flamed between streaks.

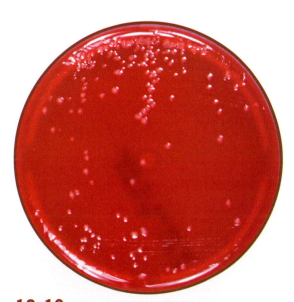

18-10 URINE STREAK ON SHEEP BLOOD AGAR This plate was inoculated with a 0.01 mL volumetric loop. The cell density (in CFU/mL) can be determined by dividing the number of colonies by 0.01.

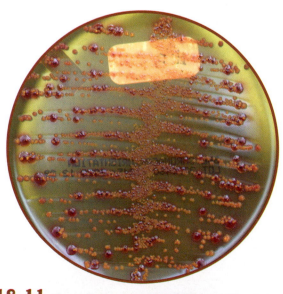

18-11 URINE STREAK ON CHROMAGAR ORIENTATION MEDIUM This medium enables differentiation of bacterial species or genera by color production. The rose-colored colonies are *Escherichia coli;* the brown colonies are *Proteus mirabilis*. Both organisms are common urinary pathogens.

Medical, Environmental, and Food Microbiology

Antimicrobial Susceptibility Test (Kirby-Bauer Method and E Test)

● Purpose

Antimicrobial susceptibility testing is a standardized method that is used to measure the effectiveness of antibiotics and other chemotherapeutic agents on pathogenic microorganisms. In many cases, it is an essential tool in prescribing appropriate treatment.

● Principle

Antibiotics are natural antimicrobial agents produced by microorganisms. One type of penicillin, for example, is produced by the mold *Penicillium notatum* (Figure 15-25). Today, because many agents that are used to treat bacterial infections are synthetic, the terms **antimicrobials** or **antimicrobics** are used to describe all substances used for this purpose.

The Kirby-Bauer test, also called the disk diffusion test, is a valuable standard tool for measuring the effectiveness of antimicrobics against pathogenic microorganisms. In the test, antimicrobic-impregnated paper disks are placed on a plate that is inoculated to form a bacterial lawn. The plates are incubated to allow growth of the bacteria and time for the agent to diffuse into the agar. As the drug moves through the agar, it establishes a concentration gradient. If the organism is susceptible to it, a clear zone will appear around the disk where growth has been inhibited (Figures 19-1 and 19-2).

The size of this **zone of inhibition** depends upon the sensitivity of the bacteria to the specific antimicrobial agent and the point at which the chemical's **minimum inhibitory concentration (MIC)** is reached. Some drugs kill the organism and are said to be

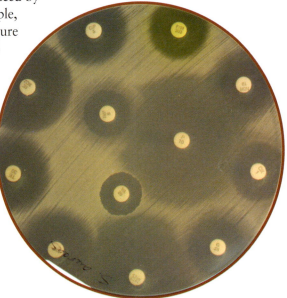

19-1 DISK DIFFUSION TEST OF METHICILLIN-SUSCEPTIBLE *STAPHYLOCOCCUS AUREUS* This plate illustrates the effect of (clockwise from top outer right) Nitrofurantoin (F/M300), Norfloxacin (NOR 10), Oxacillin (OX 1), Sulfisoxazole (G .25), Ticarcillin (TIC 75), Trimethoprim-Sulfamethoxazole (SXT), Tetracycline (TE 30), Ceftizoxime (ZOX 30), Ciprofloxacin (CIP 5), and (inner circle from right) Penicillin (P 10), Vancomycin (VA 30), and Trimethoprim (TMP 5) on Methicillin-resistant *S. aureus*. Compare the zone sizes with those in Figure 19-2, paying particular attention to Ceftizoxime, Oxacillin, and Penicillin.

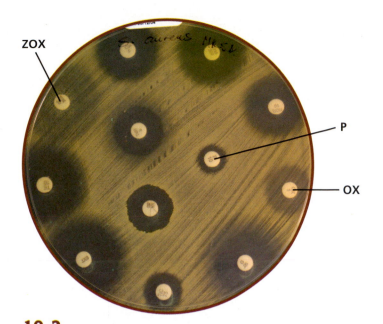

ZOX

P

OX

19-2 DISK DIFFUSION TEST OF METHICILLIN-RESISTANT *STAPHYLOCOCCUS AUREUS* **(MRSA)** The Kirby-Bauer test illustrating the effect of the same antibiotics as in Figure 19-1 on Methicillin-resistant *S. aureus*. Compare the zone sizes with those in Figure 19-1 and note the breakthrough growth surrounding Ceftizoxime (**ZOX**) and Oxacillin (**OX**) and the significantly smaller zone surrounding Penicillin (**P**).

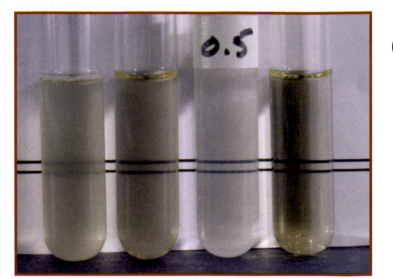

19-3 MCFARLAND STANDARDS This is a comparison of a 0.5 McFarland turbidity standard to three broths with varying degrees of turbidity. Each of the 11 McFarland standards (0.5 to 10) contains a specific percentage of precipitated barium sulfate to produce turbidity. In the Kirby-Bauer procedure, the test culture is diluted to match the 0.5 McFarland standard (roughly equivalent to 1.5×10^8 cells per mL) before inoculating the plate. Comparison is made visually by placing a card with sharp black lines behind the tubes. The 0.5 McFarland standard is marked in the photo. Notice that the turbidity of the second tube matches the McFarland standard exactly, whereas the first and fourth tubes are too turbid and too clear, respectively.

bactericidal. Other drugs are **bacteriostatic**; they stop growth but don't kill the microbe.

All aspects of the Kirby-Bauer procedure are standardized to ensure reliable results. Therefore, care must be taken to adhere to these standards. Mueller-Hinton agar, which has a pH between 7.2 and 7.4, is poured to a depth of 4 mm in either 150 mm or 100 mm Petri dishes. The depth is important because of its effect upon diffusion. Thick agar slows lateral diffusion and thus produces smaller zones than plates held to the 4 mm standard. Inoculation is made with a broth culture diluted to match a 0.5 McFarland turbidity standard (Figure 19-3).

The disks, which contain a specified amount of the antimicrobial agent (printed on the disk) are dispensed onto the inoculated plate and incubated at $35 \pm 2°C$ (Figure 19-4). After 16 to 18 hours of incubation, the plates are removed and the clear zone diameters are measured.

Normally, the zones around each antibiotic disk will be distinct and separate. Occasionally a **synergistic effect** of two antibiotics will produce a clear area between the disks extending beyond the perimeters of the otherwise circular zones (Figure 19-5). In this area between the zones both antibiotics are below MIC, but bactericidal in combination with each other.

The **E-test** system for determining antibiotic sensitivity, illustrated in Figure 19-6, is an alternative to the Kirby-Bauer method and has the added advantage of allowing the MIC to be determined. It consists of a paper strip with a gradient

of antibiotic concentrations on one surface and a printed scale on the other. After an agar plate is inoculated with a lawn of bacteria (as in the Kirby-Bauer method), the strip is placed, antibiotic side down, on the agar surface. During incubation, the antibiotic will diffuse into the agar (higher concentrations traveling farther than lower concentrations) and an elliptical zone of inhibition will develop. The point at which the inhibition zone intersects the scale printed on the strip is the MIC.

19-4 DISK DISPENSER This antibiotic disk dispenser is used to uniformly deposit disks on a Mueller-Hinton agar plate.

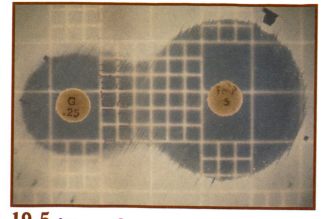

19-5 ANTIBIOTIC SYNERGISM This is an example of synergism between the antibiotics Sulfisoxazole (**G**) and Trimethoprim (**TMP**). The numbers on the discs represent micrograms (μg) of antibiotic.

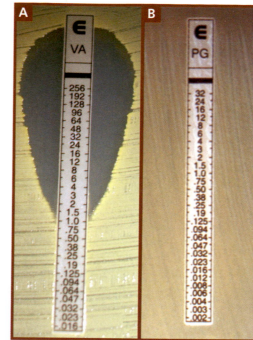

19-6 E-TEST The E-test is a procedure in which susceptibility to a particular antibiotic can be quantified as a Minimum Inhibitory Concentration (MIC). After incubation, the MIC is determined by where the zone of inhibition intersects the scale printed on the strip. **A** Shown is the zone formed by the antibiotic vancomycin when incubated with Methicillin-resistant *Staphylococcus aureus* (MRSA). **B** The antibiotic penicillin is generally not effective against Gram-negative bacteria. Shown is *Escherichia coli* grown with a Penicillin G strip. Note the absence of an inhibition zone.

Sample Collection and Transport

● Purpose

Proper collection and transport of patient specimens are crucial to the correct identification of pathogens by a clinical laboratory.

● Principle

Sample collection and transport are the first steps in identifying pathogens from patients, and their importance cannot be overstated. Improper collection and transport can make microbial identification by the laboratory more difficult assuming that the sample is even usable.

First and foremost, collection of patient specimens for laboratory diagnosis requires that the site sampled has an active infection. Collection of patient specimens may involve tissue removal, collection of sputum, urine or feces, fluid aspiration, venipuncture, or a surface swab. The method of choice is dictated by the body region and suspected pathogen, but regardless of the patient's normal flora, environmental surroundings, or the sample taker must not contaminate the sample. Further, the appropriate sampling instrument and transport medium must be used. Proper training of medical staff in sample collection and transport is imperative, because the laboratory can do little when the sample is contaminated or is not transported properly.

Samples are frequently obtained with swabs. Swabs come in a variety of types—wooden, plastic, or metal shafts and cotton, Dacron, or calcium alginate tips (Figure 19-7).

Plastic swabs are used most often because wooden swabs may harbor toxins that interfere with microbial growth. Flexible wire swabs are recommended for nasopharyngeal

19-7 COLLECTION AND TRANSPORT MEDIA Various collection swabs and transport media are shown. The tube with the maroon cap contains a plastic shaft with a polyurethane tip. Because the polyurethane tip is nontoxic, no transport medium is necessary. The red cap double swab has a rayon tip. The tube to the left contains Stuart's Liquid Transport medium, a nonnutritious, buffered medium that keeps the sample moist. The orange-capped swab has a regular aluminum wire with a Dacron tip. The green-capped swab has a soft aluminum wire with a Dacron tip. Both can be transported in the tube between them, which contains Amie's medium. So far, all tubes are for transport of aerobic organisms. The last system on the right is for transporting anaerobes. See Figure 19-8 for more information.

and male urethral samples. Cotton tips are useful in collecting nonfastidious organisms but may contain chemicals that are inhibitory to fastidious ones. Dacron tips have the widest application and may even be used for collecting viral samples. Calcium alginate-tipped swabs are best used to sample for *Chlamydia*. Once collected, the sample must be labeled with all relevant information, including patient name and ID number, sample site, date and time of collection, and collector's initials.

Various guidelines have been developed for transporting samples within a hospital or between locations, but are beyond the scope of this book. It stands to reason, though, that the sample be in a leak-proof container and in an environment that is suitable for survival of its contents. A third consideration is time: The faster the sample gets to the laboratory for processing, the better. Bacterial samples should be transported within 2 hours, if possible; the sample probably will be useless after 24 hours. And fourth, once in the laboratory, the sample should be processed in a timely fashion. In some cases, refrigeration is acceptable for a given amount of time before processing.

Various transport media are available depending on the application. Amies, Stuart's, and Cary-Blair are commonly used, and we will focus on Amies here. Amies is a defined medium with a variety of chloride salts to maintain osmotic pressure. Phosphate buffers maintain the pH, and thioglycollate produces a reduced environment to minimize oxidative damage to the cells. Some formulations contain charcoal to neutralize fatty acids and bacterial toxins. Note the absence of a carbon or nitrogen source. This medium is designed to maintain the bacteria, not provide for their growth.

Transport of anaerobes requires a special container that produces anaerobic conditions inside when the swab is inserted. A color indicator is used as a control to assure that the inside is anaerobic (Figure 19-8).

19-8 TRANSPORT SYSTEM FOR ANAEROBES This is a close-up view of two anaerobic transport tubes. They are the same as the tube shown at the right of Figure 19-7. The sample is taken and inserted into the tube, where it breaks open a vial that produces anaerobic conditions. A color indicator turns pink if oxygen is present, making the sample useless.

Environmental Sampling: The RODAC™ Plate

● Purpose

The RODAC™ (Replicate Organism Detection and Counting) plate is used to monitor contamination of surfaces in food preparation, veterinary, pharmaceutical, and medical settings. The plates also can be used to assess the efficiency of decontamination of a surface by taking a sample with different plates before and after decontamination.

● Principle

Monitoring of microbial surface contamination is an important practice in medical, veterinary, pharmaceutical, and food preparation settings. Often, the RODAC™ plate is used. It is a specially designed agar plate into which the medium is poured to produce a convex surface extending above the edge of the plate (Figure 19-9). The special design allows support of the lid above the agar without touching it. As a result, the sterile plate may be opened and pressed on a surface to be sampled. Most are 65 mm in diameter, which is smaller than standard-sized 100 mm Petri dishes. The smaller size makes it easier to apply uniform pressure across the entire plate when taking the sample. In addition, the base is marked in sixteen 1 cm squares, allowing an estimate of cell density on the surface (Figure 19-10).

The plate can be filled with a variety of media, the choice of which depends on the surface being sampled and the microbes to be recovered. For instance, plates with Trypticase™ Soy Agar, a good, general-purpose growth medium, are used. Because the surface sampled may have been disinfected recently, Polysorbate 80 and Lecithin are added to counteract the effect of residual disinfectant. The medium can be supplemented with 5% sheep blood to improve recovery of fastidious bacteria. Sabouraud Dextrose Agar is often employed when monitoring yeast and mold contamination.

The acceptable amount of growth on a RODAC™ plate is determined by the surface being sampled. It stands to reason that a surgical area would have a lower limit of acceptability than a food preparation area. Table 19-1 provides some guidelines.

19-9 RODAC™ PLATE Notice that the agar extends above the edges of the plate to allow contact with the surface to be sampled.

19-10 GRID ON THE RODAC™ PLATE Typically, RODAC™ plates are 65 mm in diameter. A grid of 16 squares is molded into the base, each with an area of 1 cm². Colonies growing in the grid can be counted and an average number of CFU per cm² of surface can be determined.

TABLE 19-1	Interpretation of RODAC™ Plate Colony Counts	

TABLE OF REPRESENTATIVE RESULTS[1]
(Colonies in 25 cm²)

Interpretation	Critical Surfaces[2]	Floors
Good	0–5	0–25
Fair	6–15	26–50
Poor	>16	>50

[1] Adapted from BBL™ Trypticase™ Soy Agar with Lecithin and Polysorbate 80 package insert.

[2] Critical surfaces include those in operating rooms, nurseries, table tops, toilet seats, and other nonporous surfaces.

Colilert®* Method for Testing Drinking Water

● Purpose

The Colilert® test is a commercial preparation that examines drinking water for the presence of total coliforms (in general) and *Escherichia coli* (specifically).

● Principal

Colilert® reagent contains nutrients and salts which favor the growth of coliforms and inhibit the growth of noncoliforms. It also contains the indicator nutrients, *o*-Nitrophenyl-β-D-Galactopyranoside (ONPG) and 4-Methylumbelliferyl-β-D-Glucuronide (MUG). The test is conducted by adding Colilert® reagent to a nonfluorescing bottle containing a 100 mL sample of drinking water. The sample is incubated at 35°C for 24–28 hours and then compared to the control.

All coliforms ferment lactose using the enzyme β-galactosidase. ONPG is an artificial substrate of the same enzyme and, when hydrolyzed, produces the yellow compound *o*-Nitrophenol. Refer to Figure 7-73 for this reaction and Figure 19-11 for the test results. If the test bottle is as yellow or more yellow than the control, the first portion of the test is positive and reported as "total coliforms present." MUG acts as a substrate for the *E. coli* enzyme β-glucuronidase, from which a fluorescent compound is produced. A positive MUG result produces fluorescence when viewed under an ultraviolet lamp (Figure 19-12). If the test bottle fluorescence is equal to or greater than that of the control, the presence of *E. coli* has been confirmed. This portion of the test is reported as "*E. coli* present." A sample that is not as yellow and does not fluoresce is considered negative and is reported as "total coliforms absent" and "*E. coli* absent."

*Colilert® is a registered trademark of IDEXX Laboratories, Inc.

19-11 COLILERT® ONPG This is a Colilert ONPG (*o*-Nitrophenyl-β-D-Galactopyranoside) test for total coliforms. The bottle on the left is negative; the bottle in the center is positive; the control "comparator" is on the right.

19-12 COLILERT® MUG This is a Colilert MUG (4-Methylumbelliferyl-β-D-Glucuronide) test for *Escherichia coli seen* under a UV Lamp. The bottle on the left is negative; the bottle in the center is positive; the control "comparator" is on the right.

Membrane Filter Technique

● Purpose

The membrane filter technique is commonly used to identify the presence of fecal coliforms in water.

● Principle

Fecal contamination is a common pollutant in open water and a potential source of serious disease-causing organisms. Certain members of *Enterobacteriaceae*, (Gram-negative facultative anaerobes) such as *Escherichia coli*, *Klebsiella pneumoniae*, and *Enterobacter aerogenes*, are able to ferment lactose rapidly and produce large amounts of acid and gas. These organisms, called **coliforms**, are used as the indicator species when testing water for fecal contamination because they are relatively abundant in feces and easy to detect (Figure 19-13). Once fecal contamination is confirmed by the presence of coliforms, any noncoliforms also present in the sample can be tested and identified as pathogenic or otherwise.

In the membrane filter technique, a water sample is drawn through a special porous membrane designed to trap microorganisms larger than 0.45 µm. After filtering the water sample, the membrane (filter) is applied to the surface of plated Endo Agar and incubated for 24 hours (Figure 19-14).

Endo Agar is a selective medium that encourages Gram-negative bacterial growth and inhibits Gram-positive growth. Endo Agar contains lactose for fermentation and a dye to indicate changes in pH. Because of their vigorous lactose fermentation resulting in acid and aldehyde formation, coliform colonies typically appear red and/or mucoid with a gold or green metallic sheen. Noncoliform bacteria (including several dangerous pathogens) tend to be pale pink, colorless, or the color of the medium.

After incubation, all red or metallic colonies are counted and are used to calculate "coliform colonies/100 mL" using the following formula:

$$\frac{\text{Total coliforms}}{100 \text{ mL}} = \frac{\text{Coliform colonies counted} \times 100}{\text{Volume of original sample in mL}}$$

A "countable" plate contains between 20 and 80 coliform colonies with a total colony count no larger than 200 (Figure 19-15). To assure that the number of colonies will fall within this range, it is customary to dilute heavily polluted samples, thereby reducing the number of cells collecting on the membrane. When dilution is necessary, it is important to record the volume of *original sample* only, not any added water. **Potable water** contains less than one coliform per 100 milliliters of sample.

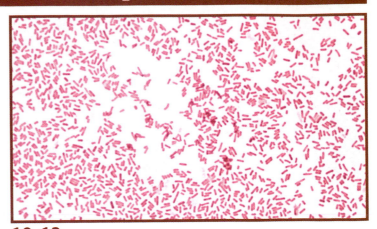

19-13 GRAM STAIN OF *ESCHERICHIA COLI* *E. coli* is a principal coliform detected by the membrane filter technique.

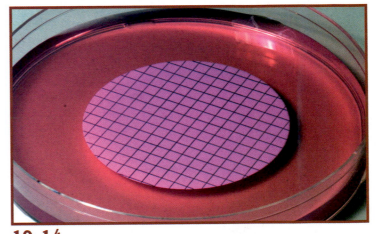

19-14 FILTER MEMBRANE This porous membrane will allow water to pass through but will trap bacteria and particles larger than 0.45 µm.

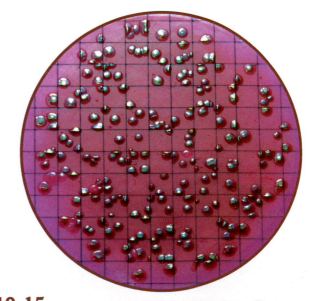

19-15 COLIFORM COLONIES ON A MEMBRANE FILTER Note the characteristic dark colonies with a gold or green metallic sheen, indicating that this water sample is contaminated with fecal coliforms. Potable water has less than one coliform per 100 mL of sample tested.

Multiple Tube Fermentation Method for Total Coliform Determination

● Purpose

This standardized test is used to measure coliform density (cells/100 mL) in water. It may be used to calculate the density of all coliforms present (total coliforms) or to calculate the density of *Escherichia coli* specifically.

● Principle

The **multiple tube fermentation method**, also called **most probable number**, or **MPN**, is a common means of calculating the number of coliforms present in 100 mL of a sample. The procedure determines both **total coliform** counts and *Escherichia coli* counts.

The three media used in the procedure are: Lauryl Tryptose Broth (LTB), Brilliant Green Lactose Bile (BGLB) Broth, and EC (*E. coli*) Broth. LTB, which includes lactose and lauryl sulfate, is selective for the coliform group. Because it does not screen out all noncoliforms, it is used to *presumptively* determine the presence or absence of coliforms. BGLB broth, which includes lactose and 2% bile, inhibits noncoliforms and is used to *confirm* the presence of coliforms. EC broth, which includes lactose and bile salts, is selective for *E. coli* when incubated at 45.5°C.

All broths are prepared in 10 mL volumes and contain an inverted Durham tube to trap any gas produced by fermentation. The LTB tubes are arranged in up to ten groups of five (Figure 19-16). Each tube in the first set of five receives 1.0 mL of the original sample. Each tube in the second group receives 1.0 mL of a 10^{-1} dilution. Each tube in group three receives 1.0 mL of 10^{-2}, etc.[1] (**Note:** The volume of

---

[1] The number of groups, number of tubes in each group, dilutions necessary, volume of broth in each tube, and volumes of sample transferred vary significantly, depending on the source and expected use of the water being tested.

broth in the tubes is not part of the calculation of dilution factor. Dilutions of the water sample are made using sterile water prior to inoculating the broths. One milliliter of diluted sample is added to each tube in its designated group.)

After inoculation, the LTB tubes are incubated at $35 \pm 2°C$ for up to 48 hours, then examined for gas production (Figure 19-17). Any positive LTB tubes then are used to inoculate BGLB tubes. Each BGLB receives one or two loopfuls from its respective positive LTB tube. Again, the cultures are incubated 48 hours at $35 \pm 2°C$ and examined for gas production (Figure 19-18). Positive BGLB cultures then are transferred to EC broth and incubated at 45.5°C for 48 hours (Figure 19-19). After incubation the EC tubes with gas are counted. Calculation of BGLB MPN and EC MPN is based on the combinations of positive results in

19-17 **LTB Tubes** The bubble in the Durham tube on the right is *presumptive* evidence of coliform contamination. The tube on the left is negative.

19-16 **Multiple Tube Fermentation** This a multiple tube fermentation of a sea water sample contaminated by sewage. The test photographed contains six dilution groups (the standard for heavily contaminated samples) rather than three, as described in Table 19-2. The tubes contain Lauryl Tryptose Broth and a measured volume of water sample as described in the text. Following incubation, each positive broth (based on gas production) will be used to inoculate a BGLB broth.

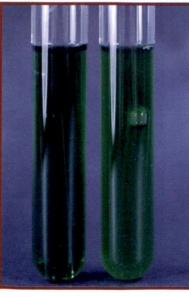

19-18 **BGLB Broth** The bubble in the Durham tube on the right is seen as *confirmation* of coliform contamination. The tube on the left is negative.

19-19 EC BROTH The bubble in the Durham tube on the right is seen as confirmation of *Escherichia coli* contamination. The tube on the left is negative.

the BGLB and EC broths, respectively, using the following formula:

$$MPN/100 \text{ mL} = \frac{100P}{\sqrt{V_n V_a}}$$

where

P = total number of positive results (BGLB or EC)

V_n = combined volume of sample in LTB tubes that produced negative results in BGLB or EC

V_a = combined volume of sample in all LTB tubes

It is customary to calculate and report *both* total coliform *and E. coli* densities. Total coliform MPN is calculated using BGLB broth results, and *E. coli* MPN is based on EC broth results.

Using the data from Table 19-2 and the formula above, the calculation would be as follows:

$$MPN/100 \text{ mL} = \frac{100P}{\sqrt{V_n V_a}}$$

$$MPN/100 \text{ mL} = \frac{100 \times 9}{\sqrt{0.24 \times 5.55}}$$

$$MPN/100 \text{ mL} = 780$$

This calculated value is reported as 780 total coliforms per 100 mL of water.

TABLE 19-2 BGLB Test Results

The results shown here are of a hypothetical BGLB test using three groups of five tubes (A, B, and C). A separate table would be produced using EC broth results. In this example, the original water sample was diluted to 10^0, 10^{-1}, and 10^{-2}. The three dilutions were used to inoculate the broths in groups A, B, and C, respectively. The first row shows the dilution of the inoculum used per group. The second row shows the actual amount of original sample that went into each broth. The third row shows the number of tubes in each group (five in this example). In the fourth row the number of tubes from each group of five that showed evidence of gas production has been recorded. This total (in red) inserts into the equation. Recorded in the fifth row are the numbers of tubes from each group that did *not* show evidence of gas production. The sixth row is used for calculating the "combined volume of sample in negative tubes" and refers to the inoculum that went into the LTB tubes that produced a negative result. (This is calculated by multiplying the number in Row 3 by the number in Row 5 of the same column.) This total (in red) inserts into the equation. The seventh row is used for calculating the "combined volume of sample in all tubes" and refers to the total volume of inoculum that went into all LTB tubes. (This is calculated by multiplying the number in Rows 2 and 3 of the same column.) This total (in red) inserts into the equation. As you can see, the undiluted inoculation (Group A) produced five positive results and zero negative results; the 10^{-1} dilution (Group B) produced three positive results and two negative; and the 10^{-2} dilution (Group C) produced one positive and four negative results. The total volume of original sample that went into LTB tubes was 5.55 mL, 0.24 mL of which produced no gas (shown in red in rows 7 and 6, respectively).

	Group	Group A	Group B	Group C	Totals (A+B+C)
1	Dilution (D)	10^0	10^{-1}	10^{-2}	NA
2	Portion of dilution added to each LTB tube that is original sample (1.0 mL × D)	1.0 mL	0.1 mL	0.01 mL	NA
3	# LTB tubes in group	5	5	5	NA
4	# positive BGLB (or EC if that is being calculated) results	5	3	1	9
5	# negative BGLB (or EC if that is being calculated) results	0	2	4	NA
6	Total volume of *original sample* in all LTB tubes that produced negative BGLB (or EC if that is being calculated) results (D × 1.0 mL × # negative tubes)	0 mL	0.2 mL	0.04 mL	0.24 mL
7	Volume of original sample in all LTB tubes inoculated (D × 1.0 mL × # tubes)	5.0 mL	0.5 mL	0.05 mL	5.55 mL

Bioluminescence

● Principle

A few marine bacteria from genera *Vibrio* and *Photobacterium* are able to emit light by a process known as **bioluminescence**. Many of these organisms maintain mutualistic relationships with other marine life. For example, *Photobacterium* species living in the Flashlight Fish receive nutrients from the fish and in return provide a unique device for frightening would-be predators.

Bioluminescent bacteria are given the ability to emit light because of an enzyme called **luciferase** (Figure 19-20). In the presence of oxygen and a long-chain aldehyde (*e.g.*, glyceraldehyde), luciferase catalyzes the oxidation of reduced flavin mononucleotide (FMNH₂). In the process, outer electrons surrounding FMN become excited. Light is emitted when the electronically excited FMN returns to its ground state (Figure 19-21).

It is estimated that a single *Vibrio* cell burns between 6000 and 60000 molecules of ATP per second emitting light (ATP hydrolysis occurs in conjunction with synthesis of the aldehyde). It also is known that their luminescence only occurs when a certain threshold population size is reached

$$FMNH_2 + O_2 + R - \overset{\overset{\displaystyle O}{\|}}{C}H \xrightarrow{\text{Luciferase}} FMN + H_2O + R - \overset{\overset{\displaystyle O}{\|}}{C} - OH + Light$$

19-20 CHEMISTRY OF BIOLUMINESCENT BACTERIA

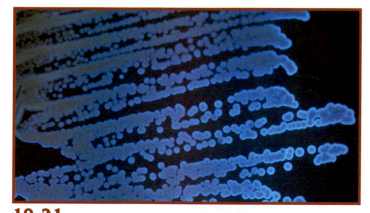

19-21 BIOLUMINESCENCE ON AN AGAR PLATE This is an unknown bioluminescent bacteria growing on Seawater Complete (SWC) Agar.

in a phenomenon called **quorem sensing**. This system is controlled by a genetically produced **autoinducer** that must be in sufficient concentration to trigger the reaction.

Winogradsky Column

● Purpose

The Winogradsky column is a method for growing a variety of microbes with uniquely microbial metabolic abilities. Bacterial photoautotrophs, chemolithotrophs, and photoheterotrophs may be found in a mature column. And more "typical" chemoheterotrophs and photoautotrophs also are likely to be found. A mature Winogradsky column is a good source for studying these organisms in the laboratory.

● Principle

The Winogradsky column bears the name of its developer, Sergei Winogradsky (1856–1953), a Russian microbiologist and pioneer in microbial ecology. He studied sulfur bacteria because of their ease of handling and cultivation, and then moved on to bacteria associated with the nitrogen cycle. One of his major discoveries was finding microorganisms (*Beggiatoa*) capable of the unheard of type of metabolism that came to be known as chemolithotrophic autotrophy (see below). Until he made his discovery, only photoautotrophs—those performing photosynthesis—were known to be autotrophs.

As a result of his work and the work of others, metabolic categories of microorganisms have been identified based on their carbon, energy, and electron sources. These are listed below. Note that in practice, terms are combined to describe the organism more fully.

Autotroph: an organism capable of obtaining all of its carbon from CO_2.

Heterotroph: an organism that can only get its carbon from organic molecules.

Chemotroph: an organism that gets its energy from the oxidation of chemicals.

Phototroph: an organism that gets its energy from light ($h\nu$).

Organotroph: an organism that gets its electrons from an organic molecule.

Lithotroph: an organism that gets its electrons from an inorganic molecule.

Winogradsky pioneered this method of growing microbes in the late 19th century. It was (and is) used as a convenient laboratory source to supply for study a variety of **anaerobic**, **microaerophilic**, and **aerobic** bacteria, including purple nonsulfur bacteria, purple sulfur bacteria, green sulfur bacteria, chemoheterotrophs, and many others (Figure 19-22).

The basis for the Winogradsky column is threefold. The first two factors involve opposing gradients that impact the types of organisms that can grow. The first is the oxygen gradient, which decreases (gets more and more anaerobic) toward the bottom. As a result, obligate aerobes, microaerophiles, facultative anaerobes, and obligate anaerobes are found in different locations in the column. The second is the H_2S gradient, which runs opposite in direction to the O_2 gradient. The third factor is the diffuse light shined upon the column. This promotes growth of phototrophic organisms at levels where they are adapted to the opposing gradients of O_2 and H_2S. These layers of phototrophs occur in natural ecosystems but are extremely thin because light doesn't penetrate mud sediments very far. But with the transparent column, thicker layers develop and it is easier to obtain samples for cultures or microscopy (Figures 19-23 and 19-24).

19-22 AN ARTIST'S RENDITION OF A WINOGRADSKY COLUMN What you put into a Winogradsky column dictates what you grow. Any well-constructed column has an oxygen gradient from top to bottom, with the aerobic zone penetrating perhaps only as much as 20% of the total depth. The remaining portion of the mud column becomes progressively more anaerobic. The different amounts of oxygen lead to layering of microbial communities adapted to that specific environment. This illustration is a generalized picture of the layering that you might see in a mature column. (The column often produces intermixed patches rather than distinct layers.) Starting at the top and working downward, the layers are: air, water (containing algae and cyanobacteria), aerobic mud (sulfur oxidizing bacteria), microaerophilic mud (nonsulfur photosynthetic bacteria), red/purple zone (purple sulfur photosynthetic bacteria), green zone (green sulfur photosynthetic bacteria), and black anaerobic zone (sulfur reducing bacteria).

Labels in figure 19-22: Plastic wrap; Air; Water; Aerobic zone; Microaerophilic zone; Anaerobic zone; O_2 dominated mud; Rust colored zone; Red zone; Green zone; Anaerobic H_2S dominated zone (black); Diatoms Cyanobacteria Protists; Aerobic sulfur oxidizing bacteria; Photoheterotrophs Non-sulfur bacteria; Purple sulfur bacteria; Green sulfur bacteria; Sulfur reducing bacteria

19-23 A FRESHLY MADE WINOGRADSKY COLUMN The black layer comprising the majority of the column is the unenriched mud. The lighter gray area at the bottom contains mud, $CaCO_3$, $CaSO_4$, and shredded paper mixed into a slurry. Note the absence of air spaces.

19-24 A MATURE WINOGRADSKY COLUMN AT EIGHT WEEKS Notice the layers and colors! Also notice that the layers are not as well defined as in Figure 19-22. In fact, some look mixed (*e.g.*, the rust and red portions appear mixed in some regions). But the dark, anaerobic zone above the whitish layer at the bottom is well defined. The remainder is—pardon the expression—clear as mud.

Nitrogen Cycle

Biogeochemical cycles, such as the carbon cycle, the nitrogen cycle, and the sulfur cycle, are characterized by **environmental phases**, in which the element is not incorporated into an organism, and **organismal phases**, in which it is. All are important, but because the nitrogen cycle has so many parts in which bacteria participate, it will be discussed here. It will be helpful for you to look at Figure 19-25 as you read the following.

Organisms require nitrogen as a component of the 20 amino acids, purine and pyrimidine nucleotides, and other

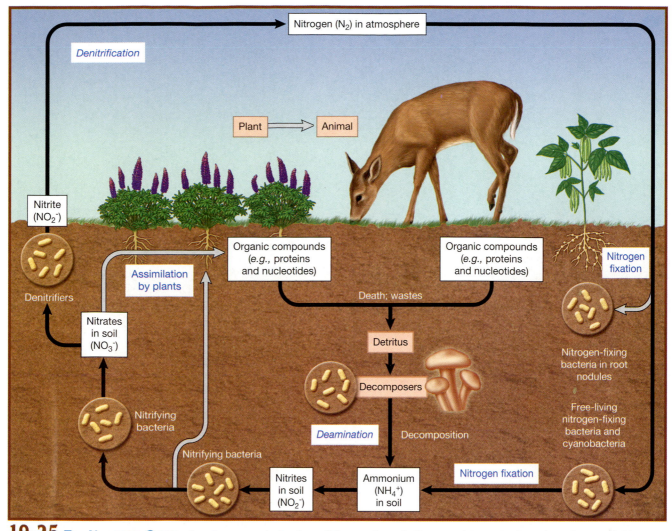

19-25 THE NITROGEN CYCLE The nitrogen cycle involves all forms of metabolism: aerobic respiration (chemoheterotrophic metabolism), anaerobic respiration, and chemolithotrophic metabolism, in addition to nitrogen fixation. And microbes are participants in all the steps.

compounds. These organic forms of nitrogen do not occur outside cells. Most of the air (approximately 80%) is nitrogen gas (N_2), but this is a form of nitrogen that is not usable by any organisms except nitrogen-fixing bacteria. Some nitrogen-fixing bacteria (*e.g., Rhizobium*—Figure 19-26) are symbionts of certain legumes and form nodules in their roots (Figures 19-27 and 19-28). Other nitrogen-fixing bacteria are free-living in the soil (*e.g., Azotobacter*—Figure 19-29) or water (*e.g., Anabaena*—Figure 19-30). The process of nitrogen fixation is highly endergonic, requiring about 16 moles of ATP per mole of N_2 reduced to ammonia (NH_3).

Because nitrogen fixation requires so much energy, the **nitrogenase** enzyme is not active if other forms of nitrogen are available. In addition, nitrogenase is inactivated by oxygen, so a variety of mechanisms have evolved to protect it from oxygen, including the heterocysts of filamentous cyanobacteria.

Some **chemolithotrophic** bacteria are capable of **nitrification**, in which ammonium ion acts as an electron and energy source when it is oxidized to nitrite, and then to nitrate.

Organisms such as *Nitrosomonas* oxidize ammonium to nitrite; then, other nitrifiying organisms, such as *Nitrobacter*, continue the oxidation of nitrite to nitrate. The same organisms do not do both.

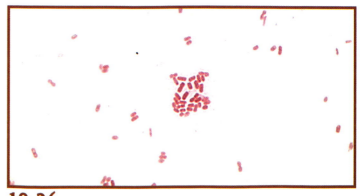

19-26 RHIZOBIUM GRAM STAIN *Rhizobium* occurs naturally as a nitrogen-fixing symbiont of leguminous plants. This Gram stain was made from a culture. *Rhizobium* and other symbionts are the major nitrogen-fixers on land.

19-27 CLOVER ROOT NODULES The roots of this small clover have been infected with *Rhizobium* that causes the formation of tumor-like root nodules (four are circled).

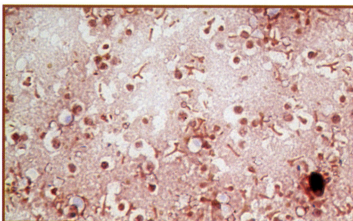

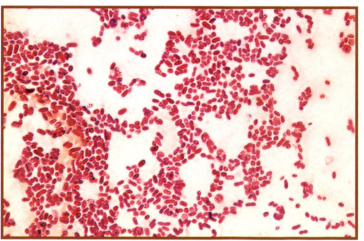

19-28 ROOT NODULE SECTION Symbiotic nitrogen-fixing bacteria, such as *Rhizobium*, induce tumor formation in the roots of certain legumes. Once in the nodule, infected cells become filled with differentiated forms of the bacterium called bacteroids. Uninfected cells are white in this preparation.

19-29 AZOTOBACTER GRAM STAIN Plump, Gram-negative rods characterize the free-living, nitrogen-fixing *Azotobacter*. These cells were grown in culture.

Once nitrogen gas has been reduced to ammonium ion, it becomes available for **assimilation** into amino acids by green plants and other bacteria. It then enters the food chain as various forms of organic nitrogen, the only form of nitrogen consumers can use. **Oxidative deamination** of amino acids during heterotrophic catabolism (including decomposition by bacteria and fungi) results in the formation of ammonium ion once again.

Denitrifying bacteria use nitrate as the **final electron acceptor** of **anaerobic respiration**. The end products of nitrate reduction include nitrogen gas, nitrite, and ammonium ion.

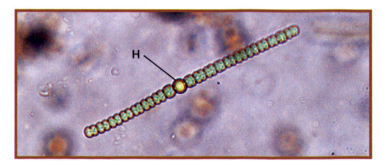

19-30 HETEROCYST IN *ANABAENA* *Anabaena* is a filamentous cyanobacterium. Specialized, thick-walled cells called heterocysts (**H**) are involved in nitrogen fixation. The oxygen-sensitive nitrogenase enzyme is protected from oxygen in these cells because they lack Photosystem II, which produces oxygen from water during photolysis, and oxygen diffusion from the environment is apparently limited by the thick wall. Cyanobacteria are the primary N-fixers in aquatic environments.

Sulfur Cycle—Introduction

Sulfur is one of the most abundant elements on Earth. Having oxidation states from -2 to $+6$, it is able to form many different compounds usable by living things. Most of the sulfur compounds used by microorganisms are inorganic molecules, used strictly for energy or to be incorporated into organic molecules in biosynthetic processes. Table 19-3 summarizes some important sulfur compounds and their oxidation states.

The sulfur microorganisms are a diverse group and include both *Bacteria* and *Archaea*. They live in habitats as diverse as freshwater ponds, lakes, and rivers (especially where there is sewage contamination), water-saturated soils, saltwater lagoons, sulfur solfaturas as in Yellowstone National Park, and in and around deep ocean hydrothermal vents. This vast group includes photoautotrophs, photoheterotrophs,

chemolithoautotrophs, chemolithoheterotrophs, obligate aerobes, facultative anaerobes, and obligate anaerobes.

Many sulfur oxidizers and reducers live **syntrophically** in mutually dependent communities, in which sulfur is converted back and forth between reduced and oxidized forms. Conversely, sulfur oxidizers living in and around hydrothermal vents, although still part of a complex community, have an abundant source of reduced sulfur flowing up from the vents. These microbes, receiving no biologically reduced sulfur, thrive in the ecosystem and produce large living mats that cover surrounding surfaces.

Sulfur bacteria fall into three major categories—photoautotrophs, chemolithoautotrophs, and the sulfur reducers. Table 19-4 lists the major groups of sulfur bacteria and some

TABLE 19-3 Sulfur Compounds and Sulfur Organisms That Use Them

Sulfur Compound	Chemical Formula	Oxidation State	Used By Oxidizers	Used By Reducers
Organic sulfur	R–SH	-2	+	+
Sulfide	H_2S, HS^-, S^{2-}	-2	+	
Elemental sulfur	S^0	0	+	+
Thiosulfate	$S_2O_3^{2-}$	$+2$ per S	+	+
Sulfur dioxide	SO_2	$+4$		
Sulfite	SO_3^{2-}	$+4$		+
Sulfate	SO_4^{2-}	$+6$		+

TABLE 19-4 Major Sulfur Bacteria Reactions

Microbial groups	Representative Organisms	Habitat	Reactions	Representative Summary Reactions
Photoautotrophs	*Chromatium, Chlorobium*	Anoxic	Anoxygenic photosynthesis	$H_2S + CO_2 \rightarrow S^0 + [CH_2O]$ $S^0 + CO_2 \rightarrow SO_4^{2-} + [CH_2O]$
Chemolithoautotrophs	*Beggiatoa, Macromonas, Thiobacillus, Thiobacterium*	Anoxic/oxic interface where H_2S and O_2 meet	Sulfur/sulfide/ thiosulfate oxidation	$HS^- + \frac{1}{2}O_2 + H^+ \rightarrow S^0 + H_2O$ $H_2S + 2\,O_2 \rightarrow SO_4^{2-} + 2H^+$ $S^0 + 1\frac{1}{2}O_2 + H_2O \rightarrow H_2SO_4$ $S_2O_3^{2-} + H_2O + 2\,O_2 \rightarrow 2\,SO_4^{2-} + 2H^+$
Sulfate/sulfur reducers	*Desulfovibrio, Desulfobulbus Desulfobacter, Desulfuromonas*	Either oxic or anoxic	Assimilatory sulfate reduction	$SO_4^{2-} \rightarrow S^{2-} + $ O-acetyl-L-serine $\rightarrow$ L- cysteine + acetate + H_2O
		Anoxic	Dissimilatory sulfate reduction	$SO_4^{2-} \rightarrow S^0$ $S^0 \rightarrow H_2S$
Many groups	Many organisms	Either oxic or anoxic	Desulfuration	Organic sulfur compounds (R–SH) + $H_2O \rightarrow$ R–OH + H_2S

summary reactions they perform. Figure 19-31 illustrates the major biogeochemical transformations.

The photoautotrophs (Figures 19-32 and 33) are anoxygenic photosynthesizers, that is, they perform a type of photosynthesis that does not produce oxygen. These organisms reside in the anoxic zone of a pond or other aquatic ecosystem close enough to the surface to use the sun's energy to fix carbon from CO_2. Rather than chloroplasts, as in green plants, anoxygenic phototrophs contain membrane-bound bacteriochlorophyll. In sulfur bacteria, bacteriochorophyll traps light energy and converts it to ATP, which ultimately is used to fix CO_2. Oxidation of H_2S or elemental sulfur provides electrons for CO_2 reduction. These reactions are analogous to the oxygenic photosynthetic reactions performed by cyanobacteria and eukaryotes.

photosynthetic eukaryotes:

$$CO_2 + H_2O \longrightarrow [CH_2O] + O_2$$

photosynthetic sulfur bacteria:

$$CO_2 + H_2S \longrightarrow [CH_2O] + S^0$$

The chemolithoautotrophs (Figures 19-32 and 19-34) are aerobic organisms that oxidize reduced sulfur compounds as an energy source and use it to fix CO_2. Because the most common form of reduced sulfur is sulfide gas (S^{2-}, HS^-, H_2S) produced in anoxic sediments, oxidation by these bacteria must occur as the gaseous sulfur rises and meets the oxic zone.

Sulfur reducers (Figure 19-35) perform two important reduction reactions: dissimilatory and assimilatory sulfate reduction. Assimilatory sulfate reduction is the production of sulfide in the form of the –SH groups of biochemicals. Dissimilatory sulfate reduction is a purely energy releasing respiratory reaction, where sulfate acts as a final electron acceptor in anaerobic respiration. Finally, desulfuration (sulfur mineralization) is the reversal of assimilatory reduction and involves the release of H_2S to the environment.

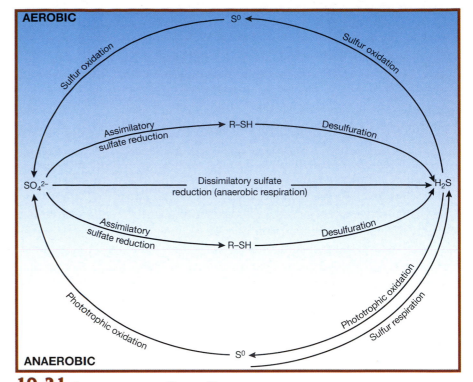

19-31 **BIOGEOCHEMICAL SULFUR TRANSFORMATIONS** These are the major sulfur transformations in the sulfur cycle. Refer to Tables 19-3 and 19-4 for details.

19-32 **MICROBIAL MAT OF SULFUR BACTERIA** The layers of this microbial mat formed at the edge of the Salton Sea contain sulfur bacteria. The chemoautotroph *Beggiatoa* is found in the lighter, surface mat. A portion of the surface mat has been removed to reveal the black mud less than 1 cm below in which sulfur reducing bacteria reside. Green sulfur bacteria (photoautotrophs) are found in between.

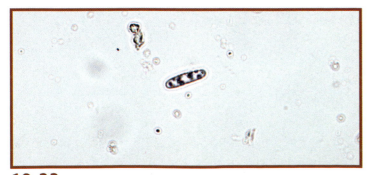

19-33 **PHOTOAUTOTROPHIC SULFUR BACTERIUM** This organism was provisionally identified as *Allochromatium*, purple sulfur bacterium. Note the evenly distributed sulfur granules in the cytoplasm.

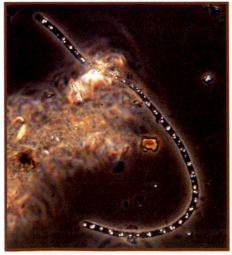

19-34 **CHEMO-AUTOTROPHIC SULFUR OXIDIZING BACTERIUM (PHASE CONTRAST)** This gliding bacterium, provisionally identified as *Beggiatoa*, shows numerous sulfur granules in the cytoplasm. These are the by-product of H_2S oxidation, the method by which *Beggiatoa* obtains energy.

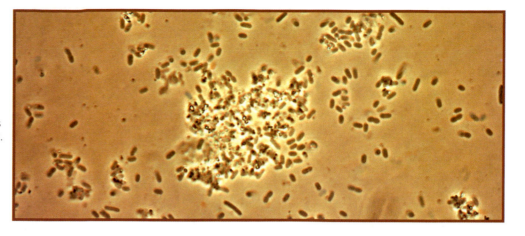

19-35 PHASE-CONTRAST IMAGE OF A SULFUR REDUCER This is a phase-contrast photomicrograph of unknown sulfur reducers recovered from black (anoxic) pond sediment.

Methylene Blue Reductase Test

● Purpose

This test is helpful in differentiating the enterococci from other streptococci. It also tests for the presence of coliforms in raw milk.

● Principle

Methylene blue dye is blue when oxidized and colorless when reduced. It can be enzymatically reduced either aerobically or anaerobically. In the aerobic electron transport system, methylene blue is reduced by cytochromes but immediately is returned to the oxidized state when it reduces oxygen. Anaerobically, the dye is in the reduced form, and in the absence of an oxidizing substance, remains colorless.

The reduction of methylene blue may be used as an indicator of milk quality. In the methylene blue reductase test, a small quantity of a dilute methylene blue solution is added to a sterilized test tube containing raw milk. The tube then is sealed tightly and incubated in a 35°C water bath.

The time it takes the milk to turn from blue to white (because of methylene blue reduction) is a qualitative indicator of the number of microorganisms living in the milk (Figure 19-36). Good quality milk takes greater than 6 hours to convert the methylene blue.

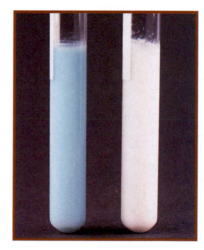

19-36 THE METHYLENE BLUE REDUCTASE TEST The tube on the left is a control to illustrate the original color of the medium. The tube on the right indicates bacterial reduction of methylene blue after 20 hours. The speed of reduction corresponds to the concentration of microorganisms present in the milk.

Snyder Test

● Purpose

The Snyder test is designed to measure dental caries (tooth decay) susceptibility, caused primarily by lactobacilli and oral streptococci.

● Principle

Snyder Test Medium is formulated to favor the growth of oral bacteria (Figure 19-37) and discourage the growth of other bacteria. This is accomplished by lowering the pH of the medium to 4.8. Glucose is added as a fermentable carbohydrate, and bromcresol green is the pH indicator. Lactobacilli and oral streptococci survive these harsh conditions, ferment the glucose, and lower the pH even further. The pH indicator, which is green at or above pH 4.8 and yellow below, turns yellow in the process. Development of yellow color in this medium, therefore, is evidence of fermentation and, further, is highly suggestive of the presence of dental decay-causing bacteria (Figure 19-38).

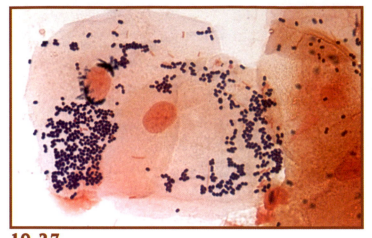

19-37 GRAM STAIN OF ORAL BACTERIA Note the predominance of Gram-positive cocci. Also present are a few Gram-negative rods and very few Gram-positive rods (*Lactobacillus*). Note also the size difference between the large epithelial cells in the center and the bacteria.

The medium is autoclaved for sterilization, cooled to just over 45°C, and maintained in a warm water bath until needed. The molten agar then is inoculated with a small amount of saliva, mixed well, and incubated for up to 72 hours. The agar tubes are checked at 24-hour intervals for any change in color. High susceptibility to dental caries is indicated if the medium turns yellow within 24 hours. Moderate and slight susceptibility are indicated by a change within 48 and 72 hours, respectively. No change within 72 hours is considered a negative result. These results are summarized in Table 19-5.

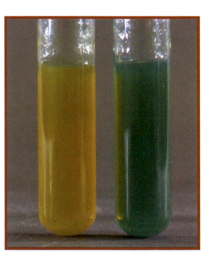

19-38 SNYDER TEST RESULTS A positive result is on the left, and a negative result is on the right.

TABLE 19-5	Snyder Test Results and Interpretations	
TABLE OF RESULTS		
Result	**Interpretation**	
Yellow at 24 hours	High susceptibility to dental caries	
Yellow at 48 hours	Moderate susceptibility to dental caries	
Yellow at 72 hours	Slight susceptibility to dental caries	
Yellow at >72 hours	Negative	

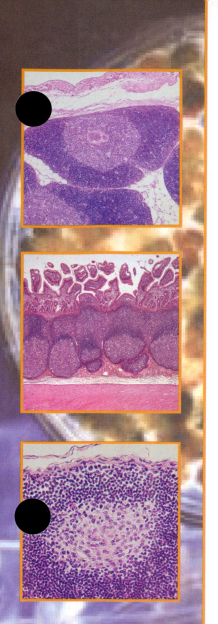

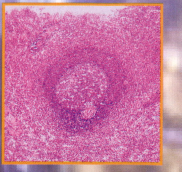

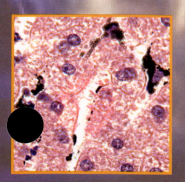

Host Defenses

Differential Blood Cell Count

● Purpose

A differential blood cell count is done to determine approximate numbers of the various leukocytes in blood. Excess or deficiency of all or a particular group is indicative of certain disease states.

● Principle

Leukocytes (white blood cells or WBCs) are divided into two groups: **granulocytes** (which have prominent cytoplasmic granules) and **agranulocytes** (which lack these granules). There are three basic types of granulocytes: **neutrophils, basophils,** and **eosinophils.** The two types of agranulocytes are **monocytes** and **lymphocytes.**

Neutrophils (Figure 20-1) are the most abundant WBCs in blood. They leave the blood and enter tissues to phagocytize foreign material. An increase in neutrophils in the blood is indicative of a systemic bacterial infection. Mature neutrophils are sometimes referred to as **segs** because their nucleus is usually segmented into two to five lobes. Because of the variation in nuclear appearance, they are also called **polymorphonuclear neutrophils (PMNs).** Immature neutrophils lack this nuclear segmentation and are referred to as **bands.** This distinction is useful, because a patient with an active infection will be producing more neutrophils, meaning a higher percentage will be of the band (immature) type. Neutrophils are 12–15 μm in diameter, about twice the size of an erythrocyte (RBC).* Their cytoplasmic granules are neutral staining and thus do not have the intense color of other granulocytes when prepared with a Wright's or Giemsa stain.

---

* It is convenient to discuss leukocyte size in terms of erythrocyte size because RBCs are so uniform in diameter. In an isotonic solution, erythrocytes are 7.5 μm in diameter.

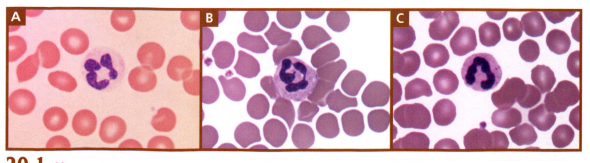

20-1 NEUTROPHILS **A** and **B** The segmented nuclei of these cells identify them as mature neutrophils (segs). About 30% of neutrophils in blood samples from females demonstrate a "drumstick" protruding from the nucleus, as in **B**. This is the region of the inactive X chromosome. **C** This is an immature band neutrophil with an unsegmented nucleus. Micrograph **A** was stained with Giemsa stain; the others were prepared with Wright's stain. Neutrophils are approximately 12–15 μm in diameter.

Eosinophils are phagocytic, and their numbers increase during allergic reactions and parasitic infections (Figure 20-2). They are 12–15 μm in diameter (about twice the size of an RBC) and generally have 2 lobes in their nucleus. Their cytoplasmic granules stain red in typical preparations.

Basophils (Figure 20-3) are the least abundant WBCs in normal blood. They are structurally similar to tissue mast cells and produce some of the same chemicals (histamine and heparin), but are derived from different stem cells in bone marrow. They are 12–15 μm in diameter. The nucleus is usually obscured by the dark staining cytoplasmic granules, but it either has two lobes or is unlobed.

Agranulocytes include monocytes and lymphocytes. Monocytes (Figure 20-4) are the blood form of **macrophages**. They are the largest of leukocytes, being two to three times the size of RBCs (12–20 μm). Their nucleus is horseshoe-shaped and the cytoplasm lacks prominent granules (but may appear finely granular).

Lymphocytes (Figure 20-5) are cells of the immune system. Two functional types of lymphocytes are the **T-cell**, involved in cell-mediated immunity, and the **B-cell**, which converts to a **plasma cell** (Figure 20-6) when activated and produces antibodies. The nucleus is usually spherical and takes up most of the cell. Lymphocytes are approximately the same size as RBCs or up to twice their size. The larger ones form a third functional group of lymphocytes, the **null cell**, many of which are **natural killer (NK) cells** that kill foreign or infected cells without antigen-antibody interaction (Figure 20-5b).

In a differential white cell count, a sample of blood is observed under the microscope and at least 100 WBCs are counted and tallied (this task is automated now). Approximate normal percentages for each leukocyte are as follows: 55–65% neutrophils (mostly segs), 25–33% lymphocytes, 3–7% monocytes, 1–3% eosinophils, and 0.5–1% basophils.

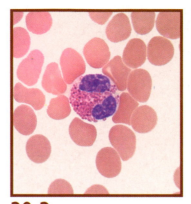

20-2 **EOSINOPHIL (GIEMSA STAIN)** These granulocytes are relatively rare and are about twice the size of RBCs. Their cytoplasmic granules stain red, and their nucleus usually has two lobes.

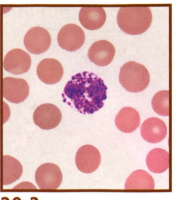

20-3 **BASOPHIL (GIEMSA STAIN)** Basophils comprise only about 1% of all WBCs. They are up to twice the size of RBCs and have dark purple cytoplasmic granules that obscure the nucleus.

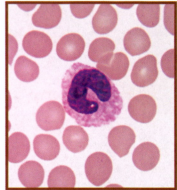

20-4 **MONOCYTE (GIEMSA STAIN)** Monocytes are the blood form of macrophages. They are about two to three times the size of RBCs and have a round or indented nucleus.

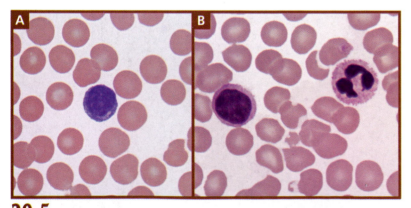

20-5 **LYMPHOCYTES** Lymphocytes are common in the blood, comprising up to 33% of all WBCs. Most are about the size of RBCs and have only a thin halo of cytoplasm encircling their round nucleus. They belong to functional groups called B cells and T cells (which are morphologically indistinguishable). Micrograph **A** is a small lymphocyte and was prepared with Giemsa stain. Some lymphocytes are larger, as in micrograph **B**. These are natural killer (NK) cells or some other type of null cell. Also visible is a neutrophil.

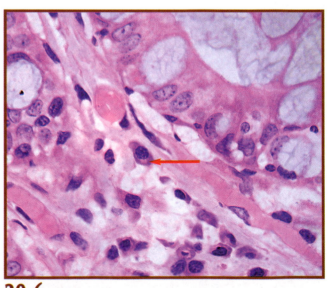

20-6 **PLASMA CELLS** B-lymphocytes develop into plasma cells when stimulated by the appropriate antigen. Plasma cells secrete protective antibodies against the antigen. This plasma cell (arrow) is recognizable because of its elongated shape, eccentric nucleus with "clock face" chromatin, and a pale region near the nucleus (which is the site of a Golgi apparatus). This specimen is from the colon.

Other Immune Cells and Organs

Cells of the **reticuloendothelial system** and **immune system** are involved in host defense and are found scattered throughout the body. Examples are shown in the following photomicrographs (Figures 20-7 through 20-16).

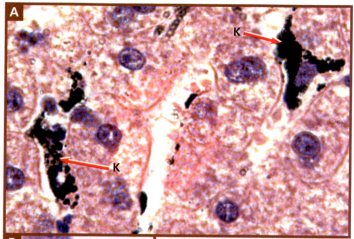

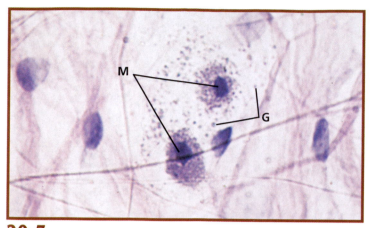

20-7 MAST CELLS Two mast cells (**M**) of loose connective tissue are shown. The cytoplasmic granules (**G**) contain histamine and other chemicals involved in inflammation as a result of tissue damage. The mast cells may also be coated with IgE antibodies, which cause degranulation when they bind antigen—as in Type I hypersensitivity (allergic) reactions.

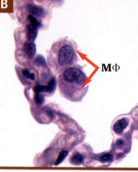

20-8 MACROPHAGES Macrophages either remain attached to a surface and are called **fixed macrophages**, or enter tissues and scavenge foreign material as **wandering macrophages**. **A** This section of the liver shows two Kupffer (**K**) cells that have ingested a dye. Kupffer cells are fixed macrophages that reside in liver sinusoids. **B** The arrows indicate two alveolar macrophages (**MΦ**) of the lung. They are wandering macrophages.

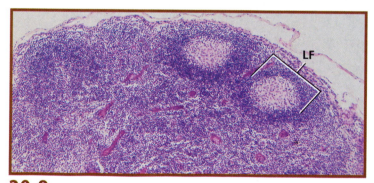

20-9 LYMPH NODE This is a section through a lymph node. The large spherical purple objects are masses of lymphocytes called **lymph nodules** or **lymph follicles** (**LF**). As lymph passes through the sinuses (channels) within the node, antigens may contact a lymphocyte with the ability to produce antibodies against it. This provides the stimulus for cloning of the lymphocyte and conversion of some clones into antibody-secreting **plasma cells**. Other clones become **memory cells** and reside in lymphatic tissue around the body. Macrophages are also found in the node's sinuses.

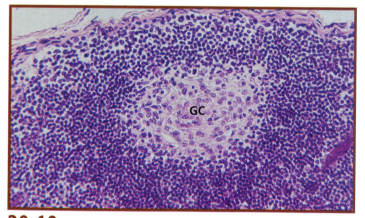

20-10 A SINGLE LYMPH FOLLICLE (SECTION) The light germinal center (**GC**) is occupied by lymphoblasts and medium-sized lymphocytes. More mature lymphocytes are found in the darker, outer portion of the follicle.

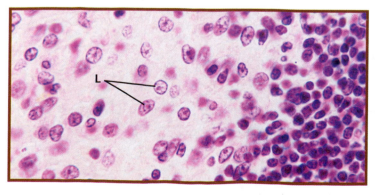

20-11 THE GERMINAL CENTER OF A LYMPH FOLLICLE Medium-sized lymphocytes (**L**) are abundant in the lighter region, whereas mature lymphocytes predominate in the darker region. Their differences in size and nuclear staining are apparent.

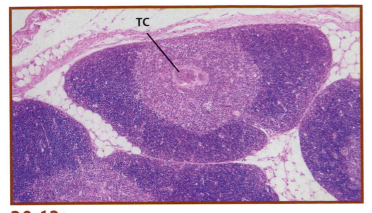

20-12 **A SECTION THROUGH THE THYMUS** One lobule (composed of lymphocytes) with its **thymic corpuscle (TC)** is shown. The thymus is the site of T-lymphocyte maturation.

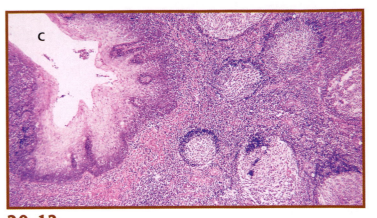

20-13 **A SECTION THROUGH A PALATINE TONSIL** Palatine tonsils are found on either side of the oral cavity's opening into the throat. Two other sets of tonsils are also found in the throat: the pharyngeal tonsils (adenoids) are posterior to the nasal cavity and the lingual tonsils are in the base of the tongue. Tonsils act much like lymph nodes in that they are composed of lymph follicles (evident in the right half of the field) that contact fluids passing through them. A **tonsilar crypt (C)** is also visible.

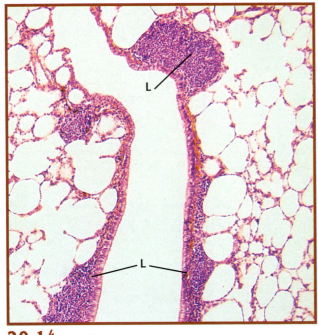

20-14 **MALT OF A BRONCHIOLE** Lymphatic tissue is found in many places besides the lymph nodes. Shown is a section through the lung with lymphatic tissue (**L**) in the wall of a bronchiole. Such tissue is referred to as *Mucosa Associated Lymphatic Tissue*, or **MALT**.

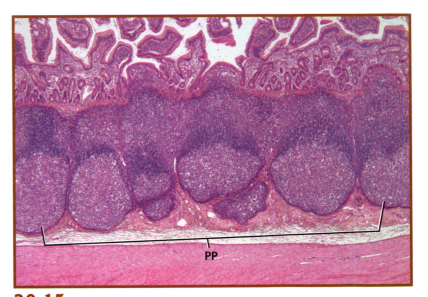

20-15 **MALT OF THE SMALL INTESTINE** This is a section through the ileum showing a **Peyer's patch (PP)** of lymph follicles. Peyer's patches may consist of 10 to 70 follicles separated from the intestinal lumen only by a single layer of epithelial cells.

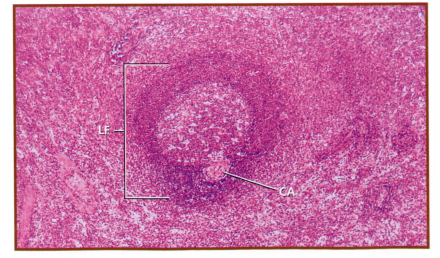

20-16 **THE SPLEEN** This is a section through a spleen. In addition to being a blood filter and reservoir, the spleen contains lymph follicles (**LF**) referred to as **white pulp**. Lymphocytes of white pulp respond to antigens in the blood. The portion of the spleen devoted to blood-vascular functions is referred to as **red pulp**. A single follicle with its central artery (**CA**) is shown surrounded by the red pulp.

Biochemical Pathways

So much of what is done in microbiology relies on an understanding of basic biochemical pathways. It's not as important to memorize them (although, with exposure they will become second nature) as it is to understand their importance in metabolism and to interpret diagrams of them when available. The following discussion is provided so you can see how the various biochemical tests presented in this manual fit into the overall scheme of cellular chemistry.

Oxidation of Glucose: Glycolysis, Entner-Doudoroff, and Pentose-Phosphate Pathways

Most organisms use **glycolysis** (also known as the "Embden-Meyerhof-Parnas pathway, Figure A-1) in energy metabolism. It performs the stepwise disassembly of glucose into two pyruvates, releasing some of its energy and electrons in the process. The exergonic (energy-releasing) reactions are associated with ATP synthesis by a process called **substrate phosphorylation**. Although a total of four ATPs are produced per glucose in glycolysis, two ATPs are hydrolyzed early in the pathway, leaving a net production of two ATPs per glucose. In one glycolytic reaction, the loss of an electron pair (oxidation) from a three-carbon intermediate occurs simultaneously with the reduction of NAD^+ to $NADH + H^+$. The $NADH + H^+$ then may be oxidized in an electron transport chain or a fermentation pathway, depending on the organism and the environmental conditions. The former yields ATP, and the latter generally does not. In summary, each glucose oxidized in glycolysis yields two pyruvates, $2 NADH + 2 H^+$, and a net of 2 ATPs (Table A-1).

Although the intermediates of glycolysis are carbohydrates, many are entry points for amino acid, lipid, and nucleotide catabolism. Many glycolytic intermediates also are a source of carbon skeletons for the synthesis of these other biochemicals. Some of these are shown in Figure A-1. *Note*: For clarity, many details have been omitted from these other pathways in Figure A-1. Single arrows may represent several reactions, and other carbon compounds not illustrated may be required to complete a particular reaction.

The **Entner-Doudoroff pathway** (Figure A-2) is an alternative means of degrading glucose into two pyruvates. This pathway is found exclusively among prokaryotes (*e.g.*, *Pseudomonas* and *E. coli*, as well as other Gram-negatives and certain *Archaea*). It allows utilization of a different category of sugars (aldonic acids) than glycolysis and therefore improves the range of resources available to the organism. It is less efficient than glycolysis because only one ATP is phosphorylated and only one NADH is produced. Table A-2 summarizes this pathway.

The **pentose-phosphate pathway** is a complex set of cyclic reactions that provides a mechanism for producing five-carbon sugars (**pentoses**) from six-carbon sugars (**hexoses**). Pentose sugars are used in ribonucleotides and deoxyribonucleotides, as well as being precursors to aromatic amino acids. Further, this pathway produces NADPH, which is used as an electron donor in anabolic pathways. Unlike NADH, produced in glycolysis and Entner-Doudoroff, NADPH is not used as an electron donor in an electron transport chain for oxidative phosphorylation of ADP.

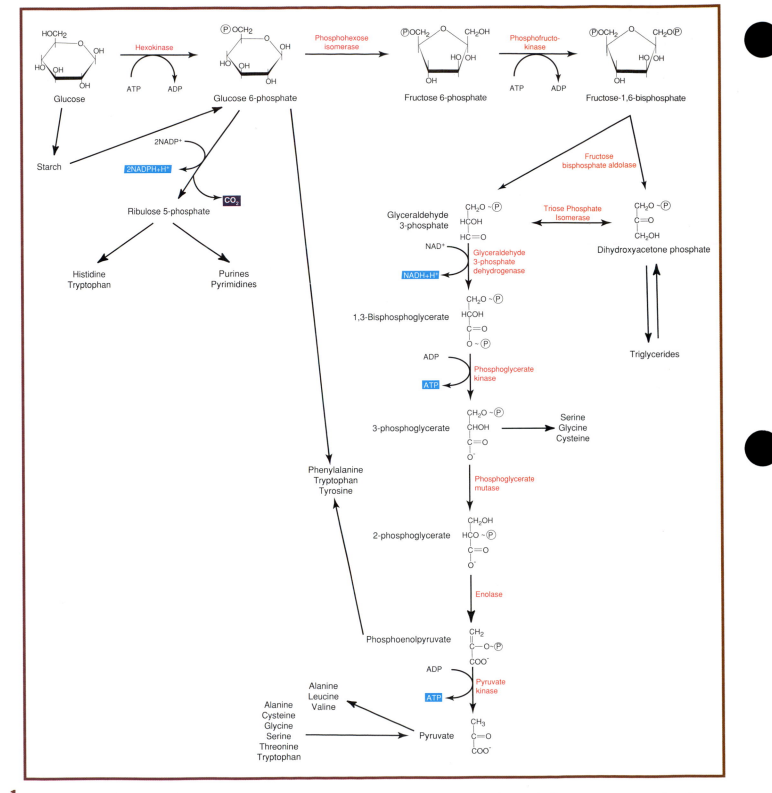

A-1 GLYCOLYSIS AND ASSOCIATED PATHWAYS The names of glycolytic intermediates are printed in black ink; the enzyme names are in red. Reducing power (in the form of NADH+H+) and ATP are highlighted in blue. The major key to getting product yields correct is to recognize that *both* C_3 compounds (Glyceraldehyde 3-phosphate and Dihydroxyacetone phosphate) produced from splitting Fructose 1,6-bisphosphate can pass through the remainder of the pathway because of the triose phosphate isomerase reaction. The conversion of each into pyruvate results in the formation of 2 ATPs and 1 NADH+H+ (Table A-1).

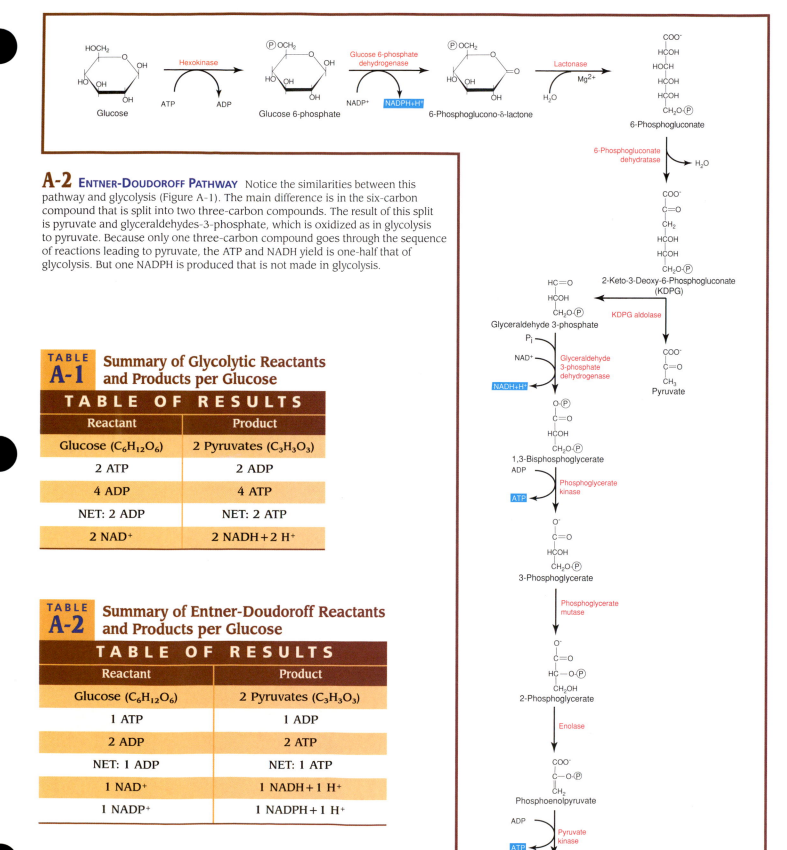

A-2 ENTNER-DOUDOROFF PATHWAY Notice the similarities between this pathway and glycolysis (Figure A-1). The main difference is in the six-carbon compound that is split into two three-carbon compounds. The result of this split is pyruvate and glyceraldehydes-3-phosphate, which is oxidized as in glycolysis to pyruvate. Because only one three-carbon compound goes through the sequence of reactions leading to pyruvate, the ATP and NADH yield is one-half that of glycolysis. But one NADPH is produced that is not made in glycolysis.

TABLE A-1 Summary of Glycolytic Reactants and Products per Glucose

TABLE OF RESULTS	
Reactant	Product
Glucose ($C_6H_{12}O_6$)	2 Pyruvates ($C_3H_3O_3$)
2 ATP	2 ADP
4 ADP	4 ATP
NET: 2 ADP	NET: 2 ATP
2 NAD+	2 NADH + 2 H+

TABLE A-2 Summary of Entner-Doudoroff Reactants and Products per Glucose

TABLE OF RESULTS	
Reactant	Product
Glucose ($C_6H_{12}O_6$)	2 Pyruvates ($C_3H_3O_3$)
1 ATP	1 ADP
2 ADP	2 ATP
NET: 1 ADP	NET: 1 ATP
1 NAD+	1 NADH + 1 H+
1 NADP+	1 NADPH + 1 H+

The pentose-phosphate reactants and products are listed in Table A-3, and the overall path is shown in Figure A-3. To completely oxidize one hexose to $6CO_2$, a total of six hexoses must enter the cycle as glucose-6-phosphate and follow one of three different routes (notice the symmetry of pathways as drawn). Notice in Figure A-3 that each hexose loses a CO_2 upon entry into the cycle, but at the end, five hexoses are produced. Thus, the net reaction is one hexose being oxidized to $6CO_2$. Notice also the reactions that transfer two-carbon and three-carbon fragments between the five-carbon intermediates. **Transketolase** catalyzes the two-carbon transfer, whereas **transaldolase** catalyzes the three-carbon transfer. Alternatively, the five-carbon intermediates can be redirected into pathways for synthesis of aromatic amino acids and nucleotides (not shown).

TABLE A-3	Summary of Pentose Phosphate Reactants and Products per Glucose-6-phosphate	
TABLE OF RESULTS		
Reactant	Product	
Glucose-6-phosphate (C_6)	$6 CO_2 + 1 P_i$	
12 $NADP^+$	12 NADPH + 12 H^+	

Oxidation of Pyruvate: The Krebs Cycle and Fermentation

Pyruvate represents a major crossroads in metabolism. Some organisms are able to further disassemble the pyruvates produced in glycolysis and Entner-Doudoroff and make more ATP and $NADH + H^+$ in the **Krebs cycle**. Other organisms simply reduce the pyruvates with electrons from $NADH + H^+$ without further energy production in **fermentation**.

The Krebs cycle is a major metabolic pathway used in energy production by organisms that respire aerobically or anaerobically (Figure A-4). Pyruvate produced in glycolysis or other pathways is first converted to acetyl-coenzyme A during the **entry step** (also known as the **intermediate** or **gateway step**). Acetyl-CoA enters the Krebs cycle through a condensation reaction with oxaloacetate. Products for each pyruvate that enters the cycle via the entry step are: 3 CO_2, 4 $NADH + H^+$, 1 $FADH_2$, and 1 GTP. (Because two pyruvates are made per glucose, these numbers are doubled in Table A-4). The energy released from oxidation of reduced coenzymes ($NADH + H^+$ and $FADH_2$) in an electron transport chain is then used to make ATP. ATP yields are summarized in Table A-5.

Like glycolysis, many of the Krebs cycle's intermediates are entry points for amino acid, nucleotide and lipid catabolism, as well as a source of carbon skeletons for synthesis of the same compounds. These pathways are shown, but details have been omitted. Single arrows may represent several reactions, and other carbon compounds, not illustrated, may be required to complete a given reaction.

Figure A-5 illustrates some major fermentation pathways exhibited by microbes (though no single organism is capable of all of them). Pyruvate (shown in the blue box) is typically the starting point for each. End products of fermentation are shown in red. Fermentation allows a cell living under anaerobic conditions to oxidize reduced coenzymes (such as $NADH + H^+$ and shown in blue) generated during glycolysis or other pathways. Some bacteria (aerotolerant anaerobes) rely solely on fermentation and do not use oxygen even if it is available. Table A-6 summarizes major fermentations and some representative organisms that perform each.

Notice that fermentation end products typically fall into three categories: acid, gas, or an organic solvent (an alcohol or a ketone). The specific fermentation performed is the result of the enzymes present in a species and often is used as a basis of classification.

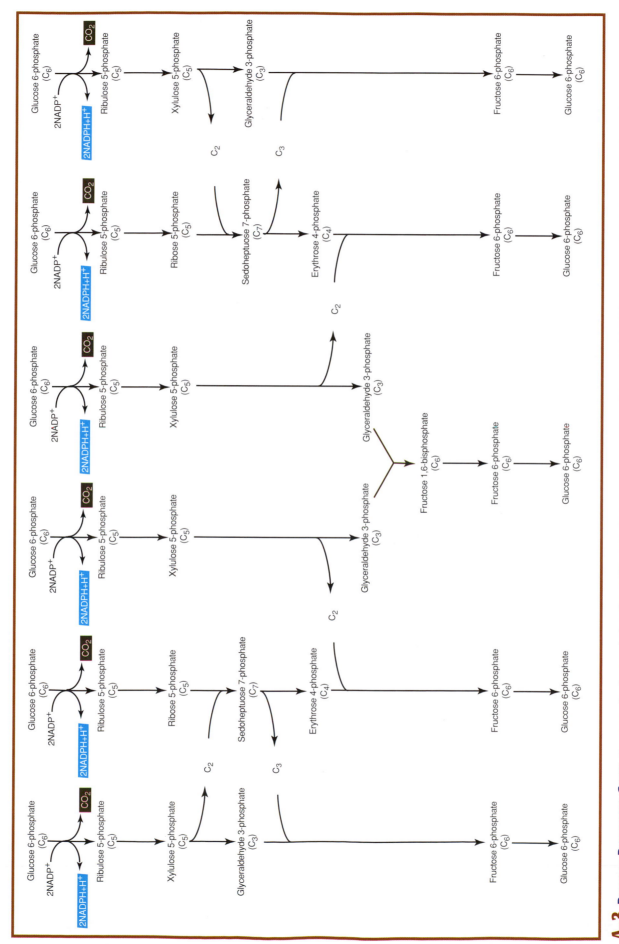

A-3 **PENTOSE-PHOSPHATE CYCLE** For every six glucose-6-phosphates that enter and complete the cycle, 6CO₂ and 12 NADPH + H⁺ are produced. Some of the five-carbon intermediates, however, may be redirected into synthesis of aromatic amino acids and nucleotides. If the cycle is performed as shown, 36 carbons enter as six glucose 6-phosphate (6 × C₆ = 36C). Six CO₂ are immediately lost, leaving a total of 30C to get shuffled around by the remaining reactions to form five glucose 6-phosphates (5 × C₆ = 30C).

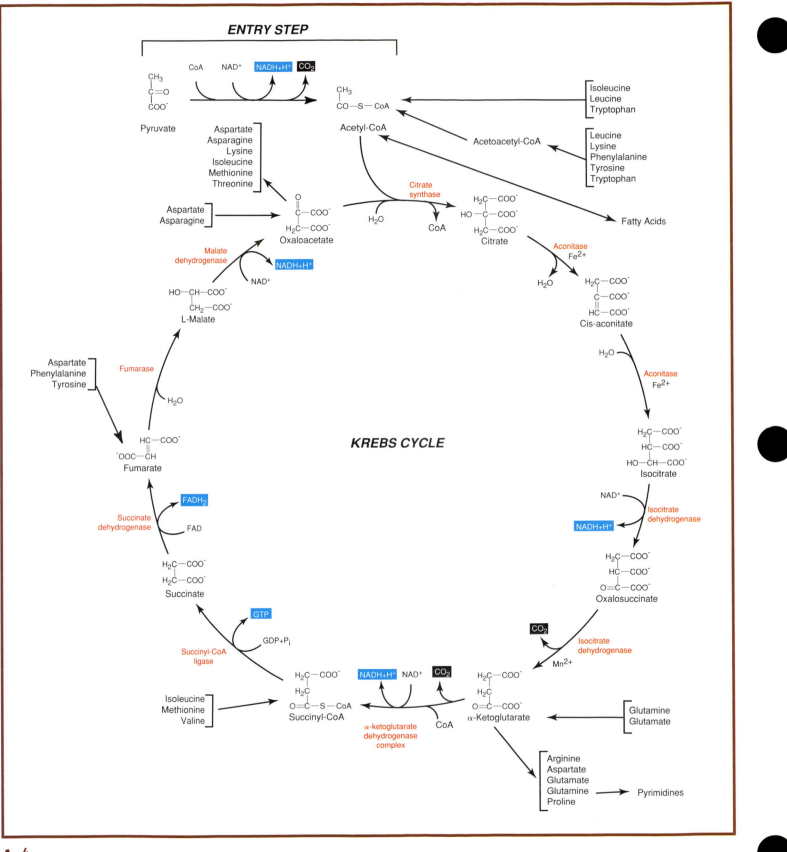

A-4 THE ENTRY STEP AND KREBS CYCLE The names of intermediates are printed in black ink; enzymes are in red. Reducing power (in the form of $NADH + H^+$ and $FADH_2$) and GTP are highlighted in blue. CO_2 produced from the oxidation of carbon is highlighted in black.

TABLE A-4 Summary of Reactants and Products per Glucose in the Entry Step and the Krebs Cycle

Entry Step		Krebs Cycle	
Reactant	Product	Reactant	Product
2 Pyruvates	2 Acetyl CoA + 2 CO_2	2 Acetyl CoA	4 CO_2
2 Coenzyme A			2 Coenzyme A
2 NAD^+	2 NADH + 2H^+	6 NAD^+	6 NADH + 6H^+
		2 GDP + 2 P_i (= 2 ADP + 2 P_i)	2 GTP (= 2 ATP)

TABLE A-5 ATP Yields from Complete Oxidation of Glucose to CO_2 by a Prokaryote Using Glycolysis, Entry Step, and the Krebs Cycle with O_2 as the Final Electron Acceptor

Compound	Number Produced	ATP Value in the Aerobic ETC	Total ATPs per Glucose
NADH + H^+	10	3	30
$FADH_2$	2	2	4
ATP (by substrate phosphorylation)	4		4

TABLE A-6 Major Fermentations, Their End-Products, and Some Organisms That Performed Them

Fermentation	Major End Products	Representative Organisms
Alcoholic fermentation	Ethanol and CO_2	*Saccharomyces cerevisiae*
Homofermentation	Lactate	*Streptococcus* and some *Lactobacillus*
Heterofermentation	Lactate, ethanol, and acetate	*Streptococcus, Leuconostoc,* and *Lactobacillus*
Mixed acid fermentation	Acetate, formate, succinate, CO_2, H_2, and ethanol	*Escherichia, Salmonella, Klebsiella,* and *Shigella*
2,3-Butanediol fermentation	2,3-Butanediol	*Enterobacter, Serratia,* and *Erwinia*
Butyrate/butanol fermentation	Butanol, butyrate, acetone, and isopropanol	*Clostridium, Butyrivibrio,* and some *Bacillus*
Propionic acid fermentation	Propionate, acetate and CO_2	*Propionibacterium, Veillonella,* and some *Clostridium*

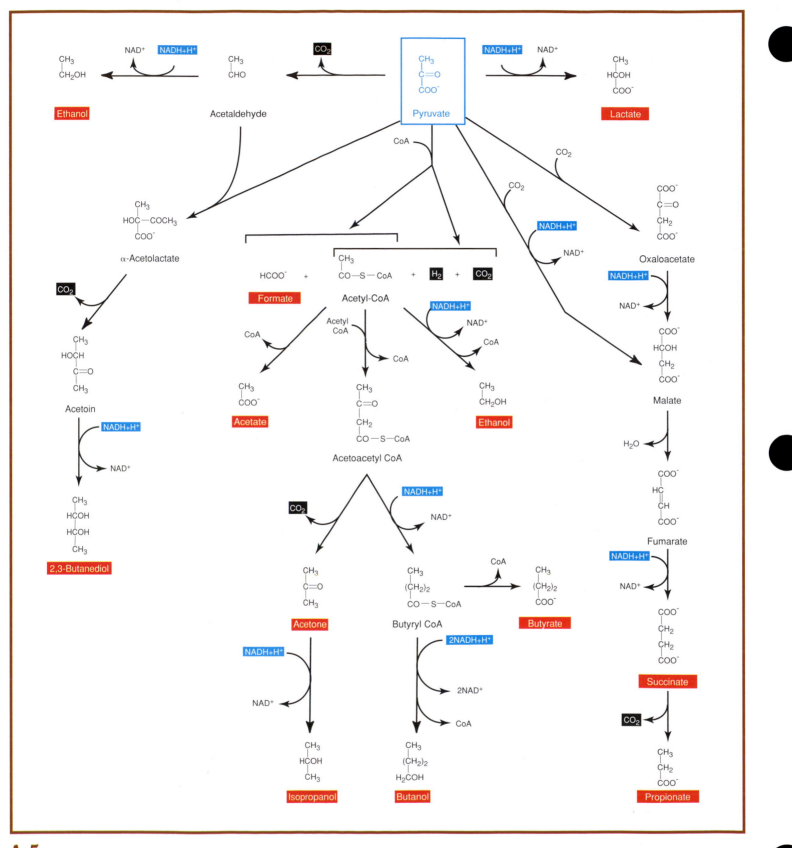

A-5 **A SAMPLING OF FERMENTATION PATHWAYS** Note that all pathways start with pyruvate, have a step(s) where NADH + H⁺ (in blue) is oxidized to NAD⁺, and produce end-products falling into one of three categories: acid, gas, or alcohol.

Selected References for Further Reading

Ash, Lawrence R. and Thomas C. Orihel. 2007. *Atlas of Human Parasitology, 5th Ed.* ASCP Press. Chicago, IL.

Bradbury, S. and B. Bracegirdle. 1998. *Introduction to Light Microscopy (Microscopy Handbooks 42).* Springer-Verlag New York Inc. New York, NY.

Brooks, Geo. F., Karen C. Carroll, Janet S. Butel, Stephen A. Moore, and Timothy A. Mietzner. 2010. *Jawetz, Melnick & Adelberg's Medical Microbiology, 25th Edition.* McGraw Hill Medical Publishers, New York, NY.

Fisher, Fran and Norma B. Cook. 1998. *Fundamentals of Diagnostic Mycology.* W.B. Saunders Company, Philadelphia, PA.

Forbes, Betty A., Daniel F. Sahm, and Alice S. Weissfield. 2007. *Bailey and Scott's Diagnostic Microbiology, 12th Ed.* Mosby, Inc. St. Louis, MO.

Garcia, Lynne Shore. 2006. *Diagnostic Medical Parasitology, 5th Ed.* ASM Press, Washington, D.C.

Garrity, George M. (Editor-in-Chief). Volume Editors: David R. Boone and Richard W. Castenholz. 2001. *Bergey's Manual of Systematic Bacteriology, 2nd Ed., Volume 1: The* Archaea *and the Deeply Branching and Phototrophic* Bacteria. Springer-Verlag, New York, NY.

Garrity, George M. (Editor-in-Chief). Volume Editors: Don J. Brenner, Noel R. Krieg, and James T. Staley. 2005. *Bergey's Manual of Systematic Bacteriology, 2nd Ed., Volume 2, Parts A, B and C. The* Proteobacteria. Springer-Verlag, New York, NY.

Gorbach, Sherwood L., John G. Bartlett, and Neil R. Blacklow. 2004. *Infectious Diseases, 3rd Ed.* Lippincott Williams & Wilkins, Philadelphia, PA.

Larone, Davise H. 2002. *Medically Important Fungi, A Guide to Identification, 4th Ed.* ASM Press, Washington, D.C.

MacFaddin, Jean F. 2001. *Biochemical Tests for Identification of Medical Bacteria, 3rd Ed.* Lippincott Williams & Wilkins, Philadelphia, PA.

Mescher, Anthony L. 2009. *Junqueira's Basic Histology, 12th Ed.* McGraw-Hill Medical Publishers, New York, NY.

Moat, Albert G., John W. Foster, and Michael P. Spector. 2002. *Microbial Physiology, 4th Ed.* Wiley-Liss, Inc. New York, NY.

Murray, Patrick R. (Editor-in-Chief). Volume Editors: Ellen Jo Baron, James H. Jorgensen, Marie Louise Landry, and Michael A. Pfaller. 2007. *Manual of Clinical Microbiology, 9th Ed.* ASM Press, Washington, D.C.

Nelson, David L. and Michael M. Cox. 2008. *Lehninger's Principles of Biochemistry, 5th Ed.* W. H. Freeman Publishers, New York, NY.

Sheehan, Kathy B., David J. Patterson, Brett Leigh Dicks, and Joan M. Henson. 2005. *Seen and Unseen–Discovering the Microbes of Yellowstone.* Falcon Guides, The Globe Pequot Press, Guilford, CT.

Shors, Teri. 2009. *Understanding Viruses*. Jones and Bartlett Publishers LLC, Sudbury, MA.

Southwick, Frederick. 2008. *Infectious Diseases—A Clinical Short Course, 2nd Ed.* McGraw Hill Medical Publishers, New York, NY.

Struthers, J. Keith and Roger P. Westran. 2003. *Clinical Bacteriology*. ASM Press, Washington, D.C.

White, David. 2006. *The Physiology and Biochemistry of Prokaryotes, 3rd Ed.* Oxford University Press, Inc. New York, NY.

Whitman, William B. (Director of the Editorial Office) and Aidan C. Parte (Managing Editor). Volume Editors: Paul De Vos, George M. Garrity, Dorothy Jones, Noel R. Krieg, Wolfgang Ludwig, Fred A Rainey, Karl-Heinz Schleifer, and William B. Whitman. 2009. *Bergey's Manual of Systematic Bacteriology, 2nd Ed., Volume 3: The* Firmicutes. Springer-Verlag, New York, NY.

Winn, Washington, Jr., Stephen Allen, William Janda, Elmer Koneman, Gary Procop, Paul C. Schreckenberger and Gail Woods. 2005. *Koneman's Color Atlas and Textbook of Diagnostic Microbiology, 6th Ed*. Lippincott Williams & Wilkins, Philadelphia, PA.

Yellowstone National Park. 2010. *Yellowstone Resources & Issues*. Mammoth, WY/Division of Interpretation.

Zimbro, Mary Jo and David A. Power, editors. 2003. *Difco™ & BBL™ Manual—Manual of Microbiological Culture Media*. Becton, Dickinson and Company. Sparks, MD 21152.

Index

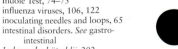